RECLAIMING CHARLES WEIDMAN
(1901-1975)

(1) Cover and Frontispiece:
Charles Weidman in *Danse Profane,* ca. 1930.
Photograph by Helen Hewett. Reproduced through the courtesy of the Jerome Robbins Dance Division, The New York Public Library, Astor, Lenox, and Tilden Foundations.

RECLAIMING CHARLES WEIDMAN (1901-1975)
An American Dancer's Life and Legacy

Jonette Lancos

With a Foreword by
Sondra Horton Fraleigh

The Edwin Mellen Press
Lewiston•Queenston•Lampeter

Library of Congress Cataloging-in-Publication Data

Library of Congress Cataloging-in-Publication Data

Lancos, Jonette.
  Reclaiming Charles Weidman (1901-1975) : an American dancer's life and legacy / Jonette Lancos ; with a foreword by Sondra Horton Fraleigh.
     p. cm.
  Includes bibliographical references and index.
  ISBN-13: 978-0-7734-5463-7
  ISBN-10: 0-7734-5463-2
  1. Weidman, Charles. 2. Dancers--United States--Biography. 3. Dance teachers--United States--Biography. I. Title.
  GV1785.W42L33 2007
  792.802'8092--dc22
  [B]
                                                    2007023384

hors série.

A CIP catalog record for this book is available from the British Library.

The Edwin Mellen Press   The Edwin Mellen Press
        Box 450   Box 67
  Lewiston, New York   Queenston, Ontario
  USA 14092-0450   CANADA L0S 1L0

The Edwin Mellen Press, Ltd.
Lampeter, Ceredigion, Wales
UNITED KINGDOM SA48 8LT

Printed in the United States of America

Dedication

To my grandmother
Catherine Franzetta Gottuso
and my mother
Helen Gottus Lancos
and my mentor
Nona Schurman

for their grace and courage

Table of Contents

List of Illustrations

1. Frontispiece. *Danse Profane*, Charles Weidman, ca. 1930, photograph by Helen Hewett

2. Little Charles Weidman sitting on a fire truck with his Daddy, ca. 1905

3. Charles Weidman performing a Russian dance, ca. 1919

4. Charles Weidman, ca. 1921, photograph by Sissman Studio

5. Ruth St. Denis, *Burmese Solo*, ca. 1923, photograph by Nickolas Muray

6. Charles Weidman, *Pierrot Forlorn,* ca. 1921, photograph by George Bockman

7. Charles Weidman and Martha Graham, *Arabic Duet*, ca. 1921

8. *Siamese Ballet*, Paul Mathis, Lenore Scheffer, Ted Shawn, Charles Weidman, ca. 1922, photograph by Nickolas Muray

9. *Sonata Tragica*, ca. 1923, photograph by White Studio

10. *Sevillanos*, Georgia Graham, Ted Shawn, Anne Douglas, Charles Weidman, ca. 1923, photograph by Maurice Goldberg

11. Charles Weidman in Kabuki makeup, *Momiji Gari*, ca. 1926

12. Sun Bathers in Sunny Florida, ca. 1930. George Eastman House

13. Martha Graham and Charles Weidman, *A Pagan Poem*, ca. 1930, photograph by Nickolas Muray

14. Charles Weidman, *A Pagan Poem*, ca. 1930, photograph by Nickolas Muray

Permissions

Foreword

If the legacy of Charles Weidman were not somewhat eclipsed by Doris Humphrey and José Limón, his two famous colleagues, this book would need no foreword. But this is far from the case. Dance historians have glossed over the work of Weidman, with the exception of this very full account by Jonette Lancos, who has made every effort to open the way to an understanding of Charles Weidman's life and dance. Her book represents careful scholarship and unflagging attention to all aspects of his choreography and performance.

Lancos is in a unique position to write about Weidman because she herself has learned much of his repertory through several dancers who worked with him. Her grasp of the scope and meaning of his work, and her detailed account of his life brings Weidman the attention he deserves. I am fascinated to learn about early modern dance through his life and the perspective Lancos provides, because the history of modern dance and Weidman are intimately interwoven.

I am surprised by how many contemporary dancers have been influenced by and acknowledge the influence of Weidman, including Bill T. Jones. Lancos takes us on a journey from Weidman's work through that of contemporary dance, including Weidman's artistic vision and his pioneering spirit from his Nebraska roots to Panama and the American West, from 1850 to 1920. His embrace of global influences on American dance from 1890 to 1930 is of particular significance today and includes the effect of vaudeville. Lancos gives a very full account of the nineteenth-century fashion for *Japonisme*—crossing from Japan to Europe and America in modern dance—a phenomenon I also include in my study of present-day Japanese *butoh* with its East/West amalgamations. Further, Lancos explores the new religious doctrines in the background of modern dance and of Weidman's—American transcendentalism and the embodiment of spirituality.

We see through Lancos' study of modernism and globalization how the movement principles of François Delsarte, as well as pantomime and gesture in the work of Ruth St. Denis and Ted Shawn, entered into Weidman's perspective at the Denishawn School. Lancos writes about Weidman's tours with Denishawn and imprints a view of early modern dance as music visualization with global assimilation of styles; this was apparent in the Denishawn Asian tour of 1925-26.

We cannot forget that Weidman danced with Martha Graham between 1920 and 1930, functioning as a link between her and Denishawn. Global dance dramas and orchestral dramas were created in the lexicon of modern dance at that time. Weidman broke from the Humphrey-Weidman alliance that lasted more than a decade from 1928-44, beginning his solo and group choreography and creating a manner of dance all his own, even as he continued to develop Humphrey-Weidman techniques based on rebound and fall and recovery principles. Eventually he shaped his own movement style and technique, as Lancos demonstrates in her study of the evolution of his personal style. We learn through Lancos how Weidman used such concepts as *center of weight,* use of the foot, and body bends; how he used hands and arms; choreographed archaic stylizations, tempo and rhythm; and how he developed musical theme-and-variation as a dance form.

The author also shows how aesthetic values and democracy are related in modernism. Several of Weidman's dances provide examples of a decade of democracy and patriotism in dance from 1930-40. Here we become acquainted with his works *Lynchtown* and *Quest: A Choreographic Pantomime.* One of the major contributions of Lancos' book is her capture of Weidman's classroom structure and his lecture-demonstration format, and no less valuable are her descriptions of a full decade of his dances beginning in 1938. Extending beyond this is her pursuit of Weidman's work on Broadway and with the New York City Center Opera Company during 1930 to 1960.

Weidman's work was voluminous and varied, as this book shows; he touched on many American institutions. Several of his works are preserved in dance notation. Lancos has created a wonderful tribute to Weidman and to modern dance through her in-depth accounts of Weidman's reconstructed works and her adroit scholarship as she follows him up to 1975 and the work *Submerged Cathedral*. This would have been the time when postmodern dance was gaining prominence; Weidman was still teaching an occasional guest artist class for college students. I took a class with him around 1960—just before the onset of the postmodern period. I remember his quick wit, our exploration of the intersection of pantomime and dance, and how much I enjoyed his humor and skill.

As Lancos witnesses the work of Weidman, she creates a generous circle of other witnesses of which I now feel as one. They are: Janet Towner, Deborah Carr, Margaret O'Sullivan, Robert Kosinski, Rosalind Pierson, Deborah Jowitt, Nona Schurman, and Dot Virden. I recommend reading this book with attention to how Lancos honors her teachers and her own dance history. May the reader discover the same joy I felt in achieving a fuller view of Weidman and modern dance history through this well-rounded study by Jonette Lancos.

Sondra Horton Fraleigh

Sondra Horton Fraleigh is Professor Emeritus in the Department of Dance at State University of New York College at Brockport, and Founding Director of the *Eastwest Institute for Dance and Somatic Studies*. She is author of *Dance and the Lived Body: A Descriptive Aesthetics* (University of Pittsburgh Press, 1987), *Dancing Into Darkness: Butoh, Zen and Japan* (University of Pittsburgh Press, 1999), *Researching Dance: Evolving Modes of Inquiry* (Dance Books, 1999), and *Dancing Identity: Metaphysics in Motion* (University of Pittsburgh, 2004). She is a recipient of the 2003-04 Congress on Research in Dance *Outstanding Service to Dance Research Award*.

Acknowledgements

Writing this book has meant searching the memories of others. Since I did not work directly with Charles Weidman, nor did I witness the first performances of his innovative dance compositions, the words of those who did, have provided me with the historical resources to trace his dance journey. I am gratefully indebted to them for their guidance in giving me the opportunity to recognize the significance of Charles Weidman's remarkable life.

My sincere gratitude to Nona Schurman for her unquenchable love of dance, which she so generously shared with me. Her endless hours in the rehearsal studio coaching Weidman's works, so skillfully restaged by Deborah Carr, made it possible for me to "continue in the long line" in American dance.

For their inspiring interviews and remarkable memories my sincere appreciation goes to Deborah Carr, Beatrice Seckler, and Janet Towner. I extend my gratitude to Sondra Horton Fraleigh for her guidance in showing me how to translate into words my study of Charles Weidman and his dances.

My thanks to the dance faculty of the State University of New York at Brockport, where this research began in earnest, especially to Jacqueline Davis, Garth Fagan, Santo Giglio, Clyde Morgan, Susannah Newman, and James Payton, whose expertise and guidance encouraged this research.

Many thanks to my colleagues of the State University of New York at Geneseo for their support, especially those whose theatrical designs brought Weidman's works to the stage. My appreciation goes to Alan Case for his dedication and skill in performing the musical scores to Weidman's dances. Many thanks to the dance faculty and student dancers who shared my enthusiasm for performing in Weidman's dances, especially to Jacqueline McCausland, Angela Amedore Caplan, Barbara Ball Mason, Joe Langworth, Christine Loria,

Laura Mosscrop, Mindy Franzese Wild, Deb Scodese French, Tari Karbowski, George Karl, Ambre Emory Maier, Tom Masters, Liz Lucena Moore, Merete Muenter, Melanie Aceto, Mark Broomfield, Victoria Baeder, Tom Coppola, Eileen Hegmann, Anne Irwin, Heather Klopchin, Christine Labeste, Melissa Murfin, Frank Paterno, Noel Raley, Diana Ricotta, Elizabeth Teegarden, Courtney Belloff, Kelly Campione, Kristi Condidorio, Kaleigh Schwarz, Kate Pistey, Heather Acomb, Chukwuma Obasi, and, numerous other dedicated students.

I am grateful to the State University of New York College at Geneseo for sabbaticals and grants that made this work possible. I would like to give special recognition to Professor of Art Thomas MacPherson for his figure drawings, and extra thanks to Jack Johnston, Lori Morsch, Cathy Reinholtz, and the School of the Arts for their generous assistance and in-kind services. I would also like to acknowledge Edward Antkoviak, Odette Blum, Christine Goff, Nancy Johncox, Bill T. Jones, Deborah Jowitt, Robert B. Kosinski, Mimi Muray Levitt, Karen Maccarone, Janet and Lloyd Morgan, Dot Virden Murphy, Margaret O'Sullivan, Norwood "PJ" Pennewell, M. Rosalind Pierson, and Sean Shanahan for their kindness and helpfulness.

My thanks to College librarians Bill Baker, Rich Dreifuss, Sonja Landes, Martha Reynolds, Harriet Sleggs, and especially Melissa Heald, my student research assistant. I extend my thanks to Sylvia Pelt Richards for writing her research dissertation on Charles Weidman, which proved to be a valuable resource carrying Charles Weidman's stamp of approval.

I express my sincere appreciation to Melanie Aceto, Deborah Carr, Bill Evans, Marie Henry, Heather Klopchin, Clare Lowsby, Ambre Emory Maier, Barbara Palfy, Mary DiSanto Rose, Nona Schurman, Kay Thomas, and Janet Towner for reading drafts of this manuscript and offering suggestions. My thanks to production editor Patricia Schultz for her support and guidance and to Dr. Doris L. Eder for her editing expertise.

For their support of this manuscript, my appreciation to Charles Humphrey Woodford, the son of Doris Humphrey, for reading and editing my first draft of this manuscript and to Charles Wilson, administrator of the Estate of Charles Weidman.

I am indebted to the fine staff at the Dance Collections in the New York Public Library for the Performing Arts, especially to Madeleine M. Nichols, Curator, Philip Krug, Tom Lisanti, Monica Mosley, and Charles Pierrier. The Charles Weidman Papers is an excellent resource. Weidman's original handwritten notes are valuable because of their authenticity. I have occasionally rephrased his writing for intelligibility, allowing Weidman's voice to be heard.

Finally, I express my heartfelt gratitude to my husband, Carl Shanahan, for his thoughtfulness, artistic vision, and loving support. I thank my parents, John and Helen, who encouraged my dancing since the age of seven; my brother John, my stepsons Sean and Shane, and my extended family and friends, all of whom have attentively supported me in my creative projects throughout the years.

Introduction

Journey to Weidman

My teaching of dance history at the State University of New York College at Geneseo spurred this investigation into the creative life of Charles Weidman. My colleague, Nona Schurman,[1] professor emeritus at Geneseo, was the pivotal individual inspiring this detailed search. A noted dancer, choreographer, and teacher, Schurman began training with Doris Humphrey and Charles Weidman in 1936. She joined their company in 1939 and during her tenure performed in their most notable works. By 1940, she had become a principal teacher at their school and was an assistant to both Humphrey and Weidman until 1943. While studying the Humphrey-Weidman dance technique, Schurman's exhilarating teaching style fostered my imagination and propelled me into this research.

Without Schurman's generosity in sharing her knowledge and experience of Weidman's dance technique, movement style, and choreography, I would not have had the opportunity of understanding this great lineage of American modern dance. She also introduced me to Deborah Carr,[2] who trained with Harriette Ann Gray, a teacher of Humphrey-Weidman dance technique at Stephens College. Carr eventually joined Charles Weidman's Theatre Dance Company in 1973. Through Schurman, many of Weidman's dances have been performed by the Geneseo Dance Ensemble and enjoyed by western New York audiences.

Having had the pleasure of directing and performing in Weidman's works with the Geneseo Dance Ensemble, I have established a historic perspective and a clear understanding of Weidman's significance as an artist. Within a fifteen-year period, performances of *Lynchtown* (1936), *Bargain Counter* (1936), *Opus 51, Opening Dance* (1938), *Brahms Waltzes* (1961), *The Christmas Oratorio,*

1

Excerpts (1961), and *Saint Matthew Passion, Four Excerpts* (1973) had been restaged by Carr and coached by Schurman. These dances exhibited a breadth of Weidman's artistic work that spanned his forty-seven year career.

While performing these works in 1990, I had an opportunity to collaborate with Schurman in restaging her 1957 Humphrey-Weidman technical demonstration *From Studio to Stage*.[3] This is a beautifully constructed twenty-minute dance originally created for the New Dance Group Studio in New York City, where Schurman taught from 1939 to 1965. When she composed it, she was directing the New Dance Group Studio's Young Concert Dancers Lecture Demonstrations (1956-64). Our reconstruction clarified similarities and differences in the movement styles of Weidman and Humphrey, illustrating the historic importance of the lecture-demonstration during this period.

To celebrate twenty-five years of Geneseo Dance Ensemble in 1993, Schurman and I used a Labanotation score to restage Humphrey's *The Shakers* (1931). Schurman had danced in *The Shakers* from 1939 to 1943, alongside Humphrey, Weidman, José Limón, Katherine Litz, Beatrice Seckler, and Lee Sherman, among others. Restaging this historic work with Schurman recalled my earlier directorial experience at the Wilkes-Barre Ballet Theatre, where I learned *The Shakers* from Ray Cook, a notator from the Dance Notation Bureau in New York City. Later, I learned *The Shakers* from notators Odette Blum and John Gilpin at Ohio State University where, in 1995, the centennial of Humphrey's birth was celebrated in a summer program. At this time, I also learned Humphrey's *Passacaglia in C Minor* (1938) from Gilpin, who restaged it using a Labanotation score. That summer I was Schurman's teaching assistant and demonstrator in her Humphrey dance technique course.

Earlier in my career, I had an opportunity to learn Humphrey's dance technique from Ernestine Henoch Stodelle, teacher, scholar, and dance critic. Stodelle was a member and soloist of the Doris Humphrey Concert Group from

2

1929 to 1935. Learning early Humphrey technique from Stodelle, illustrated in her book *The Dance Technique of Doris Humphrey*, strengthened my understanding for later study with Schurman.

While in New York City studying Weidman's technique in 1992, I had the good fortune to stay with Beatrice Seckler,[4] an exceptional dancer performing alongside Schurman in the Humphrey-Weidman Company from 1935 to 1944 and with Weidman's Theatre Dance Company. Seckler was a captivating storyteller, having found myself absorbing from her details of Humphrey-Weidman history for this research. At the same time, I was learning Weidman's dance technique and sections of his *Easter Oratorio* from Janet Towner,[5] Weidman's leading dancer and rehearsal assistant from 1969 to 1975. Studying with Towner would guide my clarification of the stylistic and technical traits specific to Weidman's art, recognizable in the creative work of José Limón.[6]

My study of Limón's technique began fifteen years before my meeting Schurman and my discovery of the Humphrey-Weidman techniques. Limón studied and performed with Humphrey and Weidman from 1929 to 1940, forming his own company in 1945. His system of dance technique is considered to be an extension of both Humphrey's and Weidman's original techniques. I had many opportunities to study Limón's technique with former Limón dancers Betty Jones, Pauline Koner, Susannah Newman, James Payton, Jennifer Scanlon, Nina Watt, and Chester Wolenski. Studying with these teachers, along with Schurman, Stodelle, Seckler, Carr, and Towner, gave me a sharply defined understanding of the Humphrey, Weidman, and Limón lineage that I delineate in my research.

Studying Humphrey-Weidman-Limón dance techniques and performing in Weidman's works enlivened my inquiry. I wanted to know Charles Weidman. In my exploration of Weidman's creative life, I have come to admire and respect his achievements and recognize his significant artistic contributions to American modern dance.

3

Chapter One offers a detailed overview of Weidman's creative life and his legacy to American dance. Using his ninth-grade essay *My Vocation*, this chapter highlights his vision of dance and his accomplishments during his fifty-five-year career. This chapter recognizes Weidman's contributions, examining his concert works, Broadway shows, and opera productions. It outlines his technique, stressing its historic lineage. Through my research I have discovered that most texts inadequately represent Weidman, though he is recognized as an originator of American dance. This chapter fully demonstrates Weidman's significance and will be useful as a supplement to courses in dance history and technique.

Chapter Two depicts Weidman's early years growing up in the Midwest at the turn of the twentieth century and through 1920, with his inspired departure for Los Angeles to study at Denishawn. After seeing Ruth St. Denis perform in his hometown, Weidman's vision of becoming a dancer, along with his strong sense of purpose, motivation, and work ethic made it possible to realize his dream. His Nebraska roots and family are given particular prominence.

Chapter Three follows the global influences on early modern dance that Weidman was a part of and which were a motivating factor in his artistic development. Research brought to light the importance of the internationalization of the arts through world trade and travel, with examples from vaudeville to the effects of French Impressionist and Japanese art that are evident in the works of noted choreographers of this period. New global religious doctrines affected Weidman and Humphrey's choreography, as seen in their themes of spiritual transcendence.

Chapter Four outlines Weidman's training at the Denishawn School. Special consideration is given to the movement theories of François Delsarte, music visualization, gesture and pantomime, modified ballet, yoga, and ethnological dances, all of which became embedded in Weidman's teaching and artistic work. This chapter establishes the similarities in Denishawn's training to

4

fundamental principles used in Humphrey-Weidman technique. Through a sketch of Denishawn's Asian Tour (1925-1926), the global and historic influences evident in Weidman's work are defined.

Chapter Five describes Weidman's partnership with Martha Graham. From their first encounter in Shawn's ballet *Xochitl* through their Denishawn tours until 1923, when Graham left to begin her independent career, they were good friends. Weidman was Graham's only partner, besides Shawn, until she met Erick Hawkins. After Graham left Denishawn, she and Weidman re-established their partnership in the early 1930s at the Neighborhood Playhouse, where they were leading dancers in Alice and Irene Lewisohn's orchestral dance dramas. As partners they gave stunning portrayals of the new modern dance. While doing my research, I wondered what path dance history would have taken if Weidman had not developed a strong affection and devotion to Doris Humphrey.

Chapter Six examines Weidman's partnership with Humphrey and Pauline Lawrence in establishing their Humphrey-Weidman School and Company. This chapter describes the circumstances that forced them to leave Denishawn; their first independent works; forming their own movement style and training system; and Lawrence's significant contribution to their theatre productions. It also gives special consideration to Weidman's men's group, his rebound principle, floor work movements based on Japanese Kabuki dance-drama, distinctive use of drums and rhythm, and his unique nonrepresentational *kinetic pantomime*.

Chapter Seven outlines how the content of Humphrey and Weidman's dances expressed social issues and provoked a mutable shift in the social and political climate in America. It was as partners that Humphrey and Weidman composed their most relevant works such as *Traditions, New Dance, Quest: A Choreographic Pantomime, With My Red Fires*, and *Lynchtown*; many have their first performances at Bennington College Summer School of Dance. These historic works of the 1930s and 1940s permanently changed the perception of

5

what constitutes contemporary dance. This chapter stresses why these American dancers wanted to express the lived experience of a modern democratic society in their works.

Chapter Eight delineates Weidman's movement style and technique system. Since he and Humphrey were partners for twenty years, they believed in similar fundamental ideals and worked from identical technical and stylistic tenets. I also acknowledge differences characteristic of Weidman and recognizable in José Limón's style and training system. I describe Weidman's formulated technical studies, or series, and how he subsequently organized many of Humphrey's exercises into a distinct form. The importance of the lecture and technique demonstration to this period is indicated by showing comparable aspects of the technique demonstrations in Weidman's *Classroom, Modern Style* and Schurman's *From Studio to Stage*.

Chapter Nine depicts Humphrey and Weidman's artistic activities at their Studio Theatre on West Sixteenth Street. It highlights their artistic work in the midst of their difficult lives and straitened circumstances during the period bridging the years of the Depression and World War II. Within the Studio Theatre Weidman composed his best works: *On My Mother's Side, And Daddy Was a Fireman,* and *Flickers.* When Humphrey considered retirement due to an injury, Weidman organized his Theatre Dance Company. In 1948 the Humphrey-Weidman partnership ended. Subsequently Limón formed his own company, with Humphrey as his advisor and choreographer. For the first time in nearly thirty years, Weidman had to pursue artistic endeavors on his own.

Chapter Ten outlines Weidman's achievements on the Broadway stage. He created nearly twenty Broadway productions—many in collaboration with Humphrey. Weidman worked with such theatrical greats as Norman Bel Geddes, Harold Arlen, Johnny Mercer, Michael Myerberg, Hassard Short, Ethel Waters, Sam H. Harris, Lawrence Langer, Ira Gershwin, Bert Lahr, George M. Cohan,

6

Moss Hart, George S. Kaufman, Richard Rodgers, E. Y. Harburg, and Langston Hughes, among others. He worked in one successful show after another—and some failures—from 1930 to 1958. Besides his teaching, choreography of concert works, and Broadway productions, Weidman was resident choreographer of the New York City Opera, where his modern dance ideas revitalized the dancing and staging of traditional opera.

Chapter Eleven focuses on Weidman's artistic achievements from 1960 to 1970. This chapter highlights the formation of the Expression of Two Arts Theatre with visual artist Mikhail Santaro, and eventually the incorporation of the Charles Weidman School of Modern Dance and the Charles Weidman Foundation. Weidman worked on numerous projects simultaneously—making new dances, such as *Brahms Waltzes* (dedicated to Humphrey), performing every Sunday evening with his company, teaching and restaging his works at more than two hundred colleges and universities, and directing a reconstruction of Humphrey's *New Dance*. Weidman, with his energy, vitality, and sense of purpose, was constantly looking ahead to the next project.

Chapter Twelve outlines Weidman's artistic projects in the last five years of his life, including *Saint Matthew Passion* and his last work, *Visualization, or From a Farm in New Jersey*. This chapter takes into account Weidman's collaboration with the Dance Notation Bureau in preserving his works for future generations, and lists the numerous projects left unfulfilled by his untimely death.

Chapter Thirteen offers an opportunity to those dancers who have studied and performed with Weidman to share their impressions of Charles with us. Through their recollections we can come to a deeper understanding of his influence and legacy in modern American dance.

From Weidman to Contemporary Dance

The *Dance Heritage Coalition* recently announced their selection of what they called *America's Irreplaceable Dance Treasures: The First 100*. The coalition's aim is to honor the outstanding contributions of these one hundred dance treasures by showing their importance to American life and to draw public attention to those who may be endangered or in need of preservation. To be honored on this prestigious list means being accorded a significant place in the history of dance in America. Charles Weidman is on this list of luminaries. Throughout the twentieth century, these artists made their indelible imprint on modern dance technique for men: Ted Shawn, Charles Weidman, José Limón, Lester Horton, Alvin Ailey, Daniel Nagrin, Alwin Nikolais, Murray Lewis, Paul Taylor, Merce Cunningham, Garth Fagan, Bill T. Jones, and Mark Morris, among others. All enjoyed illustrious performing careers, along with remarkably prolific, choreographic lives. Influenced by their teachers, they in turn influenced others.

While tracing each of these artists' remarkable careers, we should take note of how they furthered dance as a performing art. Each imparted a marked, individual way of moving or dancing (movement style); a distinct manner of organizing movement within stage space; a particular way of tying movement in dance to music; the content of their dances appealed to audiences; and the progeny of company members launched individual careers by using their teachers' methods, expanding upon or deviating from them. Ponder the idea that each individual dancer today is part of an extended dance family influenced by their ancestry. As a dancer whose career spanned fifty-five years, Charles Weidman used to tell his students, "You're in the long line."

For Weidman, the line moves like this: Ruth St. Denis' mystical performances inspired Ted Shawn to travel across the United States to New York City to audition as her partner. Joining their names they opened a dance school,

8

and company in Los Angeles called Denishawn. Their company's performance of excerpts from their dance pageant of Egypt, Greece, and India was seen by young Weidman in Lincoln, Nebraska, in 1916, inspiring him to embark on a dance career. He traveled halfway across the United States to Los Angeles to study with Shawn and St. Denis. Weidman met Martha Graham who, in 1920, became his first dance partner in Shawn's Toltec ballet *Xochitl*. At Denishawn, Weidman encountered his first teacher, Doris Humphrey, a leading dancer who became his associate and dance partner from 1928 to 1945 in their Humphrey-Weidman Company and School. Pauline Lawrence, whom Weidman met on the *Xochitl* tour, was an accompanist and dancer who would join their partnership as company manager, costume designer, and pianist.

As a young dancer steeped in theatrical experience, Weidman performed for eight years with the Denishawn Dancers, the first American modern dance company made up of women and men. He was unmistakably influenced by Shawn's dance technique and choreography. Upon Weidman's arrival at Denishawn in 1920, he became Shawn's assistant in technique classes and taught it at the New York Denishawn School in 1927. Shawn created several solos for Weidman that capitalized on his brilliant pantomimic skills: *Danse Américaine* and *The Crapshooter*. Later in his career, Weidman devised his own unique, nonrepresentational gestures and actions called *kinetic pantomime*.

Weidman's high-school friend Perkins Harnley introduced José Limón to Weidman and, in 1929, Limón began his training with Weidman and Humphrey. Limón became Weidman's assistant in technique classes by 1932 and performed in Broadway shows choreographed by Weidman. After performing with the Humphrey-Weidman Company for eleven years, Limón originated his own dance company in 1945, continuing this lineage. Humphrey eventually retired from her performing career and became choreographer and artistic advisor to Limón's dance company until her death in 1958. Lawrence became Limón's wife in 1941, performing similar duties for his company as she had for Humphrey-Weidman, such as designing costumes and attending to pragmatic details of company management. Ruth St. Denis, Martha Graham, Doris Humphrey, and Pauline Lawrence, influential women in American dance, played prominent roles in the development of the remarkable towering men of twentieth-century modern dance.

Spanning the entire twentieth century, the Shawn-Weidman/Limón line of men dancers is one of the most recognized links in American modern dance. Each of these men greatly influenced the others, creating a lineage. This Shawn-Weidman/Limón lineage is traceable from Denishawn to Shawn's Men's Group to the Humphrey-Weidman Company (1928-45), then to Weidman's Dance Theatre Company (1945-75), and finally to Limón's own company. Even today, Limón's dance company and institute maintain his technique and repertory for current and future generations to study. This lineage, with its remarkable system of training, has developed hundreds of striking performers and produced extraordinary male dancers.

These men made many significant contributions to twentieth-century American modern dance. First and foremost, they taught technique systematically, performed, and gave lectures and demonstrations. Secondly, they evolved movement styles or dance techniques based on individual points of view and aesthetic or artistic values. Thirdly, they expanded a community of dancers, composers, pianists, costume designers, company managers, visual artists, lighting designers, stage managers, scenic designers, dance notators, friends, and families. They also created unique bodies of work performed by their companies in concert with their artistic collaborators. This study helps to clarify their dance techniques, features their innovative works, and shows their integral role in educating dancers and audience members.

Similarities in movement styles and dance techniques are recognizable throughout the twentieth century. Numerous historic institutions promoted these dance artists through summer schools of dance: The Ted Shawn School of Dance, the Denishawn School of Dance, Bennington College, Mills College, Perry-Mansfield School of Theatre and Dance, Connecticut College, Springfield College, Colorado College, Jacob's Pillow, the Juilliard School, and the American Dance Festival at Duke University. These institutions, along with many others, artistically and financially supported these artists by granting such celebrated men and women of twentieth-century American modern dance the opportunity to "create their long line."

Before the Denishawn Dancers embarked on their Asian Tour in 1925, Ruth St. Denis left Denishawn House in New York City in the hands of capable teachers with her trusting, carefree, departing statement, "Carry On." St. Denis and Shawn had faith that their institution and techniques would be continued for the two years they were gone. Perhaps Weidman first heard this line from St. Denis, since Weidman often signed letters with "his valiant and optimistic slogan."[7] The Charles Weidman School of Modern Dance Newsletter was entitled "Carry On . . ."

Weidman wished to perpetuate his dances and technique. Several factors indicate his sense of purpose regarding this. Early on, Weidman initiated his interest in recording his works for future generations through scores written by the Dance Notation Bureau. Weidman, throughout his career, gave to his young dancers opportunities to try their hands at teaching and choreography " a generous move which only the great can afford to take."[8] Among teachers who have carried Weidman's and Humphrey's legacy forward are: José Limón, Nona Schurman, Lee Sherman, Harriette Ann Gray, Eleanor King, Ernestine Stodelle, Letitia Ide, William Bales, Katherine Litz, Peter Hamilton, Saida Gerrard, Craig Gabrian, William Matons, Carol Mezzacappa, Betty Osgood, Carl Morris, David Wynn, Anne Dunbar Williams, Elina Mooney, Dorothy Virden Murphy, Deborah Carr, Janet Towner, and, many others. These teachers developed their own

11

technical studies or extended movement phrases built on the Humphrey-Weidman technique. In addition to the aforementioned dancers and teachers, many noted performers were part of the Humphrey-Weidman Company such as Jack Cole, Beatrice Seckler, Anna Halprin, Katherine Manning, Sybil Shearer, and Frank Westbrook.[9] Weidman formed his own Theatre Dance Company in 1948 after Humphrey retired as a dancer. Among Weidman's dancers and students were Alvin Ailey, Bob Fosse, Gene Kelly, Jerome Robbins, Toni Charmoli, Lee Sherman, Emily Frankel, Mark Ryder, Peter Hamilton, Marge Champion, Melissa Hayden, and Charles Moore.[10] Clearly, Weidman has not only been a guiding force to modern American dance, but he has also influenced dance in musical theatre, jazz dance, and ballet.

Even those who only briefly worked with Weidman were impressed by his teaching and choreography. Besides the legendary Limón, other luminaries of dance were also guided by him. Alwin Nikolais studied with Weidman at Bennington College and said: "It was with Charles that I decided to become a dancer."[11] Paul Taylor said: "People forget I studied at Juilliard, worked with Charles Weidman, with Doris Humphrey, . . . Katherine Litz, others."[12] Garth Fagan worked with Weidman as a student at Wayne State University; his principal dancer and artistic associate Norwood Pennewell studied the Humphrey-Weidman technique with Nona Schurman at the State University College at Geneseo, where he performed with the Geneseo Dance Ensemble in Humphrey's *The Shakers*. In a recent interview, Mark Morris was asked to reveal his thoughts about the future of dance. Morris professed: " . . . at the turn of the century, mime will come back. Mime will come back as a reaction to increased technology. Mime, the simplest sort of street theatre, will come back."[13] Bill T. Jones, who studied with a Humphrey-Weidman/Limón teacher in college, said that, as a young dancer, the classic moderns were inspiring to him "for their lyricism and clarity of styles . . ."[14] Jones has been affected by Humphrey's and

12

Weidman's movement philosophy of "fall, recovery, and rebound" as well. Now, thirty years after his death, evidence from these celebrated contemporary dance artists begins shedding new light on Weidman's enormous influence.

Chapter One

A Vocation

My Vocation
As long ago as I can remember I have cherished the vision of becoming
an artist . . . to succeed . . . through my hard work and efforts to build my
own palace of my own thoughts and ideas so that I can live in it in peace
and comfort and not be a parasite in name or reality.

Charles Weidman
(Ninth-Grade Essay)

Fifteen year-old Charles Weidman already realized when he wrote his ninth-grade essay that for him to succeed in a dance occupation would require "hard work and efforts."[1] Through earnest persistence and energy, Weidman would succeed not only in his desire to become an artist, but would become a major figure in the development of twentieth-century American dance. As a child growing up in Nebraska, he learned that his striving required his taking on many jobs such as delivering newspapers, ushering at a movie theatre, working for the telephone company, teaching dance lessons, performing in community opera productions—all to bring him closer to his "cherished vision of becoming an artist." Weidman believed he was destined to become a dancer, and he did everything in his power to accomplish his destiny.

15

Vision of Becoming an Artist

Weidman grew impatient with others who did not have his strength of purpose. He wrote, "I condemn one if that one does not fulfill his or her destiny according to that persons possibilities or limitations [sic]."[2] He expected this same uncompromising attitude from his students and company members. "In his role as teacher and director," wrote David Wynn, who danced with Weidman in the 1950s, "he was very demanding, always insisting on sincerity and hard work."[3]

Young Charles, as avowed in his ninth-grade essay *My Vocation*, already knew that arduous activity and exertion are keys to success. In the environment of his dance studio, he expressed his idealistic views; in the theatre where his performances presented his artistry to the public view, and in rich personal relationships with family he built a palace of his imagination.

After high school graduation in 1920, nineteen-year-old Charles left his family in Lincoln, Nebraska, to pursue his dream of becoming a dancer. He traveled to Los Angeles to study at the Ted Shawn Dance Studio. After one month, Shawn sent him on tour to replace injured Robert Gorham in the lead role opposite Martha Graham in *Xochitl*. Weidman spent the next eight years dancing with the Denishawn Dancers alongside Shawn, Ruth St. Denis, Martha Graham, Doris Humphrey, Georgia Graham, Jane Sherman, and others. He danced to the musical accompaniment of Louis Horst, Pauline Lawrence, and Clifford Vaughan, all historic contributors to American dance. For the first three years of their careers, Graham and Weidman were partners in many of Shawn's ballets, including *Xochitl* and *Arabic Duet*. "Charles Weidman was my friend," Martha Graham wrote in 1989, "and as a deeply sensitive artist gave to me many gentle and performing moments during my life at Denishawn [sic]."[4] Even though Charles was at times financially poor—as he expressed in his ninth-grade essay, "my aims are not to become rich . . . but to succeed in making my thoughts and

16

ideas come true"—he was always artistically and spiritually wealthy. Weidman's artistic wealth characterizes his legacy to American dance.

After fifty-three years in the dance profession, Weidman received one of his greatest honors on June 3, 1973, when the Jersey City State College in New Jersey made him a Doctor of Humane Letters. Weidman's citation summarized his legacy to American dance:

> A legend in dance, pioneer of modern dance, comic genius, foremost male dancer-teacher-choreographer of his era, father of modern dance, Charles Weidman almost single handedly lifted his art to a high place when the male was still an oddity, and modern dance itself in danger of being engulfed in gloom and lost in mediocrity. The instincts and needs of the pioneer has colored his dancing, teaching and choreography for more than four decades, defining him as one of the major figures in American modern dance. [sic][5]

As a distinguished choreographer, dancer, teacher, and writer of twentieth-century America, Weidman was admired for his unique sense of humor; he created amusing, clever, lighthearted dances. These qualities set him apart from his contemporaries and gave him distinction; he was applauded by his fellow dancers, audience members, and critics. Beatrice Seckler, a longtime leading Weidman dancer, remembers what she thought made Weidman a comic genius: "He had a very special understanding of what was ridiculous in people and society that made for his ability and his approach to comedy."[6] José Limón, who knew Weidman for over a decade, agrees with Seckler's opinion. "He had a natural gift for satire," Limón writes, "a capacity to distill the essence of comedy from the human condition."[7] Weidman's humor defined his dancing and choreography, but his teaching manner and methodology were the foundations of his art.

Weidman's principal dancer and teaching assistant during the 1970s, Janet Towner, recalls why so many college students were drawn to him and his work: "There was something about Charles that was compelling . . . his joy and warmth was an inspiration from the very first day."[8] Weidman's artistry and teaching have distinctive traits. In her book *Modern Dance Fundamentals,* Nona Schurman, dancer and principal teacher at the Humphrey-Weidman school, writes: "With his musical sensitivity and wonderful sense of form," he used basic "principles to design technical studies of breath-taking interest and vitality."[9] Weidman's technical exercises, called "studies" or "series," were repeated in each class. Through repetition a dancer developed clarity of line and muscle strength. His technique has a definite physical development. Weidman also used choreographic principles (direction, change of front, design, rhythm, contrast) in his studies or series. Along with these technical studies he taught phrases from his dances. Deborah Carr recalls Weidman's teaching: "The way Charles taught class, we would work on strictly technical things and then he had what he called movement sequences where he actually took bits and pieces of the repertory that he taught us and these were very isolated."[10] Weidman had a prolific choreographic life, composing over one hundred dance works. Being completely absorbed in the creative process, he expected his dancers to invest wholeheartedly in his inventiveness. Towner writes: "He had little patience with dancers whose worry and concern over technicalities stood in the way of their ability to join in the spirit of what he was offering them. He didn't denigrate them, he simply ignored their worries, and went about his business of creating dances."[11]

Building His Own Palace

Humphrey and Weidman, as colleagues and dance partners from 1928 to 1948, founded their own school, theatre, and company—or institution. They joined together their names just as their teachers at Denishawn, St. Denis and Shawn, had done before them. Dancers who studied the techniques of Humprey and Weidman and danced their dances during the period 1935-1948 are considered Humphrey-Weidman.[12] Today, the Humphrey-Weidman dance technique practiced during this period, along with Graham's and Limón's, is considered "classic" modern dance. As contemporary trends in dance evolved, the dance technique systems of Taylor, Cunningham, Nagrin, Nikolais, and Horton could be also termed traditional or "classic" modern dance.

Weidman created a distinctive dance technique that is based on fundamental movement concepts that he shared with his colleague Humphrey. Their basic principles of body movement are suspension, fall, recovery, rebound, succession, opposition, metric rhythm, and breath rhythm. Weidman's technique includes the lyricism of Humphrey's dance style, along with his own powerfully vigorous approach to jumps, turns, and floor-work. It is the joining together of their techniques that makes it so rich in scope. In contrast to other dance techniques, the Humphrey-Weidman technique "had a breadth about it that many others didn't have," recalls Bill Hooks, former Weidman dancer in the 1950s. "Doris and Charles felt free to pick up elements from any culture and use them."[13] Hook's statement seemingly refers to their Denishawn experiences that brought a global approach to their technique. In *Modern Dance Fundamentals*, Schurman explains numerous cultural dance phrases that she devised for training dancers to perform in Humphrey-Weidman works; among them are Highland, Basque, Tartar, Israeli, and Spanish.[14] Weidman, inspired by ethnological dances with their complicated rhythms and uneven phrase lengths, features these in his dances and technical exercises.

Using expansive movements at a fast tempo, Weidman's dance training was physically challenging. He encouraged dancers in a way that was uniquely Weidman. "He made you feel that it was possible, that you could do it," Towner recalls.[15]   While teaching class, Weidman used humorous remarks to foster confidence in dancers, as exemplified in Towner's description: "In class he had his standing drums and hand drum. He had a little stool with his cigarettes and ashtray. He'd be drumming and lighting cigarettes, while the dancers were moving across the floor. You'd be struggling and he'd say, 'It's not yet a poem.'"[16] When teaching class, Weidman had a penchant for dramatic humor, especially when directing his remarks to veteran dancers. David Wynn recalls a specific instance during one of Weidman's classes: "Charles was also fond of gently teasing us by stopping the drum in class and looking fixedly at someone, who then thought he must have done something wrong. Charles would wait a moment, then say, 'That was pretty good. You should study dance, take lessons.'"[17]

Weidman was engaging as an artist because he not only created comedy, through what he calls *kinetic pantomime*, but also composed beautifully constructed, abstract concert dances such as *Quest: A Choreographic Pantomime* (1936), *A House Divided* (1945), *Brahms Waltzes* (1961), *The Easter Oratorio* (1967), and *Saint Matthew Passion* (1973). Weidman choreographed Broadway musicals, operas, and revues. Not many of his contemporaries ventured into all of these theatrical modes. Deborah Carr, former dancer with Weidman, agrees: "Charles was so totally involved in theatre that I don't think he felt that any one corner needed to be left unexplored."[18] Weidman's artistry and movement style was suitable for the Broadway stage, and he choreographed fifteen Broadway productions, many in collaboration with his partner, Humphrey. Celebrated examples are *Lysistrata* (1930), *Americana* (1932), *As Thousands Cheer* (1933), *Life Begins at 8:40* (1934), *I'd Rather Be Right* (1937), *New Faces* (1942), *Sing Out, Sweet Land!* (1944), *The Barrier* (1950), and *Portofino* (1958).[19] With the success of these Broadway shows, Charles was able to fulfill his dream and buy a farm in Blairstown, New Jersey, where he, José, Doris, and Pauline spend many

20

summer vacations. "Charles, in particular, was to function successfully in the Broadway arena," writes Limón, "presaging the later success of Hanya Holm, Helen Tamiris, Agnes de Mille, and Jerome Robbins."[20]

Weidman was considered one of the major choreographers for opera along with ballet choreographers George Balanchine, Ruth Page, and Antony Tudor.[21] He was resident choreographer from 1949 until 1955 for the New York City Opera Company at City Center in New York. In Chicago, he shared the ballet mastership of the New York City Opera Company with Grant Mourdadoff.[22] Weidman considered creating new ballets for grand opera "a decisive and important step in bringing modern dance into the realm of the lyric theatre."[23] He created dances for Sergei Prokofiev's *Love For Three Oranges*, Giacomo Puccini's *Turandot*, Umberto Giordano's *Andrea Chénier*, Ermanno Wolf Ferrari's *The Four Ruffians*, Giuseppe Verdi's *La Traviata* and *Aida,* Georges Bizet's *Carmen*, and Richard Wagner's *Die Meistersinger.* Charles was persuaded by conductor Leopold Sasche to mime the role of Leopold (the bastard son of Baron Ochs) in the opera *Der Rosenkavalier* by Richard Strauss.[24]

Pioneering the Dance Plain

Humphrey and Weidman organized their own school in 1928, composed mostly of women dancers. With Weidman's interest in ancient civilizations and tribally based societies, he wanted to recapture in modern times the idea of dance training as a valuable part of education for young men.[25] Charles began offering free lessons to men, with the stipulation that once they enrolled they would pay $2.00 for missed lessons. Weidman's idea was turning out to be what he had envisioned and hoped for—an all-men's company.

Weidman launched on a productive period creating works for men. During the Experimental Years of the Dance Repertory Theatre, 1930 to 1933, he choreographed dances such as *Steel and Stone* and *Ringside* for himself, Charles

Lasky, and José Limón, as well as *The Marionette Theatre* for him, Sylvia Manning, Eugene Le Sieur, and George Steares, a dancer from his Denishawn days. During this time, Weidman's company was composed of men while Humphrey's company was composed of women; they combined their companies for special dances.

One occasion to combine their companies was offered by Weidman's 1931 undertaking of *The Happy Hypocrite*, or *A Fairy Tale for Tired Men*, by Max Beerbohm. With music composed by Herbert Elwell, who suggested the idea for the dance, the tale was "wittily told in a pantomime dance of three scenes," Winthrop Palmer observes.[26] *The Happy Hypocrite* was Weidman's first major modern dance that humorously communicated through Weidman's distinctive gestures what had previously been mastered as a literary work. In *The Borzoi Book of Modern Dance*, Margaret Lloyd writes of her pleasure at seeing *The Happy Hypocrite*: "The discourse was pantomime in the same inimitable manner, dance and pantomime flowing logically, the one out of the other, and the whole high comedy of the most delectable flavor."[27] By 1934, Charles and Doris were famous. In *Days On Earth*, Marcia Siegel confirms this fact when she writes: "They had their pictures in slick magazines, eminent Broadway producers were said to be looking for starring vehicles for them, and they were acknowledged, with Graham, as leaders and spokesmen for American dance."[28]

The American modern dance movement grew from adolescence to maturity when, in 1934, Vermont's Bennington College, a progressive college for women, offered its facilities for a Summer School of Dance under the direction of Martha Hill and Mary Josephine Shelly. Students in small towns and big cities from all across the United States came to Bennington College to study with the originators of the new American modern dance. They were either dance or physical education teachers or those aspiring to become professional dancers. Weidman was established as one of the Bennington Group, of recognized

22

"pioneers" of modern dance: Graham, Humphrey, and Hanya Holm. These pioneers, along with composers Louis Horst and Norman Lloyd, scenic designer Arch Lauterer, historian John Martin, and photographer Barbara Morgan, disseminated their techniques and were given opportunities to create new works.[29] Among the artistic works they created during seven summers at Bennington College were Weidman's *Quest: A Choreographic Pantomime* (1936) and *Opus 51* (1938); Humphrey's *New Dance* (1935) and *Passacaglia in C Minor* (1938); Graham's *American Document* (1938) and *Letter to the World* (1940); and Holm's *Trend* (1937).

Throughout 1935, Humphrey and Weidman composed their most significant concert works: *Duo-Drama*, *New Dance*, and *Traditions*. The success of their collaboration derived from their intuitive ability to compose dances together. Their artistic partnership, now at its peak, finds expression in a controversial duet, *Duo-Drama*, a poignant portrayal of a relationship between a man and a woman. Their next collaboration, *New Dance*, was a large ensemble work in which the leaders, danced by Humphrey and Weidman, harmoniously united various individuals to represent a utopian society. *New Dance*, in theme-and-variations form, is Humphrey's choreographic poem distinguished by its lofty expression of the noble spirit of humankind, its elaborate form, and its dignified style.[30] Weidman collaborated with Humphrey to invent the movement themes of *New Dance*; he also created the *Third Theme* using male dancers. Bennington College's Summer Dance Festival gave the official premiere of *New Dance* on August 3, 1935, with music by American composer Wallingford Riegger. On completion of their *New Dance*, Humphrey was inspired by the subject to compose her second masterwork, *Theatre Piece*, while Weidman completed the distinctive work, *Traditions*.

Weidman's *Traditions* is a men's trio that was first performed on October 12, 1935, to a musical score by the young American composer, Lehman Engel. It highlights Weidman's talent for high comedy as he portrays three figures, symbolic of three different characters within the confines of tradition, represented by a recurring movement theme. Using theme-and-variations form, Weidman shows the violent struggle of two figures to break the bonds of tradition. With contempt, these two figures boldly attack the third, also danced by Weidman. Their opposition to this third figure, who upholds tradition, is so strong that they forcibly topple him and he dies an elaborate humorous death—only to revive to coerce his two antagonists into resuming the movement theme symbolizing tradition. In these works, *Duo-Drama*, *New Dance*, and *Traditions*, both Humphrey's and Weidman's artistry is inseparable from their humanism.

At the Bennington Summer Dance Festival in 1936, Weidman presented *Quest: A Choreographic Pantomime*, a topical work with the music of Norman Lloyd. It portrays the "adjustment of an artist to the unsympathetic environment of the present-day world," Lillian Moore writes.[31] *Quest's* main theme, however, concerns the role of the artist in society. In *The New York Times*, John Martin writes, "the work as a whole is a new milestone in the career of this genuinely brilliant young artist."[32] Winthrop Palmer agrees with Martin's statement that *Quest* represents a major accomplishment on Weidman's part. In her book, *Theatrical Dancing in America*, Palmer writes: "With *Quest*, Charles Weidman seemed to have ended his apprenticeship. Allegory and fantasy no longer occupied him. He began to study the life of the people around him."[33] At this same time, Weidman developed his own unique movement style that Martin calls *kinetic pantomime*. Olga Maynard considers Weidman to be "a comic genius, inventive, fresh and clever."[34] Limón agrees with Maynard's observation of Weidman's genius: "He was peerless as a comedian. His comic genius, completely spontaneous and instinctive, had a flavor, precision, and subtlety unmatched by anyone, anywhere, in his time."[35]

24

Through his dance compositions, Weidman became known for portraying human weakness through humorous situations with biting jest. His signature work, *Atavisms*, created in 1936, comprises three separate dances: *Bargain Counter*, *Stock Exchange*, and *Lynchtown*. In this trilogy, Weidman symbolically stresses human imperfections through reversion to a primal mode. In *Bargain Counter*, greed for material wealth is shown as women frantically shop in a discount department store. In *Stock Exchange*, a business executive, dependent on others for his success, saves himself at the expense of others when the stock market crashes. In *Lynchtown*, the intolerant bigotry of an angry mob is fuel for a horrific lynching.

Weidman capitalized on his unique movement style in the 1937 theatre work *Candide, A Dance Interpretation of Voltaire's Candide*. As part of the Federal Dance Theatre, *Candide* shared an evening's program at the Nora Bayes Theatre with Helen Tamiris' *How Long, Brethren?* Using the music of Wallingford Riegger and Genevieve Pitot, Weidman adapted Voltaire's fanciful tale. He played the leading role of Candide with a cast of twelve principal players and twenty-five dancers. Limón, who was a featured dancer in this unique theatrical work, remembered Charles' performance in *Candide*: "He captured with great sensitiveness the pathos and naïve charm of Voltaire's hero."[36]

In the Bennington College Summer Dance Festival in 1938, Weidman created a delightful new work, *Opus 51*, comprising six variant sections on an inventive score by Vivian Fine that is aptly titled *Opus 51* since this was his fifty-first dance. In *Opus 51*, Weidman elaborates on *kinetic pantomime* or nonrepresentational pantomime, his original method of using gestures—in this case, functional gestures—to create a humorous, fast-paced, free-for-all.

Weidman's teenage experiences in community opera productions and his work in Broadway musicals offered him a way to uniquely blend his dance with theatrical narrative in concert choreography. He became versed in comical and dramatic dances pulling from real life situations for many. Remembering his family and stories of his kinfolk vividly, Weidman paid tribute to them in several artistic works. As miniature biographies, *And Daddy Was a Fireman* (1943), a dramatic paternal portrayal, and *On My Mother's Side* (1940), a maternal pioneer portrait, each offer renderings of Weidman's own family. The appeal of his biographical works is that everyone can relate to these funny, poignant relationships and apply them to their own families. These dances also gave Weidman an opportunity to exhibit his remarkable performing ability—one of his greatest assets as a dancer.

Saving money to study at Denishawn as a teen, Weidman worked as an usher at a local motion picture theatre, where he also changed the billboards at the front of the theatre.[37] Weidman happily watched films over and over again. He came to know all the film celebrities and their famous movies, subconsciously absorbing movement nuances of the silent film genre that he would use again later in his career. Fascinated with the art form of theatre out of which motion pictures developed, Weidman was drawn to every aspect of drama revealed in motion pictures: comedy, tragedy, melodrama, musical comedy, Western and vaudeville. He experienced firsthand the delight of the mass movie audience at the antics in the slapstick comedies of Mark Sennett's famous Keystone Cops; their excitement during action-filled westerns starring G. M. "Broncho Billy" Anderson and wild-West show performer Tom Mix; and their reactions to the suspense of movie serials starring Mary Pickford, Douglas Fairbanks, and Buster Keaton. Later Weidman observed the public's fascination with Hollywood stars Gloria Swanson, Rudolph Valentino, and the great comic actor, Charlie Chaplin. Using his kinetic memory, Weidman created his impressions of the plots and stars of silent films in his signature work *Flickers*, a delectable comic dance with a piano score by Lionel Nowak. Weidman wrote the scenario in 1942, using *kinetic pantomime* to conjure up plots of four typical silent movies: "Hearts Aflame," based on the story of a hero, a girl, and two villains; "Wages of Sin," featuring Doris Humphrey as Theda Bara, the American actress whose fame as a motion-picture vamp epitomized scandalous sex appeal; "Flowers of the Desert" showing a Rudolph Valentino-style sheik separating young lovers, Beatrice Seckler and Lee Sherman with a tantalizing tango; and "Hearts Courageous" depicting a pioneer family defending their homestead in the Midwest.[38] Weidman portrayed the loutish hero in the first section and the diabolical sheik (a masterful man to whom women are irresistibly attracted) in "Flowers of the Desert." His capacity for characterization through narrative form and his stellar performance in *Flickers* are recognized in *The Complete Guide to Modern Dance*, Don McDonagh noting: "Weidman's talent for pantomime dance was never better than in his small and perfect replica of early movie days."[39]

Weidman composed his imaginative dance *David and Goliath* (based on the Biblical story) to a score by Johann Kuhnau. Against a backdrop of Israelites and Philistines, this modern rendering featured Weidman as the huge, "dumb" Goliath and Peter Hamilton as David, the sprightly "wonderboy." Within sections of *David and Goliath* Weidman combined multi-layered movement sequences in variegated dance styles joining motifs from ancient, tribal-based and baroque dancing with Humphrey-Weidman techniques and *kinetic pantomime* to compose this hilarious work. In 1993, the Purchase Dance Corps was the recipient of Peter Hamilton's reconstruction of Weidman's 1945 work *David and Goliath*.

Weidman was awarded a Simon Guggenheim Fellowship in 1947 to compose his most celebrated dance, *Fables for Our Time*. When Weidman's company danced *Fables for Our Time* at the Jacob's Pillow Summer Dance Festival in Lee, Massachusetts, he told *Time Magazine* that, after Doris Humphrey was forced to curtail her performing career due to an injury, he decided to compose a dance "as understandable and popular as the movies."[40] This renowned work is based on a book written by James Thurber called *Fables for*

27

Our Time (1939-40). The dance narrates four animal stories through a series of pantomimic episodes that dramatically meld the story with music by American composer Freda Miller. In his review, Walter Terry appreciates her music and Weidman's artistry: "The Thurber tales are wonderfully suited to Mr. Weidman's matchless kinetic humor and pungent pantomime."[41] Weidman continued to popularize modern dance in two other Thurber works, *The War Between Men and Women* (1954) and *Five Further Fables* (1960), drawing upon James Thurber's *Further Fables for Our Time*. In her review of *Five Further Fables* in *Dance Magazine*, Doris Hering concludes: "Mr. Weidman's delicacy of gesture and his sense of whimsy made us wonder why American audiences do not surround him with the adulation they confer upon Gallic mimes."[42] Hering is referring to French pantomimists such as Marcel Marceau, who began his own troupe in 1947 and, like Weidman, had great success performing solo sketches that portrayed a remarkable emotional range.

Interested in the preservation of his and Humphrey's dances through notation, photography, film, and videotape, Weidman was supportive in developing a center for dance notation; courses in notation were taught at his studio. The Dance Notation Bureau, founded in New York City in 1940 by Ann Hutchinson (Guest), Helen Priest Rogers, and Eve Gentry, remains the international center for dance notation research.[43] The Bureau bases its research on the dance notation system called Labanotation, also known as Kinetography Laban, conceived by Rudolf Laban (1879-1958), dancer, teacher, and choreographer. The Dance Notation Bureau continues to be instrumental in developing the application of the Labanotation system through the preparation of teaching materials, workshops, and correspondence courses; preserving dances through writing of nototion scores; restaging dances from notation scores, creating an Internet Website, and establishing a professional organization (ICKL) the International Council of Kinetography Laban.[44] To preserve his dances for future generations to perform, Weidman arranged for the Dance Notation Bureau to notate the scores of his compositions *Song of Songs* and *Lynchtown*. Jessie Burchess notated Labanotation scores for Weidman's works and Ann Hutchinson (Guest) notated the score for Humphrey's *The Shakers*. In 1950, these historic dances by Humphrey and Weidman were performed by the dancers of New York City Dance Theatre at the City Center Theatre in Manhattan.[45]

Expression of Two Arts

For several years during Weidman's mid-career in the 1950s, financial burdens made his studio small and shabby; some critics note this in their reviews. These were trying years in his life, a time when grief became overwhelming. Many factors seemed to overpower him: the loss of his dancing partner and collaborator Humphrey, forced to retire due to an injury; the subsequent disbanding of the Humphrey-Weidman company; the closing of the Humphrey-Weidman Studio Theatre at 108 West Sixteenth Street; and the loss of family members. These hardships sent Weidman spiraling into depression. He compromised his physical and mental health by needing to escape his pain through alcohol. Without his studio to teach in or a company to compose new works for he was not able to think about the future, just trying to get through each day with the help of alcohol. He spent his days in a neighborhood tavern or secluded in his room. Because of his depression and addiction, no new Broadway shows and few teaching assignments were offered him. He subsequently had to give up his apartment and move into the Woodward Hotel. During these difficult years, slowly Weidman's Nebraska temperament gives him a renewal of human strength against these obstacles. Weidman feels "a person should be like a spring, like a coil."[46] He calls this resilience "rebound" in his dance technique. Rebound might be termed his philosophy of life and work. Slowly he began to gather his energy and was able to eventually spring into action with vitality and humor, to

29

continue to teach and create new works. By 1955 he was once again able to contribute to the dance field as a prominent dancer, choreographer, teacher, and writer.

Weidman spent several weeks in residence at Wayne State University in 1960 where he taught dance technique classes and restaged *Lynchtown* with the college dancers. During Weidman's stay, a young art student asked him if he could observe his technique class and draw. The young student was Mikhail Santaro, a Russian-Japanese-American painter.[47] This initial introduction began a long artistic partnership; together Weidman and Santaro established a studio and performance space called the Expression of Two Arts Studio and Theatre at 102 West Twenty-Ninth Street in New York City. In their first performance on July 1, 1961, they performed a program of duets combining dance and painting. While Charles danced, Mikhail interpreted his motions through painting and calligraphy. Among their artistic works were *To Make a Form - To Give It Life*, *Commedia*, and *Calligraphy Of The Dance*.[48]

In 1961, with newfound vigor, Weidman composed a work dedicated to his dance partner Doris Humphrey, who died of stomach cancer in 1958. His *Brahms Waltzes*, set to Gina Bachauer's recording of Liebeslieder Waltzes, opus 39 by Johannes Brahms, became one of his most enduring works. With dancer Elina Mooney, Weidman created the sixteen *Brahms Waltzes* by incorporating movements that he remembered Humphrey performing so beautifully. The *Brahms Waltzes* are unique because the dancers never leave the stage but stand in a semi-circle watching each other perform sections of solos, duets, trios, and quartets. The movements are representative of Humphrey's, but Weidman incorporates his own *kinetic pantomime* section titled "Eyes," and the entire *Brahms Waltzes* are creatively composed without one waltz step.

In that same year, Weidman created a solo to Gina Bachauer's rendition of Alexander Scriabin's Suite of 24 Preludes, opus 11 that he called *Saints, Sinners*

30

and Scriabin. Charles danced these very diverse historical portraits: Buddha, Saint Francis, Savonarola, Rasputin, and Jesse James. To celebrate the forming of the Charles Weidman Theatre Dance Company in 1961, Weidman, Santaro, and eleven dancers prepared for the first performance in December at the Expression of Two Arts Theatre. The concert featured Weidman's *The Christmas Oratorio* to the choral music of Johann Sebastian Bach. Santaro created the sets and lighting for the three-part dance that includes "The Coming of Christ," "His Birth," and "His Crucifixion and Resurrection."[49]

In a concert scheduled with his company in July 1962 at the Expression of Two Arts Theatre, Weidman presented a new solo, *In the Beginning* to Albert Ferbers' interpretation of Claude Débussy's First Book of Preludes. For this impressionistic suite about the beginning of American modern dance, Santaro designed a set of ropes and a mobile that Weidman used as he danced portrayals of historic dancers Harald Kreutzberg, Doris Humphrey, Helen Tamiris, Martha Graham, and La Argentina.[50] The following year, the first performance of *King David* was given on July 11, 1963, at the Expression of Two Arts Theatre. Weidman used the 1921 oratorio by Arthur Honegger, *Le Roi David*, with a text by Andre Morax. He composed his dance using a narrator with seven dancers to dramatize the conflict between the Biblical characters and their historic situations.[51]

Throughout 1964, Weidman composed three extremely diverse dances. One composition was an abstract solo, *Study*, to the well-known Adagio for Strings by Samuel Barber. Performing to the unusual music, Symphonies of Wild Instruments by Igor Stravinsky, Weidman created another work, a duet with Santaro: *A Chinese Actor Prepares for the Role of the God of War*. Weidman also composed a fascinating dance titled *Suite Intriga* to Wolfgang Amadeus Mozart's Flute Quartets in A Major and D Minor. The four sections of *Suite Intriga* are titled: "Opening (and Something Found)," "About a Box," "Two

31

Pantomimes—one Kinetic, one Representational," and "Behind Fingers and Closing."[52]

During 1965, Weidman created dances for a smaller company on a May tour to London, England, and Norway. He composed a new solo *A Letter to Mrs. Bixby - A Lincoln Portrait* and an ensemble work to music by Ludwig van Beethoven, the *Diabelli Variations*. He created *The Easter Oratorio* to music by Johann Sebastian Bach in three sections,"Opening," "Adagio," and "Rejoicing."[53] Weidman's visit with his company to London to the Commonwealth Institute Theatre was his first visit since he had danced in London with Denishawn. In his review, Fernau Hall notes the significance of Weidman's visit as "something of a landmark in the history of dance in this country . . . this visit helped us to see the great variety of American modern dance as it exists today in perspective."[54]

With the establishment in 1969 of the Charles Weidman Foundation and the Charles Weidman School of Modern Dance, Incorporated, tax-deductible contributions were made to support his school and choreographic projects. In the spring of that year, Weidman received a grant from the National Council on the Arts to assemble a small company and create a new work. Charles titled his new composition *A69-I-123*, the grant's identification number. Dedicated to James Thurber, who died in 1961, Weidman used some of the shorter Thurber fables to compose *Of and Out of This World* to music by Camille Saint-Saens.[55]

Mikhail Santaro ended ten years of artistic collaboration with Weidman when he, along with his wife and son, moved to Hong Kong in the fall of 1970. By 1971 Weidman had received a grant to reconstruct Humphrey's *New Dance* with assistance from Beatrice Seckler, Edith Orcutt, Miriam Raphael (Cooper) and Joan Levy Bernstein. The reconstruction process relied on the kinetic memory of Seckler, Orcutt, Cooper, and Bernstein. In addition, they reviewed a two-minute film clip, studied fifty photographs, mostly Barbara Morgan's from its 1935 premiere at Bennington College, and restaged the work with Weidman's company. (*New Dance* had last been performed about twenty-five years ago during the break-up of the Humphrey-Weidman Company.) The complete historic reconstruction of *New Dance* premiered at Barnard College in 1972 and featured the following Weidman dancers: Janet Towner, Shelby Beebe, Joanne Edelmann, Myra Hushansky, Donna Mondanaro, Margaret O'Sullivan, Jan Wodinski, Barry Barychko, Robert Ghigliotti, Robert Kosinski, and Paul Wilson.[56] *New Dance* was performed that summer at the American Dance Festival at Connecticut College.[57]

With his company, Weidman created *Saint Matthew Passion* in 1973 to the grand choral and instrumental music of J. S. Bach. In this rendering of the crucifixion of Jesus Christ according to the gospel of Saint Matthew, Weidman used the subtlety of contrapuntal form in the dance. *Saint Matthew Passion* is a beautifully crafted abstract dance. The next year, Weidman created an enduring work as a dedication to Ruth St. Denis and his formative years at Denishawn called *Visualization, or From a Farm in New Jersey*. The work, considered his last, was staged in 1974 to Saint-Saens' Concerto No. 4 in C Minor, Opus 44; it is composed of two parts. Part One is a portrait of St. Denis that was danced by Janet Towner; Part Two is a montage of dances from the Denishawn repertory featuring the historic figures of St. Denis, Shawn, Humphrey, Graham, Robert Gorham, and Weidman.[58]

Kudos—Awards and Honors

Weidman won the prestigious *Dance Magazine Award* in 1950 for performance and choreography. He was not cited for a particular work, as were the other recipients, but was recognized for his versatility: "Charles Weidman—in almost anything he does."[59] On November 25, 1958, Weidman, along with his colleagues Humphrey, Graham, Holm, and Tamiris, received the Awards of Honor at the Second International Festival of Dance sponsored by the

Women's Division of the Federation of Jewish Charities of New York. The awards, presented by John Martin, dance editor of *The New York Times*, were given these five distinguished choreographers and dancers for their contributions to the development of an indigenous American art form, modern dance.[60]

For his contributions to American dance as a dancer, teacher, and choreographer Weidman received The Dance Heritage Award from the Dance Division of the American Association for Health, Physical Education and Recreation, in 1970.[61] Jersey City State College made Charles Weidman a Doctor of Humane Letters on June 3, 1973, in recognition of his legacy and contributions to American dance. On May 25, 1975, Weidman's Theatre Dance Company received a special award from the City of New York for its outstanding artistic contributions to the cultural life of New York City.[62]

Beginning at Denishawn, then at Bennington College and, indeed, throughout his extended career, Charles Weidman was an avid educator. He conducted master classes and workshops, restaging his dances at over two hundred colleges and universities in the United States.[63] Through these college dance residencies, he influenced at least 300 teachers and 6,000 students. This constitutes a remarkable contribution to American dance; Weidman can rightfully be called the "Father of Modern Dance."

In the last few decades, dance in America has undergone an astonishing renaissance in the techniques and aesthetics of classic modern dance. The technical systems of Graham, Holm, Humphrey, Limón, Tamiris, Weidman, and others are studied in colleges and studios around the world. Reconstructions of their classic works flourish, especially in college dance programs. Many of Weidman's works are restaged and performed by college dancers, such as *Brahms Waltzes*, *Lynchtown*, *Bargain Counter*, *Traditions*, and excerpts from *The Christmas Oratorio*. *Brahms Waltzes*, one of eight scores available from the Dance Notation Bureau, is the most popular.[64] More than seventy summers have passed since the Bennington College days, but the legacy of dance pioneers Graham, Holm, Humphrey, and Weidman remain the foundation of American modern dance. Their significance in the history of American dance is simply set forth in the narration to the conclusion of the 1965 WNET film *Dance: Four Pioneers*: "Wherever a dancer is trained in America he [she] is aware of these four, and consciously or unconsciously he [she] takes from them."[65]

In *The Borzoi Book of Modern Dance* (1949), Margaret Lloyd writes a witty description of Charles Weidman as dancer and choreographer:

> He delighted in incongruities, in fragmentary, mercurial movement, ringing abrupt changes of tempo, rhythm, and dynamics in the broken pieces he let the spectator put together as he would. . . . He jested in stroke and curlicue, lampooning right and left with his pencil-slim body, making jokes with his fingers and witty observations with his bare toes. And his mouth . . . was a cave of comedy in itself. He could always be counted on to do the unexpected thing.[66]

John Martin, historic figure in dance criticism, commented in 1968 on Weidman's unparalleled greatness: "His art is utterly underivative; there has been nobody in the dance before him to pattern after, and certainly there is nobody even remotely like him in the dance today."[67] Throughout Weidman's career audiences around the world recognized with delight the characters portrayed in his dances. In her book, *Theatrical Dancing in America*, Winthrop Palmer observes of Weidman's legacy:

> In summing up Charles Weidman's contribution to the art of theatre and dance in the United States, it is the opinion of the writer that he defined the stock characters of the classic comedy in the contemporary idiom . . . the urchin boy . . . half satyr, half hooligan, who can fish and also shoot crap, the dandy who will abandon any fashion as soon as it becomes commonplace, who is perhaps the archetype of the American man.[68]

35

Celebrated choreographer Alvin Ailey dedicated his company's season in April 1975 to his former teacher Weidman, in a salute to "one of the extraordinary papas of American dance."[69] To celebrate Weidman's life and contributions, the American Dance Festival at Duke University in Durham, North Carolina, marked the tenth anniversary of his death in June 1985 with a three-day tribute of films, panel discussions, and performances of Weidman's works. "The reason we're doing this tribute is that Charles was greatly underrated," said Charles Reinhart, director of the American Dance Festival. Deborah Carr's Theatre Dance Ensemble performed Weidman's *Flickers, Lynchtown, Brahms Waltzes*, and sections of *The Christmas Oratorio*, staged with the assistance of Beatrice Seckler.[70]

On July 11, 1987, Weidman was posthumously inducted into Mr. and Mrs. Cornelius Whitney's *Hall of Fame* at the National Museum of Dance in Saratoga Springs, New York. Weidman was an honored recipient with his artistic partners Humphrey and Limón of the American Dance Festival's Ninth Annual Samuel H. Scripps Award in June 1989 at Duke University. The American Dance Festival Award honors choreographers who have made significant lifetime contributions to the field of modern dance. Weidman's citation noted that his "sly and sometimes slapstick humor belies the serious human concerns that were the underpinning of his work. His choreographic reconciliation of wit and tragedy offered yet another dimension to American dance."[71] Perhaps because of his college training in Humphrey-Weidman/Limón technique, Bill T. Jones was selected to perform in their honor. Bill T. Jones/Arnie Zane Dance Company performed Jones' celebrated dance, *D-Man in the Waters*, a work for which Jones received a 1988-89 Bessie Award. In 1988, Deborah Jowitt, a former dancer with Weidman and a well-known critic and writer, recognized his stature in American dance: "Weidman, with his lean, clever body and mobile face, was a masterful comedian as well as the modern equivalent of the *dancer noble*."[72]

One week before his seventy-fourth birthday, on Tuesday, July 15, 1975, the dance community mourned the loss of Charles Weidman. His obituary in *Variety* noted that he was "considered by most dance world followers [as] the dean of modern dance."[73] Weidman's final performance with his company was presented on Sunday, July 13, at his studio in the Expression of Two Arts Theatre. "Three months after his death," wrote Jennifer Dunning, "public response was such that a memorial to Weidman had to be moved to Broadway's Majestic Theatre from the Library Auditorium at Lincoln Center."[74] For more than half a century, Charles Weidman had sustained his calling, or summons, by entering wholeheartedly into the dance career he so eloquently anticipated in his ninth-grade essay, *My Vocation*. His artistic prowess and accomplishments are undeniable.

Chapter Two

Early Years

(1850-1920)

I inhale great draughts of space,
The east and the west are mine, and the north and the south are mine.

Walt Whitman
Song of the Open Road

The expansiveness of space and the human spirit's desire to fill it represent a kind of heroism.[1] Growing up in the wide-open spaces of Nebraska, with its unprecedented human migration and vast frontier, influenced the young lives of famous dancers Charles Weidman and Fred Astaire, who were both born there at the turn of the twentieth century. Both had a tremendous capacity to dance on stage or in film in a remarkably free and generous manner. Each became a hero of the American people. Other legendary actors born in Nebraska were Marlon Brando and Henry Fonda, while William "Buffalo Bill" Cody, who called North Platte his home for forty years, made Nebraska famous in his Wild West and vaudeville shows.[2] As a third-generation American, Charles Weidman's early years in Nebraska affected his development and left distinctive traits in his personality.

Nebraska, a midwestern state about halfway between New York City and San Francisco, was the stopping point for people from the East traveling to the Western frontier. Throughout his artistic career, from 1920 to 1975, Weidman traveled between Los Angeles and New York City, two cultural centers that offered him unimaginable professional opportunities. His birth in the state of Nebraska conveniently placed him at an equal distance from these two metropolitan cities.

Part of the Great Plains, land in the state of Nebraska is devoted to agriculture, producing corn as its leading crop to supply feed for livestock. Farming and raising cattle have been at the core of its identity, so much so that Nebraska is nicknamed the "Cornhusker State." It has a colorful history of native Pawnee Indians, fur traders, settlers, homesteaders, wagon trains, cowboys roaming the open range on horseback, and expeditions by Captains Meriwether Lewis and William Clark. During the Gold Rush of 1849 thousands of people—or, 49ers—traveled the Nebraska Platte River valley route to the West.[3] Weidman's great-grandparents were part of Nebraska's history.

Nebraska Roots

In 1929, after eight years dancing with Ruth St. Denis and Ted Shawn and their company, Weidman began his independent career by creating *Cowboys*, a work reflecting his Nebraska heritage. Cowboys were cow herders who tended cattle until they reached the stockyards and markets. During the early nineteenth century they moved onto the plains of Nebraska northward to Montana and westward to southern California. The cowboy advanced the civilizing of the Western frontier becoming an American hero.[4] Weidman became a master of *kinetic pantomime*; as a historic figure, the cowboy offered him immense possibilities for characterization. With his six-foot tall, lean body, Weidman transformed himself into a cowboy with a swagger and rolling gait. Through *Cowboys*, his humorous and poignant kinetic dance, Weidman told the story of a true hero of our nation.

Both of Weidman's great-grandfathers, Hoffman and Walcott, were pioneers of Iowa. Perhaps they were given an opportunity, like other immigrants,

40

to settle the lands of the Great Plains by the Homestead Act of 1862, "heralded as the greatest democratic measure of all history."[5] The act gave ownership of public lands west of the Mississippi River to those with the pioneering spirit to settle and establish farms.[6] Free Western land for homesteaders proved attractive to immigrants from northern Europe—German, Bohemian, Swedish, Danish, English, Irish, Polish—many of whom were ill-prepared for the hardships of pioneering on the Great Plains.[7] Winters were bitterly cold, while summers were hot, dry, dusty, and windy. Crops were often burned up by the sun, the dry soil blowing away in the wind.

Charles Weidman's robust ancestors endured the staggering burdens of a pioneering life in the American Midwest. It was their resolution to remain on the land, requiring an endless effort of human power and self-direction against natural obstacles that characterizes the Nebraska temperament.[8] Weidman inherited this determination of body and mind. His Nebraska roots gave him the strength, will, and self-direction to become one of the "pioneers" of American dance.

By the 1870s the Great Plains were peopled by farmers. They cleared acres of timber or brush land, and put up fences to protect their crops from herds of roaming, grazing cattle. "The prairie grass was plowed under," writes Roy Robbins in his definitive book on the history of the public lands of the United States, "and the land on which buffalo and cowboys had roamed was turned into homesteads."[9] After farmers planted corn and wheat, the fragile water table of this semi-arid land was threatened as they used windmills and well-drilling machines to water acres of crops.[10] Corn-picking machines and the McCormick reaper were invented to make harvesting of crops easier.

At this time American productivity, reflected in the landscape of the Great Plains, prompted Weidman to create *Dance of Work* (1932) to the music of Henry Cowell, an American composer. As noted by Margaret Lloyd, in the structure of *Dance of Work*, Weidman uses the motions and rhythms of labor to mold his idea into a distinct abstract form.[11] Possibly, the essence of *Dance of Work* represents the heroic scope of the American work code exacerbated by the Great Depression. Through *Dance of Work* Weidman mines the unprecedented work ethic of his kinfolk in pioneering the Great Plains.

The construction and completion of a transcontinental railroad brought fuel and commodities into the Midwest and carried out agricultural products to the East. With federal land grants and money loans, the railroad advertised to people in northern Europe that they might migrate and settle the land bordering the railroad tracks. Robbins explains that the United States government "joined hands with the railroads in promoting settlement of the desert country."[12] By 1890, this great expansion of the American West was considered to be the largest migration in the history of the frontier.[13] During 1889 Weidman's twenty-year-old father traveled from northwestern Illinois to Lincoln, Nebraska in search of a new life.

Despite the wealth of opportunities this great migration offered, it fraught with an abundance of obstacles. For example, during treaty negotiations with the government over their fertile lands, the native Indian tribes were moved to specific tracts of land called reservations. This infringed on their traditional nomadic way of life and their ability to hunt buffalo for food. Violent conflicts arose between native Indian tribes, farmers, and ranchers over grazing land for cattle and buffalo. By the late nineteenth century, the nation's natural resources, Robbins notes, "were being exploited in such an alarming fashion . . . that these vast resources would be completely under the control of a few . . . who had no regard . . . and little respect for laws . . ."[14] One man was able to implement conservation projects to protect America's natural resources.

The year Weidman was born, President Theodore Roosevelt took office and, with his typical confidence and vitality, reclaimed land for great storage reservoirs to save water for irrigation and acres of timberland for national parks and national forests. His efforts initiated the passage of the Newlands Act by Congress in 1902 that made provision for the protection and conservation of the nation's natural resources.[15] Migration, expansion, and settlement of the vast Great Plains ushered in the twentieth century. It was at this time that Charles Weidman was born.

"Western States Still Under a Burning Sun," the city newspaper wrote on July 12, 1901.[16] The Midwest was sweltering from the longest heat wave in American history. While crops and livestock languished, the city newspaper remained optimistic: "No Serious Damage Yet: Nebraska Corn Crop Withstands the Heat."[17] Under the relentless sun, it seemed that life had slowed to a snail's pace. "Heat Mounts High: 15-year record broken in Lincoln . . . temperature exceeding 100 degrees," the *Nebraska State Journal* noted.[18] On Monday, July 22, 1901, one of the hottest days on record, Charles Edward Weidman, Junior was born in the family home on 319 North Eleventh Street in Lincoln, the capital of Nebraska.[19] His parents, Charles Edward Weidman and Vesta Walcott Hoffman, were of English, Dutch, and German descent.[20] The announcement of Charles' birth in the *Nebraska State Journal* reads: "Captain C. E. Weidman of Fire Department Engine House Number 1, treated his brother firemen and friends yesterday. Mr. Weidman is the happy father of a baby boy that arrived at his home Monday night."[21]

Charles' father was the Captain of the Lincoln City Fire Department, and that fact in itself would make his childhood an interesting one. Like other boys who were named after their fathers, his family called him "Sonny." Two years before Charles was born, almost to the day—July 23, 1899—his sister LaVone was born. LaVone would have had two baby brothers, but in 1900 a baby boy died shortly after birth. This tragic event caused his parents to worry about the birth of their third child, Charles. To complicate matters, their infant was affected with spasms and, in the doctor's opinion, their baby could be destined to live a short life.[22] Spasms, or intermittent involuntary contractions of one or more muscles, agitated the baby as if he were being shaken. In due time, Charles outgrew these spasms and developed into a healthy toddler, but when learning to talk his family noticed he stammered or stuttered.

The cause of childhood stuttering is unknown; however, there are many theoretical indicators.[23] A temporary stage or developmental stuttering is a phase a toddler goes through; however, this does not necessarily mean that a child will stutter all of his or her life.[24] During a recorded interview in 1975, Shirley P. Manasevit asked Weidman if it was strange to hear his voice on tape? He answered: "No, no—not at all but I always, I always stutter."[25] Perhaps his infantile spasms were a factor in the onset of childhood stuttering, causing hesitation in the fluency of his speech.

Before first meeting Charles in 1969, Janet Towner spoke to him on the telephone regarding a secretarial job: "I told him I was very interested in applying for the position and he said in his stuttering fashion, 'Oh, ho, very good!'"[26] There are techniques that can be practiced to reduce stuttering, and Weidman used these.[27] Margaret O'Sullivan, who danced with Weidman in the 1970s, says: "I wouldn't say Charles stuttered. He sometimes (in talking to audiences particularly) sort of sputtered, as his thoughts flowed out more quickly than the words."[28] In a conversation with Nona Schurman, she thought Weidman had a speech hesitation and believed his shyness was a factor in his stuttering.[29] In a letter from Deborah Carr regarding this topic she notes:

> Charles stuttered only when he got very excited and it was more part of his charm than anything else. It wasn't as if he had a speech impediment. He was capable of speaking perfectly well. He spoke in a stream of consciousness manner. It seemed he had many different ideas going on in his head and he tried to get them all out at once. Sometimes he stuttered a bit then and if you read some of his interviews, they are even more hilarious because he is all over the map jumping from story to story.[30]

Professor of Communicative Disorders and Sciences Linda House notes that there is a commonality in people with fluency problems "to seek methods other than speech to communicate."[31] These may be explanations for the reason that as a youngster Charles excelled in drawing, comic pantomime, costume design, music, and dancing. These are all nonverbal modes of expression.

At the turn of the twentieth century when Charles was born, Lincoln, Nebraska's capital, was a large, prosperous, bustling city, but the prairie remained close upon its borders. Immigrants from about fourteen different nations came to Lincoln; those of German descent were the largest group. They traveled to Lincoln by covered wagon, stagecoach operated by the Wells Fargo Company, the Burlington & Missouri River Railroad, the Union Pacific Railroad, or by the Missouri and Platte Rivers—major waterways for commerce. The city of Lincoln offered unimaginable economic and social opportunities for these diverse people.

Cultural and educational development had to keep pace with Lincoln's growing population. Education began with missionaries who were the first teachers among the Pawnee Indians. The year after Charles' father was born, the University of Nebraska was founded in 1869, along with the College of Agriculture; higher education developed with individual charters for seventeen denominational colleges.[32] The city had about forty churches; the largest religious group were Roman Catholics, then Lutherans, Methodists, Presbyterians, Baptists, Seventh-Day Adventists, Mennonites, Quakers, Unitarians, Christian Scientists, and Jews.[33] Charles was baptized and confirmed in the Episcopal Church. Lincoln's early history was noted for its tolerance of religious and cultural differences, and throughout Charles' life he was accepting of other's religious and ethnic beliefs.

The city had numerous schools, banks, businesses, factories, and thirteen temperance societies. The temperance movement, dominated by the Woman's

Christian Temperance Union which organized in 1874, declared complete abstinence from alcoholic beverages.[34] The temperance movement had a strong hold on Lincoln, and this struggle proved to be a topical political issue in the city. Charles' conservative unbringing probably dominated his outlook on life until he attained a global perspective by traveling with the Denishawn Dancers across the United States and Canada, England, and the Orient. As a boy Charles would enjoy many opportunities to attend theatrical performances in Lincoln and to perform in community opera productions.

The Temple Theatre, part of the University of Nebraska, was built with a gift from John D. Rockefeller, Jr.[35] Used by the University Players, a group of university teachers and students who produced a season of plays, the Temple Theatre was also used by community theatre groups. As a teenager, Weidman performed at the Temple Theatre in operas directed by Madame de Vilmar that were produced for a combined group of community and university members. In addition to the Temple Theatre, the elaborate Liberty Theatre, a grand opera house, was built in 1891. At the turn of the twentieth century, the Lansing Opera House was built and proclaimed the most ornate Romanesque building west of Chicago.[36] The Orpheum Theatre was built in 1905 to provide for vaudeville tours and was, at times, used for community productions. Vaudeville consisted of variety acts that toured American cities performing in the vaudeville theatres along the circuit. From jugglers and acrobats to actors, singers, comedians, and dancers, many entertainers including Ruth St. Denis, Charles Weidman with the Denishawn Dancers, and Adele and Fred Astaire became famous on the vaudeville touring circuit.

Family Matters

Weidman's mother, Vesta Hoffman, was born in Sioux City, in northwestern Iowa.[37] As one of five children born to Mr. and Mrs. R. W.

Hoffman, she had a close relationship with her sister Jessica, whom Charles called Aunt Jessie.[38] Vesta's grandparents were part of the Hoffman and Walcott families, immigrants from northern Europe who settled in the Midwest.[39]

The Hoffman children enjoyed swimming in the Missouri River during hot summers and skating on its ice during cold winters. In their teens, Vesta enjoyed roller-skating and Jessie relished dramatic acting and dancing. At one time Jessie had been a dancer in the *King Dodo Vaudeville Company* and Vesta had been a Midwest roller-skating champion.[40] (Roller-skating became a year-round pastime with the invention of the ball-bearing skate in 1863 by James Leonard Plimpton. The introduction of the ball-bearing shoe skate in 1880 caused a great surge of interest and enthusiasm for this sport.) By the 1890s, indoor roller-skating rinks were being built in many American cities.[41] Vesta probably excelled at figure skating; Weidman remarked that his mother loved to dance the popular social dances.[42] Vesta's dedication and enjoyment of roller-skating propelled her into regional and state competitions.

Vesta's mother, (Weidman's grandmother Hoffman) was accomplished in the craft of needlework, an American folk art. Grandmother Hoffman's needlework included embroidery, quilting, appliqué, and needlepoint lace that she used to decorate functional objects such as bedcovers, tablecloths, and clothing. Later in his life, Weidman would tenderly imitate his grandmother as she sat sewing in one of his most enduring dances, *On My Mother's Side*. Grandmother Hoffman was skilled in quilting, the art of stitching two pieces of material together in a variety of decorative patterns with an interlining usually of cotton, down, or wool. In nineteenth-century America, the common technique of quilting was an elaborate patchwork of geometric designs.[43] Grandmother Hoffman began to lose her eyesight as a result of her continual needlework projects, also poignantly portrayed in *On My Mother's Side*. One special quilt designed with "H's" for Hoffman was given to Weidman as a gift from his grandmother.[44] He was quite proud of this quilt and kept it in his possession until the end of his life. Grandmother Hoffman's finely crafted quilts were used during the cold winters, and her needlework activities became a sizable part of family life.[45]

Vesta's father, (Weidman's grandfather Hoffman) was a skilled carpenter who assembled and repaired wooded structures and was most capable at building houses and barns. In *On My Mother's Side*, Weidman sketched a tragic situation in the Hoffman family when his grandfather, after losing his total financial investments in a fire, suffered severe depression and drowned himself.[46]

Weidman's father, Charles Edward Weidman, Sr., was born in Mount Carroll, near the Mississippi River in northwestern Illinois, on September 18, 1868. At twenty years of age, in 1889, he traveled about 400 miles to Lincoln, Nebraska, to attend the State Fair and to study at the Lincoln Business College under the management of D. R. Lillebridge.[47] While enrolled as a student he applied for work in the Lincoln Fire Department and began to train as a firefighter at Engine House Number 2, where he excelled as plug-man, pipe-man, and assistant driver. Remarkably, on May 5, 1892, he was appointed Captain of Engine House Number 3. After one year, Captain Weidman was transferred to Engine House Number 1, and by July 17, 1897, Lincoln's Mayor Graham appointed him Fire Chief.[48] As a child, Charles was surrounded by a great class of American heroes—firefighters.

Vesta and Jessie customarily traveled from Sioux City, Iowa, to visit family relatives in Lincoln, Nebraska.[49] At times they would travel down the Missouri River to the Platte River, or by the Union Pacific Railroad to Lincoln. They enjoyed visiting Nebraska's capital with its various social activities, including ballroom dancing and theatrical events. Both lovely young women with their vivacious personalities attracted many male suitors. Their relatives resided near Engine House Number 1. During afternoon walks, Vesta and Jessie would pass the fire station, where the recently appointed Chief Weidman became smitten with Vesta.[50]   After a respectable courtship, Vesta and Chief Weidman were married and settled into their family home near the fire station, where visits from Jessie were frequent.

Panama Visits

On special occasions, little Charles would accompany his father to Engine House Number 1, where he would have fun riding in a horse-drawn fire wagon while sitting next to his father, Captain Weidman (pronounced Weedman in Lincoln). Captain Weidman's skill and courage as Fire Chief received local, state, and national notice. When Charles was four years old, in 1905, a significant honor was bestowed on his father: President Roosevelt had appointed his father Chief of all the fire stations to be built and organized in the Panama Canal Zone.[51] The twenty-sixth President of the United States, from 1901 to 1909, Theodore Roosevelt advocated expansion into Panama. The Panama Canal, a waterway constructed from 1904 to 1914 by the United States across the Isthmus of Panama, connects the Atlantic and Pacific Oceans. In 1903 a ten mile-wide strip of land across the Isthmus of Panama, the Canal Zone, provided United States civilian services, such as schools, post offices, police, fire protection, and courts.[52] With travel preparations for an ocean voyage and visions of a new home in a faraway place, this was an exciting time for the Weidman family.

Fire Chief Weidman arrived in Panama, the largest city and capital of the Republic of Panama, on December 1, 1905. Originally called Panama Vieja, the city was founded in 1519 as one of the first Spanish settlements in the New World.[53] In late January of 1906, Mrs. Weidman, four-year-old Charles, and six-year-old LaVone joined Chief Weidman to establish their new home in San Cristobal, a city on the Gulf side of the Caribbean Sea.[54]

Charles and LaVone made many new friends and enjoyed their adventures in Cristobal. After one year in Panama, Charles and his sister returned to Lincoln

49

with their mother. In October 1907, when Charles was six years old, his parents marriage ended in divorce.[55] Charles revealed later in life his thoughts about the divorce of his parents. It could have been due to their differing life styles. While his mother loved social dancing, his father didn't dance at all. Charles thought another reason was that Vesta was an attractive woman with a sparkling personality; Chief Weidman may have been jealous of her popularity with their male friends.[56] Nonetheless, the social stigma of divorce in 1907 was probably traumatic for little LaVone and Charles.

From his seventh to twelfth birthday, young Charles spent alternate years in Lincoln with his mother and in Panama with his father.[57] In the summer of 1911 ten-year-old Charles traveled by boat to the Isthmus of Panama, accompanied on this long journey by his cousin Ruth and her mother. Charles thoroughly enjoyed the boat trip to Panama. He remembered entertaining the passengers by telling them humorous stories, probably accompanied by explanatory gestures. He thought he inherited his story-telling skills from his father, who was always telling tales of firefighting. Charles spent a year with his father in the Canal Zone, where he was enrolled in the fourth grade. Among his many playmates was his cousin Ruth, daughter of his Uncle Frank Weidman, who was also employed in the Canal Zone. With his cousin Ruth, Charles had fun making costumes and props for their enactments of biblical stories. During this year, Charles made his first public performance when he sang for his peers "Work for the Sun is Shining," using a handsaw and hammer as props.[58]

Charles had many exciting adventures while visiting his father in Panama; however, a year was a long time for him to be away from his family, and he must have dearly missed his mother.[59] At age ten, Charles had an unforgettable experience while visiting his father. Every year the firemen in the Canal Zone demonstrated their skill in fighting fires by competing in various events to the amazement of the community, who gathered to witness these daredevil stunts.

50

Charles remembered how his own fear of heights made the last event performed by the firemen extra fearful. In her doctoral dissertation, Sylvia Pelt Richards describes the firemen's final event, as recounted by Charles in 1970:

> One of the firemen climbed to the top of the practice tower and, with a harness around his body, he attached a hook to a rope stretched diagonally between the tower and the ground. On a given signal, the fireman pushed off from the tower and "zoomed" to the ground while the anxious crowd below watched, anticipating an impending disaster. Chief Weidman decided that, as an added attraction, his son would be outfitted with a small harness and would perform the foregoing feat with a selected fireman. In recalling this episode, Charles says, "I was very much opposed to doing this, and I told Daddy that I did not want to, but nothing could dissuade him." So Sonny, assisted by one of his father's firemen, ascended to the top of the tower, hooked the harness attachment to the diagonal line, and jumped. Today he remembers that as being ". . . the most horrifying experience I have ever had."[60]

At the end of the summer Charles made the long journey home to Lincoln. Construction of the Panama Canal was nearing completion, and soon the United States civilian service employees would complete their tour of duty. Charles enrolled in the Bancroft School in 1914, completing his studies there with the ninth grade, in 1918.[61] He was looking forward to having his family together once again in Lincoln.

Childhood Dreams

As with most children growing up during the 1900s, the center of Charles' life was his family. Later in his career he was able to honor his family in his artistic works: *On My Mother's Side* (1940) and *And Daddy Was a Fireman* (1943). It is, perhaps, significant that his family-based dances had much to do with his early life, for the simple reason that his extended family was all part of the same household. Grandparents were part of most households during this period. It was a way of life that helped shape many of his opinions and thoughts.

As a child, Charles displayed a talent for drawing and a gift for caricature; his father believed that he could have been a successful cartoonist. "My father wanted me to be a cartoonist," Charles said, "because cartoonists, he thought, made a lot of money."[62] Perhaps his father was familiar with the drawings of Nebraska's best-known cartoonist, Clare Briggs, whose drawings appeared in the Lincoln *Evening News*, or with the drawings of Herbert Johnson, Rollin Kirby, John Cassel, or Hy Gage, all noted Nebraska cartoonists.[63]

Being a precocious child, Charles recalled: "I was artistically inclined at a very young age, and thought I would become an architect."[64] Charles' enthusiasm for architecture extended into the history of architecture. He made many visits to the Lincoln City Library (built with funds from Andrew Carnegie) and opened to the public in 1902.[65] At age eleven, Charles read about one of the seven wonders of the ancient world, the Hanging Gardens of Babylon, in the city of Babylon on the Euphrates River, and also read about Greece and Egypt. Charles was fascinated by the biblical Tower of Babel and the Istar Gate of Babylon, the Acropolis of Athens, and the pyramids of ancient Egypt.[66] "The history began to occupy me," Charles said; he thought he wanted to become an archaeologist or historian.[67] He was also fascinated by theatrical dance because his Aunt Jessie told him stories about her career and showed him dances from vaudeville productions, and he was kept abreast of the latest trends in social dance because his mother enjoyed ballroom dance. "In the meantime I liked the dance," Charles remembered. "I didn't care much for folk dance but the Castles were in vogue then, and having long legs I could do all those things. I liked that."[68]

Vernon and Irene Castle, famous exhibition ballroom dancers of the early twentieth century, made social dances like the polka, tango, and waltz admired throughout Europe and America. "Everyone identified with them," exclaimed

Walter Terry, "for they popularized not only special dances . . . but dancing itself."[69] Under their tutelage modern social dancing became fashionable, artistic and refined, as noted by Marcia Siegel who writes, "the Castles projected themselves as exemplars of elegance and propriety."[70]

By 1912, Americans had discovered the pleasures of participating in social dancing. "Women, emancipated by the bicycle and bloomers, adopted ballroom dancing as their badge of liberation, and their antics shocked their more conservative countrymen who still questioned the propriety of the waltz," Suzanne Sheldon writes.[71] Various American religious leaders strongly cautioned that participating in social dancing might result in "pregnancy, venereal disease, and . . . the ultimate decay of American society."[72] Ever watchful of criticism, the Castles promoted the health benefits of dancing, proper manners, decent moral judgment, and suitable clothes for the purpose. Siegel affirms these points when she writes: "Exquisitely and expensively gowned, Irene Castle seemed a lithe younger sister to the society matrons who were her sponsors; Vernon was tall and elegant, with impeccable manners."[73] With his tall, slim body and long limbs, it appears Charles certainly matched the body type of Vernon Castle. Perhaps he could imitate dancing in an elegant style, but having "impeccable manners" was probably a stretch for him—and most boys his age.

Even Ruth St. Denis gave into the social dancing mania. In a performance in 1913 at Chicago's Ravinia Park, "she broke into an impromptu encore," Sheldon writes, ". . . kicked up her heels in a stylish cakewalk-cum-tango. The crowd went wild and made her repeat it . . ."[74] During this time in the urban United States, South American dances, the tango and maxixe, were in fashion. St. Denis cynically observed: "There were no waiters anymore, they had all turned into tango teachers. Every vaudeville house, every restaurant depended for its life on a pair of tango or maxixe dancers."[75] Ruth St. Denis, "lone lady, needed a partner . . . she needed Karsavina's equivalent to Nijinsky, Irene's equivalent to

53

Vernon," Walter Terry writes.[76] "I sent out a call for young men dancers . . . intending to use modern ballroom dance in between my numbers," writes St. Denis.[77] To her disappointment, those who responded were not serious or adequately trained, and she had decidedly given up the idea—when Edwin Myers Shawn walked into her life.[78] Ruth St. Denis, considered the grande dame of American dance, married her dance partner Ted Shawn, considered the papa of American dance, in 1914. They combined their names and founded the Denishawn Dancers, a large company in Los Angeles that became the training ground for celebrated modern dancers until 1932. They danced in vaudeville and on the concert stage in the United States, England, Canada, Cuba, and the Far East.[79] Charles was inspired to become one of their company.

Charles knew about Vernon and Irene Castle, and he took great pleasure in social dancing as well. He and his sister LaVone learned all the popular dances. "We used to go to the big ballroom at Castle Beach which was not too far from home," Charles said, "and dance the Fox Trot, the Bunny Hug, and the Argentina Tango which Vernon and Irene Castle made so famous [sic]." [80] Of course his mother enjoyed dancing, and his Aunt Jessie was a dancer in vaudeville—so dancing seemed to be a considerable part of his childhood. But at this time, Charles' passion was ancient history and archeology. He saw an advertisement announcing a *Dance Pageant of Egypt, Greece, and India* to be performed by Ruth St. Denis and her company. He recollected: ". . . Ruth St. Denis . . . it seemed that I'd heard the name but I asked my Mother who she was . . . I went to see Miss Ruth dance and that was the whole thing."[81]

The colloquialism "and that was the whole thing" is used to describe this artistic performance that encompassed his every passion. If there was one day that would change Charles' life forever, it was on October 1, 1916,[82] when he witnessed excerpts of a three-part dance pageant depicting episodes in ancient civilizations with their religious beliefs. He remembered this day, observing:

"Then Ruth St. Denis came to the Orpheum Theatre in Lincoln, Nebraska, with her pageant of India, Egypt, and Greece, and there was my history, dancing before me. I just put two and two together, and from then on I wanted to do that kind of dancing."[83]

The *Dance Pageant of Egypt, Greece, and India,* composed of cultural dances ethnically inspired, choreographed by St. Denis and Shawn, was first performed at the University of California at Berkeley in the Greek Theater, on July 29, 1916.[84] Louis Horst conducted the San Francisco Symphony in a score comprising miscellaneous compositions by Walter Meyrowitz, Arthur Nevin, and the Comtesse Ada de Lachau.[85] St. Denis decided to use the entire Denishawn School in this production. Among the students was twenty-two-year-old Martha Graham dancing a small role in *Egypt*—her first professional appearance.[86] After the premiere, the company resumed a ten-month tour on the Orpheum Theatre circuit to cities including Denver, Omaha, Minneapolis, St. Paul, Memphis, New Orleans, and Montreal.[87] In her book *Divine Dancer: A Biography of Ruth St. Denis*, Sheldon describes their pageant as including "Dance of Day" and "Dance of Night" from their longer work *Egypta*; a feast in honor of Bacchus; a dance portrayal of the Greek myth Orpheus and Eurydice; a dance story about an East Indian couple's journey through life to find self-realization; and selections from other East Indian dances composed by St. Denis.[88] At the age of fifteen, Charles decided he wanted to be a dancer and began in earnest to find a way to study at Denishawn.

Saving up to Go to Denishawn

From that point on young Charles spent hours in the University of Nebraska library reading history books on the ancient cultures of China, Egypt, India, Japan, Mesopotamia, and Mexico. At this early age, he read books that postgraduate students and professors used for their research.[89] He began to design costumes for dances, real and fictitious, and frequently presented solo recitals in the family parlor featuring his improvised "impressions of Ruth St. Denis."[90] At this time, Charles also wrote a letter to the Denishawn School of Dance in Los Angeles requesting information about their summer course and enrollment fees. The response stated that three months of study cost $300.[91] His sincere hope was to study at the Denishawn School but he needed money to pursue his dream.

As a teenager, Charles was well behaved and trustworthy. He said, "I was never in a gang, we didn't have things like that in Lincoln . . ."[92] At fourteen, Charles walked two newspaper routes, one for the *Lincoln State Journal*, the other for the *Evening News*.[93] "I had learned to make money at a very early age," he pointed out, "helping support Mama but the thing that I hated was that newspaper route."[94] His mother took great care of him when he delivered daily newspapers during frigid winter months, when it was not uncommon for air temperatures to dip into the minus 30 to minus 50 degree Fahrenheit range across the Midwest. Drifting snow could be four feet high: "In the winter, Mama used to rub my legs with coal oil while I sat in front of a big pot-bellied stove early every morning before I went out to deliver the papers."[95] These jobs taught young Charles discipline, responsibility, and perseverance.

Charles also had a job sorting magazines and newspapers at a place that would be known today as a recycling center. While he sorted magazines, he would flip through the pages, finding stunning photos of ancient civilizations, travelogues, and vaudeville stars: actresses Nora Bayes and Sarah Bernhardt, whom he saw in a performance at the Orpheum Theatre; dancers Irene and Vernon Castle, Loïe Fuller, and Gertrude Hoffman, whom he saw performing in Lincoln; and Metropolitan Opera star Geraldine Farrar, who was an inspiration to him because he loved opera. He began to collect articles on art, architecture, dance, vaudeville, and opera. This proved a gold mine for this youth who was stimulated by visual images. Charles began to collect these articles in a scrapbook that he carried in a briefcase—quite novel in 1916.[96] Along with stunning performances by St. Denis, Bernhardt, and Hoffman, this scrapbook inspired him along his path to becoming an actor and distinguished dancer.

During World War I, Charles probably saw the Denishawn Dancers featuring St. Denis and Doris Humphrey at the Orpheum Theatre on November 28-30, 1918. A patriotic endeavor, this vaudeville tour would earn money to buy Liberty Bonds that St. Denis had pledged herself as well as other donations to the war effort. The company was under the musical direction of Louis Horst, a pianist who got his start playing the musical scores for silent movies; St. Denis noticed what a dexterous pianist he was. In her definitive book on Louis Horst, Janet Mansfield Soares describes why St. Denis wanted to employ Horst as a musical director:

> He played from "mood" music collections and worked with "cue" sheets, which were usually handed to pianists just before the theatre went dark. The player often had to improvise on the spur of the moment, using these "pasticcios" of small pieces of musical themes that already existed while synchronizing sound to the image on the screen.[97]

Skilled in improvisation and synchronism, Horst joined the Denishawn Dancers and spent the next ten years as their musical director. At the Orpheum Theatre, the Denishawn Dancers performed these dances: *Dance of Theodora*, a solo composed and danced by St. Denis; *Serenata Morisca*, a solo composed by Shawn and danced by Betty Horst (later danced by Martha Graham and Doris Humphrey); *Greek Scene: Pas de Trois,* composed by St. Denis to music of Louis Horst and danced by Humphrey, Horst, and Edna Malone; *Greek Veil Plastique,* danced by St. Denis; *Greek Dancer in Silhouette*, danced by Malone; *Dance of Sunrise*, danced by Humphrey; *Dance of the Royal Ballet of Siam*; and *Spirit of Democracy*, both composed by St. Denis and danced by the company.[98]

57

For Charles, these global dances reflected his love of ancient civilizations and piqued his desire to train as a dancer at Denishawn.

To save money to go to Denishawn, Charles worked many hours as an usher at a local motion picture theatre.[99] Silent films provided entertainment for people of all ages from every occupation. As Charles changed the billboards in front of the theatre and ushered, he had an opportunity to watch films over and over again. Since he came to know all the film stars and their famous movies he became a keen mimic and imitator; more important, he learned about gesture and mime. It was, perhaps, this early teenage experience that influenced Charles to create, later in his artistic career, his impressions of the stars of silent films in the dance he called *Flickers*. Charles wrote the scenario to this dance that includes four reels, or plots; *Flickers* features him as Rudolph Valentino and Humphrey as Theda Bara.

During his high school years (1917-20), Charles' mother married Jack Varner and moved to Canada, while his father married Carrie Berrie, and bought a house at 1029 R Street in downtown Lincoln, where Charles and LaVone lived.[100] Childhood friend Perkins Harnley remembers that Chief Weidman's house was "crammed full of heavy teak wood furniture which he had purchased in the Panama Canal Zone . . ."[101] When Charles went to live with his father (Daddy, as Charles called him) and his stepmother Carrie, he was relieved of his responsibility of financially supporting his mother and could more clearly focus on his mission to become a dancer. Daddy wanted him to become a partner in a small business venture, but Charles stubbornly replied: "No Daddy, I'd like to try this [a dance career] and so, he was all for it. Even if he'd objected I think I would have run away from home."[102]

From that point on, Charles' father was supportive of the idea, and he began to collect a scrapbook of programs, newspaper clippings, and photos of his son's career. As proud as he could be, Firechief Weidman continually brought

58

these scrapbooks to the Lincoln City Fire Station touting his son's praises to his fellow firemen and friends. During this time, Charles worked for the Nebraska Telephone Company, saving up to go to Denishawn.[103] His job was to order and keep in stock the thousands of parts needed to repair a telephone.[104] This job paid an hourly wage ($12 - $14 per week) that gave him an opportunity to save more money.[105] To earn money for his train fare to Los Angeles, Charles began to design and make batik lampshades, and his homeroom teacher bought one.[106] Every extra hour was needed to attain his dream, so he was constantly running to school from work. After school he would rush to work, then rush to dance class with Eleanor Frampton, or to rehearsal with Madame de Vilmar, and finally dash home to help with chores and finish his homework.

Charles' homeroom teacher at Lincoln High School, Miss Esther Lefler, took a liking to young Charles and empathized with his endeavor to become a dancer. Lefler believed in Charles; she recognized his unremitting drive to attain his dream, so she appealed to the high school principal for him to be enrolled in the fine arts curriculum. Permission was granted and Charles selected his own courses of study: art, music and history.[107] Lefler's modern approach to education, along with the principal's unusual flexibility, made it possible for young Charles to be steeped in the knowledge necessary to fulfill his vision of becoming an artist.

Charles had many childhood friends who became high school friends: Ralph Bowers, Perkins Harnley, and Varney Ferris. Ralph played the piano and wanted to be an opera singer. He and Charles performed in numerous operas directed and produced by Madame de Vilmar and her husband, who was an orchestral conductor. Many of these operas were performed at the Temple or Orpheum Theatres. Varney was a balletomane; he and Charles attended every professional and community dance event in Lincoln. Perkins was an aspiring artist who eventually went to New York City to study art. He met another

59

ambitious painter while there, José Limón, and he introduced José to Charles in 1928. Charles, who had made up his mind to become a dancer, and his artistic friends—Ralph, Perkins and Varney—were quite a clique. These high-school friends played a large role in Charles' life and they became a part of his improvised performances in the Weidman family living room, in his backyard, or in a horse barn. Charles and the neighborhood kids created fairy tales and ballets—Ralph and Varney were the producers. Perkins recalled that even at a young age, Charles' sensibility for satire was exceptional. "Their costumes were made from tinted cheesecloth and Christmas tree tinsel," Perkins wrote. "This primitive attempt at theatricality matured until Charles's name appeared in lights at the old Madison Square Garden . . ."[108]

In his junior year of high school, Charles received permission from the Board of Education of the Lincoln Public Schools to use the Bancroft School Auditorium for an 8:00 p.m. dance recital on February 18, 1919. LaVone helped Charles write the invitations to his "first solo" public performance. Charles created his dances and costumes, while his sister LaVone and his friend Ralph helped as a stage crew.[109] LaVone operated the victrola borrowed from a high school teacher, and Ralph played the piano between dances. His first dances were made from his impressions of Ruth St. Denis, but they also reflected his global study of ancient cultural history. He used books to study the *mudras*, or hand gestures, used in the dances of India.[110] Charles' recital consisted of nine extremely varied cultural dances to the music of nine different composers. He created and performed the following dances: *Russian* (Crakon), *Aztec* (Grieg), *Greek* (Liszt), *Spanish* (Moszkowski), *Impressions of Ruth St. Denis* (Joyce), *Egyptian* (Tschaikowsky), *East Indian* (Cui), *Javanese* (Maloof), and *American Indian* (Herbert).[111] Charles' first recital had exhibited self-taught dances rooted in ethnological sources. Ester Lefler invited many teachers to Charles' recital. Eleanor Frampton and Helen Hewett, physical education teachers, attended his recital. They were impressed with Charles' originality and natural ability, since he never took formal dance lessons. Frampton, taken with Charles' sincere artistic recital, invited him to study at her dance studio, where Hewitt was an assistant teacher. Charles could teach ballroom dance in exchange for his lessons in classical ballet, and he could use her studio for practice and creative work.[112] Frampton's gift of this opportunity was a dream come true for Charles.

Charles began private ballet lessons with Eleanor Frampton. Through his goal and her encouragement and generosity they developed an enduring student-teacher relationship. Charles was exceedingly fond of Frampton, or "Frampie," as he affectionately called her, as he embarked upon a dance career. He gave her a photograph of himself in Ted Shawn's dance *Boston Fancy—1854* and wrote: "To Frampie, with loads of love and admiration, from your step-son, Charles."[113] Originally from Lincoln, Frampton was only five years older than Charles and had earned a B.A. in physical education from the University of Nebraska in 1918, going on to study dance at the Perry Mansfield Summer Dance camp in Steamboat Springs, Colorado. Directly after her college graduation she came to teach at Charles' high school and opened a dance studio. She and her college friend, Helen Hewett from Alliance, Nebraska, left Lincoln in 1920 to study at the Denishawn School where they went into vaudeville with a "sister" duo-dancing act.[114] Ted Shawn even composed several dances for them. Later in her career (from the 1930s through the 1940s) she danced in the Humphrey-Weidman Company. Frampton represented Humphrey-Weidman dance at the Cleveland Institute of Music in Cleveland, Ohio where, in 1964, she was awarded The Cleveland Arts Prize.[115]

Another woman who had considerable influence on Charles was opera singer Madame de Vilmar, who directed an opera class at the university and for community productions; Charles handled the choreography. He also painted scenery for Vilmar's productions and made his own costumes.[116] He sang and

61

danced in the opera *Faust* and also danced with his sister LaVone in the ballroom scene in *Romeo and Juliet*. These experiences, Charles said, "gave me an artistic beginning. I was only a kid of fifteen or sixteen . . . but I was given an opportunity of expressing myself on stage."[117] Vilmar exposed Charles to the grandeur and drama of opera with its emphasis on the beauty of song and music. Charles was especially attracted to the voices of female opera stars. Later in his career, he created numerous dances using vocal and choral works.

At the age of nineteen, Charles was accepted into the Denishawn School with a scholarship; his duties included costuming and teaching.[118] Frampton and her colleague Hewett were enrolled in the summer course at the Denishawn School as well. They left a few weeks before Charles and rented a small room, where they invited Charles to stay until he moved into the residence at the Ted Shawn Studio that included room and board.

Weidman's last few months in Lincoln were hectic. His final dance appearance was in Frampton's Dancing School Recital at the Temple Theatre. For this performance Charles composed these three diverse solo dances: *Aztec Dance, Spanish Dance,* and *Hari-Kari.*[119] *Hari-Kari* reflects his fascination with the ceremonial rites of ancient Japan and was a pantomime based on the act of upholding one's honor by committing suicide with one's own dagger. Charles portrayed a young Japanese man; the circumstances surrounding the death of a friend made him choose between a life of bereavement or freedom from his grief in death. He summons his ancestors to the sound of a gong and purifies the space with burning incense, commiting his final act.[120] *Hari-Kari* was a preliminary Asian composition for young Charles. Beginning with the next decade, the diverse Oriental repertory composed by St. Denis and Shawn would influence Weidman's artistic work throughout his life.

On Monday, May 31, 1920, young Charles, grasping his briefcase and his luggage, climbed aboard a train and traveled halfway across the United States to

Los Angeles, California.[121] Waving goodbye to his father, stepmother, and many friends, he eagerly anticipated arriving in Los Angeles to study at the Ted Shawn Studio, where he would meet artists who would touch his life indelibly.

His good friend Ralph Bowers could not bring himself to see Charles off at the train depot. Later, in a letter to Ralph, Charles wrote, "Trains and time wait for no man."[122] Charles considered this period in association with Ruth St. Denis, Ted Shawn, and the Denishawn Dancers (1920-28) a fascinating time full of extremely favorable circumstances. He observed: "As you know, one achieves things with or in association with either places or with people."[123] It would be a wonderful beginning to a distinguished career.

Chapter Three

The Global Influence
(1890-1930)

Why not evolve a form of dance which is indigenous to this country?
. . . We wanted to do something that would be of the world today,
modern. Modern, that was the whole idea.

Charles Weidman

As Charles Weidman was growing up in the Midwest, he didn't know he wanted to be a dancer; it was the combination of ancient history and culture personified in performances by Ruth St. Denis and the Denishawn Dancers that inspired him to pursue a career in dance.[1] The only opportunity for young boys to dance at the turn of the twentieth century was in vaudeville. A young boy could dance a waltz clog with wooden shoes or a sand jig dance, fine sand, being sprinkled on the front of the stage while the boy performed shuffles and slides to 4-4 time ballroom schottische music.[2] Another option would be a song-and-dance routine like *Dreamland Waltz,* performed in a vaudeville show in 1905 by fellow Nebraskans Fred and Adele Astaire.[3] Charles Weidman's highly motivated vision of becoming a dancer enabled him to pave the way for further opportunities for other young men to embark on dance careers. The results of his work would not be noticed until 1930, with development of his independent career and his men's group. In the meantime, dance comprised a women's art.

American Vaudeville, Cradle of Dance

At the turn of the twentieth century a young woman who wanted to be a dancer could be a vaudeville or ballet girl, which amounted to the same thing. The American vaudeville or variety show was probably inspired by visiting English performers and developed into American burlesque. This was sometimes called a "leg show" or "cancan," as girls wearing ruffled bloomers kicked their legs high, the main point of the humor being centered on "the apertures of the human body."[4] Vaudeville was also inspired by big ballet spectacles performed by European stars—such as *The Black Crook* that ran for sixteen months beginning in September 1866 at Niblo's Garden in New York City.[5] In his book, *A Pictorial History of Vaudeville*, Bernard Sobel describes the grand scope of American vaudeville: "The assorted acts, or specialities, borrowed liberally from the native American variety entertainment, as exemplified in minstrel or medicine show, circus concert, dime museum, town hall entertainment, beer hall or honky-tonk, and . . . from the legitimate stage, concert hall, grand opera, ballet, musical comedy, and pantomime."[6] During vaudeville's heyday, from 1880 through the late 1920s, there were two kinds of two-a-day variety shows—those for men and those for mixed audiences. "Vaudeville was the theatre of the people," wrote Douglas Gilbert in his definitive book *American Vaudeville* remarking, "its brassy simplicity was as naïve as a circus."[7]

In 1904, at the Victoria Theatre on Broadway and 42nd Street, Princess Rajah performed an oriental dance with snakes. Her other routine, described by Gilbert, was a dance with a kitchen chair: "She would take hold of it with her teeth and, gliding about the stage, sway it forward and backward with arc-like movements that finally restored it to the stage on its legs."[8] Princess Rajah made $400 per week to start, but as audiences flocked to see her performances, her salary was raised to $750 per week.[9]

66

Gradually, such shallow acting and dancing sketches grew into one-act plays featuring English actress Sarah Bernhardt with Maurice Barrymore; musical comedy acts featuring Fanny Brice and Adele and Fred Astaire; and dance acts featuring ballroom dancers Vernon and Irene Castle, Gertrude Hoffman, performing Salome's *Dance of the Seven Veils*, and Loïe Fuller, an innovative skirt dancer who used fabric and colored lights to create spectacular effects. According to Bernard Sobel, the most important figure to further dance as an art was Ruth St. Denis, who danced "with exotic creations based on scholarly research, skilled technique and aesthetic ideals."[10]

While touring as a dancer/actress in David Belasco's productions of *ZaZa* and *Madame Dubarry*, twenty-two-year-old Ruth Denis maintained her innocence and would not be tempted by the sexual advances of Belasco or Stanford White, so Belasco nicknamed the young dancer/actress Ruth "Saint" Denis. It was during these tours that she discovered her true spiritual dance which took shape in the Hindu goddess *Radha*. This seventeen-minute dance opened in vaudeville at the Hudson Theatre in New York City. St. Denis describes the idea behind her dance thus: "Radha, who descended from her pedestal and signified to her worshipers that she had taken this human form in order to give them a message. This she would convey through a mystic dance, the meaning of which was that they must not seek permanent happiness in an impermanent world."[11]

St. Denis took her inspiration from another vaudeville star, Sarah Bernhardt, whom she saw appear in the melodrama *The Sorcerer* at Hammerstein's Victoria Theatre in New York City. During the performance St. Denis said to her friend Pat, "Put your fingers in your ears so that you can't hear her, and you will see that she is dancing."[12] St. Denis testified she was influenced by Sarah Bernhardt's artistry in quite a remarkable way when she wrote, "I feel that my picturesque posings on stage, . . . stem from watching this performance of Bernhardt."[13]

Another American dancer, Isadora Duncan, who had also danced in theatre productions, went with her family to Europe in 1899, where she discovered the origin of her artistic dance. In her book *The Visions of Modern Dance*, Jean Morrison Brown writes: "Isadora believed that dance should come from and be an expression of the spirit, inspired by nature; anything else was stilted and artificial."[14] Duncan was impassioned about dance as an art of human expression, and herself produced an astonishing effect on dancers, artists, and society as a whole. In August 1908, Isadora returned to the United States for a six-month tour, performing at the Criterion Theatre in New York City, then in Brooklyn, Boston, Philadelphia, Chicago, Syracuse, and Rochester. Of her performance the *Syracuse Post's* music critic wrote:

> The fascination of Miss Duncan's exquisite movements lies in their perfect naturalness. Despite the years of careful conscientious work she has given to her art, there is nothing studied or stilted about it . . . Every muscle of her body lends itself to the poetry of motion which she so charmingly realizes. Miss Duncan dances in bare feet and limbs but there is absolutely no suggestiveness in her movements, which are as chaste as they are classical in conception and execution. The matter of sex is entirely eliminated and one thinks only of the art which she illuminates. One seems to recognize her at once, not as a person but as a familiar figure often seen in painted colors or in marble. She seems less the individual and more the embodiment of artistic ideas.[15]

Isadora Duncan's premise of submerging her personality in order to transcend it as the embodiment of artistic ideas may be seen as allied to Loïe Fuller's formula of becoming the essence of motion in her floating, funneling fabrics accented with colored lights. Comparatively, Ruth St. Denis became a Hindu goddess in *Radha,* transformed into a corporeal form to dance her mystical message.

St. Denis, Fuller (or La Loïe as the French called her), and Duncan performed their dances in Paris, where French sculptor Auguste Rodin sculpted

Isadora and Russian ballet dancer Vaslav Nijinsky as twin artists. In a color lithograph in 1893, French Impressionist painter Henri de Toulouse-Lautrec captured Fuller's *Fire Dance* as she performed at the Folies-Bergère. Fuller also attracted other artists to render her dancing image on posters, including Jules Chéret and Manuel Orazi, among others. French sculptor François-Raoul Larche created four gilt bronze table lamps that capture how Loïe Fuller "effectively used huge quantities of silk to create movements and shapes from nature," in the sinuous lines of the Art Nouveau.[16]

While St. Denis was touring with David Belasco's production of *ZaZa* in London in 1900, she went to the Paris Exposition to visit Loïe Fuller's tiny theatre, where Fuller was appearing with a remarkable little Japanese artist, Sada Yacco. The longest lines anywhere were those outside Le Théâtre de la Loïe Fuller, where thousands of people waited to see her perform her "psychedelic light-and-motion dance show."[17] St. Denis saw La Loïe perform and called her "an inventive genius," but she was literally awestruck during the performance of the Japanese company. St. Denis wrote: "My real excitement and wonder was stirred to an unbelievable pitch by the extraordinary acting [dancing] of Mme. Sadi Yaco [sic]. For the first time I beheld and understood the beautiful austerities of Japanese art. . . . Her performance haunted me for years, and filled my soul with such a longing for the subtle and elusive in art that it became my chief ambition as an artist."[18] Through the Japanese minister in London, Fuller had negotiated to engage the Japanese troupe whose star, Sado Yacco (a minuscule, twenty-eight-year-old former geisha, born in Tokyo) would perform *The Geisha and the Knight*, a love story about a geisha and a samuri. Fuller's great success in bringing Sada Yacco to perform at the Paris Exposition "helped to advance the cause of women's rights," Richard and Marcia Current write in their definitive book on Loïe Fuller.[19] Up to this time, women had been barred from the stage in Japan, where traditionally male actors played female roles.

Richard and Marcia Current conclude: "The Japanese government finally opened the acting profession to women because of Sada Yacco's brilliant success in New York, London, and above all, Paris."[20]

The Nineteenth-century Fashion for *Japonisme*

French Impressionist art and early American modern dance were influenced by Japanese culture, as seen in Japanese woodcut prints, or *ukiyo-e*. Analogous design elements and subject matters employed in Japanese prints, French Impressionist art, and early American modern dance, reflect changing aesthetic values resulting from world trade, travel, and the internationalization of the arts. The transference of Japanese design principles to French Impressionist art was noted in the dances of St. Denis, Shawn, Fuller, Humphrey, Graham, Michio Ito, and Weidman. Selected examples of *ukiyo-e* prints will be described to illustrate their importance in documenting events in Japanese culture and their inspiring effect upon European and American art and dance.

The Japanese woodcut artist used a flat block of wood to create a print. The standard size, or *oban*, was 15 x 10 inches.[21] Negative areas where there was to be no line, shape, or color were cut away, leaving the positive image to be printed—the reverse of a line or pen-and-ink drawing.[22] Early prints were monochromatic, with design laid out in bold black lines—striking black-and-white prints. Depending on the number of colors, a separate block would be cut for each color. Exactness of registration of each block was essential to the final product.[23] During the early nineteenth century, Hokusai and Hiroshige revived the art with a new approach to landscape based on themes such as scenes of the Tokaido, or views of Mount Fiji, favorites of Japanese and Western collectors.[24] *Ukiyo-e* masterfully documented daily life, historic events, and old and new Japan.

Ukiyo-e flourished when the merchant class prospered in the cities of Osaka and Edo between 1688-1703. A new culture was born representing the hedonism of the merchant class, with gaiety and humor as a central theme in life. This lifestyle permeated society and was called the "floating world." Fun, lightheartedness, and exuberance reigned in the theatre, literature, and the arts. In these cities, leisure and amusement were centered in the courtesan section and the Kabuki theatre. During this time the suffix *-e* (pictures) was added to the word *ukiyo* to become *ukiyo-e*, or "floating-world pictures."[25]

In medieval Japan, the word *ukiyo* appeared as a Buddhist expression meaning "this world of pain," symbolizing a transitory, impermanent life represented by the image of floating weeds drifting on the water, or "where the water may take me." This meaning, with its pathos could be seen in the difficult life of the geisha, courtesan, and actor.[26] (In her 1906 mystical Hindu dance *Radha*, St. Denis conveyed this identical message—the futile attempt to attain happiness in an impermanent world.) The broad appeal of diverse images depicted in the "floating-world pictures" made them appreciated by Japanese upper, middle, and lower classes and even more valued by Western collectors.

In Japan and Europe the popularity of *ukiyo-e* prints was noted by Jules Heller in his book *Printmaking Today*: "The prints appeared in every household and, like Currier & Ives prints in America, were hawked on the streets, even pasted on walls of buildings. Japanese prints – their strong decorative design and brilliant, flat colors – had a profound influence on modern European art after they were discovered as wrappings for objects imported from Japan."[27] World trade and travel greatly influenced the internationalization of the arts. Early twentieth-century American culture reflected a noticeable change in aesthetics or artistic values. Japan's arts and culture were affected by this interchange as well. During an interview in 1989, Japanese *butoh* dance artist Natsu Nakajima commented that the opening of Japanese ports and world trade more than one hundred years

71

ago greatly influenced Japanese art, and Japanese dance was influenced by American and German modern dance.[28] American modern dance was equally affected by this cultural exchange, playing a significant role in the global development of both art and dance during the twentieth century.

The historic event that brought about this internationalization of the arts was the forced opening of Japan by America in 1854. Access to Japan's harbors would prove to be difficult because, in 1640, in fear of infringing colonial empires, Japan's feudal rulers, the shoguns, cut off their nation from the rest of the world. This policy (*sakoku,* or National Seclusion), maintained for over two centuries, was the result of national discord and trade along the Silk Road. In 1542 the Portuguese, trading in Chinese coastal towns, were blown off course and arrived in Japan, introducing gunpowder, firearms, and Christianity—all of which had devastating effects on traditional Japanese culture. During the period of *sakoku* the only European merchants permitted to trade directly with Japan were the Dutch, but their Dutch East India Company was "confined to Deshima, a man-made island in the harbor of Nagasaki."[29]

American merchant ships were able to sail to Japan under the auspices of the Netherlands. In 1799, a large Western ship called the *Franklin*, captained by James Devereux and registered in Boston, Massachusetts, entered Nagasaki Harbor flying the Dutch flag. In 1800, when the *Franklin* returned to America, its cargo contained spices, lacquerware, decorative objects, and five Japanese woodblock prints. Devereux gave these prints to the East India Marine Society Museum in the seaport town of Salem, Massachusetts, where they were displayed to public view. In her article, "The accessioning of Japanese art in early nineteenth-century America; *Ukiyo-e* prints in the Peabody Essex Museum, Salem," Nicole Coolidge Rousmaniere noted: "These [Japanese prints] . . . set the stage for the collecting and use of things Oriental, as well as significantly predating the later nineteenth-century fashion for *Japonisme*."[30]

72

During the 1840s the United States sought to expand trade in the Far East. First America needed to secure coaling stations in Japan for the inauguration of a steamship line across the Pacific Ocean and to expand whaling operations to produce oil for U.S. machinery and factories. Competition to open a Japanese port was fierce. At the end of the eighteenth century Russia, under Catherine the Great, made several attempts to open trade with Japan, and Great Britain's attempts from 1820 to 1830 proved unsuccessful.

The United States government sent Naval Commodore Matthew C. Perry on a diplomatic mission to Japan. In 1853 he arrived at Edo Bay with four black steamships. The Japanese called them "black ships of evil appearance."[31] Five thousand samurai surrounded the shore, blocking Perry's entrance; the Japanese people were fearful but at the same time fascinated. Perry returned within a year with more ships, and this time a treaty of friendship, the Kanagawa Treaty, was signed, ending Japan's two hundred year policy of seclusion.

In 1858, four more ports opened to United States trade, and by that fall four European nations—England, France, Russia, and the Netherlands—had followed the United States' example in completing trade treaties. The Five Nations, as they were called throughout Japan, became centers of attraction. Japan became the focus of attention in America when, in 1860, a dramatic visit by the first Japanese embassy to the United States toured San Francisco, Washington, D.C., Baltimore, Philadelphia, and New York.[32] This visit created a commotion everywhere, prompting Walt Whitman to write a special poem, "The Errand-Bearers," in honor of their visit.[33] Three Japanese ambassadors, with an entourage of seventy-seven officials, delivered a letter from the Shogun to President James Buchanan formally establishing treaty sanctions.

The opening of Japan to the world forced the Tokugawa shogunate to surrender its power in 1867 to the young Emperor Meiji, who vowed that Japanese security and prosperity would be achieved through modernization and economic development. Experts from the Five Nations and Italy were invited to Japan as advisors. Large numbers of students were sent to the West to be educated and trained, initiating a global exchange of new artistic values. This cultural interaction enabled Japan to present the first exhibition of Japanese art, including woodcut prints, at the Paris Universal Exposition in 1867.

Scholars and collectors became connoisseurs of the *ukiyo-e* prints depicting ordinary situations and events in landscapes, seascapes, village scenes, actors, dancers, and women in activities from daily life.[34] In his book *L'Art Français in 1872*, Jules Claretie nicknamed the cult of Japan "Japonisme."[35] Subsequent Japanese exhibits at the Paris Universal Expositions in 1878 and 1889 captivated the Parisian public. They were fascinated by the Japanese prints of artists like Kitagawa Utamaro (1753-1806), Katsushika Hokusai (1760-1849), and Ando Hiroshige (1797-1858), whose prints became wildly fashionable in Europe. In America, Japanese imports were sold at the 1903-04 American Exposition held in St. Louis. It was here that Japanese classical dancing was first introduced into America. In his article, "The First Japanese Dance Performed in America," Clay Lancaster writes: "Japan outdid herself, showing that she was second to no country in the world in either technological or artistic pursuit."[36]

During the late nineteenth and early twentieth centuries, the transference of Japanese art to the United States, and French Impressionism in art, music, and literature exhibited a fascination with the Orient with its ritual, exotic culture. French Impressionist painters Edouard Manet, Edgar Degas, Henri de Toulouse-Lautrec, Paul Gauguin, and the American Mary Cassett, and others shared an admiration of the *ukiyo-e* Japanese prints. These artists adopted similar subjects in their works and mastered the printing techniques of the Japanese masters with soft-ground etchings, aquatint, and color lithography.

More importantly, Impressionist art and early modern dance adopted the design principles employed in *ukiyo-e* prints. Through personal observation these design principles are noted as follows: an emphasis on one or two figures seated on the floor or on a low platform; figures positioned at opposing levels; contrast in line—straight or angular against curving lines; color contrast—black against white or bold color differences; asymmetry; and two-dimensional proportions.

In her book, *The Great Wave: The Influence of Japanese Woodcuts on French Prints*, Colta Feller Ives considers these design principles by comparing the *ukiyo-e* print *Kayoi Komachi* by Suzuki Harunobu to Degas' print *At the Louvre: Mary Cassatt in the Paintings Gallery*: "(*At the Louvre*) contains the Japanese characteristics most frequently pointed to in Degas's art: aerial perspective, asymmetrical composition, and a casual snapshot effect aided by cutting off figures by the picture's edge."[37] The figures are seen in an aerial perspective similar to viewing dance from a box or balcony in a theatre. The angularity of the room creates a frame for the figures similar to dancers framed by a proscenium stage. Comparable design elements are noted in Utamaro's *Woman dressing a girl for the sanbaso dance* and Cassett's *The Fitting*, where the figures are positioned at opposing levels. (This reflects a characteristic principle of opposed or opposite movements, used by French acting teacher François Delsarte and adopted in 1918 by St. Denis and Shawn in their *Siamese Ballet*.) Compare Cassett's *The Letter* and Utamaro's *Portrait of the oiran Hinzauru*. One notices the angularity of the letter and desk. The straight line of the headpiece forms a dramatic contrast to the curves of kimono, dress, and flowered wallpaper. (Contrast, an important design principle, was used in early modern dance and illustrated in the Japanese dance-drama *O-Mika*, created by St. Denis in 1913.) Consider the design of the traditional Japanese headpiece in Utamaro's *Portrait of the oiran Hinzauru*. It resembles the manner in which Graham dressed her hair for the role of Jocasta in *Night Journey* (1947); a photo portrait by Chris Alexander in 1950 shows Graham with branches in her hair that she had found on the street while she walked to the photo session.[38]

75

In his prints Toulouse-Lautrec used numerous customary design elements recognizable in the *ukiyo-e* actor prints—highly "stylized poses, bold colors and patterning, flattened perspective, and asymmetrical composition."[39] Consider the angularity of the woman's body in Toulouse-Lautrec's print *The Seated Clownesse*. Similar straight and angular lines were used in early twentieth-century American dance, which rejected the curving movements used in European classical ballet. In *The Seated Clownesse* Toulouse-Lautrec shows the figure sitting on a low platform as in Japanese prints. Michio Ito created the character Pierrot in a pantomime-play *The Donkey* in 1916, and Shawn created *Pierrot Forlorn* for Charles Weidman in 1921. The dances show similarities in their movement styles as follows: angularity of limbs, turned-in legs, curved torso, a shoulder rotated inward, and one figure seated on the floor. These characteristics illuminate the vulnerability of Pierrot, a standard comic character of the old French pantomime. The design principles presented in these dances were also employed in Japanese *ukiyo-e* prints. Japanese elements of design were quickly incorporated into the works of American artists.

According to renowned architect and collector Frank Lloyd Wright, who in 1907 gave an exhibition of Hiroshige prints at the Art Institute of Chicago, one underlying and overriding design principle used in Japanese prints is "simplification."[40] Carl Shanahan, professor of art, calls this "economy."[41] Both terms may also be called "abstraction," as Wright states about Japanese prints in his book *The Japanese Print: An Interpretation*: "Beauty abstract in immaculate form."[42] The term abstraction refers to the "essence" of an idea, or the molding of an idea into movement, thus communicating an idea to an audience. The new American dancer or modern dancer used abstraction, as Paul Love further explains:

The modern dancer works in movements constructed on physical rhythms and built into phrases and themes, varied in accent, shifted in space, repeated or discarded. He is not telling you a story from which you could get as adequate a response through reading; he is abstracting, distorting and emphasizing known motor patterns, so that his assemblage and presentation of them in their new pattern will give you a new perception, enlarge your vision, refocus your eye.[43]

The design principle of economy is recognized in Toulouse-Lautrec's print *Jane Avril* and Torii Kiyotada's *An actor of the Ichikawa clan, probably the second Danjuro, in a dance movement of violent motion.* In these prints the subject is a dancer's movement caught in performance, Jane Avril at the Moulin Rouge and a Kabuki actor in a dance-drama. In both prints the dancer's body is totally enclosed within the cloth of her or his costume, while the head is framed within the cloth. Each artist uses economy, simplification, or abstraction to present the "essence" of motion. Regarding this point Ives notes: "In the Japanese prints, as in Lautrec's, the motion of the dancer is caught still, as if by a camera. The dancers' costumes are seen whipped about, overwhelming their wearers to the extent that only heads and feet are visible beyond turbulent cloth."[44]

In 1892, Fuller became an overnight sensation in Paris when she performed *The Basket, The Spiral, Serpentine,* and other dances at the Folies-Bergère, where skillful use of fabric and colored lights heightened the sheer excitement of movement. In a solo titled *Scarf Dance* in 1919, Humphrey used fabric to enlarge her movements in space. Her aim of using a scarf to increase vertical space was seen in her dance *Soaring,* composed with St. Denis in 1920. Consider the resemblance in movement style shown by Jane Sherman in *Soaring* and Michio Ito in the *Greenwich Village Follies in 1919.* Each dancer (balanced on the left leg, with the right leg forward at a right angle, the chest lifted and arched) shows a suspended movement into vertical space. St. Denis' *Valse à La Loie* delighted audiences at every performance by Geordie Graham and Anna

Douglas, from their first performance in 1924, to their last in 1927. St. Denis greatly admired Fuller's use of fabric and stage lighting, and she created *Valse à La Loie* as a tribute to her fellow American dancer. Jane Sherman's account of *Valse à La Loie* describes how the two dancers in flesh-colored leotards convey an image of Fuller's dancing: "Around the shoulders . . . suspended a floor-length, very full circular white silk cape . . . In the changing colors of the lights and the figurations of the material, even faces were often invisible . . . as they . . . raise and lower their arms like butterfly wings . . . the lighting changes to flame. The dancers spiral swiftly in place . . ."[45] Graham said of her performance in *Moonlight Kisses* in the *Greenwich Village Follies of 1923:* "I danced in floating yellow chiffon, very Loïe Fuller."[46] Seven years later, Graham further developed abstraction in her famous dance *Lamentation,* where her body was encased in a tube of fabric.[46] She forced the observer to focus on her body's movement within the fabric, along with her expressive face, hands, and feet. Graham's *Lamentation*, St. Denis' *Valse à La Loie*, and Fuller's *The Spiral* are substantially allied to Kiyotada's *An actor of the Ichikawa clan, probably the second Danjuro, in a dance movement of violent motion* and Toulouse-Lautrec's *Jane Avril.*

In a 1966 interview with Weidman, Marian Horosko suggested that he was influenced by Michio Ito.[47] Possibly Ito's artistic work was affected by Weidman's art as well. After all, Ito worked with Louis Horst and was in New York during 1927-28, when Humphrey and Weidman were teaching and creating their first compositions. It is interesting to speculate whether one influenced the other and where and when; perhaps it was essentially changing aesthetics that affected all of them.

Born in Tokyo in 1892, Michio Ito, "whose talents were admired by Debussy and Rodin in Paris, by Yeats and Shaw in England, and by thousands in the United States," touched many modern dancers, including Weidman.[48] His paternal grandfather was a samurai who opposed Commodore Perry's opening of

Japan to the West; his father was an architect and friend of Frank Lloyd Wright.[49] Michio, the eldest son, at age eighteen left Tokyo to explore Europe's art; at twenty-two he became a professional dancer.[50] He choreographed and directed plays, operas, operettas, pantomimes, musical revues, and motion pictures in New York, Hollywood, Los Angeles, and Washington. In New York City he worked in the *Greenwich Village Follies* and at the Neighborhood Playhouse. Ito presented major recitals in New York in 1927-1928, with Louis Horst as his pianist. Considering the diversity of Ito's creative work and the cities in which he worked, he was undoubtedly inspired by dancers of his period, Shawn and Weidman, St. Denis and Graham—and these dancers were inspired by him. In her book, *Michio Ito*, Helen Caldwell affirms the *ukiyo-e* influence on Ito's *Spring Rain* of 1928:

> A Japanese print come to life for a moment in new colors; a young man (or maiden) folding and opening his umbrella at the whims of the weather, displaying his many-colored finery to April's soft rain and sun. As idea, it is a brief thing of innocent vanity: youth's evanescent beauty ready to shield itself from life's showers with a huge, many-splendored paper umbrella.[51]

Jane Sherman's use of her umbrella in *A Burmese Yein Pwe*, choreographed by St. Denis and Humphrey in 1926, reflects Caldwell's account of Ito's dance, and also exhibits the philosophy of youth Caldwell presents in her description. Comparable aesthetic values are shown by Ernestine Day in *Momiji Gari*, choreographed by Matsumoto Koshiro and arranged by Shawn in 1926, and by St. Denis in *Burmese Solo* in 1923. Shawn's *Japanese Spear Dance* of 1919 and Ito's *Japanese Spear Dance* of 1923 show a direct link to Japanese Kabuki actor prints. Weidman created his *Japanese Actor* and *Singalese Drum Dance* in 1928, inspired by his work with Japanese Kabuki actor Matsumoto Koshiro, and

79

Chinese opera actor, Mei-Lan Fang, during Denishawn's 1925-26 Asian Tour. Similar dance titles and composers used by St. Denis, Shawn, Graham, Humphrey, Ito, and Weidman clearly reflect the influence of Japanese culture and Japanese *ukiyo-e* woodcut prints upon early American modern dance.

Not only has Japanese culture affected the development of American dance in the early years of the twentieth century, but Japanese choreographers of the twenty-first century have been influenced by Commodore Perry's historic visit as well. Saeko Ichinohe's Dance Company celebrated 150 years of U.S./Japan Relations on April 13, 2004, in a performance at the Kaye Playhouse in New York City. Born and raised in Japan, Saeko Ichinohe graduated from the Juilliard School and lives in New York City. For this artistic celebration Ichinohe created *Utamaro*, given a New York premiere. The publicity notes state: "This work was inspired by the woodblock prints of Utamaro (1753-1806), who designed his prints in *Ukiyo-e* (means the floating world). His portraits of courtesans, lovers, working girls, tea-house girls, and mothers and children, were indicative of the lives of people, who lived in the Edo period (1603-1867)."[52] For this celebration, Ichinohe recreated *Stars & Stripes and Cherry Blossoms* (1984), a work that "reflects the changes that took place after the arrival of Commodore Perry. This work, divided into *Village, Confusion, Relationship, and Freedom*," is indicative of what this historic event represents in Japanese culture. In Ichinohe's *Stars & Stripes and Cherry Blossoms* "modern dance and Japanese dance were fused."[53]

American and European intoxication with travel to the Orient and the tropics could be captured, if not literally, then through imagination in the paintings of José Tapiró Baró, Paul Gauguin, and in the novels or descriptive travelogues of Pierre Loti. Spanish artist Baró painted a number of Oriental images. Baró's stunning painting *A Tangerian Beauty* (ca. 1876) was the result of time spent in Tangier, the capital of Morocco, just across the Strait of Gibraltar.

Both Gauguin's and Loti's works reflect a steamy exoticism. Loti's travelogues took one to such distant places as China, Palestine, India, and Tahiti, and expressed the "profound melancholy of an eternal wanderer seeking an earthly paradise in primitive societies."[54] Exotic places and aboriginal peoples had been an important part of Gauguin's life.

When Gauguin was an infant and his sister a toddler, his parents emigrated to Lima, Peru, the country of his mother's family. His father did not survive the ocean journey and the family returned to France when Paul was six-years old. He joined the navy at seventeen years of age; as a young sailor his ports of call were Rio de Janeiro, Bahia, Panama, and Martinique. He married a young Danish girl settling in Paris, where he began collecting art and studying painting. His studio was decorated with the *ukiyo-e* woodcut prints of Utamaro.[55] Artistic pressure from Impressionist painters prompted Gauguin to flee Paris to exotic Martinique and Tahiti to live among the natives or "savages," as the French high society called them, where naked Tahitian women dominated his work. *Still Life with Head-Shaped Vase and Japanese Woodcut* (1889) is a work that reflects Gauguin's world in Tahiti. It bursts with color—a pink table; a sunny yellow wall; lush, vibrant, colored flowers; and a *ukiyo-e* woodcut print of a Kabuki actor on the wall, exemplified his admiration of Japanese art. About the head-shaped vase, Gauguin said: "It represents vaguely the head of Gauguin the savage."[56] *Still Life with Head-Shaped Vase and Japanese Woodcut* reinforces previous statements about popular fascination with the Orient, specifically *ukiyo-e* prints. At the same time, this work shows a fascination with indigenous or tribally based society. The head-shaped vase in Gauguin's image shows three-dimensionality akin to the carvings and sculpture in Balinese art. The aboriginal subject of the painting with the vibrant-colored, exotic, lush flowers transports one to tropical Tahiti.

In Europe during the 1880s and 1890s, it was not unusual for ballets to be based on Japanese motifs. For example, *Le Rêve* (*The Dream*), based on a Japanese theme, was a ballet in two acts and three scenes that had a libretto written by E. Blau. The choreographer of *Le Rêve* Joseph Hanson, a Belgian dancer who, in the course of his career, was ballet director at Russia's Bolshoi Theatre in Moscow, ballet master at London's Alhambra Theatre, and ballet master at the Paris Opéra.[57] Hanson enjoyed creating ballet productions with colorful national themes. *Le Rêve* was performed in 1885 at the Académie Nationale de Musique. The lithographic poster advertising *Le Rêve* was designed by Théophile-Alexander Steinien, a native of Switzerland, and depicts a Japanese scene on a scroll, mounted on a bamboo frame. The natural scene shows a full moon in the top left corner. Above a windswept pine tree, the ballet's title is printed in a muted orange color and hangs in a bamboo frame in the top right corner. A large, muted, orange-colored Japanese fan covers the entire mid-section of the poster, with a corps de ballet flanking the front of the fan in two symmetrical lines. On the poster, whose style is indicative of the ballet, the men are costumed in short kimonos and the women in short tutus, with their heads adorned in Japanese-styled wigs. They all use Japanese fans as props. A prima ballerina poses in the left foreground. She is wearing a short, pastel-colored tutu with a long, opened, orange-and-white kimono. She wears a Japanese wig and holds an open Japanese fan behind her head. *Le Rêve* truly represents a Japanese print come to life through the European classical ballet.[58]

During the first decade of the twentieth century, European and American dance art centered around Asian inspired choreography in the forms of ballet, interpretive, and Delsarte-Orientalism.[59] The world seemed intoxicated with all things exotic and Oriental (from Spain to the Far East).[60] The early Universal Expositions in Paris encouraged this. In his book, *The Banquet Years*, Roger Shattuck's account of the 1889 Universal Exposition gives further details of

Oriental influences on dance and music: "A Cairo street scene was constructed with authentic imported Egyptians to live in it and perform the *danse du ventre*. The Javanese dancers became the rage of Paris, influenced music-hall routines for twenty years, and confirmed Debussy in his tendency toward Oriental harmonies."[61]

In 1910 the famed Russian Ballet (or Ballets Russes), under the direction of Serge Palovitch Diaghilev, encouraged Michel Fokine to create his exotic ballets *Scheherazade*, *Cleopatra*, and *L'Oiseau de Feu*. In 1906, St. Denis created *Radha*, based on a Hindu legend, and in 1913 she premiered *O'Mika*, a Japanese dance drama. Maude Allen and Gertrude Hoffman became overnight sensations in 1908 with individual performances of *Salome* and imitations of Isadora Duncan's interpretive antique Greek dances. The famous Russian ballerina Anna Pavlova, with her partner Mikhail Mordkin, gave performances at the Metropolitan Opera, dancing to the music of Frederick Chopin in Greek "draperies" ending with a wildly exciting *Bacchanale*.[62] Shawn created his archaic dance *Gnossienne* (1917) and Ito composed several dances in ancient Greek style. In a New York performance in 1928, Ito danced *Warrior* to Rachmaninoff's music. "Ito was a Spartan reincarnate in a picturesque costume," critic Nickolas Muray writes.[63] Ito created and performed his dances *Gnossiennes I & II* in 1933-34 as interpretations of Erik Satie's music. Caldwell's description of Ito's works noted their similarity to Shawn's work as "reminiscent of Minoan and archaic Greek art. *Gnossienne I* recalls the gaudy dances, processionals, banqueting . . . that enliven Etruscan tomb paintings—the spirit of life lived well on earth in contrast to a dank hereafter in the tomb; *Gnossienne II*, a Cretan religious celebration . . ."[64] During his years as a teacher in New York and California, Ito trained a number of students who contributed to American dance including Lester Horton, Pauline Koner, and Angna Enters. Ito's suite of Spanish dances *Malaguena* (1928), *Bullfighter* (1920), and *Tango* (1927) seem closely akin to Shawn's *Flamenco Dances* (1919) and *Cuadro Flamenco* (1923), where Shawn's portrayal of a bullfighter recreates the atmosphere of exotic Spain. In *Cuadro Flamenco* Shawn used traditional Flamenco dances as the foundation for the four sections of the dance: *Seguidilla, Flamenco Solos, Shawl Plastique*, and *Malaguena*. Weidman danced in these works and incorporated the stylistic arm positions of Flamenco dancing into his movement style.

At the turn of the twentieth century, America's fascination with the picturesque customs of ancient civilizations and exotic cultures were Orientalized through images from the visual arts continued in French Impressionists paintings and Japanese *ukiyo-e* prints. Perhaps it was the totality of these arts that had a keen impact on America and on the development of modern dance, specifically in the works of St. Denis, Shawn, Graham, Humphrey, and Weidman.

Miraculous Visions, New Religious Doctrines

Spiritual enlightenment was absorbing interest in the initial decades of the twentieth century. Several religious doctrines, such as Shakerism, Christian Science, and American Transcendentalism, formulated in the late eighteenth and nineteenth centuries, became significant denominations by the early twentieth century. As a young man, Weidman's exposure to various religious doctrines offered him chronicles to use in his dances, and his associates involved him in the creation of their dances.

Modern dance as a concert art was expanded in 1931 when Humphrey set to work with the Humphrey-Weidman dancers to compose *The Shakers*, a work that includes narrative. Humphrey, inspired by the stylistic dance form that dominated the Shaker religious service, was equally fascinated by their philosophy of life. The key to the Shakers' lives was their belief in the transformation of earth into heaven, "to reconcile meaningfully the human and the divine, the temporal and the eternal."[65] Humphrey, along with Weidman and their dancers, studied the historic development of the Shaker religious sect in order to fully realize this composition. Ann Lee, founder of Shakerism, or the Shaking-Quakers in America, was born in Manchester, England. In 1770, she had a vision of Jesus, a "revelation." Lee claimed to be the embodiment of the promised Second Coming of Christ, representing the Mother, or female principle in God, just as Jesus represents the male Father principle. In 1774, with eight followers, Mother Ann Lee founded an American Shaker colony at Watervliet near Albany, New York. The Shakers were gentle, hardworking people who considered all work an act of worship. Celibacy was at the core of their religion, since they believed it brought them closer to God's image. In the Shaker community men and women worshipped, worked, ate, and slept separately, even using different stairs within their communal houses. They were pacifists who believed in equality between men and women and people of color. During the 1930s these Shaker beliefs were equally important to Weidman, Humphrey, and their dancers. The Shakers practiced frenzied dancing as a part of their formal ritual of worship, but the separation of genders was upheld throughout their religious worship. The Shakers believed that they could rid themselves of sin by shaking it from their bodies.[66] The Shakers practiced a form of trance or ecstatic dancing, in which worshippers transcended their corporeal bodies to attain spiritual enlightenment. Humphrey capitalized on this aspect with her masterful use of climatic phrase lengths in her rendition of a Shaker religious service.

American Transcendentalists

The basic belief of the American Transcendentalist movement was mystical. For them knowledge of spiritual truths was acquired through intuition and meditation. American poets Ralph Waldo Emerson and Walt Whitman were exponents of American Transcendentalism. Considered by his contemporaries to be the doyen of American Transcendentalism, Emerson believed that "truth was apprehended not by rational means, but by intuition; spirit was more real than matter; and the spirit, which was God, was in all men and revealed itself in all things."[67] Emerson's ideas paralleled those of the Shakers; he was interested in their conceptualization of spiritualism, and visited the Hancock Shaker village in Massachusetts for a closer look. In his essay "Self-Reliance" (1841), Emerson's visionary ideas on how the divine manifests itself in the individual are clarified. Emerson writes: "Trust yourself. Know that what is true for you in your own heart is inevitably true for other men, because a common spirit dwells in all men and speaks to them, when they will listen, in the same voice."[68]

With Emerson's encouragement, Whitman wrote his collection of twelve poems, *Leaves of Grass,* in 1856. A new poem, "Crossing Brooklyn Ferry" is considered by James E. Miller, Jr. to constitute a "transcendental drama of the spiritual unity of all objects and beings, including poet and reader."[69] In his third edition of *Leaves of Grass* in 1860, Whitman's brilliant poem "Out of the Cradle Endlessly Rocking" relates an emotional experience common to everyone. Miller suggests it is a poem "of mystical insight into love and death narrated by the poet-become-boy as he observes a mocking bird on the seashore singing for his lost mate."[70] Shawn had the idea of creating a great American production based on Whitman's *Leaves of Grass.* His project never materialized, but Shawn believed that *Leaves of Grass* was "one of the greatest books of any time, age or people."[71]

The first poet to cultivate the full potential of free verse, Whitman created a structure to serve the content of his work. This same idea was at the root of American modern dance—free form evolved to serve the content of the dance. Free form helped shape the individual movement styles in the dances of Duncan, St. Denis, Shawn, Graham, Humphrey, and Weidman. Miller concludes that Whitman's popularity was due to the fact that he presented themes of "democracy and the individual, science and spirit, body and soul, love and death, in a refreshing untarnished language common to man but new to poetry."[72] While delivering a series of lectures at the George Peabody College for Teachers in Nashville in 1938, Shawn wrote: "Walt Whitman is not only the greatest American and the greatest poet that ever lived, but probably the supreme example in the world's history of cosmic consciousness."[73]

Dance and the Embodiment Of Spirituality

An interpretation of the Bible is what distinguishes most Western religions, but what seems intriguing about the previously mentioned denominations is the core idea of spiritual transformation. Be it through trance dancing, as in the Shaker religion, or prayer healing, as in the Christian Science Church, or intuition, leading to union with the oversoul as in the American Transcendentalist movement, a notion of spiritual transformation is evident.

St. Denis was clearly touched by the doctrines of the Christian Science Church. One Sunday afternoon she discovered a brown-covered book by Mary Baker Eddy in their small family library. St. Denis was so entranced with Eddy's religious premises that she reads the entire book. Mary Baker Eddy, founder of Christian Science, had been born in New Hampshire. As a young woman, sickness, death of loved ones, and despair caused her to search for a deeper understanding of God as the key to the problems of pain, evil, and hatred in life. After a near-death accident in 1866, she began to read the Bible and, while reading an account of Jesus healing a paralyzed man in the St. Matthew's gospel, she received spiritual illumination and was suddenly healed. She spent the next three years in concentrated study of the scriptures. She published her finding as a textbook, *Science and Health with Key to Scriptures*, that explained her doctrine of healing through prayer and laid the foundation for the Christian Science religion. Christian Scientists rely upon prayer to solve human problems; a part of their religious service is retained for spontaneous testimonies of healing.

St. Denis felt a need for reformation in her spiritual life, but thought the next level of spirituality should be attained in the arts, not in an established church. "The discipline of spiritual consciousness," wrote St. Denis, "is the only force that can enlarge the artist's capacities and free him from his own temperamental limitations."[74] In her book *Time and the Dancing Image*, Deborah Jowitt explains that most of St. Denis' dances encompass "ideas of evolution, transformation, and the circular nature of existence."[75] Part of her public appeal was her ability to transcend herself and become the female divinities she was dancing: Radha, Isis, Ishtar, and Kuan Yin. Jane Sherman maintains that St. Denis had one great message: "The expression of God through Dance."[76]

Certainly Shawn's training for the ministry and subsequent rehabilitation after diphtheria was carried directly into his work as a dancer. Themes of transformation were woven into Shawn's dances, especially *Gnossienne,* a Cretan ritual performed before the altar of the Snake Goddess. "Gnosis is a Greek word meaning positive knowledge, especially of spiritual truth," writes Sherman.[77] In Shawn's *The Cosmic Dance of Siva* of 1926, Sherman observes that the choreography "revealed the contradictions that make up India: its contemplation versus its violence, the subtle beauty of its art versus its often vulgar manifestations."[78] But at the root of India's culture is the quest for spirituality, whether through Hindu, Muslim, Buddhist, or other religions.

Humphrey seemed drawn to the Shaker religion when she created her dance *The Shakers,* originally titled *Dance of the Chosen.* Like St. Denis and Shawn, Humphrey uses her superb sense of theatre to make a point. The dance appears to be a historical adaptation of the path toward spiritual enlightenment attained during an actual Shaker prayer meeting. For musical accompaniment Humphrey and Lawrence use a traditional Shaker hymn performed with voice, harmonium, and percussion. In the dance, men and women never cross the centerline of the dancing space. With the women dancing on stage right and the men dancing on stage left, they rhythmically walk in lines and circles, shaking their hands, and thus, the sins from their bodies. This rhythmic walking builds into larger ecstatic movements of falling and recovering, Humphrey's basic movement tenet. Humphrey uses the spoken word as "divine revelations" of the spirit of God. In a testimonial, a man points up to heaven and shouts: "My Life. My Carnal Life! I Will Lay It Down Because It Is Depraved." The worshippers rush to center stage where the Eldress, representing Mother Ann Lee, stands on a bench rhythmically clapping her hands to get their attention until they fall to their knees. "It Hath Been Revealed—Ye Shall Be Saved When Ye Are Shaken Free Of Sin," the Eldress exclaims.[79] The Eldress begins leading her followers into the climax of the service. In the trance dance sections that follow, Humphrey shows spinning, with a climax of frenzied, ecstatic, jumps reaching upward to heaven and the attainment of spiritual enlightenment. Humphrey crystallized the essence of the Shaker's spiritual transformation in her dramatization *The Shakers*.

Weidman danced in *The Shakers*. He also composed numerous Biblical chronicles through abstract dance, such as *David and Goliath* (1947), *The Christmas Oratorio* (1961), *King David* (1963), *The Easter Oratorio* (1967), and *Saint Matthew Passion* (1973). Weidman's *Rose of Sharon* and *Song of Solomon* in 1949 were based on those Psalms in the Bible. Religious concepts of spiritual transformation were dominant themes in his modern dance choreography. Apparently Charles was an extremely spiritual man. Regarding this evolution of his spiritual life, Weidman wrote:

> I probably am quite a religious person. I was baptized and confirmed in the Episcopal (High) Church. When Daddy married again his wife, Carrie Berrie, was a Seventh-Day Adventist, and she explained their doctrines. Then I have been exposed at Denishawn with Miss Ruth and Martha [Graham], and then later with many of my dancers to Christian Science. However, my religion is art—in the things I have chosen to project it is

not so much the Biblical chronicles and their achievements, but the artist's interpretation of the deeds.[80]

Weidman's diverse religious experiences culminated in his later works: *The Christmas Oratorio, The Easter Oratorio*, and *Saint Matthew Passion.* These works, choreographed to the music of Johann Sebastian Bach, use a full chorus in which the voices support the strength of the contrapuntal movement as exemplified in the ensemble sections. Weidman's use of a large dance group balances the chorus with an equal dynamic; the orchestral instrumentation aids in the drama of Weidman's skillfully crafted works for large ensembles. In these dances Weidman's own fascination with spiritual transformation render these passion plays of Christ mostly abstractly, few sections relying on Weidman's pantomimic craft. When interpreting numerous Biblical chronicles, Weidman's spiritual life guides him toward choreographic clarity, resulting in formal compositions and inspiring performances.

Chapter Four

Dancing with Ted Shawn and Ruth St. Denis
(1920-1928)

For we are witnessing the birth and adolescence of a true American art,
the dance, which, with the metaphysical thinking which stemmed from
our New England atmosphere, constitutes the only indigenous
expression of our native consciousness.

Ruth St. Denis
An Unfinished Life

Ruth St. Denis believed in building an endurable American dance,
combined of the fertile past, with fresh new ideas provided by younger dancers.[1]
Arriving at Denishawn in 1920, Charles was accepted into the summer training
program on a scholarship—his duties included costuming and teaching. Without
jeopardizing his opportunities at Denishawn, Charles made a point to study at the
Theodore Kosloff Ballet School located near Grand Street. Denishawn was an
institution, both a school and a company. Located on South Grand Street in Los
Angeles, Denishawn was housed in a large pseudo-Greek structure surrounded by
a colonnade. "It had a beautiful big studio, all white, even the piano, the living
room, shiny black with green in Egyptian—all things about the stars," Weidman
said.[2] Denishawn provided the technical training and theatrical experience for
emerging dance artists Weidman, Graham, Humphrey, Lawrence, Louise Allen,
Louise Brooks, Marion Chase, Jack Cole, Ernestine Day, Anne Douglas, Robert
Gorham, Barton Mumaw, Klarna Pinska, Jane Sherman, and many others.
Denishawn was cofounded by two of the most prominent American dance artists

91

St. Denis and Shawn, along with musical director Louis Horst, who "became one of the chief architects of modern dance in the twentieth century."[3] Charles' first teacher at Denishawn was Doris Humphrey who was substituting for Shawn. At once Charles decided, "Oh, I don't like her at all."[4] Martha Graham, whom he did not meet at this time, was rehearsing a Toltec ballet of Shawn's called *Xochitl*. Charles did not finish the summer training course because Robert Gorham, a handsome, talented dancer, had broken his foot and young Charles was sent to Tacoma, Washington, to replace him as Graham's partner in the role of King Tepancaltzin in *Xochitl*.[5] "Graham took him in hand," wrote José Limón, "hurriedly rehearsed him, and pushed him onstage to dance opposite her as the Aztec emperor."[6] Weidman spends the next eight years as a member of the Denishawn Dancers, performing with them in 720 cities on all of their vaudeville tours.

Movement Principles of François Delsarte

Training at the Denishawn School of Dance was based upon a system of expressive gesture used by French acting teacher François Delsarte (1811-71). As a child growing up on a farm in New Jersey, Ruth St. Denis was exposed to Delsarte's ideas by her mother, who had studied with Delsarte's disciples Madame Poté and actor Steele Mackaye.[7] Ruth's mother graduated from the University of Michigan as a doctor; she practiced in a clinic in Philadelphia. Unfortunately, after one year, she suffered an emotional and physical breakdown from overwork and had to give up her practice, but she vowed to keep herself in good health from that point on.[8] Ruth's mother and father (who was born in England) met at Perth Amboy, an art colony where Steele Mackaye, a genius of the American theatre, was a principal contributor.[9] Mrs. Dennis found one key to good health was to discard her corset and practice Delsarte's relaxation exercises and Mackaye's "Harmonic Gymnastics," which she taught to her daughter.[10] In her bedroom, with her mother sitting holding a Delsarte manual, Ruth wrote: "I grasped the rail of the bed, swinging my long legs to and fro, doing the numberless exercises that were the actual beginning of my dancing."[11]   Ruth enjoyed practicing Delsarte's exercises based on his theory of succession, which she noticed made the joints and muscles of her body more fluid.   She spontaneously practiced these exercises while doing chores or playing in the yard; one of the summer boarders in the Dennis home nicknamed her "Delsarte."

A major part of Delsarte's theoretical stance rested on the Law of Trinity rooted in the established canon of Christianity. He further developed the Ninefold Accord based on life, mind, and soul comprising a trinity. Delsarte's Law of Correspondence operated simultaneously with the Law of Trinity and referred to the concept that spiritual and emotional states are reproduced in bodily attitude, gesture, and facial expression.[12] Delsarte's comprehensive system of physical training was valued by both St. Denis and Shawn and was embedded in their teaching methodology at Denishawn.

As a young woman, St. Denis saw a performance given by a noted Delsarte disciple, Genevieve Stebbins, that made a lasting impression on her. Of this performance she wrote: "The image of her white, Grecian figure became so indelibly printed on my mind that everything I subsequently did stemmed from this revelation. . . . She moved in a series of plastiques [poses] which were based upon her understanding of the laws of motion discovered by Delsarte. Her poses were derived from Greek statuary and encompassed everything from the tragedy of Niobe to the joyousness of Terpsichore."[13]

St. Denis began to "evolve meaningful movement in dance in an era when dance, in the Western world, was devoid of meaning," Walter Terry wrote.[14] When she met Shawn in 1914, she encouraged him to learn about the laws of motion designed by Delsarte, and he studied intensively with Mrs. Richard Hovey, a pupil of Delsarte's son, Gustave.[15] Shawn invited Hovey to the

Denishawn School to give a series of lectures on Delsarte's theories. Subsequently, when Graham, Humphrey, and Weidman embarked upon their own careers, they continued to make use of Delsarte's theories—especially the Law of Expressive Gesture. These three originators of modern dance created historic works that reflected Delsarte's basic underlying idea—one must have motivation for the use of gesture. In his book *How to Look At Dance*, Walter Terry writes that this was the time American dancers heightened their use of expressive gesture as "an integral part of an evolving American dance process which has long demanded that choreographers and dancers go below the surface attraction of the human body in movement and probe the meaning of movement."[16]

While probing the meaning of expressive gesture, Shawn developed pantomimic movement that he defined as "how to convey realistically emotions, dramatic episodes, human situations and activities, without the use of words."[17] While using pantomimic movement, Shawn recognized a natural comic temperament in Charles Weidman. To utilize Weidman's natural talent, Shawn choreographed three special solos for him: *The Crapshooter, Pierrot Forlorn,* and *Danse Américaine.* In *The Crapshooter,* Charles played a "small-town smart aleck who boasted he could win in a game of craps," Jane Sherman writes.[18] With the unprecedented success in American and Asia of both *The Crapshooter* and *Danse Américaine,* Weidman revealed his mastery of pantomimic movement and "established his reputation as a comic interpreter."[19]

Among other significant Delsartean doctrines incorporated into classes and choreography at Denishawn were the notion that all movements may be divided into three major categories: *oppositions, parallelisms,* and *successions.*[20] In his book *Every Little Movement,* Shawn defined oppositions as "two parts of the body moving in opposite directions simultaneously . . . expressive of force, strength, physical or emotional power."[21] Weidman used oppositions in his technique series *Body Bends, Hop Series, Free Kicks,* and in his works *Danse*

94

Profane, Traditions, and *A House Divided,* as Humphrey did in *Opposition Study* and *Side Fall.* Shawn defined parallelisms as "two parts of the body moving simultaneously in the same direction . . . stylized movements along the line of Egyptian or Cretan wall-paintings."[22]

In an interview with Marian Horosko in 1966, Weidman spoke about his affiliation with Denishawn and the Delsarte training he received from Shawn: "He was from Delsarte. I am also from Delsarte . . . it's got to come from way within . . ."[23] In his statement, Charles stressed that gesture and movement must be motivated from an interior center, a clear motivational source. This trait was recognizable in his dances and characterizations of historic figures. Weidman further observed how Delsarte's theories influenced Humphrey's choreography: "She got a great deal out of my little old book on Delsarte which I still have; on folding successional movement, unfolding and oppositions—all those oppositions—all those things.[24]

The Delsarte fundamental movement principles taught at Denishawn became equally distinctive in Weidman's and Humphrey's techniques, movement styles, and choreographic principles. Shawn defined successions as "any movement passing through the entire body, or any part of the body, which moves each muscle, bone, and joint as it comes to it—that is the fluid, wavelike movement."[25] Successions were used in Weidman's *Body Bends, Push-Up,* and *Knee Fall* and in Humphrey's *Side Fall, Back Fall, Back Succession,* and *Water Study.*

Delsarte's Law of Velocity suggests that the speed of movement is in direct correlation between the weight of the body and the distance in space it will move. Expressions of profound emotions and serious subjects "require slow and large movement patterns; emotions that are petty, light, trivial, nervous . . . take on small and quick movement patterns," Shawn wrote.[26] Delsarte's Law of Velocity, as described by Shawn, was recognizable in Weidman's *Fables for Our*

Time, Flickers, and *Saint Matthew Passion* and in Weidman and Humphrey's *Duo-Drama.*

Gesture and Pantomime

A gesture is a motivated movement developed to communicate a thought or expression. Pantomime conveys through gesture human situations, emotions, and dramatic events.[27] Shawn choreographed a solo for Weidman called *Pierrot Forlorn* in 1921 to the music of De Acevas. In 1923, *Pierrot Forlorn* became part of a suite of dances titled *In the Garden.* Charles also performed *Pierrot Forlorn* in his first independent concert in 1928. According to Barton Mumaw, a noted Denishawn dancer, *Pierrot Forlorn* was a cliché set to ordinary music, "of which Charles made a Chaplinesque gem of wit and poignancy."[28] *Pierrot Forlorn* copied the conventional mime drama of the character Pierrot with Harlequin and Columbine. In her book *The Drama of Denishawn,* Jane Sherman describes *Pierrot Forlorn,* a dance she watched Charles perform more than one hundred times during an Asian Tour.

Pierrot steps through the split black velvet back curtain into a blue moonlight spot. He dances a few steps, then, holding one of his long sleeves as if it were a neck of a guitar or a mandolin, he strums across its invisible strings with his other hand while he stands beneath an invisible window to serenade his love. Miming his plaintive song, his wide mouth moves, his dark eyes stare upward. He stops. He listens with head cocked for a response. Shrugging his shoulders at the silence, he plays some more. Then, rejected and dejected, poor Pierrot dances his sorrow, wiping away his tears first with one sleeve, then the other. He pauses often in a bent-kneed, pigeon-toed stance, arms hanging limply at his sides, head tilted up as if to listen again for the beloved voice that refuses to speak. In a burst of despairing activity, he moves with trailing sleeves flung above one long-legged *arabesque* after another, before he resumes his fruitless serenade. Finally convinced it is useless, he is left standing, truly forlorn, at stage center when the lights black out.[29]

Weidman unveiled his intuitive talent for pantomime, drama, and characterization in *Pierrot Forlorn*—these gifts that he would develop throughout his career. Sherman's description of Weidman's performance notes the unfolding of the dramatic situation and the complexity of Pierrot's story. Weidman's innate talent was evolved and enhanced with Shawn's knowledge and coaching. Shawn's study of Delsarte with Hovey led him to realize that nine basic problems need to be solved in creating a successful pantomime: "It must imitate or describe objective forms . . . relations between forms . . . spatial dimensions . . . weight; make comparisons in spatial dimensions and sizes . . . weight . . . speed; indications and illustrations of action; characteristics of action."[30] Keeping these in mind Shawn created another solo especially for Weidman in 1923 called *Danse Américaine.*

Danse Américaine, a highlight in Shawn's dances based on American themes, was set to the music of American composer Dent Mowry. After Weidman's first performance on October 15, 1923, at the Apollo Theatre in Atlantic City, New Jersey, the audience's response was so overwhelming that he had to give an encore.[31] Two years later, Weidman's performance of *Danse Américaine* had become such a favorite with audiences that in June 1925 an article "Popular Sport Steps" appeared in *Dance Lovers Magazine*, giving Weidman an opportunity to share the steps of *Danse Américaine* with his public.

In his introduction to the article Byrne MacFadden, writer for *Dance Lovers Magazine,* expresses his desire to master the steps of *Danse Américaine:* "One of the first real American dances we have ever seen was Charles Weidman's 'Danse Américaine,' presented in the Denishawn program. There was something about it so different, so clever and so catchy that it seemed you must see it over and over again until you grasped every detail. Then you want to go home and try its popular sport steps yourself." MacFadden was so enthusiastic about *Danse Américaine* that he arranged to visit the Denishawn School. Arriving early,

97

MacFadden was able to observe a dance class in process, and declares: "Such a lovely big room! Even on this hot day it seemed cool and airy. We could see about a dozen boys and girls, all in plain black bathing suits, who didn't seem to appreciate the fact that the room looked cool, for the perspiration was pouring down their faces as they worked. No wonder, for they weren't doing ordinary technique of the average dancing class, but all kinds of difficult leaps and beats. We could feel ourselves getting rather warm from just looking at them." After the class, MacFadden spoke to Weidman about *Danse Américaine*. "'Don't you think you could write it out for our readers? It is so unique and just the thing that many amateurs are wishing for.' 'I certainly will,' Weidman replied. I am fond of the magazine myself and would like to contribute something to help my fellow readers.'"

Danse Américaine

Created by Mr. Shawn and Danced by Charles Weidman of Denishawn

This dance is purely pantomime, which is the most important thing to remember throughout. Pantomime is, as a rule, a gift. Some dance students never become proficient in that art, others find it comes to them naturally. Pantomime is one of the greatest aids to moving-picture actors and actresses, and one of the main reasons for the many failures in the pictures is due to the lack of this natural art.

Every dancer should try to perfect his pantomime. It is not necessary in ballet work, but for character dances and Oriental interpretations it is absolutely essential. If you are not good in pantomime, if you fail, as a rule to put it over, you will find practicing this little dance will help you a great deal.

The costuming is important. You must put your audience in the spirit of the dance from the moment you appear on the stage, and the only way to get this effect is to have music and costuming absolutely suitable. . . . The suit is tight-fitting and small; a vivid shade of tan is the most effective color. The shoes are the "bulldog" type, of the color known as "yellow" tan. Light socks, striped shirt, bright tie and a derby complete the ensemble.

The character is a small mill-town "dude." He is the sport of the town and knows it! He is afraid of nothing on earth—but the "skoits"! Remember to keep this spirit of bravado throughout the entire dance.

The dance itself can be done without knowledge of technique. There are no regular fixed steps to it; it is merely the interpretation of a story, by gestures, to suitable music.

As you walk on the stage you are supposed to be coming down the street, all dressed up in your best clothes, with an eye opened to everyone's envious glance, your hands in your pockets, chest thrown out and a real swagger. Over to the right you see a friend. You motion to him with your hand, and at the same moment you see another friend over to the other side. In a few minutes you are the center of an admiring imaginary circle, and parade about, showing off your new outfit!

Presently you suggest a game of craps. You stand still, leaning forward, hands on your hips, watching your imaginary chums try their luck. Then with a scornful gesture you place your hat on the ground, kneel down, and generally prepare for action! After much coaxing and shaking the bones you "roll'em out" and find that you have won everything.

More pleased with yourself than ever, you walk over to where a game of baseball is in progress. Your offer to pitch awhile is accepted. But you soon tire of this and ask for a chance to bat. You put your hat down for a base and after two strikes you line out one which you think is going to be a home run. However, the umpire calls you "Out" after a slide to third base, and after telling him your opinion of his judgment and threatening to "knock him for a row of ash-cans," you walk away in search of new fields to conquer.

Then you meet a beautiful girl, but fear of her is uppermost, and you start to walk away. She smiles encouragingly and, conquering your embarrassment, you ask her to come to the dance with you. To your great delight, she accepts. You take your imaginary partner in your arms and dance for a moment, but your bliss is shattered by a collision with another couple. You are belligerent and start a fight, but remembering you have a lady with you, you gallantly take her by the arm and lead her away.

She is very proud of you and her praises gradually go to your head. You tell her she hasn't seen anything yet and start to dance for her. This can be any type with which you are most familiar, tap, clog, soft shoe, etc. If you prefer, you may put in a few amusing eccentric steps.

You are very pleased with the applause you receive and walk off the stage, completely forgetting your partner . . . As the applause dies down you notice your girl. Full of apologies, you take her arm and lead her off the stage with you making explanations as you go.

Never lose your character in the pantomime, and put over each idea as clearly as possible. It is not an artistic dance but in the usual recital program is a welcome novelty.[32]

In *Danse Américaine* Shawn successfully employed Delsarte's system of expressive gesture and pantomime. Weidman's description of *Danse Américaine* demonstrates that this was no ordinary pantomime. Indeed, Weidman was a rare combination of dancer and actor who was uniquely able to communicate the sundry episodes within the work.

Shawn composed a final work in the pantomimic genre for Weidman called *The Crapshooter* from a suite of dances titled *Five American Sketches*. The suite, composed by Shawn, included *The Crapshooter, Around the Hall in Texas, Gringo Tango, Boston Fancy—1854,* and *Invocation to the Thunderbird.*[33] *The Crapshooter*, created in 1924 to music by Eastwood Lane, was first performed on October 6 at the Academy of Music in Newburgh, New York. Weidman, wearing a similar costume as he wore in *Danse Américaine,* performed this comedic pantomime emulating a conventional character. In *The Crapshooter* Shawn and Weidman seem to have expanded upon the same character portrayed in *Danse Américaine*. Weidman entered an empty stage giving an impression he was arrogantly strutting down a city street. He eagerly gathered his companions for a gambling game of rolling dice. He squatted to his knees as his imaginary fellow-players encircled the game spot. In *The Drama of Denishawn*, Sherman describes Weidman's performance in *The Crapshooter:*

He placed his derby on the ground beside him, shook the dice close to his ear, then rolled them out so convincingly that the audience saw the imaginary ivories as clearly as they saw the imaginary companions.

100

When he won his bet, he swept up the money from the ground and pocketed it in one triumphant gesture. Putting his derby back on, he rose, dusted off his knees, and paraded around the admiring girl onlookers like a rooster among his hens. Then he knelt to play again, first looking over his shoulder to spot a possible passing constable. Cradling the dice in his cupped hands, shaking them, talking to them, he finally rolled them straight toward the footlights with outstretched hand. Balanced on his right knee with his left knee bent upward to support his left hand, his open mouth and wide eyes mimed a yell for the right number to come up. When, in spite of his arrogant confidence, it failed to do so, his chagrin was painful but funny.

He pulled his pockets inside out to prove he had no money. He begged to be allowed a chance to recoup on credit. Refused, rejected, he shrugged his shoulders, cocked his derby over one eye, and swaggered off, undefeated in defeat.[34]

Both Shawn and Weidman seemed to have been experimenting with dynamic quality in *The Crapshooter*. A dramatic moment came just after the dice were thrown directly downstage and Charles was suspended in a balance on one knee, creating a sensation of temporarily hanging in time and space. In another scene, they explore the element of duration when Charles, shaking and rolling the dice, makes the movements faster, then slower, repeating the movement for emphasis. These choreographic devices clearly demonstrate Weidman's understanding of pantomime and Delsarte's expressive gesture. Later in his career Weidman developed his trademark, *kinetic pantomime*, a style of pantomime that he employed in numerous works such as *Juggler*, *Marionette Theatre*, and *Minstrels*.

Delsarte's movement principles played a major role in Denishawn dance training, not only technical training, but in choreographic form as well. Apparently no formal classes in dance composition were offered at the Denishawn School; however, choreographic concepts were absorbed through the broad principles of Delsarte used in Denishawn compositions. Conjointly, the

101

craft of composition employed through the development of the concept of "music-visualization" brought into play the use of musical form as a choreographic device for example, recurring motifs, ABA form, and theme-and-variations form.

François Delsarte's movement theories totally transformed the art of dance in the early twentieth century. His theories provided dance makers with useful methods of crafting innovative compositions, thereby evolving a fresh new technique with its special vocabulary. According to Shawn, it "completely changed the caliber, quality and significance of dancing in the 20th century."[35] During their school's seventeen years of operation, Shawn and St. Denis pledged their full commitment to the validity of Delsarte's laws of movement as part of new American dance. They taught every student at the Denishawn School the principles of François Delsarte. Shawn felt strongly about certain aspects of Delsarte's laws of human movement when he wrote: "One of the vital and important differences lies in the recognition of the torso as the source . . . of true emotional expression—and equally important, the use of successions . . ."[36] Through observation, Delsarte had categorized human movement in three zones: *intellectual,* using the head and neck; *emotional*, using the arms and torso; and *physical*, using the lower extremities. The use of the torso (arms, chest, ribs, and spine) to express emotion seems quite natural because a person's vital organs of life are housed in this part of the body. Moreover, the arms were used to portray expressive gesture in dance. Isadora Duncan was known to use her solar plexus to initiate her movement, enabling her to develop her breath rhythm theory. More important, as expressionism became the new trend in dance, exploration of the torso or trunk became paramount.

Denishawn Dance Training

In the summer of 1918, two years before Charles Weidman attended, the Denishawn School brochure listed an impressive dance curriculum: Basic technique; Expressive gesture based on Delsarte's system; Oriental technique (East Indian, Arabic, Siamese, Egyptian and other hieratic dancing) under the direction of Ruth St. Denis; Ballet class with teachers trained in the French, Italian, and Russian schools; Creative dancing; Greek and esthetic dancing; Visualization of pure music themes; Plastique movements (the study of body line); Piano lessons with Louis Horst; French lessons; "Geisha dancing taught by a native Japanese lady formerly a geisha teacher in Tokyo"; Lessons in craft-work, designing and making of costumes, jewelry, properties and scenery.[37]

The summer brochure of 1918 showed the diversity of dance techniques that only Denishawn could offer. With these innovative and global perspectives, St. Denis and Shawn developed a comprehensive system of training. Barton Mumaw explains how these various methods merged to form the Denishawn technique:

> Many misconceptions about Denishawn technique still persist, but I will remember the combination of ballet, Delsarte, Dalcroze, and ethnic movements that Shawn had devised and that I learned at Greater Denishawn. From the interaction of these techniques emerged Denishawn dancing, which freed ballet from rigid bonds and westernized Oriental traditional dance to adapt to our sturdier, less pliable American bodies.[38]

When Graham, Humphrey, and Weidman, the second generation of American modern dancers, embarked upon their separate creative paths, they used movement principles learned at Denishawn as the basis for their dance techniques. In a conversation with Nona Schurman about the influence of Denishawn upon these pioneers of modern dance, she remarked that, in essence, Denishawn's technical and choreographic foundation continued until Humphrey retired in 1946.[39] Schurman's statement is relevant because it acknowledges the fact that Denishawn principles were used in the development of the movement style and technique of Humphrey and Weidman, but it does not take into account Weidman's later career or Graham's career.

Through his independent career, Weidman's work continued to expand upon Denishawn movement concepts, culminating in his final composition, *Visualization, or, From a Farm in New Jersey*, composed in 1974. Indeed, Graham's technique is rooted in Denishawn. Recently, in a Graham technique class taught by Jacqulyn Buglisi at the Alvin Ailey School, Buglisi reminded the class that Martha had studied with Denishawn, and that St. Denis was influenced by the Orient and yoga. She reminded students about the seven *charkas* of yoga. These should be emphasized, specifically with a breath when bringing the arms up through the center of the body. Buglisi urged students to pass through these seven energy points.[40] In yoga, the *charkas* are the "body's energy centers" which "run through the center of the spinal column" and "intersect with each other at seven junctions."[41] Graham's technique begins in the basic sitting position of yoga with an emphasis on inhalation and exhalation of breath. Moreover, in Graham's technique, the "turn around the spine" is rooted in yoga postures. In Weidman's training system he always emphasized breath, breath, breath—especially in his drops and rebounds into suspension movements, and one may recognize this technique in his artistic works.

The Denishawn School, as a result of a teaching philosophy that nurtured individual freedom, was democratic and in tune with concepts of modernism. Shawn affirmed their teaching philosophy when he wrote: "We stressed the individual in all our teaching. . . . The last thing we wanted to produce was a facsimile row of pupils who would be robot imitators of St. Denis and Shawn."[42] This teaching philosophy was absorbed by both Humphrey and Weidman and was at the root of their techniques. In contrast, Graham evolved an extensive codified technique, each basic exercise developed into an advanced form. American philosopher, Susanne Langer refers to techniques as "conventions"; in time such

104

conventions are no longer new ideas, but become prosaic.[43] The idea that techniques could become entrenched and unvarying seems antithetical to democratic philosophy, or exercising one's own free will by inventing new ideas and being modern. Humphrey and Weidman based their evolving techniques on what they learned at the Denishawn School.

Humphrey and Weidman devised techniques in theme-and-variations form. Instead of accumulating movement exercises through repetition, as in Graham technique, they developed variations. In discussing Humphrey-Weidman with Schurman she thought their use of variation in technique and choreography referred to the basis of progress.[44] Her concept simply points to a stylistic and philosophic difference between Humphrey-Weidman technique and Graham technique. Graham training might be considered marked by authoritative assertion because the technical movement sequences are codified and performed without change. Graham's technical sequences include development, but do not include the compositional device of variation which, according to Langer's definition, indicates a dogmatic approach to technique. On the other hand, Humphrey and Weidman teachers are given freedom to approach and develop the fundamental Humphrey-Weidman movement principles of fall, recovery, rebound, opposition, succession, suspension, and breath rhythm in their own way. Due to this individual freedom absorbed at Denishawn and perpetuated by them, variations in approach permeate the teaching methodologies of Humphrey, Weidman, and subsequently Limón.

Classes taught at the Denishawn School were based on fundamental techniques. During the 1920s, advanced students took summer classes in Studio 61 at Carnegie Hall in New York City taught by Shawn, Weidman, and Humphrey, with either Lawrence or Horst at the piano.[45] These Denishawn classes consisted of stretching, ballet barre, center work, floor work, pas de basque series, and big ballet jumps.[46] As a method of cooling down the body

105

after this physical workout, the class would practice hand gestures for their Oriental dances. Sherman describes these Oriental gestures: "We might sit down and practice Javanese arm movements, do hand stretches to force our Western fingers into some semblance of Cambodian flexibility, attempt the East Indian nautch dancer's side-to-side "cobra" head slide above motionless shoulders, or work on a pantomime assignment for Charles Weidman."[47]

Ballet terminology was used as a vocabulary, but ballet steps were modified because Denishawn dancers did not have to maintain extreme "turn-out," and, dancing in bare feet limited the amount of friction on the surface of the floor, as Sherman explains: "The traditional steps became distorted. This loosening of the strict ballet grip upon the physique . . . altered the traditional steps to such a degree that they were barely recognizable."[48]

The descriptions of "General Stretching—Standing Exercises" in *Denishawn Dancing Technique* in the Dance Collections reinforce Schurman's suggestion that Denishawn dance technique is a forerunner of Humphrey and Weidman techniques.[49] Descriptions of movement sequences in this series closely resemble the drawings titled "Body Swing" in Schurman's book *Modern Dance Fundamentals.*[50] Similar are the drawings "Successional Movement: Vertical"; "Sideways Succession with Drop and Gravitational Pull"; "The Swinging Series: Up and Forward, Down and Back" in Ernestine Stodelle's book *The Dance Technique of Doris Humphrey.*[51] Each of these examples shows a successional swing of the body forward and backward, and body side bends in a broad second position. Shawn composed a study for the body and its relationship to rising and falling called "Arms and Body."[52] Barton Mumaw, a noted dancer with Shawn's Men's Group, considered it a prototype of the modern dance warm-up: "It started with feet placed widely apart, flat on the floor. A slow, loose swinging of the body developed into even larger circles. Then came head, shoulder, and torso rolls, arms sweeping from floor to overhead . . ."[53] Shawn's

"Arms and Body" series is quite similar to Stodelle's description and drawing of Humphrey's "Vertical Torso and Head Swings" series in her book[54] and closely parallels Schurman's "Warm-Up in Standing Position," a fifteen-part series in her book.[55] Mumaw's description of "Arms and Body" is substantially allied to Schurman's "Body Circle with Leg Action"[56] and Stodelle's "Body Circle."[57]

"Delsarte Falls"—Spiral, Backward, Forward, Floor Set Number 1 and Number 2" in *Denishawn Dancing Technique*[58] reveals a likeness to Stodelle's "Floor Work" in *The Dance Technique of Doris Humphrey*,[59] and Schurman's "Floor Stretches" in *Modern Dance Fundamentals*.[60] Humphrey and Weidman used Delsarte's principle of succession in their floor work sequences. Examples of successions are illustrated in Schurman's "Outward Succession Down and Up from a Sitting Position" and "Inward Succession Arching Back from a Sitting Position" in her book *Modern Dance Fundamentals*.[61] Comparative examples of successions are Stodelle's "Backward Descent" and "Arched Ascent" in her book *The Dance Technique of Doris Humphrey*.[62] Additionally, this movement succession is recognizable in Humphrey's "Back Fall" and "Side Fall," and in Weidman's *Brahms Waltzes*. In the *Denishawn Dancing Technique*, the description of Shawn's "New Tension Set" illustrates a series that develops into a body bend side with a jump—a whipping sideways jump.[63] Shawn's description is similar to a series of Weidman's jumps that Schurman calls "Charles' Fishtail." As two distinguished teachers of Humphrey-Weidman technique, Schurman and Stodelle offer comprehensive sequences of technique exercises with a distinct correlation to Denishawn dance technique.

Historic and Global Influences

Weidman's intense training with various Asian masters on Denishawn's Asian Tour prepared him to perform in their recreations of authentic Asian dances created while on tour: *Singhalese Devil Dance* (Shawn), *A Burmese Yein Pwe*

(St. Denis/Humphrey), *General Wu Says Farewell to His Wife* (St. Denis/Shawn), and *Momiji-Gari* (Shawn). In addition to mastering these diverse Asian dance movement techniques, Weidman learned to manipulate props and fabrics, apply traditional Japanese Kabuki and Chinese opera makeup, and to make costumes—valuable skills that would enhance his creative work in his years after Denishawn. Throughout his career, he created costumes and props for most of his dance works and for Limón's first compositions. This was especially true in Weidman's later association with Mikhail Santaro and their Expression of Two Arts Theatre in New York where, in 1964, they performed a fascinating duet titled *A Chinese Actor Prepares for the Role of the God of War*. Weidman found a deep connection with the dances of Asia, especially Japanese Kabuki dance-drama. His brief biography states that he "is a member of the houses of Koshiro Matsumoto and Mme. Fujima of Kabuki—and he has his coolie coat to prove it."[64] He was fascinated by ancient Asian dance forms, yet his aims for new American dance were clear and seemed opposite—"to be ready each year to say new things and say them in new ways . . ."[65]

The content of Weidman's 1935 dance composition *Traditions* is concisely characterized by Louis Horst: "The error of ignoring tradition is as great as succumbing to it."[66] In his search for new directions, Weidman and other modern artists of the early twentieth century turned back to primordial civilizations. This was, perhaps, because their "naïve but powerful simplicity, provided the desired vigor and directness that the art pioneers needed," Horst writes.[67] From Denishawn's exoticism (Orientalism) to the primitivism of the 1930s, in such compositions as Graham's *Two Primitive Canticles*, Humphrey's *With My Red Fires*, and Weidman's *A Passion* [Savonarola] and *Dance Profane*, these artists displayed an expressive idiom based on primal art with its bluntness, awkwardness, strength, and vitality.[68] Even a work composed fifty years later, Limón's *The Unsung* (1971), danced to the rhythm of eight men representing the

108

"Pantheon: Metacomet, Pontiac, Tecumseh, Red Eagle, Black Hawk, Osceola, Sitting Bull, Geronimo,"[69] has primitive origins. As a modern artist, Paul Taylor seems particularly fascinated by the primitive in his compositions *Runes* (1975) and *Promethean Fire* (2002). For dancers who want to explore primeval possibilities in their compositions, Horst suggests: "The subject matter can be drawn out of primal experience; the mysteries of a planting ceremony, or a burial ritual, or any form of earth worship. Almost any subjective experience can be treated as primal: love, seach, fear, discovery, etc."[70] Weidman's *Lynchtown* is an example of a composition reflective of the primitive.

Weidman's creative work was also guided by Delsarte's theory of parallelisms, used as a design element in Denishawn dances, inspired by the stylized figures shown on wall paintings, bas-reliefs, and vase paintings of the ancient civilizations of Egypt, Greece, Crete, and Mesopotamia. In a conversation with Deborah Carr, she said that Charles used the term "archaic" and added that George Bockman called these stylized movements "King Tut."[71] In his book *Modern Dance Forms*, Horst uses the term archaic instead of ancient or parallel. The archaic design was "angular by nature of its two-dimensional directness," Horst writes.[72] Within this dance style, the strength of distortion was needed to mold a dancer's body into a two-dimensional design, as Horst notes: "He reduces his forms to planes, selecting what is essential and permanent and omitting the irrelevant. It is in this abridgment, this abstraction, that the contemporary artist feels very close to the archaic."[73] Denishawn's compositions *Tillers of the Soil, Gnossienne, Xochitl*, and *Ishtar of the Seven Gates* illustrate the use of archaic designs showing that figures are "stark, planal, and powerful."[74] This archetype was used in Weidman's technique (*Study in Contrast, Body Bends*) and choreography (*Saint Matthew Passion*), creating a direct link to his Denishawn experience and Delsarte's theory of parallelism.

Dance as Music Visualization

Ruth St. Denis developed a choreographic concept that was inspired by Isadora Duncan's approach to music. St. Denis termed her approach "music visualization," which she defined as "the scientific translation into bodily action of the rhythmic, melodic, and harmonious structure of a musical composition without the intention to in any way 'interpret' or reveal any hidden meaning apprehended by the dancer."[75]

While watching Duncan dance to Schubert's *Unfinished Symphony* in 1918, St. Denis realized that Duncan "stopped when the music became too complicated for the dance, and compromised by making one of her unforgettably noble gestures in complete disregard of the music."[76] Duncan interpreted and enacted the music but, as St. Denis realized, "had in no way maintained a consistent visualization of its structure or rhythm."[77] For St. Denis, this realization stimulated a germ of an idea for which Shawn coined the term "synchoric orchestra . . . an ensemble of movement, as symphonic suggests an ensemble of sound."[78] St. Denis and Humphrey created their first "synchoric orchestra" to Beethoven's *Sonata Pathétique*. St. Denis termed the genre "concert" dances and explained its significance in American dance.

> I am content to rest my claim that we began the first suggestion of what has become the American dance, that dance which owed everything and nothing to Europe and Asia. . . . Each girl was told in no uncertain terms that her personality counted for nothing. She was a member of a group, and the business of that group was to do two definite things: to reflect in as faithful a manner as possible the tempo, rhythms, and structure of the music, and to see that the patterns, space coverings, and groupings were as beautiful as possible.[79]

In Denishawn, Weidman participated in the experimental choreographic process, performed in numerous "music visualizations," observed these novel

110

performances from the wings, and was undoubtedly influenced by this new abstract, non-narrative dance. Shawn credited Delsarte: "In our 'Music Visualizations' we were the first to use 'abstract' movement. . . . In all these dances, with or without music, abstract, dramatic, or lyric, we used the principles of Delsarte as a base. . . . This was made clear and explicit to all who worked with us. . . . This basic science of Delsarte was so instilled . . . that it has continued as the core of all American modern dance."[80]

Polonaise was Ted Shawn's first ensemble "music visualization" choreographed for men: Shawn, Weidman, Robert Gorham, J. Roy Busclark, and George Steares.[81] *Polonaise*, composed in 1923 to the music of Edward MacDowell, remained in Denishawn's repertory and was performed by Ted Shawn Men's Dancers in 1938.[82] Shawn was inspired by St. Denis' concept, and created several "music visualizations" such as *Revolutionary Etude*, *Adagio Pathétique*, *Album Leaf and Prelude*, and *Voices of Spring*.[83]

Conjointly, St. Denis and Humphrey collaborated on another "music visualization": *Sonata Tragica* (1923), danced to the music of Edward MacDowell, by Humphrey and Weidman with Louise Brooks, Anne Douglas, Georgia Graham, Lenore (Martha) Hardy, Theresa Sadowska, and Lenore Scheffer. During the Second Mayer Tour (1923-24) the MacDowell music for *Sonata Tragica* was discarded and the work was performed in silence. To perform a work in silence creates several challenges for the dancers—such as establishing a tempo and, in this case, keeping eight dancers in time with each other. Humphrey would explore this same concept in *Water Study* in 1928. By initially reflecting the structure of the music and then performing the work in silence, Humphrey's concept of "music visualization" began to alter the form of her dance compositions. She, along with Weidman, began to realize that the strength and success of a work depends on its clarity of form. One of the most important choreographic concepts explored at Denishawn and used in their separate careers was "music visualization." During their alliance, Humphrey and Weidman composed numerous visualizations of pure music themes in abstract works—*Color Harmony, Passacaglia in C Minor, Brahms Waltzes,* and *New Dance.* These are all masterpieces of choreographic form.

Asian Tour, 1925-1926

Early in the month of August 1925, Charles, along with the Denishawn Company, departed on the steamship *President Jefferson* from Seattle across the Pacific Ocean to Yokohama Harbor. Their long journey was a brand new experience for the dancers: they had never been on a mammoth cruise ship before, with delicious food to eat every few hours, as well as entertainment, socializing with the crew and passengers, formal evening attire adorned for late dinners, ballroom dancing, and a dance class every morning to keep them in shape.[84] On this voyage, twenty-four-year-old Charles Weidman and thirty-year-old Doris Humphrey developed a close personal relationship; throughout the tour they were always seen together. In her journal, Humphrey wrote about how Charles' experience in ballroom dancing began one of their earliest artistic collaborations:

> Somewhere Charles had learned the newest ballroom sensation, the Charleston, and I had fun learning it from him. One night, members of the Denishawn Company were asked to entertain at a party. Charles, in a tuxedo, and I, in my new yellow evening dress, put on an exhibition Charleston, much to the astonishment of the company, and possibly to the embarrassment of its leaders.[85]

Not only did Charles and Doris deepen their partnership during this Asian tour, but, their long-standing friendship with Pauline Lawrence gave them the opportunity to form a close-knit artistic triad. As senior members of Denishawn, Charles, Doris, and Pauline were becoming known to the rest of the company as

112

the "unholy three" because they were, at times, recalcitrant toward the authority of St. Denis and Shawn, and they were inseparable. During this tour, Charles was said to act as Doris' protector by shielding her from the sun with a parasol and carrying her shopping packages. "He was tall, good-looking, and determined to be a dancer. He was fun, too," Humphrey writes.[86] Since their first meeting five years before, Charles and P'line (Charles shortened her name for easier and faster pronunciation) enjoyed each other's company; they were always charming and funny together.

As the ship neared Yokohama Harbor, Doris peered out of the porthole for her first look at the exotic, enchanting lands they were to visit, and was delighted to see a panoramic view of small boats with brown and blue sails that looked "as though they had been painted on a Japanese print."[87] Arriving on August 23, the Denishawn Dancers began their monthlong stay in Tokyo, Japan with a jinrikisha ride from the ship to the Imperial Hotel. Their voyage to the Orient would take them through Japan, China, Malaya, Burma, India, Ceylon, Indonesia, Indo-China, and the Philippines.[88] For this tour of one year and three months, the company included St. Denis and Shawn and twelve dancers: Ernestine Day, Anne Douglas, Georgia Graham, Doris Humphrey (and her mother), Pauline Lawrence, Jane Sherman, George Steares, Charles, and the new girls Grace Burroughs, Edith James, Mary Howry, and Ara Martin. The artistic staff included Clifford Vaughan, who replaced Louis Horst as musical director; Pearl Wheeler, costumer; Buzz (Ruth's brother), stage manager; Stanley Fraser, electrician; and June Hamilton Rhodes, company manager.[89]

For this tour St. Denis and Shawn decided not to perform their Asian dances; rather they performed their "music visualization" and Americana dances, along with Spanish and ancient dances. The company's repertory included *Sonata Pathétique, Boston Fancy—1854*, Shawn's *Adonis Plastique* and *Invocation to the Thunderbird*, Humphrey's *Hoop Dance* (Scherzo Waltz), and

113

Weidman's *Danse Américaine*.[90] During the tour, additional dances from their repertory were performed, such as *Soaring, Valse à La Loie, Ishtar of the Seven Gates, Xochitl, Cuadro Flamenco,* with a score arranged from Spanish folk music by Horst, *Danza de Quatro* (Pas de Quatre or Sevillanos), and others.[91] Charles was partnered by Anne Douglas in *Danza de Quatro* and Ernestine Day in *Album Leaf and Prelude*; he danced the father role opposite Georgia Graham in *Xochitl*; played the role of Zephyr, with Edith James as Primavera, in *Voices of Spring*; and was partnered by Pauline Lawrence in *Boston Fancy—1854*. With choreography by Shawn, Charles danced his three noted solos, *The Crapshooter, Pierrot Forlorn,* and *Danse Américaine.*

The phenomenal success of the Denishawn Dancers after their opening night performance at the Imperial Theatre in Tokyo was said to be one of the greatest historical events since Admiral Perry had arrived in Japan. Moreover, one newspaper review suggested that the Denishawn Dancer's appearance in Japan had completely altered the Japanese perspective toward American art.[92] Natsuya Mitsuyoshi, a critic who greatly admired Denishawn, made a formal introduction of St. Denis and Shawn to Matsumoto Koshiro, the foremost actor-dancer of the Imperial Theatre. After their meeting, Koshiro graciously offered to teach daily classes to the dancers during their stay in Tokyo.[93] Shawn wanted to restage of one of the most popular Kabuki dance-dramas, *Momiji-Gari*, which he had thoroughly enjoyed seeing in performance at the Kabuki-za Theatre. Matsumoto Koshiro agreed to teach his version of *Momiji-Gari* to the Denishawn dancers. The company took a four-hour lesson every morning for more than a month. Ted Shawn worked with Koshiro; Charles and George studied with the men teachers of the Fujima School, and the girls learned their parts from Koshiro's wife, Madame Koshiro.[94] Charles and his fellow dancers were fascinated by the strict stylistic movements of Kabuki dance-drama and, as Jane Sherman describes, they all intently focused on achieving its intricate style:

"Dressed in simple kimonos, we tried to absorb the fundamentals of Japanese technique—the art of moving gracefully in kimono, the gliding steps on flat, toed-in feet, the body sway, the sitting on folded legs, the bowing, the handling of long kimono sleeves, the manipulation of fans, the dancing to baffling rhythms."[95]

To perform *Momiji-Gari* on a Denishawn program, Shawn had to condense the fifty-minute work. The company rehearsed Shawn's version for almost ten months while on tour. When they returned to Tokyo in mid-October of 1926, Weidman had the opportunity to study with Koshiro. Shawn and the company showed his shortened rendition of *Momiji-Gari* to Koshiro, who courteously watched Shawn's rehearsal. Koshiro then performed every role for the company, while Shawn took film footage that served as a valuable guide for final rehearsals.[96]

In Peking (Beijing), China, the Denishawn Dancers were graciously given a special performance by Mei-Lan Fang, China's outstanding opera actor, accompanied by his company. Shawn invited him to teach the Denishawn dancers the intricate movements of Chinese opera dance, and to stage his version of *General Wu's Farewell to His Wife* for their American tour. Anne Douglas learned Mei-Lan Fang's part as the Princess, who is married to the General, played by Weidman.[97] The music was arranged by Clifford Vaughan for piano and Western orchestral instruments; however, throughout the tour a variety of Asian percussion instruments were added, such as drums, woodblocks, bells, and gongs.[98] The dancers had to learn how to successfully manipulate the myriad hand props used in Chinese opera such as fans, sleeves, and swords. In her part, Douglas had to master a dance using double swords. All of the props, costumes, wigs, headpieces, music, and backdrop were bought with the guidance of Mei-Lan Fang.[99] Additionally, some of the dancers had to master playing the music. In her book *Soaring,* Jane Sherman notes that, in *General Wu's Farewell to His Wife,* she and three other dancers performed a short fan dance and sleeve dance

115

and in between played in the orchestra. The complicated music and musical cues required numerous rigorous rehearsals. "I played a small cymbal, Pauline the woodblock, Mary a gong, and Geordie a smaller gong," Sherman writes.[100] *General Wu's Farewell to His Wife* premièred in Hong Kong in September 1926, where it was an instant success.

The company then played four months in India, where they gave a hundred performances in sixteen cities. They performed for seventeen days in Bombay to huge, cheering audiences; we "stopped the show with *Xochitl*," Shawn writes.[101] Miss Ruth's *East Indian Nautch* and *Dance of the Black and Gold Sari* were absolute hits and she performed them at every show. With their great success in India, the company enjoyed the beautiful historical sights, celebrated with food and drink, and kicked up their heels. But often they were too exhausted and many times were on trains or boats traveling to the next stop on their tour. This meant that often on trains they had to eat in their own compartments, where they became adept at cooking canned foods on impromptu stoves.

Men will be boys, and Charles and George Steares always seemed to be up to zany antics. They danced together, shared hotel rooms together, and urged each other into mischief. Sherman recalls how crazy Charles and George were while on a train in India: "They scared the wits out of us by leaving their compartment while the train was going full speed, inching along the narrow catwalk *outside* the train, and so climbing in through our windows!"[102]

While traveling in diverse Asian countries, the company's main quest was, of course, for basic necessities—eating and drinking. Exotic cuisines and strange languages made ordering food in restaurants difficult and sometimes quite amusing. Shawn told a funny story about when Charles wanted a glass of milk in Japan: "In a final attempt to get his order across, he dropped to all fours and realistically mooed while George Steares went through the motions of milking.

The waiter brightened with the usual, 'Ah, so *desuka*,' and served a beef steak to Charles."[103]

Arriving in Kandy, Ceylon, the company's hotel was heavenly, with "soft beds and real American food, with salads and vegetables," Sherman recalls.[104] During the company's tour in Ceylon, Shawn engaged several troupes of top-notch festival dancers to teach the men their dances. Shawn explained the process: "Charles and George and I struggled with complicated rhythms that, with authentic costumes bought in Kandy, we used in the *Singhalese Devil Dance* which I choreographed for our American tour."[105] The music was adapted from authentic sources by Clifford Vaughan and had its first performance on October 24, 1926, at the Shurahu-Kan Theatre in Kobe, Japan.[106] Charles had been influenced artistically by learning and performing in *Singhalese Devil Dance*. Weidman's use of drums and percussion instruments, along with complicated rhythms, became his hallmark as a teacher and choreographer and could be traced to his experience in Ceylon and the knowledge he gleaned from rehearsing and performing *Singhalese Devil Dance*.

The evening before the company left Kandy for Singapore, Charles happened to meet a young Singhalese man in a bookstore. Charles invited him up to his room to talk with some of the dancers. He was a Buddhist and a Theosophist who was studying for his doctorate at Oxford.[107] He stayed for hours and explained the different religious systems, especially Buddhism and Brahmanism. Charles was fascinated by the young scholar's explication of the search for divine wisdom through contemplation. Charles' spiritual yearning was captured in a photograph in Java at the Borobodur Temple, where like Buddha he sat in an alcove in full lotus position with his right hand raised in a gesture while Shawn, as a monk, stood obliquely below him with an offering.[108]

117

Chapter Five

Dancing with Martha Graham

(1920-1930)

Although cities and towns did seem to overlap and blend into
one composite American community, each new audience was distinct,
with a personality of its own that was an inspiration to us.
We were exhilarated by the knowledge that we were pioneering
for the art of dance to which our lives were dedicated.

Ted Shawn
One Thousand and One Night Stands

In the summer of 1916, Martha Graham, having just graduated from the
Cumnock School of Expression in Los Angeles, enrolled in the Denishawn
School. After seeing Ruth St. Denis perform, Graham, along with Weidman, was
inspired to become a professional dancer. Both were instructed under the tutelage
of Ted Shawn, whose pragmatic administrative skills made the Denishawn School
the most prominent dance institution in the United States.[1] But circumstances in
Europe would intrude on Graham's training at the Denishawn School.

In May of 1915, a German submarine sank the British ocean liner
Lusitania off the coast of Ireland, killing 1,200 passengers including 128
Americans. Within the next year continued incidents against neutral merchant
ships forced the United States Congress to declare war on Germany. In late
December 1917, after receiving a summons from his local draft board, Shawn
enlisted in the Army Ambulance Corps. Fortunately, he was stationed at Camp
Kearney near San Diego, where he was able to supervise the Denishawn School

119

business. From November 1918 to September 1919 St. Denis and her dancers, Doris Humphrey, Betty Horst, Edna Malone, and Pearl Wheeler, with Louis Horst as musical director, performed on a Pantages Liberty Bond Tour. When Shawn enlisted, he invited Graham to teach at his school, located in a small house on Sixth Street. Not only did Graham's teaching position bring her closer to her goal in dance, she was able to earn much-needed money to support herself and her mother. After her father's death, his estate was depleted due to living expenses and taxes on their house in Santa Barbara. Martha's sisters Georgia and Mary moved to Los Angeles, where Georgia, Martha's younger sister, worked at Denishawn while Mary found an office job.[2] Graham sent money home just as Weidman and Humphrey had done. They all supported themselves and their families through their dance careers.

Fortunately, World War I ended before Shawn was deployed overseas. Released from the army in December 1918, he began to search for a new home for the Denishawn School. He hoped that income from the school would finance his next concert tour. Shawn found an old building on Grand Avenue in Los Angeles and began renovations with Margerie Lyon as project manager. They commissioned Buk-Ulrich to recreate an Egyptian Hall and Robert Law to create a green and gold studio theatre and two exquisite black drawing rooms.[3] One month before Weidman arrived, the opulent Ted Shawn Dance Studio opened on April 6, 1920, with Graham as Shawn's assistant teacher.

While studio renovations were in progress, in 1919 Shawn was commissioned by Alexander Pantages, a famous vaudeville theatre owner to produce an extraordinary dance on a grand scale for his touring circuit. St. Denis and her dancers were just completing their Liberty Bond Tour under Pantages management. A Pantages vaudeville tour consisted of three shows a day during the week and four shows a day on Saturday and Sunday. The Pantages was considered a secondary theatre circuit, but the Orpheum had daily matinee and evening performances; Orpheum theatres were known as "top vaudeville," or what Louis Horst called "top time."[4]

Shawn's idea for his new work evolved from his fascination with the story of Julnar from *The Arabian Nights* (also known as *The Thousand and One Nights*), a celebrated collection of Eastern stories. He wove Scheherazade's tale of Julnar, a beautiful princess in a kingdom underneath the sea, who is pursued by an earthly prince, into a three-act dance drama with seventeen dancers and a storyteller. The curtain opened to reveal a "stylized oriental exterior, a drop curtain with a big central window that was a transparency through which the audience could see Scheherazade," Shawn writes.[5] Reclining on a low sofa, Scheherazade began to tell the story of the first act of Julnar to an unseen Sultan. This prelude, as Shawn describes it, "was followed by a black-out during which the divan on rubber tires was rolled off stage and the window drop pulled up."[6] The narrated part of the story was then enacted through dance. This theatrical process was repeated three times as the tale was recounted. Featuring Lillian Powell with Horst as musical director, *Julnar of the Sea* opened at the Pantages Theatre in Los Angeles in November 1919 and toured the circuit for more than twelve hundred continuous performances until March 1921.[7]

Ted Shawn's Dances for Martha and Charles

With the public success of *Julnar of the Sea,* Shawn began to stage another dance drama for the Pantages vaudeville touring circuit. Featuring Martha Graham, Shawn created one of the first dances based on the ancient Mexican story of *Xochitl*, an old Toltec legend. Shawn invited Homer Grunn, a specialist in American Indian music, to create an original score for this new work and also invited Francisco Cornejo, a Mexican artist who was also an authority on Toltec, Aztec and Mayan civilizations, to design sets and costumes.[8] Cornejo's authentic, colorful costumes were hand-embroidered and overlaid with small feathers. Cornejo's costume for the Emperor Tepancaltzin was truly spectacular: he wore a broad, hand-embroidered apron bordered with fringe over his trunks; across his tanned, bare chest hung a golden emblem of the sun covering his heart; his head bore a huge headdress of black and orange feathers; and he wore a cloak made of hundreds of vivid orange feathers falling from his shoulders in a long train to his feet.[9]

Xochitl had its premiere in Long Beach, California, in June 1920. Shawn cast Robert Gorham, a tall and handsome student, in the part of the emperor, but early in the tour he suffered a foot injury and was replaced by a new student—nineteen-year-old Charles Weidman. Having just arrived at the Ted Shawn Dance Studio a month before, Charles was summoned by Shawn to dance a leading role. Shawn was certain that Charles knew his right foot from his left, he was good-looking and, being over six feet tall, he would fit into Cornejo's costume made for Gorham. There was only one small reservation—Charles didn't know the steps of the dance. After a brief rehearsal with Shawn, Charles was on his way to Tacoma, Washington, where Gorham, Graham, and the *Xochitl* cast awaited his arrival.

With a wonderful *Xochitl* cast, Charles was fortunate to meet new colleagues who would support him in his first role and continued to support him for the next twenty years. Martha's younger sister, Georgia, was among the six young women who took the roles of the emperor's dancing girls. Shawn entrusted the music to a young pianist from California, Pauline Lawrence, who came to Denishawn straight out of a Los Angeles high school to play for classes in 1917. "She was plump and pretty," remembers Humphrey, "with cascades of black curls luxuriating on her head. She was fun to be with, and we became fast friends."[10] Pauline was reserved in public situations but outgoing and jovial among the company; Pauline and Charles got along famously. Pauline also studied dancing at Denishawn and performed small roles in Denishawn ballets. In addition to her fine skills as a pianist, she studied costuming for dance with Pearl Wheeler, Denishawn's costumer extraordinaire. As Jane Sherman notes, *Xochitl* "marked the first professional appearances of Charles Weidman, Georgie Graham, and the first time Pauline Lawrence accompanied a Denishawn program on the piano."[11] In the near future, these three would travel the world performing about 725 performances together—it all began with Shawn's ballet *Xochitl.*[12]

Act One of *Xochitl* was danced in front of a painted backdrop showing an ancient temple in the distance with large, bluish-green, spearlike, agave plants in the foreground. Xochitl, the "most beautiful of all chaste Toltec maidens," writes Graham, was seen at work tending plants.[13] Her father, a peasant, entered wearing a long leopard skin, and he was tipsy. Through mime Xochitl's father told her he had discovered how to make pulque.[14] Pulque, or the fermented juice of the agave cactus, was the only alcoholic drink known to pre-Hispanic Indian civilizations. After the Spanish conquest of Mexico, mescal, a high-proof alcoholic drink, was made through a distillation process rather than fermented as pulque. Xochitl and her father decided to take his new discovery to their emperor.

Act Two was danced in front of a painted backdrop showing the interior of Emperor Tepancaltzin's palace. Against red clay adobe bricks, a huge circular Aztec painting of the sun was displayed directly behind the emperor's throne. The emperor's dancing girls flanked each side of his throne, raised on a dais at center stage.[15] Act Two, "told of Xochitl (the flower) taking a bowl of pulque to the emperor who, inflamed by the strong liquor and her beauty, jumped from his throne and pursued the innocent."[16] The emperor chased Xochitl about the stage; once caught, she fought for her release as they tumbled to the floor, the struggle culminating in a passionate embrace. "When Xochitl's father was about to plunge a knife into the emperor," Shawn wrote, "she stopped the blow, and there followed a happy, legal ending complete with court wedding."[17]

As *Xochitl* began its tour of the Pantages vaudeville circuit, Graham took on the added responsibility of being the company's paymaster. When Charles arrived in Tacoma to join the cast, Graham was in a state of utter panic because she had lost the company's payroll. She and Gorham also had to teach Charles the role of the emperor before that evening's performance.[18] Fortunately, the Gorham family wired money to replace the payroll, and within the next few days, they had more time to rehearse Charles in their duet.

With her long black hair and exotic features, Martha Graham looked the part and was faultless in Xochitl, a role whose movements ranged from ferocious and primordial to intensely still and regal. Charles was about to encounter Graham's fury in their duet. "It was a rape scene, or an attempted rape scene, and I tried to focus all of my energy into this thought of anger and violation," Graham wrote.[19] She became enraged to be chased by the big, powerful emperor; her anger was realistically vented by repeatedly striking his chest with her fists. During this scene Graham expressed her rage with a fierce grimace. "Teeth, teeth, teeth like a shark," recalled Weidman.[28] Graham was known to pummel Weidman and Shawn, who took the role in 1921, so vehemently that they both complained of bruises, fingernail scratches, and a bleeding lip. In Charles' first performance as the emperor in *Xochitl*, he was acclaimed by the Tacoma press for his "impressive stateliness," his "praiseworthy solo work," and was declared to be "a virile and impassioned artist."[21] In these first outstanding reviews as a professional dancer, Weidman's acclamations were listed in the name of Robert Gorham whose name appeared in the program as Emperor Tepancaltzin. No matter, Charles celebrated his achievement and successful début.

After the first *Xochitl* tour, three cast members became good friends—Charles, Martha and Georgia. They all needed to save money and send it home to their families, so they decided to move into a small house in Hollywood with Martha's sister Mary and a girlfriend.[22] Yes, Charles was living with four young women. However, when he first moved to Los Angeles he had shared an apartment with his teachers, Eleanor Frampton and Helen Hewett, so he already had brief experience of living with women. His even-tempered personality made sharing a house with him enjoyable—besides, he was funny and easily made everyone laugh. In his biography of Martha Graham, Don McDonagh describes their unusual living arrangements:

> Mary and her roommate had the bedroom; Georgia slept on the porch, with the heater; and Weidman and Graham shared a bed, innocently though not without humor. Weidman characterized his role as that of a long hot water bottle for Graham when she was having her period (which she referred to, in coy terminology that perhaps reflected her straitlaced upbringing, as the "zizzlums").[23]

Martha Graham was known to be temperamental and difficult; her emotional outbursts were notorious. However, Martha and Charles were able to work together in peace and friendship. She considered him a good friend and confidant. "Martha became very fond of him," writes Agnes de Mille, "and they were always attached."[24] At the time when Charles had just arrived in Los Angeles, Martha remembered when they all lived at the Denishawn House where she was a teacher, but wanted to be a dancer—she would practice in the middle of the night. Charles "came downstairs and found me dancing but he said nothing then," writes Graham.[25] Charles reminded her of his secret observation later in their careers. "I was . . . trying to find strange, beautiful movements of my own. I would dance and rehearse in absolute darkness until dawn. When the time came for me to dance I would be ready."[26] In fact, for the first three years of their careers, Charles and Martha partnered in many Denishawn ballets including *Xochitl*, *Arabic Duet*, *The Princess and the Demon*, and group dances that included *Soaring*, choreographed by St. Denis and Humphrey.

125

Second Cross-Country Tour

Ted Shawn had made very little money on the vaudeville tours of *Julnar of the Sea* and *Xochitl*; however, the money he earned teaching gave him enough to start his next project. To establish himself as a great American male dancer and choreographer, he conceived of a cross-country tour from Los Angeles to New York City. Shawn, assisted by dancers Martha Graham, Betty May, Dorothea Bowen, and Charles Weidman, with Louis Horst as musical director and Sid Winton as stage manager, began their concert tour on September 8, 1921, at the Egan Little Theatre in Los Angeles.[27] Of the twenty-two cities on the tour, Lincoln, Nebraska, held the most excitement for Charles, as it marked his professional dance début in his hometown. With matinee and evening performances at the Orpheum Theatre, Charles probably performed with Martha in *Xochitl*, *Arabic Duet,* and A *Dance of Job*, along with new solos, *Pierrot Forlorn* and *Le Contrebandier*.[28] Charles was thrilled when his parents, his high school teachers, Miss Esther Lefler and Madame de Vilmar, and his high school friends, Ralph Bowers and Varny Ferris, attended his performances.

After a festive party in Lincoln with Charles' family and friends, the company departed for Omaha, the next stop on the tour. It was in Omaha that Martha and Louis developed a romantic relationship that launched seventeen years of living together, albeit not without conflict. Horst was ten years older than Graham and was married to dancer and teacher Betty (Bessie) Cunningham Horst who, when not teaching in her own studio in San Francisco, danced with Denishawn on various tours, including the St. Denis' Liberty Bond and Shawn's *Julnar of the Sea* tours. When Louis and Martha were employed on the same Denishawn tours as Betty, their romantic relationship made circumstances difficult for the entire company.

For this haphazard cross-country tour arranged by Harry Hall, an inept agent and manager, Shawn created about thirty-five diverse dances. Shawn

126

grouped these dances according to type: religious, represented by *A Church Service in Dance*; music visualizations, such as *Revolutionary Etude* and *Gnossienne*; romantic, such as *Pierrot Forlorn* and *Moon of Love*; Spanish, as in *Tango* and *Malagueña*; and Oriental, such as *Serenata Morisca, The Devidassi,* and *Japanese Spear Dance*.[29] Each performance used a three-section program arranged from these dance types, and each program ended with a shortened version of *Xochitl,* with Shawn as the emperor and Charles as Xochitl's father.[30]

Along with dancing, Charles served in the capacity of "dresser." Helping Shawn and others with quick costume changes, he also made sure that props and scenery were ready for each dance, working closely with Sid Winton, the stage manager. This tour proved to be a valuable apprenticeship for Charles, teaching him essential theatrical skills that would enable him to establish an independent career in 1928.

Soaring with Daniel Mayer

With their last performance at the Apollo Theatre in New York City on December 2, 1921, a "Standing Room Only" sign at the box office proclaimed the ultimate success of the concert. After a standing ovation at the end of the performance, Shawn's dressing room was filled with people offering compliments and congratulations. The most thrilling was a "contract offer from Daniel Mayer, the internationally known impresario who managed Paderewski, Pavlova, and similarly shining stars," Shawn wrote.[31]

The next morning, after signing contracts with Daniel Mayer, Shawn opened a Denishawn School in New York City at the Chatsworth on Riverside Drive. With their extended Daniel Mayer tours assured, the establishment of a Denishawn School on the East coast testified to Shawn's prudence in providing artistic and financial security for himself and St. Denis.

127

At the Chatsworth, Shawn and the company lived together and worked at necessary jobs to earn money until the tour began. Many dancers were able to find work in the movie industry. "Charles . . . took a role in Griffith's film *Orphans of the Storm*. He can be seen as a skinny little dark nineteen-year-old boy running around in the *Carmagnole*," Agnes de Mille writes.[32] Three tours from 1922 to 1925, arranged by Daniel Mayer for the Denishawn Dancers, "were the high points of Denishawn concert dancing in America," Christina L. Schlundt writes. She further notes that the vaudeville circuit intersected both large cities and small towns; thus, "a new generation became conscious of dance as an American art form."[33]

Daniel Mayer arranged a small tour of southern states from April 17 to 27, 1922, and then a month's tour to London from May 15 to June 25, 1922. On May 3 the company sailed from Boston Harbor aboard the Cunard Line's *S.S. Samaria*. This would be the first international tour for Charles; travel by ship brought back childhood memories of his numerous trips to Panama to visit his father. During the ocean voyage the dancers enjoyed a restful time in fellowship. Many tales could be told of romantic intrigues among Betty, Louis, and Martha. Arriving in London, everyone explored its historic sights and enjoyed a busy social schedule with teas, luncheons, and after-theatre parties. The company made the acquaintance of the great British author Havelock Ellis, and was frequently entertained by Maude Allen, an American dancer who was a success in London, where she now lived.[34]

During their four weeks at the London Coliseum, Charles danced the role of the father opposite St. Denis in *Xochitl*. Martha was relegated to performing as one of the emperor's dancing girls. "It was Ted's idea to put Miss Ruth in my role in *Xochitl*," Graham wrote.[35] Regardless of Miss Ruth's success in *Xochitl*, the consensus was that her temperament didn't suit the role; during the fall tour Martha resumed performing the role she had originated.

Supported by Miss Ruth, Charles had an unprecedented opportunity to perform the central role in the dance *Soaring* with Martha, Betty May, Dorothea Bowen, and Pearl Wheeler. *Soaring* (to Robert Schumann's *Aufschwung*) was "a ballet to symbolize the birth of Venus from the sea foam," writes Graham.[36] It was categorized as "music visualization," jointly composed by St. Denis and Doris Humphrey in 1920, revived for their tour of London. Graham describes her dancing in *Soaring*: "It began with an extraordinary sheer transparent piece of silk almost covering the stage, held at each end by [four] young girls . . . I was one of them. We would lift the silk to catch the air and the slim suggestion of a body beneath it was Doris, rising and falling with the silk."[37] Martha's image of Doris "rising and falling" seems to epitomize Humphrey's later fall and recovery movement theory. Perhaps her dancing in *Soaring* was the germ of Humphrey's development of her well-known movement principle. Indeed, while Charles danced the central role in *Soaring,* he came to know Doris and her movement principles through her choreography long before he would dance alongside her as a Denishawn dancer.

The first Mayer tour began on October 2, 1922, visiting 143 cities in the United States and Canada until April 21, 1923. The company performed in grand opera houses and high-school auditoriums—mostly one-night stands—rode the train in the early mornings, rehearsed in the theatre afternoons, and performed nightly. The touring company numbered twenty: eleven dancers (including Shawn and St. Denis); Horst and three instrumentalists; Sid Winton (stage manager); Walter Burke (company treasurer); St. Denis' maid; and two stage crew.[38]

Shawn and St. Denis continually gave Charles opportunities to perform new roles. It was clear to the company and the public that Charles was Denishawn's principal male dancer. In the first Mayer tour Charles danced two new Japanese solos, *The Coolie* and *Servant with a Parasol*. Additionally, he danced a new Shawn work, *Siamese Ballet* with Shawn, Lenore Scheffer, and Paul Mathis. He performed his solo *Pierrot Forlorn* (*Ne Rien Plus*), followed by a Moszkowski *Valse* with May Lynn, Betty May, Lenore Scheffer, and Paul Mathis (later replaced by Robert Gorham). He danced *Toth and Horus*, a duet with Mathis from *Egyptian Ballet*, the role of the father in *Xochitl* opposite Martha, and a Javanese dance *The Princess and the Demon*, with Martha and the company.[39]

With the great success of their first Mayer tour, the company had about six months to relax before the second Mayer tour. Of course, there would be two months of teaching classes and rehearsals. Shawn and St. Denis took a trip to Spain—Barcelona, Madrid, Toledo, and Seville—where they saw gypsy dancing, and Shawn studied with flamenco dancer Mañuel Otero. In preparation for a new dance Shawn purchased all the necessary items—combs, shawls, mantillas, castanets, shoes, flamenco and matador suits, sombreros, and sheet music—for his new ballet *Cuadro Flamenco* that would premiere on the second Mayer tour.[40]

Martha Leaves the Corps

For Charles and Martha, this would be their last performance together until 1928. Martha's mother and their family's nanny and housekeeper, Lizzie Prendergast, "were in need of help in Santa Barbara." Unfortunately, Graham wrote, "nothing could be done about the money that had been embezzled from Father's estate."[41] To remedy this dire financial situation, when Graham was offered a contract to dance in the *Greenwich Village Follies of 1923* by its producer John Murray Anderson, she had no choice but to accept his offer.[42] Her frugal existence on Fourteenth Street in New York City enabled Martha to send money home. Even during unpaid rehearsals she adopted a Spartan lifestyle with one meal a day, and she walked instead of riding a bus.

In the *Greenwich Village Follies of 1923* Martha performed solos in *The Garden of Karma, Silk and Incense*, and *Moonlight Kisses*, and Ted Shawn gave her permission to dance *Serenata Morisca*. During the second year of the *Follies* Martha worked under the direction of Michio Ito, "a Japanese disciple of Delsarte."[43] Ito had a penchant for creating what he called "dance poems," or "continuous movement, gesture moving inevitably into gesture . . ."[44] With five shows every night, dancing in the *Follies* was certainly a strenuous professional workout but for Martha, the perks outweighed the fatigue and monotony. "I had billing, and the salary was a high one," Graham writes.[45] But when she was not rehearsing or performing, she thought about her sister Georgia and all her friends in Denishawn, and probably missed performing with Miss Ruth and Charles. The person she yearned for mostly was Horst, who in 1923 left Denishawn to study music in Vienna. After two years, Graham left the *Greenwich Village Follies* to find her own way of moving, to compose her own dances, and to teach at the Eastman School of Music.

For Charles, five years passed quickly. He was consumed by dancing in Denishawn Company tours: second Mayer tour, third Mayer tour, Oriental tour, and the Arthur Judson tour. It was during this time that Charles danced with Doris Humphrey, a leading dancer, who jointly created dances with Miss Ruth and on her own. She was also the principal teacher of Denishawn dance technique. After Shawn, Charles was the leading male dancer and the principal male teacher of Denishawn technique. Together, they were the mainstay of Denishawn.

To earn money to complete the new Denishawn House, "a three-story Hollywood-style stucco palazzo,"[46] being built at Van Cortlandt Park in New York City, Shawn and St. Denis, along with their company, embarked on their last extensive tour, the Ziegfeld Follies tour of 1927-1928. During this time,

Charles and Doris were given the responsibility of teaching classes and running the New York Denishawn School, or what Shawn called "Greater Denishawn."

With Lawrence at the piano, Charles and Doris taught classes at Studio 61 in Carnegie Hall. In 1928, Doris found a new studio for the Denishawn School on the fifth floor at Nine East Fifty-Ninth Street in Manhattan. She and Charles prepared for a dance performance presented by the students of the Denishawn School, to be given on March 24 at Brooklyn Little Theatre.[47] This year would be a turning point in Charles' career—for the first time since high school he began to create his own dances. Away from Shawn's directorial authority, Charles and Doris were free to discover their own way of moving and to devise their own solo, duet, and group compositions. Charles and Doris had new opportunities working in New York City, center of the arts. These, coupled with other circumstances, led to their eventual break from the Denishawn dancers and school.

St. Denis and Shawn gave America the next generation of dance "greats:" Charles, who was the only male dancer of his caliber in New York City; Doris, who was searching for her own style through masterful choreography; and Martha, who had already given her own independent recital in 1926 with Horst at the piano. While these three dominant figures struggled to establish dance as an American art form, others took the lead in establishing the arts as a social force. Among noteworthy contributors to this social effort were Alice and Irene Lewisohn who, in 1915, founded the Neighborhood Playhouse located on the lower East Side of Manhattan. In addition to their affiliation with social worker Lillian Wald at the Henry Street Settlement School, and their father's financial support, the Lewisohn sisters provided for underprivileged children an array of social and creative activities. Through their philanthropic efforts they soon realized that, in addition to social welfare programs, the arts could bring beauty to the lives of immigrant poor, thereby enriching them.

132

Neighborhood Playhouse

The Neighborhood Playhouse School, a nonprofit organization located at the corner of Grand and Pitt Streets, included dance, music, and theatre, and was administered by social worker Rita Wallach Morgenthau. The Neighborhood Playhouse came into being at a time "when lyric forms expressed through the dance, or through song," as Alice Lewisohn Crowley explains it, "were relegated to the music hall, opera bouffe, or opera ballet."[48] Their idea of a Neighborhood Playhouse sprung from the children's festivals at the Henry Street Settlement. Although naïve and crude, "the festivals were motivated by myth and ritual associated . . . with the people of the neighborhood," Crowley writes.[49] Thus, dance, music, and theater became the expression of the collective history of this diverse community.

In concert with Lillian Wald, the Lewisohn sisters began to produce festivals and street pageants at the Henry Street Settlement, with the "wholehearted cooperation of city, school, and library authorities."[50] These festivals led to later festivals and lyric productions given at the Neighborhood Playhouse. Irene, who had studied Delsarte's theories of motion with Genevieve Stebbins, trained the Festival Dancers. "She designed and directed the choreography, and the casts were drawn from her classes in dance," Crowley wrote.[51] Alice traveled extensively to arrange for guest lecturers and teachers, while Irene worked on artistic planning and pragmatic details with Morgenthau. They hired prominent teachers of dance (including Graham and Horst) and they offered innovative and historic performances. In the Neighborhood Playhouse School students were chosen both for their talent and their character and were given full scholarships. Highly regarded teachers and performers taught students how to move, sing, speak, and perform all aspects of theatre arts. Dorothy Bird, Jane Dudley, Sophie Maslow, Anna Sokolow, and Blanche Talmud were some of these who became notable in dance.

From 1917 to 1927, productions at the Neighborhood Playhouse Theatre were conceived and directed by the Lewisohn sisters, who invited guest directors, lecturers, and performers to collaborate on their productions. Irene served as choreographer, assisted by Blanche Talmud, a member of Irene's dancing classes from their inception at the Neighborhood Playhouse. Not only did Irene direct and choreograph, she also performed in plays and ballets. The Lewisohn sisters produced many children's ballets. Irene choreographed these children's ballets, along with several Russian ballets such as *Petrouchka*, with dances arranged by Louis Chalif, a Russian émigré who taught classical ballet and Russian folk dance. Irene performed the role of the puppet figure in *Petrouchka* under the name of Ivan Litvinoff.[52] She also choreographed *La Boutique Fantasque* and *The Royal Fandango*, a Spanish ballet in which she performed a leading role. In addition, the Lewisohn sisters produced innovative plays and dance dramas based on Oriental themes.

Global Dance Dramas

When Michio Ito arrived in New York City in 1916, the Lewisohn sisters invited him to collaborate and perform in their production of *Tamura*. Ito played the role of the Cherry Sweeper opposite Irene, who played the role of the pilgrim monk or Waki, in their 1917-18 production of *Tamura*. A Japanese Noh play, *Tamura* was their first Asian production inspired by Irene's visit to Japan. She had embraced the spirit of Noh drama, the religious drama of Japan, and was able to study with Kongo San, a distinguished teacher of Noh.[53]

In 1923-24, after the Lewisohn sisters traveled to Arab countries, they produced *An Arab Fantasia*, an impression of Arab life with scenario and choreography by Irene and Alice. They commissioned music by a young Syrian composer, Anis Fuleihan, who was studying music in Boston. One rehearsal of

An Arab Fantasia had a noted invited guest—Kahlil Gibran, a distinguished Lebanese poet.[54]

After a visit to India in 1924-25, the Lewisohn sisters decided to produce *The Little Clay Cart*, a Hindu drama. During the 1925-26 season, they produced *A Burmese Pwe*, an impression of Burma, and *Kuan Yin, the Goddess of Mercy*, a Chinese fantasy. Coincidentally, during these years the Denishawn Dancers were touring Asia, studying with master teachers, and performing comparatively similar dances, such as *Momiji Gari* (Japan), *A Yein Pwe* (Burma), and *Singhalese Devil Dance* (Ceylon/Sri Lanka). As early as 1921, St. Denis danced her *Kuan Yin* and *The Nautch*, a street dance of India. During 1925 Shawn danced his *Japanese Spear Dance* among other Asian works with the Denishawn Dancers at the Lewisohn Stadium, which was donated to the City College of New York by the Lewisohn sisters' only brother, Adolph.[55] The dances and plays produced by Alice and Irene Lewisohn at the Neighborhood Playhouse further exemplified the relevance of world trade and travel and the internationalization of the arts in America.

By the 1920s, the Neighborhood Playhouse had launched a professional acting company, the Neighborhood Players and the Festival Dancers, even producing their own burlesque, the *Grand Street Follies of 1922*. On its initial success, they produced the *Grand Street Follies* for the years 1924 through 1927. Albert Carroll, Gertrude Kingston, Mark Loebell, Catherine Nesbett, Ian Maclaren, Dorothy Sands, and a young George Abbott were among their successful actors during these years. The Neighborhood Playhouse Theatre's principal set and costume designer Aline Frankau Bernstein became the first woman member of the United Scenic Art Union.[56] Through the teaching of theatre craft and production of innovative performances under the direction of Agnes Morgan and Alice and Irene Lewisohn, the Neighborhood Playhouse left a rich legacy in dance and theatre history.

135

The Neighborhood Playhouse Theatre was forced to close its doors due to financial constraints in 1927. It was, perhaps, "the realization that we had outgrown the physical dimensions of the building," Crowley wrote, which urged them to conduct a comprehensive study of the situation.[57] After considerable reflection, in 1928 Alice and Irene Lewisohn, together with Rita Wallach Morganthau, founded the Neighborhood Playhouse School of the Theatre, an institution that thrived for thirty years.

Orchestral Dance Dramas

From 1928 to 1931, a series of orchestral dance dramas conceived and directed by Irene Lewisohn provided occasions for Weidman and Graham to dance together again. Irene's conception of these orchestral dance dramas used movement as "a visualized expression of the orchestration, as if the musical structure were being interpreted through a composite orchestra of dancers . . ."[58] Here Crowley's choreographic description of orchestral dance drama is remarkably similar to the terms "music visualization" developed by St. Denis and "synchoric orchestra" employed by Shawn a decade earlier. Irene Lewisohn's method of choreography for her orchestral dance dramas was to commission Graham, Weidman, or Humphrey, to create the movement material, which Lewisohn would edit as she felt necessary. Certainly these former Denishawn Dancers were expert in the "music visualization" concept; thus they contributed greatly to the success of Lewisohn's adventurous orchestral projects, while simultaneously they strengthened their own artistic ingenuity.

Nikolai Sokoloff, director of the Cleveland Symphony Orchestra, was an ardent supporter of Lewisohn's new orchestral dance dramas. The Neighborhood Playhouse's first collaboration with the Cleveland Symphony Orchestra was Ernest Bloch's *Israel Symphony* (1916), performed in 1928 at the Manhattan Opera House. Born in Geneva, Switzerland, Bloch began his studies with

136

Jacques-Dalcroze, a music theorist whose ideas proved useful to dancers as well. When Bloch came to America in 1916 he taught Dalcroze's theories to many noteworthy composers. The scenic designs for Lewisohn's production of *Israel* were created by Jo Davidson and represented the Wailing Wall, shaped as monumental chiseled rock. Irene Lewisohn's method of directing rehearsals for *Israel* was to explain the theme of the work to the dancers and "encourage free improvisation."[59] Agnes de Mille describes one particular rehearsal for *Israel* when novice dance students learned Martha Graham's use of economy, a design element also noted in Japanese *Ukiyo-e* prints: "The students then all took off simultaneously, and there was a general writhing, crying, wringing of hands, and beating of breasts. Martha stood in their midst as a mourner, absolutely still. Inevitably it was *her* figure that everybody watched . . . . They had learned about economy."[60] Alice Lewisohn Crowley describes how the dancers, whether moving or still, were guided by the three great figures of modern dance (Graham, Humphrey, and Weidman) in creating the image of spirits floating about the "ageless sculptured edifice" of the Wailing Wall which inexplicably symbolized the "weeping heart of Israel."[61]

The second collaboration of the Neighborhood Playhouse and the Cleveland Symphony Orchestra occurred in the following year when a production of *Ein Heldenleben* (*A Hero's Life, or Hero and World*), a tone poem by Richard Strauss, opened at the Manhattan Opera House. According to Crowley, *Ein Heldenleben* is a "drama of heroic dimensions"; it featured Graham and Weidman as the central characters.[62] Weidman's performance further represented a period when he performed hero roles. In the case of *Ein Heldenleben*, the hero represented is considered to be Richard Strauss. *Ein Heldenleben* is scored in six movements each follow the other without pause: The Hero; The Hero's Adversaries; The Hero's Courtship; The Hero's Battlefield; The Hero's Works of Peace; The Hero's Retreat from the World and Fulfillment.[63]

137

Ein Heldenleben, written in 1898, is known as an autobiographical symphony characterized by lilting melodies, bravura orchestrations, and discordant counterpoint; it shows Strauss at the pinnacle of his creative career.[64] In his book *The Life of Richard Strauss*, Bryan Gilliam noted that *Ein Heldenleben* comments on "the relationship between the individual and his outer world," the protagonist struggling against divergent opponents.[65] A similar theme is addressed in Humphrey's dance *Color Harmony* (1928), Graham's *Heretic* (1929), and Weidman's *Studies in Conflict* in 1932. As in these dances by Graham, Humphrey, and Weidman, Strauss concludes *Ein Heldenleben* with the individual's yearning for peace and harmony after struggling against the world.[66] Irene Lewisohn's production of *Ein Heldenleben* used a scenic element comprising a series of leveled platforms, steps, and cubes rising to a huge pyramid. At the climax of the work, Weidman and Graham stood at the topmost center point, other characters facing them at each level of the ascending pyramid.[67] The large scale of the production's scenic design, along with the costumes, lighting, and Strauss' symphonic music enhanced the legendary import of the epic heroic tale of *Ein Heldenleben*.

A Pagan Poem

"Since leaving Ted Shawn," wrote Agnes de Mille, "Martha had never danced with a man except Charles Weidman on tour and special occasions, not even in the *Greenwich Village Follies*."[68] The orchestral dance dramas produced by the Neighborhood Playhouse offered Graham and Weidman performances in large-scale productions that they could not produce on their own, giving them occasions to gain acceptance from theatre audiences. Realizing their popularity, Irene and Alice Lewisohn created another opportunity for Weidman and Graham to dance together as partners, and for the public to witness their distinctive synergy. Furthermore, the Lewisohn sisters solidified their commitment to establishing dance as an American art through their presentation of works of epic proportions. These works: *Israel*, *Ein Heldenleben*, *A Pagan Poem*, and Ernest Bloch's *String Quartet*, with their salient social symbolism, reinforced the Lewisohn sisters' original premise that theatre arts could lift the spirit.

The performance of Charles Martin Loeffler's *A Pagan Poem* (*Poème paien*), in 1930, was a third collaboration with the Cleveland Symphony Orchestra. Produced by the Lewisohn sisters at Mecca Temple, it featured the Neighborhood Playhouse Company with Graham and Weidman in the leading roles. During the same year Lewisohn's production was invited to Cleveland as part of the gala opening or dedication program of Severance Hall, the Cleveland Orchestra's new performance hall. German-born Charles Martin Loeffler, a violinist and composer with the Boston Symphony Orchestra, scored *A Pagan Poem,* opus 14 for orchestra with piano, english horn and three trumpets obbligato in 1903.[69] Often compared to Richard Strauss, Loeffler based his work on the *Eclogues*, or *Bucolics*, ten pastoral poems written by the Roman poet Virgil (Publius Vergilius Maro). Virgil was one of the world's four great epic writers along with Homer, Dante, and Milton. Virgil's *Eclogues,* written in 37 B. C. show the idealized events in the lives of Roman shepherds with their pastoral life of song and dance.

Charles Martin Loeffler wrote *A Pagan Poem* after becoming "inspired by the Eighth Eclogue of Virgil's *Pharmaceutria* (the Sorceress)," Ellen Knight writes in her definitive book on Charles Martin Loeffler.[70] Particularly affected by a rhythmic chant the Sorceress recites in Virgil's *Eclogue*, Loeffler composed one of his "most important and popular works."[71] Describing the twenty-minute orchestral dance drama *A Pagan Poem* to Agnes de Mille, Weidman explained: "it was based on a bit from one of Virgil's eclogues, I was her [Graham's] lover who wanted to roam."[72] Irene Lewisohn's choice of scenic design was once again

139

on a monumental scale. Five ten-foot-long steps led obliquely to a large platform, then four steps mounted directly to a smaller platform, and three smaller steps led to the final pyramidal shape. Weidman explained the function of this set: "I mounted a sort of pyramid. She [Graham] started her incantation as the bereft woman and began running around its base in an enlarging circle, attracting him [Weidman] by centrifugal force, drawing him in [with] great spirals, and back to her."[73] The striking photographs of Weidman and Graham in *A Pagan Poem* by Nickolas Muray capture their economical use of design: Martha stands exalted, her solar plexus lifted toward the horizon, her arms cast sideways in space, while Charles kneels on her left side symbolically supporting her flight. These photographs reveal the reason Shawn partnered them together—together they embodied the beauty, strength, and affirmation of new American dance.

After their last performance together in *A Pagan Poem,* Agnes de Mille writes: "Charles went back under Doris Humphrey's jealous eye and obediently stayed there. He was valuable to Doris. Doris looked on Martha as a devourer."[74] Charles was valuable to Doris (and subsequently Doris was important to Charles) because they had established a five-year artistic relationship, they wanted their Humphrey-Weidman company to be representative of the Denishawn company format, and they wanted their dances to express the newly emerging ideas of American democracy and gender equality. Graham, with Horst's guidance, was creating her own dances with her first group of women dancers; "she was not prepared to choreograph for men," writes de Mille, "nor did she think in terms or pieces involving men."[75]

At this time, Weidman was exploring movements and creating dances that were instinctively male; "he had the idea that the male should and could move in patterns which were his solely, both physically and psychologically," José Limón wrote.[76] Early dances of this sort choreographed by Weidman for men were *Ringside* (1931), *Steel and Stone* (1931), *Studies in Conflict* (1935), and

140

Traditions (1935). He not only influenced the next generation of men dancers with his choreography but through teaching his technique, special men's workshops, and his repertory at the Bennington College Summer Dance School from 1934 to 1941. Charles Weidman pioneered new dance forms for men in twentieth-century American dance.

Chapter Six

The Humphrey-Weidman Alliance
(1928-1938)

To be master of one's body:
to find a perfect union between inner thought
and outer form—to draw from this a radiance and
power that makes of life a more glorious
and vital experience—this is to dance.

Humphrey-Weidman School Brochure, 1928

In September 1927, while thirty-two year old Doris Humphrey and
twenty-six year old Charles Weidman conducted classes with Pauline Lawrence at
the piano at the Denishawn School in New York City, the Denishawn Dancers
embarked on a Ziegfeld Follies tour. During this restful period away from
touring, Humphrey and Weidman were able to think about their underlying
philosophy within new movement possibilities, ultimately leading to their break
from the Denishawn School and its company of dancers.[1]

Their first concert with the students of the Denishawn School on March
24, 1928, at the Brooklyn Little Theatre (and later on April 5 at the John Golden
Theatre in New York City) was remarkable for its breadth of invention.
Humphrey's *Air for the G String* (to Bach's Air on the G String), a work for five
women, opened the performance. Eleanor King, who danced in this concert,
described the work's embodiment of classical style as "the dancers glided
upstage, long silk trains unfolding behind them. With lifted chests and opened

143

arms, they rose like waves, extending, bowing, greeting each other in Gothic curves and arches."[2] Their program included: Humphrey's *Piano Concerto in A Minor* (Grieg), a "music visualization" for thirteen dancers; Weidman performed his *Cathédrale Engloutie* (Debussy); Humphrey danced a Debussy waltz; Charles interpreted his comedic pantomime *Minstrels* with John Glenn and Eugene Le Sieur; and Doris' solo *Papillon* (Rosenthal) ended the first half of the program.

After a brief intermission, the ensemble performed Humphrey's innovative *Color Harmony*. According to Eleanor King, the work was "an abstract movement statement of the Helmholtz theory of light."[3] Humphrey decided against using precomposed music to create *Color Harmony*; instead she crafted rhythmic movement phrases, devised an original form, and later commissioned Clifford Vaughan to compose the score. Vaughan attended rehearsals and wrote his score for *Color Harmony* after he and Humphrey had completed many weeks in rehearsal with her seventeen dancers. In the future this choreographic method used for *Color Harmony* would become a dominant compositional pattern for Humphrey and Weidman.

After *Color Harmony,* six more short dances were performed. Among these was Charles' *Pierrot* (Scott), probably his own rendition of his first solo *Pierrot Forlorn,* composed by Shawn. Charles danced his comic solo *Juggler* (Borodin), in which "he juggled invisible balls and balanced non-existent feathers on the end of his nose," Lillian Moore mused.[4] A romantic duet, *Pathetic Study* (Scriabin), danced by the duo, concluded the program. This concert was a huge success and Humphrey and Weidman were hailed by the critics as consummate teachers who were opening a new chapter in the history of American dance.[5]

Cathédrale Engloutie

Weidman's first compositions, presented in 1928 and 1929, naturally reflected the influence of eight years of dancing with Denishawn. His dance,

144

Cathédrale Engloutie (Submerged Cathedral) to the music of French composer Claude Debussy, was in essence a tribute to St. Denis. Using St. Denis' idea of "music visualization" and inspired by her performance in *The Spirit of the Sea* (1915), Weidman created his *Cathédrale Engloutie*—a solo he continued to perform throughout his career. In her book *Time and the Dancing Image*, Deborah Jowitt describes St. Denis in *The Spirit of the Sea:* "draped in a stage-sized expanse of blue silk, she undulated from a prone position into the full-bodied waves of high tide, then sank back down."[6] Comparatively, Jowitt's description of *The Spirit of the Sea* is akin to Weidman's *Cathédrale Engloutie,* which symbolizes the Breton legend of a cathedral that periodically rises out of the ocean and sinks back into the sea. Jane Sherman, who saw his first performance, outlined Weidman's dancing in *Cathédrale Engloutie*: "His whole body was engulfed in a weird olive-green costume that suggested granite encrusted with barnacles. Made of a stiff material, it hung straight down from exaggerated square shoulders . . . he indicated with a truly moving quality the surge of sea depths, the rising and sinking of the submerged structure, and the tolling of underwater bells."[7] St. Denis was a master at using costume as metaphor in *The Spirit of the Sea.*[8] She and Humphrey made use of a huge square of blue silk in their "music visualization" *Soaring,* where the silk created images of the sea, a waterfall, a thunderstorm, and other phenomena. Moreover, St. Denis' artistry in using costumes and fabrics inspired the three noted modern choreographers who trained at Denishawn: Graham in *Lamentation* (1929), Humphrey in *Air for the G String* (1928), and Weidman in *Cathédrale Engloutie* (1928).

In her book *Days On Earth,* Marcia Siegel explains the musical structure of "music visualization": "Dance dynamics would reflect the score."[9] Siegel's statement is significant for an understanding of the important role "music visualization" played in the early development of dance composition. A dance

145

"music visualization" exhibits musical elements such as dynamic range, phrase length, and rhythm, several fundamentals of composition Humphrey made explicit in *The Art of Making Dances*, a book that Weidman owned, certain sections being well underlined.[10]

Charles performed *Cathédrale Engloutie* forty years later, since "at his age (74 years) he could perform it easily. It wasn't as demanding as *On My Mother's Side*, and the public came to see Charles perform," Deborah Carr said.[11] Dancing *Cathédrale Engloutie* was his way of looking back fondly on his experiences and life-long relationships that he forged at Denishawn. In 1989 Beatrice Seckler summarized her thoughts on Weidman's motive for performing *Cathédrale Engloutie:* "When you reach a certain age you like to go back to the beginning. Graham is now reviving some of her early pieces, it must be that same impulse."[12] Debussy's music with its unexpected harmonies creates an evocation of the sea, and Weidman's *Cathédrale Engloutie* reflects the legend.

Break from Denishawn

Doris and Charles urged St. Denis and Shawn to accept the new ideas of German modern dance originated by Rudolf Laban, Kurt Jooss, and Mary Wigman, which redefined the essentials of modernism in the dance. Humphrey explained the "German movement was bringing a splendid new technique to the dance . . ."[13] based on a notion of space as an intrinsic factor of movement. St. Denis was resistant: "With Wigman one is reputedly face to face with the abstract dance, stripped to its barest essentials of movement."[14] But St. Denis knew it was useless to speak against it because of the characteristic way in which cultural vogues flooded the country. So in due course Margareta Wallmann came to teach at the Denishawn House.[15] Wallmann, an Austrian choreographer and a member of Les Ballets Russes, studied with Mary Wigman and danced in her company. When Shawn brought Wallmann to teach at the Denishawn School, she was the first teacher of Mary Wigman's dance technique to come to America. She went on to become a successful director of operas around the world, including New York City's Metropolitan Opera Company.[16] At this time, Pauline Lawrence strongly felt that the only way Doris and Charles could expand artistically was through separating from the techniques of Denishawn.[17]

Doris, Charles, and Pauline were devoted to Denishawn but they also knew that to develop as individual artists they needed creative freedom. Weidman declared: "We did not wish to leave Denishawn; we wished only that Denishawn would incorporate our newer ideas."[18] Weidman explained that he, Humphrey, and Lawrence were opposed to certain ideas within Denishawn: "Humphrey-Weidman was against the theatricality of Denishawn . . . we wanted something more solid . . . to elevate [the dance] from entertainment to things of proportion which we later achieved in big symphonic ballets . . . and to get a technique . . . realize a new way of saying things."[19]

The Denishawn Dancers continued to perform their unchanging repertory, as they had on their Asian, Judson, and Ziegfeld Follies tours, something that marked for the trio Ruth and Ted's unwillingness to move into the next decade. Doris, concerned with the inevitable changes that would occur when the directors returned from their tour, would have to abide by Shawn's artistic decisions and she felt he was at least ten years behind in his movement theories.[20]

When St. Denis and Shawn returned from the Ziegfeld Follies tour, Doris received an invitation from them to attend a dinner meeting to discuss the future of Denishawn. Charles and Pauline were not invited, which was puzzling to Doris. Arriving at Denishawn House, she realized she had been summoned to appear before a newly formed board of Greater Denishawn. Shawn and St. Denis knew that Charles and Pauline would follow Doris' lead in matters concerning Denishawn; therefore they didn't want to complicate the situation by inviting them.

In attendance were St. Denis and Shawn; Olga Frye, the school secretary; Hazel Kranz, the children's teacher; Margerie Lyon, manager; and Fred Beckman, manager of public relations.[21]* Doris listened in disbelief to the new Denishawn policies outlined by St. Denis and Shawn that, to her, would control the moral and personal, as well as the artistic lives of their dancers: the number of students of Jewish descent must be limited to ten percent of the total enrollment; a committee would be formed to hear cases of immorality, such as affairs that did not end in marriage; and every dancer would have to embark on another Follies tour to help pay the mortgage on the Denishawn House.[22] After dinner and further discussion about her loyalty, Shawn asked Doris if she would go on the planned Follies tour. Doris said she would not go. Shawn asked the board to vote on Doris as a member in good standing—the board voted Doris out of Denishawn.[23]

Stunned by what had just happened, Doris said nothing to Shawn and St. Denis or the others but left, making her way home on the long subway ride from the Bronx. Arriving home at almost midnight, Charles and Pauline had been anxiously waiting for hours, eager to hear the news. They were shocked to hear Doris' story and were particularly distressed to learn that Greater Denishawn was to be 90 percent Aryan. Discussing this situation later in life, Charles recounted: "Now—that is awful because we had just done our concerts at the Golden Theatre over in Brooklyn where over half of our girls were Jewish. For people even to think that way, you would look at them just sort of amazed . . . Well, that was the strongest reason for our leaving and I would say even now, I don't want to be associated with you if you think that way."[24]

After this incident St. Denis and Shawn found it difficult to keep their company working and to balance their own personal lives. St. Denis realized her destiny when she expressed: "Since Ted's and my spiritual separation had already taken place, the going of Doris and Charles meant that the last pillar fell, and very soon Denishawn, in the form we knew it, would be a thing of the past."[25]

148

The tragic demise of Denishawn would not be abrupt; rather it was slow but laden with bitterness. After Humphrey and Weidman left the company, their solos were dropped from the repertory and Humphrey's choreography was no longer performed. With Lawrence's departure, Denishawn lost a first-rate accompanist. St. Denis recognized that their absence created a hollowness that could not be filled. This was not the case in 1924 when Graham left the company, because her sister Georgia and Anne Douglas took on her roles. Younger dancers were eager to experience the greatness of St. Denis and Shawn and their Denishawn Dancers. When Weidman and Humphrey departed, St. Denis and Shawn lost their foremost teachers.

More important, *la belle époque*—the good old days—of vaudeville touring had changed. In its heyday in 1909, St. Denis was the first dancer to schedule a week of evening performances in New York's Hudson Theatre, and the Denishawn Dancers performed in vaudeville theatres and opera houses throughout the United States. When the stock market crashed in October 1929, Shawn and St. Denis performed in high-school auditoriums—these tours were financially perilous ones. During the 1930s, St. Denis continued performing solo concerts, along with teaching, while Shawn began his Men's Group and built up the Jacob's Pillow Summer Dance Festival in the Berkshire Mountains. Today's modern dancers owe a tremendous debt to Ruth St. Denis and Ted Shawn for their pioneering spirit, which contributed much to American modern dance.

The Trio

Doris, described as "cool, detached, intellectual, always in control," and Pauline, who was "remarkably competent, efficient, and versatile," came to the Denishawn School in 1917 and developed a kinship that lasted forty years.[26] Charles came to the Denishawn School in 1920 and found there his artistic grounding. Nimble and lively, he acted on impulse. He was joyful, charming,

149

and childlike. Selma Jean Cohen depicted Charles as "gay and outgoing, full of fun. He improvised brilliantly, onstage—and off . . . He stuttered a bit, but chattered incessantly . . . [he was] childishly irresponsible. He borrowed money from everyone."[27]

Charles and Doris became one of the famous dance partnerships of the mid-twentieth century. They could be compared with other legendary partners of the century such as Vernon and Irene Castle, Anna Pavlova and Vaslav Nijinsky, Fred Astaire and Ginger Rogers, Rudolf Nureyev and Margot Fonteyn, or Mikhail Baryshnikov and Natalia Makarova. Margaret Lloyd described Humphrey and Weidman as a dynamic duo: "The partners complimented each other beautifully. Doris, whose ribbon-bound hair with its tawny waterfall set a fashion, was lyrical and lovely in her delicate, steely strength against the asseverative [sic] line of the tall, dark-haired Charles. The Humphrey-Weidman dance was good to look at from the beginning. The bloom of charm lay upon it. Everything was fresh and novel and attractive in this new theatre of the imagination."[28]

At Denishawn Pauline Lawrence served as rehearsal pianist; she was witty and a gifted musician. "With her small, fine-boned hands and endless patience," Jane Sherman recalls, "she was a deft, indefatigable pianist for class or rehearsal."[29] Pauline worked with two music masters during her tenure at Denishawn: Louis Horst, whose new musical ideas and dance composition classes impelled the modern dance forward; and Clifford Vaughan, whose ability as a composer was certainly evident through the creation of novel ethnic scores that accompanied newly-created Asian works during Denishawn's Asian and Judson tours.

The trio was literally surrounded by greatness at Denishawn. Pearl Wheeler was the costume designer and sewing mistress. Sherman depicted Wheeler as "Miss Ruth's devoted confidante, dresser, and co-creator of the highly theatrical and ethnical ballets for which Denishawn was famous."[30] Wheeler

150

taught classes in costume design, costume construction, jewelry and properties at Denishawn. Wheeler was indeed clever, while on tour she trained the dancers to be adept at their theatre crafts: the dancers had to unpack their own costumes, wigs, shoes, and makeup boxes; press their costumes and make sewing repairs; keep their shoes polished and clean; and style their many wigs.[31] Lawrence learned about costuming for dance from Wheeler and St. Denis. She not only learned about fabric and designing costumes but she also learned how to create costumes. Lawrence had a special creative process for designing and constructing costumes for Humphrey-Weidman dances, as Lloyd explains: "Pauline's costumes were brewed into life. She would stroll through the yard goods section of a department store, humming the music of the dance, until the right material called out to her, 'I am it.' With the material popped ideas for cutting. Hems were left unfinished, not only because there was no time to finish them, but because they moved better so."[32]

The trio honed their theatrical skills at Denishawn. Lawrence was certainly keen at absorbing the crucial skills she needed to manage a dance company. After their break from Denishawn, from 1928 until 1945, Lawrence played a critical role in the development of the Humphrey-Weidman Company and School. As company business manager, press agent, pianist, costume designer, seamstress, wardrobe mistress, stage manager, lighting director, and confidant, Lawrence was a pillar of strength. Her artistic integrity and protectiveness of her collaborators launched the Humphrey-Weidman Company as a first-class theatre dance company. José Limón summarized Lawrence's extraordinary ability to perform the tasks of an entire production crew while the Humphrey-Weidman Company was on tour.

> When the curtain went up, on her cue, she would double as one of two pairs of hands at the piano, give the electricians at the switchboard their

cues as needed, jump to the percussion instruments when these were indicated in the musical score, and return to the piano. Intermissions meant supervising and directing changes of scenery, refocusing spotlights, and changing colored slides [gels]. After the final curtain she would supervise the crew in packing the curtains, lights, props, and costumes, accompany the loaded trucks to the railroad station, check the baggage to the next destination, tidy up a bit, and join the company at whatever reception was being held by the local sponsors.[33]

The distinctive talents of these three friends and their devotion to each other combined with their credo to elevate their dance from entertainment to an art form; they were propelled to the forefront of emerging American dance.

Studio at Nine, Fifty-Ninth Street

In the fall of 1928 instruction in the Art of Dance was taught by Humphrey and Weidman at their first studio at Nine, East Fifty-Ninth Street. Their students took an elevator to the fifth floor to learn their innovative techniques in an oblong studio that had a parquet floor, high ceilings, and a skylight. A gold and silver Japanese folding screen separated the students' dressing area from the studio. Beyond the studio was a sitting room with several couches, a kitchen, bathroom, and several small rooms for Doris, Pauline, and Charles.[34] It was at this studio that the trio began to evolve their training methods, to develop a company of dancers, to compose their first independent works, and to produce their art in theatres. Enthusiastically they began rehearsals for their spring performance at the Guild Theatre.

Charles was inspired to compose his novel dance *Ringside* to a score by Winthrop Sargeant when Charles Laskey, a boxing instructor who also had a physical education degree, appeared at the studio for class. In *Ringside*, a choreographed boxing match, Charles found a perfect popular subject for dramatic characterization. The legalization of boxing as a commercial sport in

America during the 1920s reflected American manhood—its elemental conflict confined to a ring twenty-four feet square bounded by ropes. In large urban cities poor boys with boxing talent and dreams of becoming champions hurried into established clubs, and with the Dempsey-Carpentier fight in 1921 (the first million-dollar gate in history), boxing as a business began.

In *Ringside* Charles played the Referee and Laskey "was a natural for Weidman's new George Bellows-etching-come-to-life . . . which pitted John Glenn against Laskey," Eleanor King observed.[35] George Wesley Bellows, an American painter and lithographer born in Ohio, moved to New York City and found his niche by painting urban scenes of streets, slums, and prize fights. Bellows' colorful action paintings of fight scenes, especially of the American hero Jack Dempsey, were widely liked by the common man. Charles seems to be able to recognize such popular trends and portray them in his dances.

In their March 31, 1928, concert at the Guild Theatre, the curtain opened upon Humphrey's *Air for the G String*. Charles premiered his *Passion* and *Compassion*, contrasting character studies. In *Passion*, Charles danced Savonarola, the fifteenth-century Dominican friar whose militant crusading spirit made him one of the most controversial figures in religious history. In *Compassion*, he portrayed the gentle Christian mystic Saint Francis of Assisi. Following a brief intermission, Humphrey's *Water Study* had its first performance. With fourteen women, Humphrey explored the various vertical and horizontal planes of space as her dancers performed forward and backward spinal successions based on rhythmic breathing, to represent the ebb and flow of the ocean. In her book *Artists of the Dance*, Lillian Moore describes Humphrey's *Water Study*: "It concerned itself with the abstract representation of the movements of water, its deep slow rocking, the rise and fall of the waves and the climax of their breaking. The rhythm was established through the movement of the girls' bodies, in harmony with natural laws. There was no music, nor did it seem necessary."[36] After *Water Study*, Charles revealed his new works *Scriabin Study*, *Gershwin Preludes*, *Ringside*, and *Cowboys*. Humphrey's *Life of the Bee* ended the program. Charles illuminated prominently popular American folk heroes in his works *Gershwin Preludes*, *Ringside*, and *Cowboys*.

The following weekend (April 7) Humphrey, Weidman, and their dancers gave another performance. Their concert began with *Air for the G String* followed by Charles' version of Bach's *Jesu, Joy of Man's Desiring*, "a Flemish-style medieval nativity with Rose Yasgour as the Virgin and the three boys [Weidman, Le Sieur, Glenn] as the three kings," Eleanor King notes.[37] Weidman's *Rhythmic Patterns of Java*, a men's quartet, received its first performance. Charles danced his solo *Singhalese Drum Dance* and his quartet *Minstrels*. Moore outlines Humphrey's stark ensemble work *Life of the Bee* that ended the concert:

> It was inspired by Maeterlinck's illuminating study of the bee, and it amounted actually to a dramatic ballet, for it depicted with vivid reality the death duel between the old queen and the new. It revealed the theatrical possibilities of modern dance forms. The accompaniment consisted of continuous humming sound (obtained actually by the use of combs and tissue paper), and the beating of the dancers' wings and feet. This was a tremendously effective device.[38]

These two varied programs by Weidman and Humphrey reflected diverse historical subjects in *Passion* and *Compassion*, Bach's *Jesu, Joy of Man's Desiring*, *Ringside*, and *Cowboys*; world dance in *Rhythmic Patterns of Java* and *Singhalese Drum Dance;* and dance inspired by nature in *Water Study* and *Life of the Bee*.

154

Drums and Rhythm

On Denishawn's 1925-26 Far East tour, Weidman was exposed to two important influences: drums and intricate rhythms. In Ceylon, Shawn, Weidman, and George Steares learned the difficult steps and intricate rhythms of the "devil dancer." Shawn based his *Singhalese Devil Dance* upon the original steps that the trio had learned from several authentic sources in Ceylon.

When Weidman created his *Singhalese Drum Dance* in 1928, it showed his fascination with the complex drum rhythms of Ceylon. The next year Weidman devised *Rhythmic Patterns of Java* in which those intricate rhythms learned on the Asian tour were carried into the core element of his choreography. *Rhythmic Patterns of Java*, composed for four men, was the first performance for a young Mexican dancer named José Limón. Limón remembered the three other young men who were in his classes with Weidman as experienced dancers compared to him: "John Glenn, a miner's son from Pennsylvania, Charles Laskey, who was from Staten Island, and Gino—or Eugene—Le Sieur, a French-Canadian."[39] One important aspect, rhythmic variety, made Weidman's technical series and choreography difficult to perform, exciting to watch, and essential in mastering his movement style. He captured these complex Asian rhythms in a modern style but he also utilized various rhythms from other world dances as well.

In Weidman's training system, the rhythm he used in his *Forward Leg Whip Turn* is what he called "rumba rhythm," and it is recognizable in the men's section of Humphrey's *New Dance*. The rumba, a popular Cuban dance with African origins, was popularized in ballroom dances, musicals, and nightclub acts. Weidman utilized the rumba in his choreographed scene "Revolt in Cuba" in the Broadway musical *As Thousands Cheer* and "Shoein' the Mare" in the Broadway musical *Life Begins at 8:40*. Weidman's dance *Rumba to the Moon* was performed at the nightclub the Rainbow Room. He was fascinated by its

155

syncopated rhythm and he tended to increase the tempo of dance phrases when using the "rumba rhythm." Weidman's *Forward Leg Whip Turn* is recognizable in Nona Schurman's dance *From Studio to Stage*. Due to the meter of the music composed by John Schlenck, it is performed in a four-count phrase. During a rehearsal session with Schurman, I learned Charles' *Forward Leg Whip Turn* in the "rumba rhythm" with hands placed on the hips, as it was traditionally performed in Weidman's classes. I realized the use of the "rumba rhythm" clarified the dynamics of the turn, making it noticeably stronger with emphasis on rebound, weight, and syncopation.

Weidman's stylistic use of drums and other percussion instruments as accompaniment in his teaching and choreography became his signature. In Kathleen Cannell's 1950 article "Weidman Conducts a Master Class," she highlights his class in the Sargent School of Physical Education at Boston University. Cannell confirmed Weidman's distinctive use of drums: "Mr. Weidman conducted the master class with a drum. The rhythms, simple at first and then becoming devious and complicated, were taken up by his own pianist, Freda Miller, with precision and fire."[40] Charles considered a master class to be a lecture on dance without words, illustrated by his troupe: Jamie Bauers, Bill Hooks, Carl Morris, Lee Murray, Betty Osgood, Bob Purtain, and Nicholas Vanoff. In his hour-and-one-half master class Weidman teaches the abridged version of a course of study that takes a year and a half at Weidman's school. Cannell notes Weidman's training system: "Its technique is as arduous and strict as that of ballet and its vocabulary as varied, though less formal."[41] Weidman leads the class through three spheres into which movement is divided, as Cannell observes: "They began on the floor, slow and legato, rose through the standing position, allegro and staccato, to wild jumps and flying turns."[42] By using complex drum rhythms, Weidman was able to make classes respond to changes in dynamics and speed through his technique. Susannah Newman, who trained with

156

Weidman in the 1960s, remembers his classes: "Charles' class was a celebration; it was high energy and visceral. Weidman was hot! With drums beating, people were moving through space athletically."[43]

Dance Repertory Theatre

Weidman and Humphrey's first concert in the winter of 1928 had been an unexpected success, with standing room only available. At the Humphrey-Weidman studio at Nine Fifty-Ninth Street, classes and rehearsals continued. Their next concert was scheduled at the Philadelphia Academy of Music on May 10. Preparation for their two-week intensive course for teachers was in full swing; they needed complete enrollment to pay the summer's rent. In debt, the trio just couldn't make ends meet and decided they must find a less expensive studio. After a brief summer vacation, classes and rehearsals began in September. They had only a few months to get ready for their first season of performances under the auspices of the Dance Repertory Theatre, an innovative approach to programming conceived by Helen Becker Tamiris. The idea was to combine the efforts of the top modern companies and to produce six concerts during the week of January 5-9, 1930, at the Maxine Elliot's Theatre.[44]

The first Dance Repertory Theatre concerts, with Louis Horst at the piano, were held on the evenings of January 5 and 6, 1930. Doris and Charles performed these new duets: *A Salutation to the Depths* (Dane Rudhyar); *Choreographic Waltz* (Ravel); *Air on a Ground Bass* (Purcell); and *Suite: Poem No. 2, Study* (Charles' solo), and *Etude No. 12* (Scriabin). Doris composed a new solo, *The Call and the Breath of Fire* (Rudhyar); Charles performed his solos *Japanese Actor, 17th Century* (Horst) and *Preludes* (Gershwin). New works for their group included Weidman's *The Tumbler of Our Lady* (Respighi) and *The Marionette Theatre* (Prokofiev) and Humphrey's *Drama of Motion*. Doris' *Drama of Motion* in sonata form was performed without music. The piece comprises a formal

157

andante, a middle section with a contrasting largo, and a final part with a fast, spirited allegro; without musical accompaniment she created through pure movement a musical vision.[45]

The following week's performance was on Thursday, January 9, 1930. Several of their ensemble works were repeated (*Drama of Motion*), but in addition Humphrey showed *Color Harmony,* with Weidman and Leja Gorska dancing the leading parts with the ensemble. At this concert, Charles performed several new solos: *Three Studies: Diffidence, Annoyance, Rage* (Honegger); *Scherzo* (Borodin); and *The Conspirator* featuring Weidman with an ensemble. At their concert on Saturday, January 11, dances were accompanied at the piano by Horst, Lawrence, and Dane Rudhyar: Charles performed his solos *Passion* and *Compassion* (Satie); their duet *A Salutation to the Depths*; and Doris and Charles premiered *La Valse* (Ravel), a choreographic waltz featuring their duets and ensemble sections with their group Ruth Allred, Cleo Atheneos, Rose Chrystol, Justine Douglas, Evelyn Fields, Margaret Gardner, Leja Gorska, Ilse Gronau, Ernestine Hennoch, Letitia Ide, Eleanor King, Virginia Landreth, Dorothy Lathrop, Katherine Manning, Sylvia Manning, Betty Schlaffer, Rose Yasgour, Charles Boughner, George Esterowitz, John Glenn, Charles Laskey, Eugene Le Sieur, and Arthur Miller.[46]

During the second year of the Dance Repertory Theatre, each company was no longer featured in a separate performance; rather productions at the Craig Theatre contained several works by the participating choreographers Graham, Humphrey, Agnes de Mille, Tamiris, and Weidman. Weidman presented *Ringside,* featuring Charles Laskey and José Limón, and *The Marionette Theatre* (Prokofiev) danced by Weidman, Sylvia Manning, George Steares, and Eugene Le Sieur.[47] "Once upon a time, etc" formed the program note. In a 1942 performance of *The Marionette Theatre,* the Princess and Wandering Prince were played by Katherine Litz and Weidman, Peter Hamilton played the role of The

King, and Lee Sherman was The Retainer.[48] Weidman's intuitive feel for the ridiculous, along with his sense of style in composing the movements for wooden puppets, made *The Marionette Theatre* a charming dramatic piece with five scenes: a youthful delicate princess (perhaps Rapunzel) combing her long hair; a hero's swashbuckling entrance; a father who intervenes by summoning his rogue to fight the prince; a slow, buoyant duel; and a victorious exit of the prince with his princess.[49] On this same program, February 1, 1931, Humphrey showed her newly created *The Shakers* and *Dances of Women*. For the February 3 concert Weidman featured his new work *Steel and Stone* (Cowell), a trio with Laskey and Limón, and a new solo *Danse Profane* (Debussy). Charles' creative energy enabled him to produce one innovative work after another. Together he and Doris had a magnetic and prolific artistic partnership.

During this time Charles had been working on his first big group project, *The Happy Hypocrite* ("A Fairy Tale for Tired Men") written by Max Beerbohm to Herbert Elwell's music. It premiered on February 7, 1931, at the Craig Theatre as part of the Dance Repertory Theatre. Sir Henry Maximilian Beerbohm (1872-1956), an English essayist and caricaturist, published *The Happy Hypocrite* in 1897. Beerbohm's tale was set in England during the Restoration era and shows a parody of a stylish debauchee who deceives innocent Jenny Mere by holding a mask before his vile face, only to be reformed by pure Jenny.[50] Asian artist Nura designed the masks worn by the cast and by Charles, who played the dual roles of Lord George Heaven and Lord George Hell. Cleo Atheneos danced the role of Senora Gambogi, Letitia Ide played Jenny Mere, and Sylvia Manning danced the Merry Dwarf.[51] The entire ensemble took part in the opening banquet scene. "The low comedy mime of eating celery I remember as being particularly unrefined and absurd," Eleanor King recalls.[52] Weidman's skill in creating narrative form was hailed by John Martin, who called *The Happy Hypocrite* the first modern dance *ballet d'action*.[53]

Studies in Conflict

In her book *Time and the Dancing Image,* Deborah Jowitt mentions several works similar in conception to Weidman's *Studies in Conflict:* "Engaging parts of the body in adversary relationship to each other, accentuating the power of gravity, could express inner battles or the dancer's fight against some imagined force."[54] In 1932 Weidman created his abstract *Studies in Conflict,* a work that Limón considered "a tour de force in imposing disciplined formality on a dramatic subject."[55] With a musical score composed by Dane Rudhyar (1895-1985) and arranged by Vivian Fine with Pauline Lawrence, *Studies in Conflict* made its premiere at the New School for Social Research on January 5, 1932.[56] Weidman was strongly attracted to the music of Dane Rudhyar; he and Doris composed their duet *A Salutation to the Depths* to Rudyar's music. Dane Rudhyar was born in France, where he studied music at the Paris Conservatory; he came to America in 1916. Ardently affected by the religion and philosophy of Asia, he gave up his real name, Daniel Chennevière, for a Hindu name.[57] Rudhyar's compositions were inspired by the melodic lines and rhythmic cycles of Asian music and the principle of theme and variations to be found in East Indian music. Understandably, many modern choreographers appreciated his music, particularly Weidman and Humphrey.

In *Studies in Conflict* Limón observed that Rudhyar's music, "a striking, dynamic, and violently dissonant piece," [58] was performed three times while Weidman presented three variations on the social theme of conflict: First, the individual's conflict with himself; second, the individual's conflict with another individual; and third, the individual's conflict with a group, a quartet, or more universally, society.[59] Several movement themes presented in the first section recurr in the second and third sections.[60] Using theme-and-variations form as a structural component is typical of Weidman's compositions. Apparently

160

Rudhyar's score was adapted for Weidman's work by Fine and Lawrence. Limón recounts Weidman's use of theme and variations in *Studies in Conflict*:

> Charles danced in his strongest way a solo statement of the "conflict" theme. As in the ritual preparation for a duel, I, as the adversary, detached myself from a semicircle of eight men standing in the background. A beautifully developed two-part invention based on the thematic subject ensued. The men joined in for the third variation. This enlarged upon the theme while adhering scrupulously to the choreographic premise. It was a strong and arresting work.[61]

Studies in Conflict is related to Weidman's choreography of the men's section in Humphrey's *New Dance* in 1935. In a conversation with Deborah Carr about his composition in *New Dance*, she commented that the movements evolved from a *Primitive Study*.[62] Weidman used several movement themes from his numerous primal studies within the quartet section of *Studies in Conflict*, thereby developing these motifs more fully in the men's section, or "Third Theme" of *New Dance* in a way that was "brilliantly effective. Through dynamic movement and superb composition, he has conveyed a splendid feeling of unity, harmony and strength," Lillian Moore declares.[63] In delineating his movement style it is important to realize that Weidman was continually reworking ideas and movement themes, and it was typical of him to choreograph the men's parts in Humphrey's dances.

Floor Work

Weidman's training in Asian dance at Denishawn and on the Asian tour prepared him to develop his own unique series of exercises dancing freely on the floor (or floor work). In 1928, he devised *Japanese Actor (XVII Century)*, a work incorporating a unique use of low levels, or as Weidman described it, "using fabulous Japanese floor technique."[64] Weidman credited his work with Denishawn: "I think I was the first innovator of doing the floor things which modern dance later took on. Because I had experience in Japanese and in Oriental, all I did was to translate it into a modern man with emotions of the time."[65] Weidman's dance *Japanese Actor (XVII Century)*, set to music by Louis Horst, was affected by the Asian tour, along with other Denishawn dances he performed. In the early 1920s, as part of a *Japanese Suite*, Shawn created *Japanese Servant with Parasol* and *Coolie Dance*. Charles performed in both of these works. He performed the role of the Mountain God in the Kabuki dance drama *Momiji Gari*, a role he learned from the Japanese actor-dancer Matsumoto Koshiro, who taught Charles how to apply the complicated make-up and costume of the fierce character of the Mountain God, which is important in the presentation of the role.

To find a way to juxtapose stylistic Kabuki floor movements in a suitably modern way, Weidman's *Steel and Stone* offered him the perfect vehicle for experimentation. His abstraction of modern architecture with its thrusts of stone and steel was designed from floor level. Its emphasis was to balance on one hand and on one foot, to struggle in opposition upward. The surging of Henry Cowell's music supported the vehemently thrusting motions of the dancers, Weidman, Limón, and Laskey, symbolizing the machine age.[66] When the men dancers were working at their day jobs and Charles wanted to figure out the floor movements for *Steel and Stone,* he used Eleanor King. She noticed how strong her arms and upper body became through his creative experimentation, which culminated in *Steel and Stone.* Weidman's floor technique was initially created by and for him and his men dancers, but within a short time women dancers learned his floor technique in his classes and compositions.

Weidman developed challenging technical studies based on floor work to train the dancer's body for the demands of his new works. Weidman's *Modulation Slide Series* was designed as a transitional movement from standing level to floor level, back to standing level, and into locomotive movements.[67]

Weidman's *Modulation Slide* has been freely adapted for use in the American jazz dance technique called the *Jazz Split*. It is particularly noted in Gus Giordano's training system, where the *Jazz Split* is taught as a sequence of exercises to beginning students.[68] Weidman's *Modulation Slide* is recognizable in the section of *Brahms Waltzes* called "Soft Side Extensions and Modulations," the "Opening Dance" of *Saint Matthew Passion*, and Schurman's *From Studio to Stage*.

Another challenging technical study based on floor work was Weidman's *Knee Fall*. It begins supported on both knees and continues as follows: using a succession in a backward direction, push the hips forward, then fall forward onto the hands, ending facedown on the floor. A recovery to standing after the *Knee Fall* is usually followed by Weidman's *Hip Lift*, or *Pushing Up*. Weidman's *Hip Lift* has also been freely adapted for use in American jazz dance technique. In Giordano's technique, Weidman's *Hip Lift* is called *Pelvis Lift*.[69] Moreover, in Giordano's technique the *Jazz Split* is combined with the *Pelvis Lift*.[70] Weidman's *Hip Lift* and *Knee Fall* may be studied in Appendix B and through Labanotation in Schurman's book *Modern Dance Fundamentals*. These may be recognized in the section called "Tee-hinny" in Weidman's *Brahms Waltzes* and Schurman's *From Studio to Stage*.

Long after his career was established, Weidman held special affection for Ruth St. Denis, whom he and the Denishawn Dancers called Miss Ruth. He was her assistant in the creation of the Chinese dance drama *General Wu Says Farewell to His Wife,* which was originally choreographed by the great Chinese actor-dancer Mei-Lan Fang.[71] About forty years later Charles would perform his work *A Chinese Actor Prepares to Perform the Role of the God of War*. In her autobiography St. Denis expresses her affection for the young dancer when she writes "a kind of happy feeling comes over me when I think of Charles. His deftness and his humor always enchanted me . : . . [there is] a friendliness and mutual appreciation that is of pure gold."[72] Charles was known for his loving, comic impressions of Miss Ruth. He started to imitate her as a kid in Lincoln, Nebraska. Weidman's impressions would send the Denishawn dancers into bouts of laughter, including Miss Ruth and Ted (Papa) Shawn. One of Weidman's last dance compositions, created in 1974, was *Visualizations, or From a Farm in New Jersey: About, and Dedicated to, Ruth St. Denis.*

Kinetic Pantomime

Weidman created a delightful solo in 1934 called *Kinetic Pantomime*. John Martin mentions this dance as having "passages with music by Colin McPhee alternating with passages of completely absurd action without music."[73] To abstract the essence of an emotion through movement, Weidman explained how this gem of a solo came about:

> Instead of being frantic as, let us say, a minstrel would be when a bucket of water is thrown over him, I tried to convey the same idea without impersonating a minstrel and with no bucket of water causing the emotion. This attempt finally crystallized into a dance called *Kinetic Pantomime*. In this composition I so juggled, reversed and distorted cause and effect, impulse and reaction that a kaleidoscopic effect was created without once resorting to any literary representation.[74]

Weidman's realization of his gift as a mime was gained through the pantomimic solos created especially for him at Denishawn by Shawn, such as *Pierrot Forlorn*, *Danse Américaine*, and *The Crapshooter*. Shawn's *Pierrot Forlorn* may have been the ancestor of Weidman's trio *Minstrels* (1929), set to Debussy's music.[75] Instead of using narrative form to develop a character as he did in *The Crapshooter*, Weidman experimented with natural form by reversing the order of a normal response and distorting the movement of the human response in his dance *Kinetic Pantomime*. Don McDonagh considered Weidman's conception of *kinetic pantomime* as his major contribution to American dance because it was "a quite revolutionary approach to composition."[76] In his book *The Complete Guide to Modern Dance*, McDonagh wrote an account of Weidman's *kinetic pantomime*, and indicating its unconventional approach to nonlinear choreography: "He simply followed the trajectory of a gesture as it metamorphosed into a whole skein of movement that suggested bits and fragments of characterization as it progressed but did not tarry or linger over any. It was and is inspired foolishness that transcended the linear mode in which most dances of the time were composed."[77]

Weidman continued to develop *kinetic pantomime*, a concept that became his signature idea, using it within many of his noteworthy dances including *Quest*, *Bargain Counter*, *Opus 51*, *Flickers*, *Fables of Our Time*, and *Brahms Waltzes*. Marcia Siegel mentions that "Doris' comic style was influenced by Charles' kinetic pantomime."[78] Weidman's abstract humor moved Humphrey and others towards exploring comedy; Humphrey's *Race of Life* was one of her successful comedic works. At the suggestion of Humphrey in 1951, Pauline Koner, a leading dancer with Limón's company and a noted choreographer, invited Charles to dance in her new satire *Amorous Adventure*. Koner performed in the work with Charles and Daniel Nagrin. In her review in *Dance Magazine*, Helen Dzhermolinska observed Weidman's outstanding comedic performance in Koner's *Amorous Adventure*: "Who that has ever seen that king of comedy, Charles Weidman, can resist his inspired clowning, his miracle timing? Conceive of Weidman as the abandoned husband in this little drama, ineffectually hanging himself because his wife has left him; even the rope won't cooperate with him; it splits, laughing."[79]

Weidman's deftness in using choreographic devices to evolve his personal kinetic pantomimic style he described thus: "I utilize the natural laws that govern the body, intentionally distorting them. The idea projected causes a movement or gesture to be purely abstract or pantomimic. And no matter how pantomimic a gesture may be, it should have rhythm and design, quality and phrasing—projection—or any other quality which constitutes a pure dance movement."[80] Weidman stressed these key terms in his statement: rhythm, design, quality (dynamics), and phrasing. Moreover, these terms were emphasized in Humphrey's book *The Art of Making Dances*. However, Weidman adds the term 'projection' to his list, or what could be called performance personality. As a master of comedy, Weidman suggested that the following rules be applied to achieve humor:

1. Any extreme or exaggeration or distortion of the natural.
2. Sadistic humor—accidents and discomfitures.
3. Any extreme contrasting movement.
4. An affected person—lameness, toothache, etc.
5. Sudden changes of thought, spasmodic changes of direction, or a quick introduction of new themes.
6. Pantomimic representations of a function—juggling, fighting, eating.[81]

Weidman's suggestions on how to master *kinetic pantomime* and humor in a dance are beneficial. Of special importance on Weidman's list is how to employ abrupt changes in direction into new ideas. In a conversation with Beatrice Seckler about Weidman's particular brand of humor, she said, "I don't think anyone can do the comedy pieces of Charles unless they've worked with him . . . to get the feeling [kinetic sense] of the motivation."[82] Certainly observing Weidman performing *kinetic pantomime* and learning his comedic technique from him are beneficial to a dancer's successful performance of his historic works. Weidman expected dancers to invest totally into the kinetic process. In the 1970s, Charles didn't explain to his company how to perform *kinetic pantomime,* and when questioned by his dancers during a rehearsal, Deborah Carr dryly relayed Weidman's response: "It's not in the knowing how, it's in the experiencing of it—so just do it and don't analyze it out of existence."[83] Carr and Seckler's statements indicate the importance of absorbing the motivational thrust of *kinetic pantomime* by watching Weidman at work in his studio and in performance, exactly as he learned in Denishawn. Weidman's unique comedy may be studied as he performs *kinetic pantomime* on the videotape *Charles Weidman On His Own.*

Eighteenth-Street Studio

Doris sprained her knee during a Dance Repertory Theatre performance of *The Shakers* on February 8, 1931, at the Craig Theatre. She wouldn't be able to dance for several weeks, so Charles took on more teaching responsibilities. She was planning to visit Arizona as a guest of Mary Wood Hindman before the upcoming spring and summer performances and the intensive course for teachers in July. While Pauline and Charles were making their summer plans, Doris was looking forward to a needed rest.

When the trip to Arizona fell through, she spontaneously booked herself on a vacation Caribbean cruise—she sailed on the *S.S. Dominica* of the Furness Line.[84] On the cruise Doris read Havelock Ellis and Friedrich Nietzsche (*The Birth of Tragedy*), played bridge, began her habit of smoking cigarettes, and met her husband-to-be Charles Francis Woodford, a second-class officer and an Englishman who came into New York Harbor every three weeks. When they first met Doris observed Charles Woodford to be a calm man of strength and courage. Doris called her husband Leo since she had a close relationship with another Charles. Pauline thought Doris' marriage plans were hasty and Charles was just aggravated by the whole idea.[85] Pauline thought Leo distracted her from her work and Charles complained that they weren't dancing together as much.

During that summer Doris and Charles were hired by the Cleveland Opera Association and spent several weeks staging the dances for *Carmen* and *Aida*. Lawrence Higgins conceived of the Cleveland Opera Association as a way to

167

revitalize the arts in Cleveland during the Depression, and served as both producer and director. Under his helm every aspect of the Cleveland Opera Association's productions were theatrically fresh and innovative, including hiring Humphrey and Weidman to create new dances. Most of the dancers were from the Cleveland area but included Limón and Robert Gorham. Eleanor Frampton, who was teaching at the Institute of Music, served as dance rehearsal director. Charles and José stayed to perform and be guests of Frampton.

Charles and Doris taught their annual course for teachers in July, with Pauline accompanying the classes on the piano. With full enrollment they shared the profits, but they could still barely make ends meet. Doris and Charles were busy staging their dances for the Broadway musical *New Americana,* and shortly after the closing of Charles' original *Candide* (produced for Broadway, on July 8, 1933), Doris gave birth to a son—Charles Humphrey Woodford.

In early September Charles and Doris worked with their company on the dances for a new Broadway version of Molière's comedy *The School for Husbands.* While Pauline managed the school, nanny Lisa Alida Hein was hired to care for baby Charles. They all had formidable financial concerns so they decided to pool their resources and live together. They found a suitable place on the third floor at 31 West Tenth Street—close to the Eighteenth Street studio—with seven rooms, a fireplace, and two bathrooms. Doris and Leo had their own room; the nanny shared a room with baby Charles, and Pauline, Charles and José each had their own rooms. They moved their belongings and furniture into a place where they would spend the next seven years together as a family. To complete the living room, Charles placed his Gauguin painting of Polynesian women and his two Cambodian headdresses that he had acquired in Asia on the mantel above the fireplace.[86] With the success of *The School for Husbands* and the Broadway musical *As Thousands Cheer* Charles was able to buy a 176-acre farm in Blairstown, New Jersey, that eventually became the family's woodland haven.

Charles, Doris, and Pauline set out for Bennington School of Dance at Bennington College in southern Vermont on July 30, 1934, for the first summer school of modern dance in America. Conceived by Robert Devore Leigh, the president of this progressive women's college, the summer school was organized by Martha Hill, director of their dance program, who was joined by Mary Josephine Shelly from the University of Chicago.

The fundamental educational philosophy of this six-week intensive in modern dance was that physical education teachers from around the country could enroll to study in three-week segments with the originators of modern dance: Martha Graham, Doris Humphrey, Hanya Holm, and Charles Weidman. Additionally, students studied music with Louis Horst and dance history and criticism through lectures from John Martin. But the real icing on the cake was a concert series where by these same artists composed new works for their companies and performed them. Resident composers Horst and Norman Lloyd, who taught at Sarah Lawrence, and his wife Ruth, an accompanist, wrote music for new dances, and Arch Lauterer, who taught at Bennington College, offered innovative stage and lighting designs. Noted photographer Barbara Morgan was in residence to document this historic event. During that first year the heat and humidity were intense, but the students were soaking it all up with glee. Charles had a splendid first year teaching and performing, as Doris confirmed in a letter to Leo:

> . . . the audience was large and loyal. At least to Charles. You see he had just finished a week's work here and I'm sure half the girls are in love with him and as I was in the distasteful position of the chosen one—the partner, the lover even, they would not be very pleased with me. Please get off the stage Miss Humphrey and let me imagine myself as the

inamorata of the romantic young man with the dark eyes. Isn't he divine and cute too.[87]

During the month of January 1935 the Humphrey-Weidman Group embarked on a tour of college physical education departments throughout the Midwest and Canada. Since finances were tight, it was a lean tour, allowing for only piano accompaniment for their performances. The dancers received minimum Equity wages plus train fare while on tour, but Doris and Charles received no wages whatsoever. Their repertory comprised *Life of the Bee, Alcina Suite, The Shakers, Water Study, Dances of Women, Dionysiaques,* and *Rudepoema.*[88] They traveled with their collapsible set of platforms, boxes, and cyclorama for scenic design; Pauline was a master technician at creating atmospheric lighting for their dances. With appreciative audiences but dismal reviews, Doris became discouraged, but optimistic Charles thought they were young and strong and it wasn't so hard pioneering the dance plain.

Returning home in February, Charles and Doris were hired to choreograph nine dances for the American premiere of Gluck's *Iphigenia in Aulis* for the Philadelphia Opera Company that was conducted by Leopold Stokowski. The opera was produced by the Philadelphia Orchestra Association, directed by Herbert Graf, designed by Norman Bel Geddes, and performed at the Academy of Music.[89] Doris performed a maenadic solo; she and Charles performed a lovely duet, and their group also performed in a big lyrical dance scene in the second act. The press reviews of their work were extremely favorable.

William Kolodney, the new director of the Education Department at the Ninety-Second Street YM-YWHA, contacted Doris, Charles, and Martha Graham with his plan for developing a dance center offering a comprehensive curriculum. Kolodney had approached John Martin to be chair of the dance committee of which Doris, Martha, and Charles were members. With Kolodney's grand plan it

170

became clear that the Ninety-Second Street YM-YWHA would give them all a steady teaching salary, along with some of their dancers as their teaching assistants.

Since the year had been consumed by touring, Broadway shows, and operas, Charles and Doris decided to focus on a performance at the Guild Theatre on January 6, 1935, featuring solos and duets. Doris opened the concert with her new work, *Credo* (Chavez), "a rather vague composition that played with a variety of distortions and variations of them," Henry Gilford wrote in his review.[90] Next Charles danced his new composition *Affirmations* to music by Vivian Fine. Unfortunately, Gilford's review in *The Dance Observer* lacked insight: "The affirmations were varied; there were soft affirmations, softer affirmations, and vigorous affirmations."[91] Their first duet was the *Alcina Suite* to Handel, a graceful and formal dance in baroque style accompanied by the Gordon String Quartet, with Vivian Fine and Harry Cumpson at the piano, and Simeon Bellington on clarinet.

Memorial to the Trivial (Moross) was Charles' work intended to help the audience remember the merits of what is commonplace—humor and laughter. In his review of *Memorial to the Trivial,* Gilford seems to have missed the point completely in writing of Weidman's composition that it "draws a multitude of laughter for its all too obvious and rather pointless efforts at humor. Humor is something much too profound to be carried on inconsequential and simply inessential head wagging and finger flapping."[92]

The first half of the program closed with their duet *Rudepoema* to the music of Heitor Villa-Lobos. According to Limón, *Rudepoema* was "a primitive rite of betrothal, incantatory and mysterious."[93] In his review, Gilford describes it as being a "dance of opposition . . . the basic concept of conflict between the horizontal and the vertical planes, the conflict between the feminine and the masculine figures."[94] During the entire second half of the program, Charles and

Doris performed their new work *Duo-Drama* to a Concerto for String Quartet, Clarinet and Piano by Roy Harris. Weidman and Humphrey restated the concept they presented in *Rudepoema* in *Duo-Drama*, an abstract work with three parts: "Unison and Divergence," "Phantasm," and "Integration." According to Limón, the thirty-minute work shows a man and a woman in three historical scenes. The first section represents a primordial state, the second reflects the baroque period, and the third shows the modern era.[95] *Duo-Drama* could be considered a dramatic portrayal of the relationship between men and women through time.

For Weidman and Humphrey and their company, 1935 seemed to be a very good year. During the previous year the departure of some of their leading dancers to get married or earn a living—such as Cleo Atheneos, Ernestine Henoch, Eleanor King, Dorothy Lathrop, Sylvia Manning, and Gail Savery—had meant teaching new dancers their repertory. Now their company seemed to be a cohesive unit once again. Rehearsals and classes continued at a fast pace at their Eighteenth Street Studio. New dancers were invited into the company including some of the most noteworthy performers such as Beatrice Seckler, Eva Desca, Edith Orcutt, Katherine Litz, and Sybil Shearer.[96] Charles and Doris also established a small understudy group. In exchange for free classes, understudies learned repertory and performed in their large ensemble compositions. Doris and Charles composed three of their most important works during 1935: *Duo-Drama, Traditions,* and *New Dance.*

New Dance

New Dance was a work of epic proportions. Doris and Charles danced as soloists with twelve women and four men dancing together as an ensemble. This full-length symphonic work had a commissioned score by Wallingford Riegger. Working on the dance before the score was completed, Doris composed some of the phrases to *When Johnny Comes Marching Home* by Roy Harris. She discarded this music and composed her noted 7-7-10 variations for solos, duets, and trios in opposition to a large group of background dancers performing a 4/4 ground bass.[97] The dancers rehearsed without music, dancing only to the metric counts or a beating drum, as was often the case in the creative process of Humphrey and Weidman. When Doris and Charles completed the work, Doris asked Riegger to attend a rehearsal of the fifty-five minute dance. After he wrote the melodic lines, Riegger gave them to Norman and Ruth Lloyd to complete his score by adding his stylistic chord progressions.[98] The Riegger-Lloyd score is noted for its rhythmic use of percussion and terraced dynamics.

New Dance had its first showing on August 3, 1935, as part of the Bennington College Summer School of Dance at the Vermont State Armory. Charles and Doris danced the central roles, along with seventeen of the Humphrey-Weidman Group and twenty-four workshop dancers. Arch Lauterer designed the lighting and Pauline Lawrence designed the costumes. The women wore dark-toned, ankle-length dresses designed with scoop necklines and capped sleeves; these dresses were open on the left side to accommodate free leg gestures. The men wore basic light-colored pants and matching boat-necked, long- sleeved shirts. As central figures, Doris and Charles wore similar costumes but in a dominant color.

New Dance was an expansive work comprising six parts, each presenting a thematic movement statement. The curtain rose to show a panoramic view of a city, with its pyramidal buildings composed of various large wooden boxes placed in the strongest areas of the stage—the four corners, representing the directions North, South, East and West. The grid between these four corners appeared to represent the streets of a city whose inhabitants stood or sat surrounding their societal leaders, as symbolized by Charles and Doris, standing at center stage. After a short overture, the two began a visceral, affirmative duet, calling forth their highest ideals in a heroic movement statement representing their joint

173

credo.[99] During the next section, the woman, in increasing degrees of movement, entices the women "off the boxes and into a resonant percussive dance that ends with a flurry of propulsive rushes toward the center of the stage and whirling exits," Marcia Siegel writes.[100] Similarly, the man quickly summons the men to center stage. Sudden movements swiftly sliced though the diagonals and burst forth into runs that catapulted horizontally into crooked jumps, progressing into "leaps that ended in long strides on the knees. Here was all the dynamism and force of the male nature unleashed," wrote Limón.[101] The men and women slowly come together, guided by their leaders, in a dignified procession that became more exalted as it segued into the fugal *allegro con brio* ending the work with a celebratory, contrapuntal conclusion.

After their Bennington concert, Doris added the final section to *New Dance,* "Variations and Conclusions," where the boxes were moved to center stage and arranged to create a huge pyramidal structure for the reiteration of previous movement themes and their variations. The Humphrey-Weidman Group gave the premiere of the finale to *New Dance* at the Guild Theatre on October 27, 1935. When Eleanor King (who had just left the Humphrey-Weidman company) saw *New Dance* performed in New York City she expressed that it "deeply moved and exhilarated me."[102] When Nona Schurman (who was about to become part of the company) witnessed a performance of *New Dance,* she thought the contrapuntal action of the movement material was Humphrey's philosophy in action.[103]

In many formal discussions with their company Weidman and Humphrey stressed their absolute repugnance at the thought of living in a society under a dictatorship. They were witnessing the plague of fascism in Europe and the resulting slaughter and pillage of the Spanish Civil War that shocked and terrified the world.[104] The Humphrey-Weidman Group performed many benefit concerts appealing for financial support to aid the Spanish people. *New Dance* was an assertion of their unquestioning belief in the possibilities of a democratic society in which the individual could expand his or her own capacities in accordance with and in cooperative association with others.[105] Doris had ascertained her ideal in *New Dance*; now she felt she must portray the impediments to her credo.

Theatre Piece

In direct opposition to *New Dance,* the content of *Theatre Piece* showed the negative, destructive self-indulgence of those engaged in competitive civil or business ventures, and a plea for a noncompetitive society. Intensive rehearsals began in September for *Theatre Piece,* a lengthy artistic Humphrey-Weidman collaboration comprising eight sections. Charles and Doris danced the central roles with seventeen members of their company, to music composed by Wallingford Riegger and in costumes designed by Pauline Lawrence. At its first performance at the Guild Theatre on January 19, 1936, as the theatre curtain ascended on the forty-five minute *Theatre Piece,* the stage revealed various sized wooden blocks arranged to suggest the skyline of a modern city.[106]

Theatre Piece began with a ceremonious "Prologue," an introduction to the cast of characters, evolved into "Behind Walls," a section in which the characters portrayed the personification of the vicious competition of "Big Business." Young women work in the confines of their corporate cubicles dehumanized by their environment they appear to be mannequins with fragment body parts visible to the spectator. "In the Open" showed these office girls and their quest to find an eligible man to wed—the competition was fierce. Within the scene, an unsuspecting man (Charles) was "pursued by a pack of predatory females. Panting, pushing each other aside to gain advantage, they would fling themselves in his path in lewd abandon," wrote Limón.[107] In the final segment the pursued man stops, selects the most aggressive woman, throws her over his

175

back, and exits as the rest of the women chase after them continuing their contention.

In the third part, "In the Stadium," the boxes were arranged as bleachers, filled with spectators whose mania for competition in various sports (boxing, golf, football, soccer, track, wrestling), as exhibited through the movements of two athletes (Bockman and Limón), portrayed the public's fanatical mania for organized sports. Doris placed herself in the scene as a nonconformist whose reaction, in opposition to these competitive proceedings, was passed over in total disregard by the crazed crowd.[108]

Charles made his social commentary on competition by composing the fourth part, "In the Theatre," as a nonsensical comedy in two scenes to Riegger's jazzy percussion score. Now the boxes were arranged as a stage with the actors, (Charles, Katherine Litz and Katherine Manning) atop and the audience, played by the dancers, seated below. In the first section, the actors steadfastly "upstage" each other and jockey to be in the spotlight. The second section portrays a frenetic vaudeville burlesque. In their standard act, Charles and his leggy chorus girls allowed their rivalry to develop into such a wildly insane delirium that the "burlesque turned pandemonium, played to the shrieks and roars of the audience," wrote Limón.[109] "The Race" showed all of the characters in their greedy final contest, a madly symbolic race for life. The competitors surged from the rear of the stage forward to the footlights over and over again, until a musical fanfare brought a sudden stop to the competition. The nonconformist (Doris) summoned them to take their original places. The work's conclusion heralded a new philosophy of living as portrayed by Weidman and Humphrey in *New Dance*.[110]

This Passion

In November 1937, Charles had just finished collaborating on the Broadway musical *I'd Rather Be Right* starring George M. Cohan. Among the

176

musicals numbers he had staged for the show was a dance scene titled "American Couple," a stylized portrayal of a modern relationship. It is, perhaps, this same idea that Charles developed more fully in his next concert work.

This Passion, with music by Norman Lloyd and costumes designed by Pauline Lawrence, premiered at the Guild Theatre in New York City on January 23, 1938. The program notes state: "With three divergent themes chosen for their contrast to each other and arranged in such a manner as to present a kaleidoscopic effect. 'Tabloid' (first theme) deals with a 'domestic tragedy.' 'Air Raid' (second theme) pictures the possibility of humanity conditioned to a completely militarized environment. 'Interlude and Conclusions' (third theme) deals with the aspiration toward a saner order."[111] Each of the three themes of *This Passion* had three parts or nine scenes. According to Margaret Lloyd the three themes were not developed in a sequential manner, but were played in three parts. Weidman arranged these nine contrasting scenes by performing all of the first scenes, then all of the second scenes, and finally all of the third scenes. His arrangement created a series of occurances that mirrored world events. By using this organization, Weidman shows how the multiplication of evils lead to the perniciousness of war.[112] As a three-part fugue, each theme is contrasted in its conceptualization, development of the sequence of movements, and its manner of conveying its subject. Each theme's compositional structure is in the form of statement, development, and conclusion.[113] In creating the stage design Charles made use of essential wooden blocks of various shapes and sizes, supplemented by other pieces of scenery, to create his powerful theatre dance. José Limón describes the three themes of *This Passion:*

> The first dealt with a tawdry *crime passionnel*, where an unprepossessing husband was done to death [sic] by his sluttish wife and her lover. The second voice was a nightmarish vision of a world inured to living underground with gas masks and the threat of annihilation by poisonous

177

gases. The third was, again, the artist's call for order and sanity, the ever-recurring vision of an impossible Utopia.[114]

In *This Passion* Charles decidedly reiterated the exact theme he and Doris stated in *New Dance*, but in an episodic manner. The opening scene showed a domineering husband (Charles), with his wife (Doris), who waits on him like a handmaid, and her lover (José) with whom she escapes her dull, tedious, wearisome domestic life. In this part Lloyd's music reflected the wife's tiresome, uninteresting life and her restless desire for something more.[115]

The second scene showed a street with figures moving at a frantic pace like insects, with strikingly incongruous appearance, these were actually distorted human figures wearing gas masks.[116] Here, Lawrence's costumes placed the dance in the future, the men wearing modern jackets and the women wearing micro-mini skirts. Suddenly the stage ominously emptied—a figure appeared as a Utopian apparition and performed a heroic sarabande.

The wife and her lover enter and perform a reptilian duet as they scheme to murder her husband. "Charles used a powerful, slashing movement to indicate the crime, a sort of brutal shorthand. The husband was enticed, all unsuspecting, and gruesomely murdered, his corpse dragged into the shadows," wrote Limón.[117]

As the air raid ceased, shell-shocked humans peered out from their underground shelters and began, in degenerate fashion, to creep into view. They celebrated their survival with all the socially accepted vices—wildly danced, drank until drunk, and made seemingly lustful love—until a stripper became everyone's focus. She went into her burlesque striptease act, removing everything except her gas mask. With encouragement from the crowd, she removed her last piece of attire—her mask—and revealed her face. This act sent outbursts of lewd pleasure throughout the crowd. Then suddenly, the visionary

178

figure representing the ideal social order appeared as an illusion in her serene, peaceful dance.[118]

In the next scene the police, caricatures like large frogs, leaped off the boxes and captured the murderous couple. Next came a scene making a mockery of the justice system as an insane judge and jury sentenced the pair for their crime and dragged them away. At once the masked humans tumultuously catapulted themselves through space in sheer panic. Annihilation was in process. They died grotesque, prolonged, comical deaths. In conclusion, the Utopian vision appeared as an apparition to dance her heroic sarabande.[119] Weidman's genius as a creator of effective theatre was noted by Lois Balcom in her review of *This Passion* in *The Dance Observer:* "Its arrangement of contrasting sections to simulate the jumble of concurrent but unrelated happenings in life is ingenious."[120]

In total contrast, at this same concert Doris presented *Race of Life*, her first full-length comedy, based on James Thurber's cartoons published in *The New Yorker*. Pauline created the costumes to resemble Thurber's drawings and Vivian Fine composed a delightful musical score. Influenced by Charles' episodic comedic style, she invented the story of a family's journey through life to fulfill their dreams. Doris played the mother, José the father, and Charles the nine-year-old child. Marcia Siegel summarizes *Race of Life:* "Beset by Indians, Night Creatures, and a Beautiful Stranger, the family finally succeeds in climbing a mountain, representing material success, made of the ever-useful boxes, to plant an Excelsior banner on the top."[121]

From 1936 to 1940 the Humphrey-Weidman Company would spend the first five months of the year touring the United States. Their strenuous schedule of performances, master classes, and lecture-demonstrations mimicked their days as Denishawn Dancers, except that now Doris, Charles, and Pauline were at the helm. They would usually depart by train ahead of the company so they would be on-site to give interviews and arrange production logistics for their performances.

The main motive of their touring was to keep their dancers employed, but at the same time to exhibit their dance works to the public, thereby developing an audience for dance. Moreover, their educational work, highlighted in the Bennington Summer School of Dance, became an increasingly valued commodity.

Rebound, Falling, and Recovery Principles

Humphrey, Lawrence, and Weidman were influenced by the art and music of a new decade; moreover they drew inspiration from noted German dancer Mary Wigman and Ronny Johansson, a Swedish dancer. "It was quite a wonderful period of innovation and experimentation," exclaimed Weidman.[122] In a 1966 interview with Marian Horosko, Weidman further illuminated an innovative performance given by Ronny Johansson in New York City prior to the Denishawn dancer's departure for Asia:

> It was our first glimpse of a different way of successional movement. And then she did this one air thing and came down with a certain amount of heaviness. And I remember Ted leaned over to Doris and said, "What do you think of her?" And she says, "Oh I think she's fascinating." But he said, "Don't you think she's kind of heavy?" And Doris said, "I think she intends to be." So therefore that was a glimpse of something else to do with the gravity pulls, not to defy it always but to come down and let it enhance your movements.[123]

Johansson's new use of gravity sparked an idea for both Humphrey and Weidman in their new technique and movement style. For Humphrey it was the fall and recovery principle and for Weidman it was rebound theory. Their new movement concepts with a new vocabulary were developed from simple movement principles. "The very first thing I discovered was that the body's natural, instantaneous movement—its very first movement, is a falling

180

movement," Humphrey wrote.[124] It is interesting to note that throughout the years Humphrey's basic movement principle of fall and recovery has continued to be explored by contemporary choreographers. A recent review in *The New York Times* of Sally Gross and Company by Jack Anderson notes that her work *In Silence* showed five dancers sitting with their backs to the audience. "Occasionally, one or two tilted and toppled over, only to regain balance. Ms. Gross may have been reminding her audience that life abounds with unexpected falls and recoveries," Anderson writes.[125] Even today, almost fifty years after her death, choreographers use Humphrey's movement theory. Anderson's statement refers to her movement theory as having been a philosophy as well. Of course, Humphrey and Weidman shared artistic and philosophic ideas. In a lecture given at the George Eastman House, Bill T. Jones addressed questions of mortality and art by suggesting that his key to survival was based on the title for his speech: "Falling and Catching: Dancing through the Other Door." His lecture focused on the people in the survival workshops and making his dance work *Still/Here,* along with his personal journey in surviving the death of his partner Arnie Zane. During the lecture he revealed how he came to this title.

> Giving a name to a thing as I said when I began tonight's address is at once a wish and a statement of purpose. A title is often an impetuous act and it's only later that one can connect to and reflect on its source. Last week on a snowy afternoon in Lawrence, KS, in those limbo hours before going to the theatre, as I was working on this speech I realized that catching and falling harks back to my early training, some 30 years ago, in Humphrey Weidman Modern Dance technique. I can still hear my instructor shouting out "Fall and recover" or "Catch and release." Here was a technique built on an unending chain of loops, circles and arcs. Majesty, mystery and truth existed in the dynamic journey between the top of the arc and its bottom. The journey between was the essence of the dance.[126]

Charles didn't believe in utter relaxation after a falling movement, so he would always quickly rebound to standing movement after a fall.[127] Ernestine Stodelle poetically describes how movement rebound occurs: "When collapse is imminent, a self-protective mechanism goes into action . . . and a counter movement takes place in which the body springs back as if with renewed life."[128] Nona Schurman simply describes movement rebound in the Humphrey-Weidman technique as "a small pushing down and a corresponding spring back to create the bounce."[129] This bounce, or rebound was firmly established in Weidman's movement technique, starting with the first exercise in his class, the *Body Bends Series*. This rebound concept was enlarged in his *Modulation Slide Series, Forward Leg Whip Turn,* and *Hop Series*. Additionally, rebound is distinctive in his choreography as well, particularly in *Traditions, Lynchtown,* and in the men's section of *New Dance*. Schurman's description indicates a push against gravity to gather spring or resilience, while Stodelle's description indicates a counter movement with an emotional motivation. In two separate conversations with Elinor Rogosin, in 1972 and 1974, Weidman explained that rebound was not just a movement principle, but also a philosophy of life:

> At times it's very hard. Sometimes I feel sort of low, maybe because of an ailment or something like that. I can get depressed. And well, I always felt a person should be like a spring, like a coil. When you do get low down, then in the technique we have something that is quite . . . wonderful; it is the ability to rebound, to shift energy from a fall into action. Rebound is in the technique and in the attitude. To rebound and then to start all over again.[130]

In this quote Weidman describes rebound as both Schurman and Stodelle have defined it: a springing action and a dynamic shift of energy. Weidman spoke of rebound as a movement principle in his technique, but noted that one's attitude and motivation were equally important in performing the Humphrey-Weidman movement style and technique. The ability to rebound was an essential element in the temperaments of Weidman, Humphrey, and of the members of their company.

Chapter Seven

Democracy and Patriotism

(1930-1940)

After having achieved a new way of saying things in dance,
then, what should be said? We forsaw the coming of war
and danced against this.

Charles Weidman

. As a modern dancer of the twentieth century Charles Weidman's dance embodied a democratic ideal; he was a passionate artist who possessed the effort and freedom to develop an indigenous American dance. Walt Whitman could have been describing and affirming modern dance when he wrote the poem *One's-Self I Sing*. Whitman has defined himself and America in a modernistic mode by using these key words in his poem: the body ('top to toe'), democratic, and equality of gender.[1] No other decade in the history of modern dance in America expressed Whitman's sentiments as well as the 1930s.

The relevance of the works of Charles Weidman and Doris Humphrey and the content of their dances were critically significant as both reflection and catalyst of social and political change in the United States during the 1930s and 1940s. The Humphrey-Weidman works created under the Works Progress Administration's New York Dance Project and the New Dance League were specifically pertinent. Moreover, their works proved to be relevant because they expressed social issues and clearly altered dance as a theatre art.

185

Aesthetic Values and Democracy

Dance is cultural communication, the act of imparting concepts, arts, and traditions of a particular nation to others through human movement; it also reflects a specific epoch. Cultural heritage, consciously or unconsciously, plays a significant role in a dance artist's work. In her article "A Private View of Criticism," Deborah Jowitt affirms this point when she writes: "context seems crucial; dance does not exist in a vacuum, but reflects the traditions and world views of its culture and era."[2] As art, modern dance is human movement as conceived by dancers of the twentieth century. Weidman and his contemporaries intrinsically created dances from their own artistic values and were influenced by the conceptual thinking of modernism employed in visual art, music, and literature. Through individual discovery, they laid the foundation of American modern dance. The aesthetic values of modern dance can be viewed as inherent to this evolution and its individualism.

Aesthetic values, or the principles of beauty, are qualities in a work of art that elicit an internal sensation or response. In her book *Dance and the Lived Body*, Sondra Horton Fraleigh distinguishes and categorizes these aesthetic values as affective, subjective, and objective.[3] Affective values are those that excite an emotional response. In dance, affective values may be inherent in the subject matter presented or, as John Martin states, in metakinesis: "Movement . . . in and of itself is a medium for the transference of an aesthetic and emotional concept from the consciousness of one individual to that of another."[4] Subjective qualities stem from one's life experiences. In contrast, objective qualities are those that are learned as standards of evaluation of art objects. In his 1945 article "The Esthetics of Art" in *American Photography*, Frank Meister indicates, "esthetic perception of art includes the esthetic elements of appreciation, experience, intelligence, and judgment."[5] Meister's term "esthetic perception" appears to be a combination of the subjective and objective elements as defined by Fraleigh.

186

Affective, subjective, and objective aesthetic values are influenced by an individual's cultural heritage, social status, education, and a developed appreciation of the arts. To develop someone's aesthetic values in viewing dance, an appreciation of all of the fine arts may be necessary because dance employs music, visual art, drama and, in many instances, literature. An understanding of these various arts used in dance is beneficial in developing one's appreciation, experience, intelligence, and judgment, or in Meister's terms, "esthetic perception."

Modernism in dance adopts a novel vision and uses experimental methods. Dancers neither hesitate nor regret to discard old or proven doctrines.[6] Abandonment of old forms is especially evident in democratic nations where citizens, particularly artists, have "freedom of choice." Fraleigh compares my term "freedom of choice" to that of a "questioning attitude" when she writes: "All forms of modern dance emphasize discovery modalities—finding (or creating) value in dance through a questioning attitude and way of working, rather than assuming without question the already established models."[7] This democratic philosophy, inherent in modern dance, rejected the European classical ballet and Denishawn's Oriental dance. The modern dance was "not so much an outgrowth of Denishawn as a rebellion against it," John Martin writes.[8] Weidman explained it this way:

> We became a part of it because of two revolts: one was the revolt against the "eases"—by "eses," I mean we did Japanese, we did Chinese, we did Spanish, we did everything. We were very talented; we could do these things. However, when we went to Japan we didn't do the Japanese dances. Why not? Because they could do them better, simply being trained as little kids. Besides, they looked more Japanese than we did. So, therefore, thought one: why don't we have a dance which would be indigenous of [sic] this country, rough that it may be, that we might take it all over the world and say, "This is America dancing." That was the first revolution. The second was against the ballet. Ballet was out![9]

187

Another aspect of European classical ballet that modern dancers discard is ballet's codification and predetermined usage of classical steps called *enchaînements,* from French balletic vocabulary. The modern dancer does not use "cumulative resources of academic tradition," notes Martin in his *Book of the Dance.*[10] The modern dancer rejected ballet's rigid form, narrative content, and male dominance. In modern dance "women chose to be agent rather than object," Judith Lynne Hanna writes.[11] Nevertheless, ballet history has acknowledged the influence of modernism upon the ballets of the early twentieth century. Distinguished Russian ballet choreographers Michel Fokine, Vaslav Nijinsky, Bronislava Nijinska, Leonide Massine, and George Balanchine created new works called *neoclassic* ballets, such as *Les Sylphides*, *Le Sacre du Printemps*, *Les Noces, Choreoartium,* and *Apollo,* respectively. However, most early twentieth-century ballets never radically departed from the classical approach to beauty that uses the Golden Mean or a classical standard based on harmonious, proportional, geometric formations.

In defining the concept of beauty in a purely aesthetic sense, Wladyslaw Tatarkiewicz analyzed beauty as consisting in the "size, equality, and number of the parts and their interrelationships."[12] This idea, termed the Golden Mean, developed by the ancient Greek philosophers Plato and Aristotle, was contemplated through the ages by philosophers Plotinus, Thomas Aquinas, St. Augustine, sculptors Ghilberti and Alberti, and the painter Poussin. It was an objective theory of beauty, a classical standard of perception for evaluating beauty in art. In defining how the aesthetic judgement of movement was used by ballet theorist Jean-Georges Noverre and modern theorist Doris Humphrey, Wilfried A. Hofmann states: "The idea of natural beauty of movements that are well-proportioned, measured, organic, geometric—in short, harmonious—has remained uncontested since ancient times."[13] Hofmann's definition may be recognized in Weidman's dances, for example, *Brahms Waltzes* and *The*

Christmas Oratorio, and Humphrey's *Passacaglia in C Minor*. The success of these dances lies not in their expression of emotions but in the optical sensation they evoke.

The painter LeBrun established the term "expression" in the seventeenth century. The idea of beauty as the expression of emotions began in the nineteenth century through artists espousing the concepts of romanticism.[14] Ballet was specifically suited to express the subjective moods of romanticism, and received significant recognition when Théophile Gautier, one of the leading poets turned to writing ballet scenarios. One of his most successful ballet scenarios was undoubtedly *Giselle*. Numerous philosophers questioned an objective theory of beauty. British philosopher Hume argued: "Beauty is no quality in things themselves. It exists in the mind which contemplates them, and each mind perceives a different beauty."[15] As a twentieth-century philosopher analyzing the development of subjective and objective theories of beauty, Tatarkiewicz concluded that beauty was not the most important objective of art: "It is more important that a work of art should agitate people than that it should delight them with its beauty; and this . . . effect can be achieved by other means than beauty, including even ugliness."[16]

Accordingly, modernism in the dance aimed at immediacy, an idea present in a style guided totally by that idea. Margaret Gage writes that in modernism "abstract design is the first consideration rather than technical virtuosity or the projection of a dramatic emotion."[17] Hans Wiener (Jan Veen), a noted dancer with Mary Wigman and the first dance director of the Boston Conservatory, affirmed that within the "abstract, or absolute dance . . . [there] is a free development of an idea . . ."[21] As a modern dance artist of the twentieth century Weidman did not have to adhere to an objective theory of beauty upholding balance, harmony, and proportion. Weidman's choice of subject matter shows freedom from constraints in aesthetic and social values, freedom to develop ideas through new approaches to movement. The use of asymmetry or distortion to convey ideas was now becoming acceptable. Weidman (along with Humphrey) rejected the idea of balance as was shown through his use of oppositional design in direction and level, in the fall and recovery theory, and in the rebound principle, which countered the stability of balance and harmony. Weidman's style developed the foundations for indigenous American dance.

Modernism

The look or style of modern dance varies with each decade of the twentieth century. Modernism is a word demonstrating evolving aesthetic values inherent in all the fine arts, each medium juxtaposed. A search for the origins and a definition of modernism in the arts will lend a greater understanding of these influences upon Weidman's artistic development as a twentieth-century dancer; more important, it will offer larger scope in understanding emerging and changing trends in the aesthetics of dance in America between 1890 and 1930.

Speaking about the dance in the late 1920s, Weidman said: "We wanted to do something that would be of the world today, modern."[19] When one referred to the new American dance of the fourth decade of the twentieth century, it was simply termed "modern dance." The term "modern" itself means of the present time, and characterizes a type of dance performed during the past one hundred years in America. Changing with each decade, modern dance exhibited modernistic or contemporary trends. During the 1960s, "postmodern dance" emerged, referring to dance that evolved after the classic modern style conceived by the likes of Graham, Humphrey, and Weidman. In his *Book of the Dance*, Martin writes about what makes modern dance contemporary: "[Modern dance] is not interested in spectacle, but in the communication of emotional experiences—intuitive perceptions, elusive truths—which cannot be communicated in reasoned terms or reduced to mere statement of fact."[20]

190

Martin's statement emphasizes that modern dance rejected the concept of spectacle, which has been a significant objective of classical ballet productions since the first ballet, *Ballet Comique de la Reine,* in 1581. Furthermore, Martin stresses that what modern American dancers wanted to express in their dances was their experiences living in a modern democratic society. Julia Foulkes agrees with Martin's premise when she writes: "In their attempt to reconfigure modernism to be both confrontational and participatory, authorial and populist, modern dancers' greatest successes were in dances of America where they put forth this participatory theatrical process as an enactment of democracy."[21] In his essay *Artists and Audiences*, Charles Weidman sets forth tenets about being a modern artist.

> "Modern"—What does this word mean? The dictionary defines it as pertaining to the present time, but it is not enough to be merely existing in the contemporary world. Active life demands that we be mentally and emotionally aware of the world's continual change and realize the constant progressions and retrogressions.
>
> The artist who attempts to escape the present, either by delving into the past or the future, is running away from his center of being. But it is not enough for the artist alone to assume his responsibilities as mentor and preceptor. His audience also must do so, especially in the case of an artistic form which concerns the theatre.
>
> The concert dance lives only while it is being presented. It cannot be referred to later in files or books. Therefore, both the stage and auditorium have equal importance. Those who sit in the "house" must be of today. They also must be conscious of and sensitive to their age, for only then will the dance-work come alive and project its full meaning and value as the artist wished.
>
> Modernism in the dance requires that we, both artist and audience, be not blind to the life that summons us, nor shut ourselves off from it into fantasy and romance. It demands that we be part of it and merge with it. It calls upon us as artists to become mouthpieces for its expression; to cease being static and self-satisfied; to be ready each year to say new things and say them in new ways; to keep our mode of expression fresh and vital; and to remove the dance from pleasant entertainment that lulls

us into vague nostalgia, to a strong living art that touches us powerfully as we are today.[22]

Dance reflects the philosophy of its era. Noted critic John Martin writes: "True modernism in dance, as in the other arts, can never be reduced to a formula; it is basically an approach to art in its relation to living, a point of view."[23] The individual point of view or philosophy of dancers in the twentieth century, expressed through original movement, developed the underlying principles of modern dance through its technique and aesthetics.[24] The impetus and momentum of modern dance is its democratic philosophy; considering and treating others as one's equals, nurtures individualism and social consciousness, encouraging singularity of expression and unprejudiced acceptance of differences of expression.[25] In her book *Dance and the Lived Body*, Fraleigh suggests "modern dance forms develop through courageous individual discoveries,"[26] and by practicing one's own free will "the existential context of modern dance appears in its emphasis on the importance of the individual and the principle of creativity."[27] Considering its democratic philosophy, modern dance is expansive and highly individual in approach. Edward Mathews, in his article "Applied Modernism," suggests that "no one word expresses it quite as well as freedom."[28] In his article "The Limits of Modernism in Arts," Ralph Adams Cram supports a democratic philosophy in modern dance and recommends rejecting the standards and methods of the past "to invent something that is altogether new and therefore consonant of the time."[29] Rejecting the past, Weidman and Humphrey create dances that reflect their patriotism or loyal support of their country and its democratic philosophy.

Doris Humphrey, born in 1895 in Oak Park, Illinois, attended the Francis W. Parker School, a school based on the educational reforms of Francis W. Parker

192

and John Dewey. The school was seen as a model democracy, a place where children would learn self-control and self-government, where a spirit of adventure and self-discovery was encouraged. She was taught by extraordinary educators at the school, including Mary Wood Hinman who gave dancing lessons. Humphrey and her peers in the class of 1913 were the first pupils to attend the school from kindergarten through high-school graduation. The Francis W. Parker School and its democratic ideals influenced Humphrey's philosophy of life and her artistic career. After completing a pedagogy course with Mary Wood Hinman by 1914 she was teaching interpretive dancing and ballet.

Humphrey, at Hinman's suggestion, went to study at the Denishawn School in Los Angeles in 1917, where she met Pauline Lawrence. Three years later, Charles Weidman went to study with Ted Shawn and Ruth St. Denis; there he met Humphrey, his first teacher at the Denishawn School, and Lawrence. At Denishawn, Weidman and Humphrey sharpened their theatrical craft while Lawrence absorbed the skills needed to manage a dance company. After their break from Denishawn in 1928, Lawrence played a critical role in the development of the Humphrey-Weidman School. The three collaborators launched the Humphrey-Weidman Group to the forefront of the theatre dance scene at a perilous time in American history, as José Limón remembers: "Doris and Charles were whistling in the dark, so to speak, to keep up their spirits and courage. Things were going from bad to worse in the country. The unreal world of politics, senseless and strident, would impinge crudely on our minuscule universe."[30]

With the American stock market crash in 1929 leading to the Great Depression, the only "silver lining" was the election of Franklin Delano Roosevelt as the thirty-second President of the United States. At the time of his inauguration in 1932, most banks were closed, approximately 13 million people were jobless, and hundreds of thousands were homeless. Representing this insecure time, a new artistic work, the Ernest Bloch *String Quartet*, premiered on April 23, 1931, at the Library of Congress in Washington, D.C. Conceived by Irene Lewisohn, this work was choreographed by Humphrey and Weidman. Limón describes this dramatic work:

> Simply stated, the plot concerned a woman, Doris Humphrey, lost in a strange and forbidding landscape represented by an arrangement of steps and platforms that gradually ascended to the rim of a yawning crater. A chorus of robot-like dancers, representing the protagonist's confusions, frustrations, and torments, sought to draw her into the abyss. Charles appeared, and together, they found the courage and unity to triumph over the darkness of the pit.[31]

The New Deal

Representing the fears that all Americans faced, Weidman and Humphrey's work *String Quartet* showed how courage and unity were needed to triumph over this period of economic distress. President Roosevelt implemented his New Deal that offered two work programs for the unemployed: the Civilian Conservation Corps and the Works Progress Administration. In his article "Can Patriotism be legislated?" Daniel J. Boorstin describes these two programs:

> The Civilian Conservation Corps (March 31, 1933) for men 18 to 25 was primarily a program for unemployment and family relief. Jobless young men received room and board and medical care plus a $30 cash monthly allowance, $25 of which was sent to their families. By 1941 almost 2 million had been employed. They added 17 million acres of new forest land, fought forest fires, and plant diseases, stocked hatcheries with over a billion fish, built 6 million check dams to halt erosion and refurbished the national parks.
>
> The Works Progress Administration, created in 1935, produced substantial and enduring benefits. While employing more than 8 million jobless, it left a rich legacy in literature, music, the theatre and the arts, and provided

194

us with guidebooks to the American historic landscape that are still unexcelled.[32]

Late in the summer of 1935, four arts projects (Dance, Music, Theatre, Visual) were set up as a work relief program to employ thousands of actors, choreographers, dancers, musicians, visual artists, and writers, including technical staffs. Dance became an important part of the Federal Theatre that was headed by Hallie Flannagan. She told the editor of the *Federal Theatre Magazine* Tony Buttitta: "We have a raft of dancers and choreographers. Do a piece on how the dance is coming back to the theatre."[33] Buttitta set to work on the assignment.

> I rode all over Manhattan interviewing project choreographers. Charles Weidman spoke of his plans for *Candide* which was set to the music of Wallingford Riegger. Felicia Sorell was creating a dance production to Albert Rousell's *Suite in F*. Tamiris led her young group through a spirited performance of Whitman's *Salut au Monde*. Gluck Sandor was using the Prokofieff music for his new work, *The Eternal Prodigal*. Don Oscar Becque, head of the dance unit, was preparing *Young Tramps*, youths on the roads of America, to a new score by Donald Pond.[34]

In 1936, under the direction of Don Oscar Becque, the New York Dance Project was given federal money that paid choreographers and dancers a rehearsal salary to mount dance concerts. Historic works were composed and produced: Weidman's *Candide*, Tamiris' *How Long, Brethren?* Humphrey's *Prelude and Celebration* and *Parade*; the theme of this patriotic work was the reaction of a crowd to a passing parade.[35]

Candide and *How Long, Brethren?* shared the bill for an extended run at the Nora Bayes Theatre. *How Long, Brethren?* was performed with choral and orchestral accompaniment and "presented a full theatrical story of the plight of African Americans in the United States," Julia Foulkes wrote.[36] Weidman's 1937 interpretation of Voltaire's *Candide* was a condensed version of the production he presented in 1933. With a new musical score by Wallingford Riegger, fresh costumes, and Charles in the title role, it was destined to be a hit, as Lillian Moore confirmed: "The very absurdity of the tale made it particularly adaptable to Weidman's brand of satirical wit and caustic comment. His comedy has a certain spicy bitterness about it; it is at the opposite end of the scale from the wistful Chaplineque humor of America's other talented dance-mime, Agnes de Mille."[37] The Federal Dance Project brought dance to the public free of charge or at a minimal cost. This served a dual purpose: education of the public about dance through classes and lecture-demonstrations, and the development of a choreographic art form that focused greater public attention on modern dance.

During the 1930s radical political and social turbulence produced circumstances in which modern dance became the reflection of American social consciousness, as Olga Maynard writes: "Becoming the dance of angry protests, dancers eager to find a 'cause' sought the ills of the period, and these included the Nazi, Fascist, anti-Semitic, anti-Negro, anti-labors factions."[38] Some dancers used political fervor to forward their art; some used their dance to forward social reform.

As an expression of political unrest, picketing was used as a vehicle for social change. Weidman and Humphrey were not aligned with the left-wing group Workers Dance League, who performed at Labor Union meetings, rallying support for an eight-hour day, portal-to-portal pay (wages for workers based on the time entering a factory until leaving it), and health insurance. However, Weidman and Humphrey gave many benefit performances. In 1937, the Humphrey-Weidman Company (Beatrice Seckler and Nona Schurman were company members at this time) danced Weidman's *Quest* and Humphrey's *With My Red Fires* for over 5,000 people at the New York Hippodrome; the proceeds went to the International Labor Defense Fund.

Humphrey helped to start the Concert Dancers League in 1931. It was the first activist group in the field, formed by a majority of New York's prominent dancers, with the objectives of protection and advancement of their art. The Concert Dancers League spent two years fighting for an amendment to the Blue Law, an antiquated law passed in 1879 that forbade entertainment performances on Sundays. Through their efforts, Governor Franklin D. Roosevelt signed a bill permitting dance recitals in theatres on Sunday evening. This event made it possible for Humphrey, Weidman, and others to present new works to the public on the only day that Broadway theatres were available. "It is simply the case of classifying the dance recital as a concert instead of a theatrical performance," Elsa Findlay, the Secretary of the Concert Dancers League wrote."[39]

The New Dance League was formed in 1935 as a national dance organization. A Humphrey-Weidman Group program stated the New Dance League was for dancers who support "a mass development of the American dance to its highest artistic and social level; for a dance movement dedicated to the struggle against war, fascism and censorship."[40] In May 1936, *Men in The Dance* was produced to benefit the New Dance League. The program notes state: "It marks the definite recognition of men as an important factor in the contemporary dance, and unites these artists under the banner of two organizations [Humphrey-Weidman and New Dance League] whose basic program is against War, Fascism, and Censorship."[41] Weidman, José Limón, William Matons, and other male dancers performed works including Weidman's *Affirmations*, *Kinetic Pantomime,* and *Traditions*.

Traditions

Traditions, a men's trio created in 1935, was an example of non-representational pantomime. Weidman invented a work altogether new and relevant to this patriotic time. He collaborated with the talented, young Lehman

197

Engel who composed the score. Engel studied at Juilliard; during the 1930s he wrote scores for many modern dance choreographers including Graham and Gluck-Sandor. According to Limón, Engel wrote a rhythmic percussion score "full of wit, irony and sarcasm" for Weidman's *Traditions*.[42] In *Traditions* three figures, (Weidman, Limón and William Matons, later replaced by George Bockman) were symbolic of three distinctly different characters. They were mired down in the same traditions represented by a recurring movement theme of "elaborate manipulations of the upper body, arms, hands, and head. The feet were planted in a wide stance firmly in place. 'Here we have stood,' they implied, 'and here we stay,'" as Limón writes.[43] The first man breaks away with a new theme and incites the second man to join him. The third man, danced by Weidman, clings to the traditions until "slowly he sank to the floor . . . and expired with one last feeble flourish of an aristocratic hand." This part always delighted audiences, creating much laughter. A bizarre funeral scene followed, where the traditions are without a doubt, part of the past. Unexpectedly, the traditions begin a gradual revival "imbued with new energy and direction," to meet the challenge of the future.[44] *Traditions* was a serious work from the hand of a master of comedy. Weidman created it at a time when all American institutions faced crisis. In the dance, Limón notes Weidman's final statement symbolized that this revolutionary surge of the 1930s was upon the three men, or universally everyone, with its command, "Change, or be changed."[45]

The classification of Weidman's dances by critics and historians as only theatrical satire with ironic humor has limited the knowledge of a generation of aspiring dancers of his superbly structured abstract dances. Even Martin errs in categorizing *Traditions* as a *kinetic pantomime*: "In spite of the fact that it deals in pantomime, not a single movement from beginning to end bears any connotation of representationalism. It is non-representational pantomime, or better, kinetic pantomime."[46] In this review Martin labeled Weidman's unique manner of gesticulating in thematic movement as non-representational pantomime, and suggests Weidman abstracted the motions of these gestures.

In *Traditions* the trio, stabilized on a diagonal plane, legs widely separated, began in unison with a characteristic Weidman shift of weight and rebound. The presentation of movement included fundamental motions that epitomize Weidman style: a circling arm gesture right and left moving into a variation from the *Body Bend Series,* which segues into four sharp hand gestures that appear to be grasping; then the trio turn to greet each other with a gesture of hitting the heels of the hands together while the body bends in a forward direction.[47] These hand gestures could be seen as pantomimic, but the work conveys its idea through abstraction. Weidman used his characteristic claw hand movement that also appears in the Opening Dance of *Opus 51;* Weidman used it again in his last group work, *Saint Matthew Passion.*

A clearly distinctive Humphrey-Weidman compositional trait developed during this period was to present, at the start of a composition, a movement theme, then, develop the dance with movement variations from this original movement theme. This method was used in *Traditions,* when one dancer disrupted the unity of the theme and urged another to interrupt the repeated movement, leaving a single dancer to defiantly repeat the theme. This device effectively portrays human resistance to departing from established traditional values, and the inherent need for individuals to explore other possibilities—even if this eventually means returning undaunted to the established or traditional values.

The Democratization of Dance

A democratic philosophy nurturing individualism and social consciousness spurred Weidman and Humphrey to explore an ideal harmonious relationship between men and women through abstract dance. Their duet *Duo-*

Drama premiered on Sunday evening, January 6, 1935, at the Guild Theatre; it was their first New York performance without their company. Although Henry Gilford's review in *The Dance Observer* claimed their pre-intermission dances were mediocre, he approved of their final dance: "With the startling *Duo-Drama* . . . Doris Humphrey and Charles Weidman made significant contribution to the development of dance in America."[48] John Martin's comments in *The New York Times* noted his approval of their "program, which except for its feature number, was of great distinction."[49] In total contrast, Joseph Arnold's critique in *The American Dancer* stated "the dances which Mr. Martin praises so enthusiastically were ninety percent sheer tripe, and a deadly bore . . ."[50] The work that both Martin and Arnold agreed upon unfavorably was *Duo-Drama*, arranged to a Concerto for String Quartet, Clarinet, and Piano by Roy Harris. Martin blamed the failure of the dance on the music: "This is music, which, with all due respect, does not belong in the theatre. It is entirely unchoreographic and evocative in no way of movement. Though Miss Humphrey and Mr. Weidman have apparently worked diligently over it, it has defeated them."[51] Their accompanists were Vivian Fine and Harry Cumpson at the piano, Simeon Bellinson, clarinet, and the Gordon String Quartet. Gilford's observation was dissimilar: "*Duo-Drama* . . . in basic rhythms, moved dynamically through three movements in changing colors and patterns, posing questions, answering them, and challenging new directions for the dance."[52] Arnold thought all of the works "were trite in conception, meaningless in rendition and generally sophomoric."[53] To emphasize his point, Arnold took the liberty of printing the program notes sent confidentially to reviewers.

> *Duo-Drama*—represents in abstract form the struggle for supremacy between man and woman. The opening *Fantasia* pictures the two moving harmoniously together, absorbed in the joy of rhythmic effort. Gradually the greater vitality and daring of the man carry him beyond the reach of

the woman, resulting in the first break in their unity. The *Scherzo* finds the woman developing her own individual expression and attempting to fit into the man's original pattern, which he has resumed. Failing in this, there is a complete break between the two and the man is left alone to dream of a woman nearer his heart's desire. She appears as the incarnation of his dream, romantic and fragile, then disappears, leaving him alone as before. In the last movement the woman reappears, sure of her own identity. The struggle for supremacy is repeated, followed by an eventual understanding and harmony.[54]

Arnold was referring to the pretentiousness of their entire program but particularily to *Duo-Drama* when he wrote: "Miss Humphrey is married and has a baby, and Mr. Weidman is a grown man, but both have not yet lost their wonder at the facts of life."[55] What in the subject matter of *Duo-Drama* could have provoked Arnold to comment unethically about their personal lives? In a conversation with Nona Schurman about the content of *Duo-Drama*, she said she thought that Weidman and Humphrey were asking themselves a question about how they could say something serious about this time in history.[56] In *Duo-Drama*, Humphrey and Weidman showed their desire for harmony in society—starting at the base—a harmonious relationship between a man and a woman.

New reforms concerning the issue of equality for women are certainly topical in 1935 and still have relevance in today's world. Was Arnold warning Humphrey and Weidman about the inappropriateness of this type of sociopolitical subject matter in the theatre? He reprimanded Weidman about being a "grown man." Did he imply "don't let Humphrey dictate to you?" He indicated that Humphrey should have been emotionally mature since she was "married with a baby."[57] Arnold's motive in his review seems to be to discredit their artistry and consequently undermines their significance as harbingers of new American dance. Henry Gilford disputed Arnold's opinion in his review:

201

Duo-Drama occupied the stage for thirty minutes; it took up completely the second half of the program. The time element alone sufficiently ambitious and inspiring, certainly it is a significant note in the history of the dance when without the aid of scenery, without the artificial sustenance of story (as of literature), without the insipid interpreting of music, two dancers create composition, drama, dance of proportions approaching epic. *Duo-Drama* is a broad conception, a brave one, and it is excellently and courageously presented.[58]

Gilford recognized both their craft and their significance in the development of the history of dance. Humphrey and Weidman choose to express relevant social issues in their artistic works. Through their efforts they advanced dance as a theatre art. *Duo-Drama* provoked one critic to a prejudiced response to their work. Arnold seems biassed about Weidman's dance in writing: "This writer always had a high opinion of Mr. Weidman. It seemed to him that this dancer combined the authentic spirit of the dance with a theatricalism which found an agreeable expression in irony and burlesque."[59] In the years following Weidman would disprove Arnold's definition of his dance.

Surely Weidman and Humphrey's democratic philosophy embedded in their dance and their rejection of past standards played a role in their motivation for composing *Duo-Drama*. The struggle for supremacy between a man and a woman presented in their work offered a universal social comment. In America it was time for men and women to become equal partners in society. Only fifteen years before, in 1920, women in America had won the right to vote. In *Duo-Drama,* Humphrey and Weidman present a "dream woman," romantic and fragile, a nineteenth-century image of woman. They also present their image of woman in contemporary times, courageous and self-reliant, sure of her identity, as well as a contemporary man's unprejudiced acceptance of her identity, thus creating a harmonious relationship. The contrary opinion of these three critics—Martin,

Arnold and Gilford—illustrates conflicting public opinion regarding this topical issue.

At Bennington College in the summer of 1935, Humphrey and Weidman premiered six segments of *New Dance*, their masterpiece of symphonic, abstract dance. On October 27 at the Guild Theatre in New York, "Variations and Conclusions" to *New Dance* was premiered, completing the work. *New Dance*, performed to a piano and percussion score by Wallingford Riegger, integrated the philosophic, choreographic, and theatrical concepts that Humphrey, Weidman, and Lawrence developed during their first collaborative years. *New Dance* used ten screens (18 feet high and 5 feet wide) that could be made into flats, wings, towers, platforms, or a cyclorama, and a set of various large cubes designed by Erika Klein.[60] This design concept was influenced by modern art and became a Humphrey-Weidman trademark. In *New Dance*, the traditional Humphrey-Weidman compositional elements, such as theme-and-variations form, succession, opposition, and ground bass, were so rhythmically and successfully employed that pure form became an emotional experience for the observer. Their intent was to compose a work reiterating the theme of a noble and harmonious society. In the mid-1970s, Weidman restaged this masterwork at the American Dance Festival. Documented on film, notes on this archival videotape describe the work.

> *New Dance*—A choreographically symphonic ballet that represents a world where each person has a clear and harmonious relationship to his fellow beings. To achieve this, the leaders gradually mold and unify the group in a series of stages or "themes." The triumphant and joyous ending, "Variations and Conclusions," depicts an ideal society that allows for individual expression within group unity. The parts of the dance are titled: "Prelude," "First Theme," "Second Theme," "Third Theme," "Processional," "Celebration," and "Variations and Conclusions."[61]

Weidman and Humphrey's vision of an ideal society they had portrayed in *New Dance* was their appeal for harmony in the world. Their struggle to thrive in the turmoil of the 1930s was further acerbated by limited funding for the Federal Theatre Project.

A dramatic "sit-in" occurred in May 1937 at the Nora Bayes Theatre in New York City after the Federal Dance Theatre's performance of Weidman's *Candide* and Tamiris' *How Long, Brethren?* This protest, led by Weidman, was against "the order to fire one third of the personnel of the Federal Theatre Project because of cut backs by the United States Congress . . . The *New York Post* newspaper called it the first sit-in strike in the history of the American Theatre."[62] When the Spanish Civil War began in 1936 there were protests against fascism, and the American people financially subsidized the Lincoln Brigade to fight against fascism in Spain. Modern dance choreographers played a significant role in this movement.

A special performance *Dances for Spain* was presented on May 23, 1937, at the Adelphi Theatre in New York by the American Dance Association for the Medical Committee to Aid Spanish Democracy. Helen Tamiris, Sophia Delza, Ruthanna Boris, Anna Sokolow, and others presented dances titled *We Weep for Spain* (Delza), *Impressions of the Bull Ring* (Tamiris), and *A War Poem* (Sokolow).[63] In response to the Spanish Civil War Martha Graham composed *Immediate Tragedy* (1937) and *Deep Song* (1937). A year before Graham had premiered her work *Chronicle* at the Guild Theatre on December 20, 1936. *Chronicle* was Graham's artistic reaction to the malevolence of fascism in Europe. With a score by Wallingford Riegger, Graham's *Chronicle* showed the all-embracing tragedy of war; concluding with a plea for harmony and unity.[64] Three sections of the original forty-minute dance were reconstructed and performed by the Martha Graham Dance Company in their 2005 Season at New York City Center: "Spectre—1914" (Drums—Red Shroud—Lament); "Steps in the Street" (Devastation—Homeless—Exile); and "Prelude to Action" (Unity—Pledge to the Future).[65]

As the Spanish Civil War ended in 1939, the Second World War began in Europe. With the bombing of Pearl Harbor by the Japanese in 1941, the United States entered the war. In July 1942, soldier Harry Cable, a former dancer with the Ted Shawn Men's Group and the Humphrey-Weidman Group, wrote a letter to *Dance Magazine* that summarized this dancer's patriotism and the stance of dancers in general in the decade of 1930 to 1940. "The dancer in order to function during the past decade has had to face facts and say something about them. And no vague generalities either; topical, up-to-date facts. It is well within my memory that dancers walked in picketlines or signed petitions and participated in demonstrations to get what they wanted."[66] Indeed Humphrey and Weidman did not express "vague generalities" in their works but depicted topical issues. One of their overriding concerns was their desire for harmony in every facet of society. The content of their works was critically important as both reflection and catalyst of social and political change in the United States during the decade 1930 to 1940—a decade focused on patriotism and democracy.

Quest: A Choreographic Pantomime

At the Bennington Dance Festival in 1936, Weidman presented *Quest*, a semi-autobiographical work to a musical score by Norman Lloyd. It was the first composition to use a large group of men dancers—the cast included eleven men and fifteen women. These dancers represented an artist's obstacles as he struggled to to have his creative work accepted by society. Produced at the Vermont State Armory, Weidman's *Quest* had four main parts: "Prelude," "Kulturreinigung," "Pro Patria," and "Affirmations." As was characteristic of Weidman's work, he combined "satirical spoofing with serious purpose in an Artist's Progress over the rough road to real fruition and . . . recognition,"

Margaret Lloyd writes.[67] As he danced the "artist" with Humphrey as his "inner spirit," Weidman presented his struggles as an artist during a decade of political and social unrest. Weidman depicts his artistic journey through this decade in several scenes: searching for interpretation and recognition from the critics; seeking financial support from wealthy patrons; attempting to create art under a dictatorship; using art to overcome the evils of war; and the artist discovering a strength of purpose by understanding the responses of others to his work.[68] Along his artistic journey, Weidman was accompanied by his partner, Humphrey, who continued to be his inner strength for the next ten years. Lillian Moore describes *Quest* and Weidman's duets with Humphrey: "His experiences with patronage, dictatorship, and false patriotism offer opportunities for witty satire, while the interludes in which he receives reassurance from his inner self, personified by Doris Humphrey, are full of conviction and a certain quiet strength."[69]

In one scene the protagonist (Charles) "confronts a pyramid of haughty dowagers who end up using him as an ashtray for their cigarette butts," writes Limón.[70] In a section of *Quest* called "Transitions," Charles used the men—led by his three principal dancers: Limón, William Bales, and William Matons—to express his inner emotions "by falling, whirling, leaping, like so many tossing thoughts."[71] In another scene the artist is "forced to a crudely humorous inquisition by grim, uniformed Fascists, who dissect, weigh, measure, and probe his mind and body, leaving him, so to speak, in pieces, rejected as a 'non-Aryan,'" summarizes Limón.[72]

Throughout his early career Weidman struggled with the complexities of his relationship with women. As a lone man in a field dominated by females Weidman was the subject of the affections of many young women. In *Quest*, Weidman portrayed the artist in a scene where the men presented a woman (literally held up before him) "but he will have none of her until he realizes that she stands as co-worker, for the platonic relationship, not romance," interprets

Lloyd.[73] Could this scene be representative of his relationship with Humphrey? In numerous photographs they were pictured walking together at Bennington College, or dancing together; these captured their intense physical and spiritual bond. There were hints of romance as they first met during Denishawn's Asian tour; they also lived together (along with Pauline and José); and the first summer at Bennington, Humphrey admitted that all the girls were in love with the tall, handsome, young man with the dark eyes, and she thought everyone assumed they were lovers. This romantic period was severed when Humphrey married Charles Woodford in 1932. At that time, Weidman considered departing, but Humphrey assured him that their artistic work together was more important. So he stayed, knowing there was no chance to rekindle romance; instead he fostered her friendship and their artistic relationship.

In the next section of *Quest* a group of dancers represents the critics. With notepads and typewriters in hand (mimed), the critics watch Charles dancing. They are arrogant. They lack the power to perceive the meaning of Charles' dance and they tire from its dullness. In Charles' experience as an artist, critical opinion greatly affected his success. He became, as Lloyd wrote, "distressed by the literal-mindedness that would measure him in scales, and cut him to pattern with scissors."[74] In *Quest*, Charles was making a direct statement regarding the misunderstanding of his art by critics, including the reviews by Broadway critics of his first production of *Candide*. Joseph Arnold's callous review of *Duo-Drama* predicted Weidman and Humphrey's future demise when he wrote: "As two representative modern dancers, Miss Humphrey and Mr. Weidman are losing themselves in the fantastic labyrinth which modern dancing has erected. The sad thought—sad for the dancers, comforting for us—is that the structure is built of the thinnest material. It does not require much to blow it down. Only the support of deluded critics and parlor intellectuals have enabled it to survive to this time."[75]

Arnold's view is that Weidman and Humphrey were creating from an imaginary and isolated perspective and even encouraged by "deluded" critics and "parlor intellectuals." Paul Love's program note for *Quest* refutes Arnold's opinion: "The artist goes forth and calls others. He knows finally that the artist cannot live in an ivory tower, aloof from the masses of mankind. He is an integral part of the masses and must make that known."[76] In the last section of *Quest*, Weidman composed "a grand finale of affirmation, the artist has found himself in finding the way to the understanding response of his fellows," Lloyd writes.[77]

Atavisms: Bargain Counter, Stock Exchange, Lynchtown

Weidman's works continued to show his concern for social injustice. Interestingly, his works created during this period are perhaps equally pertinent today—particularly *Atavisms,* created in 1936. The sections of the suite are actually three separate dances depicting three situations: "Bargain Counter," "Stock Exchange," and "Lynchtown." All comment on atavism or a reversion to remote ancestral characteristics.

As a humorist, Weidman would weave a satiric tale of the typical day of a salesman in a bargain basement into a critical commentary on coveting for material wealth. In "Bargain Counter," an onset of crazed women shoppers collided with Charles, the frazzled store manager (floor-walker), exasperated with the "onrush of modern maenads."[78] Vivian Fine's notes in her piano scores for *Bargain Counter* give us an idea of Weidman's compositional structure for his work and his imaginative titles for each section:

Bargain Counter
Piano—4/4
Entrance—7/4
The Blues—Mixed Meter
Pumble—8/4

Luscious Theme—8/4
Pile Up—8/4
Roxy Chorus Line—6/4
Indian Wrestling—4/4
Football "Hike" Then Jump—4/4
Glissando—To Curtain [79]

In "Stock Exchange" Weidman exaggerated the daily activities of a businessman, showing his dependence on others for his success. On the stock market crash, he "strives to save himself at the expense of everybody else, leaving prostrate bodies in his wake . . . he collapses, sunk in his own helplessness," wrote Lloyd.[80] Weidman presented "Stock Exchange" on December 15, 1935, at Carnegie Hall in a concert presented by the Committee on Cultural Activities, International Labor Defense. Weidman's group members performing in *Stock Exchange* were: José Limón, William Matons, Kenneth Bostock, George Bockman, Morris Bakst, Jerry Davidson, Maurice Zilbert, Lee Sherman, Harry Cable, William Bales, Ezra Friedman, Gene Oliver and Joseph Belsky.[81] In his review in *The Dance Observer*, Henry Gilford described "Stock Exchange" thus:

> Using white wire props for chairs, coat tails, etc, and occasionally upsetting the props in movement, Charles Weidman (and his group of men) offer a rather comic version of what we take was the 1929 Wall Street Crash. The choreography depicts a "dog eat dog" exchange which is climaxed with the dog finally eating itself. Some good movement, some extremely comic design, and some exceedingly funny gesture and pantomime, the composition drags a bit, will undoubtedly be tightened; but such atavisms are deserving of more pungent satire.[82]

The satiric became grotesque in "Lynchtown," a dance documentary of a lynching in which the townsfolk "respond not with horror but with excitement, curiosity, eagerness, even pleasure."[83] One of Weidman's best-known dances, "Lynchtown" depicts a lynching, progressing from the townspeople's accusations, through murder, to the dragging off of the body. "Lynchtown" came into being at a time in American history when a person could be persecuted, or hanged to death, by mob action. Supposedly, as a young man Weidman witnessed a lynching in Omaha, Nebraska. When Charles created "Lynchtown" in 1936 such horrific events were common in the American South. The effect of the piece, as critic Walter Terry puts it, "was to attack the complacency of those who sit in the safety of the theatre."[84] "Lynchtown" was a reflection not just of the culture of the time but of American social consciousness as well. Lehman Engel's notes in his musical score reflect Weidman's compositional structure:

"Lynchtown"
Score for B^b Clarinet, High and Low Tom Drums, Gong
4/4—Boys entrance after 22 measures
First Duet, First Variation
Second Duet, Second Variation
Third Duet, Third Variation
Boys Second Entrance
Girls Stagger [85]

During the summers of 1936 and 1937, Limón, Weidman's leading dancer, along with Anna Sokolow and Ester Junger, received a choreographic fellowship to the Bennington School of Dance. Both Sokolow and Junger used large casts of women for their new dances. Limón selected six women and four men for his new work *Danza de la Muerte*. In the spring of 1938, Martha Graham invited Limón to dance in her new dance (*American Document*) that she was planning to present that summer at Bennington. Graham's offer was appealing to Limón; he asked Doris and Charles for guidance in making his decision. They said the choice was up to him. Limón thought: "One does not abandon one's loyalties no matter what. One does not live for gain, but for belief.

210

I owe Doris and Charles a debt. This obligation was concocted of archaic notions having to do with loyalty and honor."[86] Limón declined Martha's offer; subsequently that summer at Bennington Erick Hawkins became her partner and husband.

Opus 51

In the summer of 1938, at the Bennington Dance Festival, both Weidman and Humphrey presented new works: *Opus 51* and *Passacaglia in C Minor*, respectively. Completely opposite to Humphrey's stately, formal *Passacaglia* was Weidman's "mirthful and zany" *Opus 51*. "Idiom and bromidiom," wrote Margaret Lloyd, "it was Charles all over."[87] In the process of creating this dance, Charles was searching for a title for his new work. After he showed the work to Doris, they discussed a title. She asked him how many dances he had made so far, and he made a quick list—fifty, he noted. So she said, call it *Opus 51*. So he did.

Opus 51 was set to an inventive score composed by Vivian Fine. The six sections of the work were fairly nondescriptive: "Opening Dance," "March," "Comedia," "Solo," "Duet," and "Spectacle." Pauline Lawrence's costume designs for the work were in shades of green; Charles wore pants with a modified doublet trimmed in a lighter shade; the other men wore modified doublets with tights, while the women wore short (mid-thigh) dresses with an ankle-length, layered overskirts that they took off during the *kinetic pantomime* sections. "The work began with deceptive formality but soon burst into the maddest, merriest prank of all the Weidman years," Lloyd writes.[88] Charles used wooden blocks to set the scene. These blocks were about three-feet high, stacked one on top of another. They were precariously high for the dancers to move onto and off within the work. According to Lloyd, Weidman "tossed about queer, disconnected oddments of motion or gesture that almost told you something and then darted off

211

on another tangent."[89] In *Opus 51*, Charles increased the scope of the kinetic or nonrepresentational pantomime he explored in his 1934 dance *Kinetic Pantomime*. Lloyd describes Weidman's unique manner of inserting functional gestures into abstract humor: "There was hoeing and weeding at the farm, sewing costumes, stumbling over an obstacle that wasn't there, taking a shower, sweeping a floor, and a bit of hair-pulling that could be anybody's quarrel but wasn't. Flashes of camp meeting, circus, gymnasium stunts, acrobatics, were jumbled in with personal touches."[90] It was as if Charles had taken a silent movie and quickened the tempo of the scene two or three times faster. Lloyd was in the audience for its premiere at the Vermont State Armory, and she noted that the "dance was quicker than the eye and nobody could catch it all at once."[91] Charles acted as a master of ceremonies presiding over the zany proceedings. Noted performances in *Opus 51* were given by company members Harriette Ann Gray, Katherine Litz, Beatrice Seckler, George Bockman, William Bales, Lee Sherman, Eleanor Frampton, and Pauline Chellis.

Limón observed that *Opus 51* was on the cutting edge of Dadaism in dance. Marcel Duchamp, the early twentieth-century French painter and founder of the protest movement in art called Dadaism (c. 1916-22), preached non-sense and anti-art.[92] Limón thought the way Charles selected his title for *Opus 51* was just the perfect start for his Dadaist work.

> It was a work of delightful invention, the grandfather, I think, of Dadaism in the dance in this country. It was concocted from a species of nonrepresentational doodling. Things had a charmingly unexpected way of coming out of nothing and going nowhere, and exploding in-between into brilliant fragments of pure nonsense. His mastery of wit, irony, and slapstick were given full rein . . . The work had been composed and rehearsed with scrupulous care, yet it had the saucy spontaneity of an improvisation—an early "happening." Charles used an impressive range of gesture, movement, and dynamics. Nothing meant anything, and it was all explosively funny.[93]

The sixth annual session of the Bennington School of the Dance was held on July 1 through August 11, 1939 at Mills College in Oakland, California. Guided by both Weidman and Humphrey, Limón received a choreographic fellowship, where he presented his first major dance composition *Danzas Mexicanas* to music by Lionel Nowak. The 1939 summer dance festival concluded with a demonstration program of the techniques of modern dance given by Weidman, Humphrey, Graham, and Holm. Weidman began his demonstration with a remarkable leap study and led his dancers through a series of exercises for hops, jumps, leaps, turns, and falls. Humphrey gave her impressions of the program: "Martha was the first with something that looked very much like *American Document*, only gayer and more lyric. No more hard angles or glum faces. They smile, they run, they skip and leap. How these gals do change. Hanya too—I must say we're the only ones who appear to have made up our minds about dancing once and for all, as to theory, movement, style, focus, everything." [94] Humphrey was pleased with her group's performance and noticed that the Humphrey-Weidman dancers had a more clearly defined training than the other groups.

Weidman and Humphrey traveled from Mills College to teach at Perry-Mansfield in Steamboat Springs, Colorado. At times Doris became frustrated with her partner's free-spirited teaching. In a letter to Leo she complained about Weidman's teaching methods at Perry-Mansfield: "It's rather a mess here, as Charles, true to his nature, came one week, and threw enough difficult technique at them to floor a professional company. In his demonstration at Mills he had the same characteristics as always—the winning charm, the irresistible humor, the messy, illogical technique, much too difficult and too long for his admiring and frantic group."[95] These summer intensives at Bennington, Mills, and Perry-Mansfield gave Weidman and Humphrey an opportunity to shape their training system. Weidman was noted for his challenging movement material such as

Dance of the Elevens, and was more concerned with the spirit inherent in motions than with perfection. By the end of the decade, the Humphrey-Weidman technique had been formulated.

Chapter Eight

Shaping a Movement Style and Technique

Dance should expand the beauty, the dignity
and the mystery of man—and, at times,
when necessary, show his foibles.

Charles Weidman

By 1940 Weidman and Humphrey had solidified their dance technique. It was an expansive, exhuberant style based on natural movement principles. At Bennington Weidman diligently worked with his assistants William Bales, George Bockman, José Limón, and Lee Sherman to establish a training system for men. At the last Bennington Festival in 1941, Weidman and Humphrey featured the premiere of *Decade,* a work that retraced their joint career. That summer Weidman also taught his technique and the first repertory class, where students performed *The Shakers* and *Lynch Town* (original spelling) in the festival's culminating program. From 1939 through 1942, the weekly informal showing of student projects at Bennington highlighted choreography by Humphrey-Weidman company members William Bales, George Bockman, Katherine Litz, José Limón, Katherine Manning, and Nona Schurman. For the next thiry years Weidman taught his technique and composed more than fifty dances (such as *Classroom, Modern Style*) based on his personal movement style.[1] In his book *Prime Movers*, published three years after Weidman's death in 1977, Joseph Mazo claims: "There is no 'Weidman style' of modern dance, as there is a Humphrey style or a

Graham style."[2] Unfortunately, Mazo has rendered Weidman's movement style irrelevant to American dance. The following research will delineate Weidman's movement style and argue its significance in twentieth century American dance.

Weidman's Movement Style

Weidman's personal movement style, reflective of its historic period and his philosophy, was inextricably linked to his technique and to common movement principles he shared with Humphrey. *Style* is defined as an individual or characteristic manner of expression, execution, or design in any art.[3] In the *Handbook For the Dance Director*, dance notator Ray Cook suggests how to distinguish style in dance: "The style of a dance, dancer or choreographer is affected by the attitudes of the people involved, which is in turn affected by the social and economic conditions of a particular location and at a particular period."[4] Weidman's style was affected by the Depression and took on a theatrical simplicity that showed his affirmative attitude to the changing tide of the 1930s. Cook further affirms that the evolution of the choreographer's specific movement material will be influenced by gender and socioeconomic stratification: "Each choreographer represents a special selection of movements organized from racial, social, period, and other characteristics. Each of these movements may be seen in terms of flow, weight, time, and space . . ."[5] As a choreographer, Weidman consciously or unconsciously, made artistic decisions by selecting movement material supported by subjective qualities inherent in his life experiences, and thus expressive of Weidman. Choreographic style is influenced by temperament as well as life experience. Weidman's disposition was characterized by his pioneering spirit, earnest persistence, and energy; his belief in the multiplicity of the world; his study in libraries, museums, and art galleries; his strong religious faith; and his charm, humor, and wit. It was the balance of these ingredients or his nature that guided Weidman in his reactions to life

216

experiences and his art. "Style is not just the manner of the expression; it is the result of both movement matter and movement manner—not imposed on movement but found in it," Sondra Horton Fraleigh suggests.[6]

In his choreography Weidman used certain movement elements that were reflective of his personal style: contrast in dynamic effort (such as smooth, abrupt, rise, fall, swing, shake); clarity of form (for example, ABA, rondo, repetition, theme-and-variations); tempo and rhythm (such as accent, beat, duration, pattern); design (such as symmetry, asymmetry, straight or curved line, shape, distortion); space (direction, pathway, level); and clarity of intention or motivation (purpose, function, meaning). Cook suggests that such factors defining Weidman's movement style "are shaped by the choreographer's attitude to his art, time of creation, national heritage . . . and schooling of the dancers."[7]

Weidman and Humphrey were partners and collaborators for twenty years, from 1928 to 1948, and during the height of their artistic careers, from 1935 to 1945, their names were connected: Doris Humphrey and Charles Weidman and Group. Their company performed in dances created by both Humphrey and Weidman and studied technique in classes with Weidman and Humphrey. As partners they believed in similar fundamental ideals and worked from identical technical and stylistic movement principles: fall, recovery, rebound, succession, opposition, suspension, and breath rhythm. From these principles they developed a movement style—a style dancers still aspire to master. Weidman's movement style evolved in mid-twentieth century America during his partnership with Humphrey at their Humphrey-Weidman School of Dance in New York City. In his article "About Balanchine," George Jackson supports Cook's definition of style when he writes: "By 'style,' I mean the things that advertise authorship as well as a point of view, a hierarchy of values, the set of assumptions that define the universe of a work, of a corpus, or an entire school."[8]

Subtle differences within the Humphrey-Weidman movement style characteristic to Weidman were due to the density of his bones, body weight, body structure, and stature (height: 6 feet, 1 inch; weight: 155lbs) that all contributed to his powerful vigorous style. Weidman's solid angularity in linear movement design contrasts with Humphrey's curving designs. Additionally, Weidman's technical studies and choreography (based on a rebounding motion) showed qualities regarded as characteristic of men's movement in comparison with the series of falls used by Humphrey considered choreographically feminine.

Center of Weight and Use of the Foot

During a studio session with Nona Schurman while we were reconstructing her technique demonstration *From Studio to Stage,* our dancing paused and a discussion about movement style began. I asked, "How does one conceive of style?" Schurman's answer fell into two parts: the variety of dynamics within a given movement and the use of body weight.[9] These two points are important in recognizing and delineating any movement style, but are particularly helpful in spurring specific research into the clarification of Weidman's movement style. Schurman's explanation of how a dancer would perform movement phrases in Weidman's style stressed the movement *between* positions.[10] Schurman's stylistic ideas distinctly emphasize movement from one shape or design to the next.

These ideas were based on Humphrey's concept of gravity called the arc between two deaths, a concept she explored in *Water Study* and discovered while reading Nietzsche's *Birth of Tragedy*.[11] Humphrey felt dancing on vertical or horizontal planes for too long rendered dance theatrically uninteresting or static. She was philosophically attuned to movements between vertical and horizontal planes because, with the pull of gravity, her body tensed, causing dramatic conflict.[12] Therefore, her training system, shared by Weidman, focused on off-

218

balance and falling movements into a recovery to stability and balance. The beauty of Humphrey's movement principles was its simplicity, as Ernestine Stodelle confirms: "From such basic acts as breathing, standing, walking, running, leaping, rising, and falling came the inspiration for Doris Humphrey's theories of movement. Simple as these fundamental human motions appear to be, they contain the ever-present drama of man's struggle to gain mastery over himself and his physical environment."[13]

A ballet dancer may have difficulty mastering the Humphrey-Weidman movement style because classical ballet technique stresses clarity of body positions—*croisé, efface,* and *écarté*—along with precise foot and leg positions. Emphasis in classical ballet technique is on training a dancer to move from codified positions on a frontal, or lateral plane, which in essence creates classical ballet style. Moreover, a ballet dancer, a Graham dancer, or a Cunningham dancer may encounter obstacles in mastering Weidman's distinctive use of body weight. Since the training systems in ballet, Graham and Cunningham conceive of the center of weight as lifted up out of the legs; there is never recognition of a low center of weight in the pelvis, or an "under-curve," when moving in any given direction in space.

In Weidman's movement style, shift of weight is performed with a slide, led by the ball of the foot, the whole foot contacting the floor, and using a deep under-curve *plié* (bend of the knees) when shifting the center of weight. In contrast, in a forward walk in ballet, a dancer will extend a pointed foot forward, then, step onto the toe, then ball of the foot, or present the leg, then shift the center of weight. This procedure is similar in the movement styles of Graham and Cunningham. Stylistically, Humphrey-Weidman movements fall through the space. In comparing the Graham style to Humphrey-Weidman style, Katherine Litz writes: "They [Graham dancers] carved out space, like a sculpture. We didn't make up-and-down designs, we moved across. We used space not for display but to go through, like the wind."[14]

Moving across the space is an important trait of Weidman's movement style. It is founded on the basic principle of a fall onto the foot and a rebound or recovery. Schurman suggests that the application of the principle of fall is important to his style.[15] This recognition of body weight centered in the pelvis, the deep "under-curve," and the shift of body weight performed with a slide, the whole foot contacting the floor, takes into account the dancer's relationship to the space.[16] Using these stylistic principles, movements become rich and visceral. Walks and runs pitch forward and rush through space. Turns fall away from the body's central axis.[17]

Body Bends

While practicing the body bends that begin Schurman's Humphrey-Weidman technique demonstration *From Studio to Stage*, I start to analyze Weidman's stylistic movement quality. Her technique demonstration begins with a variation on Weidman's *Body Bends*. When practicing the body bends with Schurman, her directions about the use of the arms stress a basic characteristic: the dynamic element is a fast drop of the arms, then a slow lift of the arms.[18] Schurman coaches: "throw it down," and "pull it up."[19] In addition, this dynamic principle appears throughout Weidman's technical studies. I also begin to make distinct correlations with specific dance sequences from Weidman's choreography, particularly *Opus 51* (Opening Dance) and *Lynchtown*. In these works, using the weight of the arms falling with gravity and pulling them up with resistance strengthens the theme of the work, as in *Lynchtown,* or accents the dynamic quality of the music, as in *Opus 51* (Opening Dance). The power and muscle density of Weidman's body certainly affected his movement quality. Humphrey's contrasting dynamic quality, with its movement centered on breath rhythm and suspension, creates a style of dance that is lyrical. It expresses the strength of the human spirit to overcome opposing forces.[20]

Hands and Arms

In Weidman's movement style, the hands and arms are used in a distinct way. They are used in a contrasting stylistic manner to ballet. In ballet, the arms are curved, with the palm of the hand facing toward the body; the fingers of the hands are distinctly separated, with the thumb and third finger close together. In Weidman's movement style, the hands are used in a cupped manner, with the fingers together but not rigid. This gives generosity and strength to hand gestures without rigidity. To master this distinctly cupped hand, try exchanging a handshake with a friend.

In Weidman's movement style, when the arms are placed low at the sides of the body, the elbows are rotated forward against the natural position of the arms, similar to ballet style, and there is space under the arms to separate the arms from the body. Unlike ballet style, however, when the arms are held above the head in Weidman style, the arms bend firmly at the elbows and the palms rotate outward toward the audience, showing warmth, openness, and generosity. In contrast, in Graham's movement style, the palm of the hand is in a small contraction, conferring rigidity on the fingers and angularity on the hands. Additionally, the arms flex at the elbows and the palms turn to face the body, showing a cool, austere, and private attitude.

Weidman uses his hand on his upper thigh in a unique manner, easily recognizable in his *Traditions*, *Opus 51, Brahms Waltzes*, *The Christmas Oratorio*, and *Saint Matthew Passion*. To achieve Weidman's stylistic stance, recognizable in *Opus 51,* follow these directions: pull the ball of the right foot toward the arch of the left foot; place the palms of the hands high on the front of the thighs; bend the arms strongly; place the elbows forward; and strongly lift the rib cage. In a variation of this stance noticeable in his technical series *The Body Bends Series,* Weidman uses one hand on the thigh while the other hand gestures into oppositional space and the body bends sideways (lateral flexion). This special Weidman stance with its lift of the rib cage reflects a stable and valiant attitude.

In a conversation with Beatrice Seckler about the style used in Weidman's *Traditions* and Humphrey's *New Dance,* she described the use of the arms as "heroic, solid, stately, unbreakable but not aggressive."[21] Deborah Carr described the style as "open, optimistic, and humanistic."[22] Their words offer specific images recognizable in the movement styles of both Weidman and Humphrey. Their techniques were interwoven with a philosophical credo reflective of a historic era. "It was a very heroic period in modern dance," says Carr, "the lift of the rib cage—you see it in the technique and attitude—that incredible lift of the rib cage."[23] When speaking to Seckler and Schurman, who danced in the Humphrey-Weidman Company during its artistic height from 1935 to 1948, both said that the Humphrey-Weidman style and technique originated from these movement principles: succession, opposition, fall, recovery, rebound, breath rhythm, and metric rhythm.

In an interview in 1967, Weidman revealed what Humphrey thought about others teaching her movement theories: "Doris felt that Nona [Schurman] . . . was one of the best teachers because she understood the principles. And Doris always said, 'I don't care what you teach as long as you understand the principles.'"[24] To truly master an understanding of these movement fundamentals, one must comprehend the concepts inherent in these principles. Each principle includes a movement vocabulary, theoretical foundation, choreographic invention, and philosophic ideals. As indicated in Weidman's own words, he and Humphrey urged their teachers to invent within the guidelines of Humphrey-Weidman principles, which accounts for varied interpretations of their techniques. Dancers were drawn to work with specific choreographers because they were attracted to their choreography and because their movement style and technique felt comfortable for their bodies. Talking with Schurman about why she was drawn to study technique with Weidman and Humphrey, she indicated that the heroic quality of their style appealed to her. She also enjoyed sending her body through space in a visceral way when dancing their movement material.[25]

This stylistic quality described by Schurman is recognizable in the second section of her technical demonstration in *From Studio to Stage*. Here a series of Weidman's turns begin in the upstage corners of the stage and move diagonally to the downstage corners: *Forward Leg Whip Turn*, *Flat Turn*, *Reverse Turn*, and Schurman's "Low Forward 3/4 Leg Turn." This section shows how movement would be practiced in a Weidman classroom as dancers move through the space, one after another. In *From Studio to Stage* the movements develop vigorously into Weidman's *Side Crossing*, "Men's Elevation Solos," "Hip Hops" from *New Dance*, Runs, and Leaps, with a reiteration of these themes performed in double time or twice as fast. The conclusion of *From Studio to Stage* builds into an energetic climax just as Weidman's technique classes were structured. Schurman invented a spirited dance in the Humphrey-Weidman movement style by using their characteristic contrapuntal form and their compositional elements, such as succession, unison, half time, double time, change of front, change of meter, change of direction, phrasing, dynamic variety, and rhythmic variety.

Archaic Design and Stylistic Walk

Weidman's dance style as it developed from 1930 to 1948 was influenced by emerging ideas in theatre, art, music, and the social and political climate of this time. In breaking from the stylistic exoticism of Denishawn, Weidman, along with Humphrey and Graham, moved toward ceremonial forms or, as Schurman notes, ritual dance.[26] Ideas derived from primeval and ritual forms caused a shift in movement vocabulary, technical methods, and choreographic invention. Louis Horst explains it this way: "Primitivism had released us from the tyranny of symmetry; the question followed by the answer in music, the right hand movement to balance the left in dance. The way of the primitive is repetition rather than sequence."[27] Horst's statement indicates a distinct change in compositional structures used by Weidman, Humphrey, and Graham after Denishawn.

For Weidman, ritual form took hold in his origination of a stylistic walk—walking forward with the heel first. He used this in transitional walks only; otherwise, he used a slide onto the supporting foot into a turn. This stylistic heel walk may be noticed in his *Forward Leg Whip Turn* in rhumba rhythm, in the men's section of *New Dance*, and in the first women's entrance in *Lynchtown*. Weidman's primitive walk is in a parallel position (feet not turned-out), with the foot strongly flexed, "every step an adventure, an exploration," according to Horst.[28] Graham used this same idea, telling her students: "Come down into the earth with your heels!"[29] Weidman also used the heel of the foot in an unusual manner: by rotating or turning on the heel of the foot. This stylistic rotation, or turning on the heel of the foot, is used in his *Body Bends Series*, and a heel turn is also used in the second dance of *Saint Matthew Passion*.

As a youngster Weidman was inspired by the heroes of the ancient Greek myths he had studied, and later by the two-dimensionality of Shawn's Cretan dance *Gnossienne*. In contrast to the asymmetry of primitivism, Weidman moved toward the archaic. Horst suggests, "The pull and stress of opposition, as in the pagan Archaic, connotes strength . . ."[30] Perhaps attracted to the powerful shapes in the design principle of opposition, Weidman originated beautiful movement sequences using archaic design.

Weidman created examples of ancient movement designs in *Quest* and the "Variations" section of *The Christmas Oratorio*. These works employ a stylistic

224

Humphrey-Weidman rib-cage lift in profile, as follows: move into a characteristic Weidman forward lunge on the left foot, the body simultaneously twisting to the right and bending to the left; the left hand is on the front of the thigh, while the right hand gestures in a high forward diagonal direction, and the head is strongly turned right to show a heroic profile.

Simplicity was an aspect of such ancient designs, and in the Trio section of *The Christmas Oratorio*, Weidman invented many archaic shapes. In particular, while facing stage right, make a small jump to fourth position parallel, right foot forward while the body twists to the left, arms placed low, palms facing outward. This movement, which serves the content of the dance, gives a calm repose, and creates a "tension of arrested movement that is typical of archaism."[31]

In the second dance of *Saint Matthew Passion*, Charles invented many effective archaic designs with elevation and using floor work. (Particularly in the dance "Serpent Heart" which communicates the agony experienced by the mother of Judas, upon learning of his betrayal of Jesus.) "Serpent Heart" segues into a third dance that begins with archaic floor work symbolic of Christ's crucifixion. The archaic design provides "the distortion necessary to force the human body into a two-dimensional design and creates a tension which gives the composition great strength," writes Horst.[32]

Forced-Arch Foot Position

A stylistic foot position called "forced-arch" is used by Weidman to move through space. This step is recognizable in numerous Weidman dances: the Opening Dance of *Brahms Waltzes* as the women are moving in a small circle around a central figure; the Opening Dance of *The Christmas Oratorio* as the dancers are moving in an oblique direction; and at the conclusion of the Closing Dance of *Saint Matthew Passion,* as the dancers move in a large circle. "Forced-arch" is best described as a grapevine step from folk dance, but it is performed on the balls of the feet (*relevé*) with the knees bent. The feet keep contact with the floor by sliding into the steps. It is a rigorous step, especially when performed quickly or slowly. José Limón continued to use this stylistic "forced-arch" foot position in his choreography; it is recognizable in *Chaconne* (1942), *The Moor's Pavane* (1949), *There Is a Time* (1956), and *The Unsung* (1970).

Tempo and Rhythm

Weidman, Humphrey, and Limón employed diverse use of tempos and rhythmic variety in their technical systems and compositions. This element is notably important in delineating Weidman's movement style. His unusual application of tempo and rhythm was noticeable as a compositional tool in his technique series and choreography. Weidman's use of tempo added texture to movement, and he was especially fond of using half time and double time as a choreographic variation in his dances and technique. He was noted for his use of brisk, spirited speeds, of vivace especially in his *Body Bends Series* and *Hop Series*. This is true of his dances, particularly "Fast Turns" and "Tee-Hinny" from *Brahms Waltzes* and the "Variations" from *The Christmas Oratorio*. He was also noted for his use of legato, in *Modulations,* and in leg-circling exercises to prepare for the *Forward Leg Whip Turn* and *Reverse Turn*. Some members of the Humphrey-Weidman group referred to the leg-circling exercises that moved through space on the diagonal as the "Death March," since it was a painfully slow sequence. This certainly trained a dancer to perform the beautiful sustained "Opus Turn" from the Opening Dance of *Opus 51*, the "Soft Side Extensions and Modulations" from *Brahms Waltzes,* and the Opening Dance from *Saint Matthew Passion.*

As a choreographic device Weidman's use of rhythm was difficult to perform since it was intricate and unpredictable. His rhythmic variety employed numerous movements beginning on the "upbeat," accenting the "ands" between the counts, and unexpected "rests." A dancer has to be extremely musical to perform Weidman's dances—she/he will certainly become musical by training in his technique and dancing in his dances. For example, *Lynchtown*, only nine minutes long, is a dance that is extremely rhythmic; each movement theme is rhythmically complicated and uses contrapuntal form. It is a difficult work to master because of complex rhythms, contrasting dynamics, intricate spatial patterns, driving tempo, and demanding movements.

Theme-and-Variations Form

In dance compositions each choreographer's style shows a distinct manner of organizing movement in the stage space, a particular way of linking dance phrases to music, and of handling primary elements of dance composition. An important feature defining Weidman's style was his judicious use of choreographic form. The structure he mainly used was the theme-and-variations, "a musical form in which a theme . . . a melody that assumes importance in a composition because of its central and continued use . . . is stated then varied in a succession of statements."[33] In his book *Modern Dance Forms*, Louis Horst includes a chapter entitled "First Rules of Composition," in which he lists the prerequisite to any choreography: "To compose is not an inspirational experience. Composition is based on only two things: a conception of a theme and the manipulation of that theme."[34] In an article published in 1941 in *The American Dancer*, Charles explains the importance of form in his dance compositions:

> Clarity in the forms is essential. There are five fundamental forms, the first of which is A B A. People familiar with the construction of music or poetry know that A is one idea and B is related but a different idea. The final A would be a return to the original theme. The second form is A repetitious. The third is A B recurring and the fourth is A B C D E F G -

an unfolding theme which goes on and on without ever returning. The fifth is a broken form which necessitates the composing of the music (if any is required) to follow the composition of the dance.[35]

When working in any of these forms, it is important to begin with a workable movement theme, as Weidman explains: "One essential difference between dance composition and music composition is that the ear will stand repetition of the same music, but the eye will not stand repetition of the same movement. Each time one returns to the A, he must make a new variation of the original theme. The same is true of the B theme."[36]

To make variations on a movement theme in the Humphrey and Weidman tradition, one uses the elements of dance and the principles of composition. Elements of dance include motivation, design, rhythm, and contrast. Compositional principles are change of front, opposition, succession, unison, and ground bass. These elements of dance and principles of composition are analyzed by Humphrey in her book *The Art of Making Dances*.

The compositional principle of theme-and-variations form is presented beautifully in Weidman's abstract dances such as *Traditions, Opus 51* (Opening Dance), *The Christmas Oratorio, Brahms Waltzes*, and *Saint Matthew Passion*. Moreover, the men's section in *New Dance* may be studied for its superb use of variation. Weidman used succession as a compositional element in which a movement theme is performed once, then another dancer picks up the movement theme, and then another. Don McDonagh describes Weidman's use of succession in the Opening Dance of *Opus 51*:

> The first movement begins conventionally enough as two women walk forward and do an attitude turn followed by extensions of the leg to the side. They are joined by two other women and then a third and all turn together. Legs are extended backward and all bend forward, and the five join in a circle after stepping grandly around for a moment. In the circle

they step backward, pause for a moment, and file around slowly, swinging crooked arms right and left. All stand in a vertical line. First three jump to the side and return, and then two others follow, and the impression is of a bell tolling. One begins a turn which is then picked up by all. They bow to the center, swing their arms, extend their legs and then walk off.[37]

Weidman's Dance Technique

Technique is defined as the method or details of procedure essential to expert execution in any art or science.[38] In reference to dance, technique is considered a specific exercise or study used to train the student in finite control of bodily movements. Technique systems include a movement terminology or vocabulary that correlates to a historic period, philosophic conviction, and theoretical foundation. As a point of definition it is important to keep in mind that training systems are fundamentally based on discovering movement material inherent in a dancer's movement style. Sondra Horton Fraleigh supports this idea in writing: "These [techniques] are defined ways of moving embedded in, not imposed upon, individual movement styles."[39] At the time the innovators of American modern dance (Graham, Humphrey, and Weidman) developed their techniques, there were no established training systems except for Denishawn and ballet. Their techniques were conceived in order to break away both from the Asian emphasis of Denishawn training and the rigidity of classical ballet technique. In her article "Modern Dance—A Technique or Philosophy," Edith Stephen writes about technique and style as discovered by the originators of modern dance: "The modern dance has been so strengthened and crystallized by its original innovators that it has created an exacting technique within the styles of each school. When these innovators were first evolving their individual techniques, there were no set precedents, the field was open and free, and the creative climate was of a pioneering spirit."[40]

In talking about his technique with Marian Horosko in 1967, Weidman remarked that Humphrey would teach her class and he would teach his class, and to keep in training both he and Humphrey would take each other's classes, "but I never got into the thing, as a Humphrey dancer," Charles said, "because I was always keeping my own feelings about things."[41] One of the fascinating points about their artistic partnership was that they thought alike, and because they didn't discuss or analyze, they worked intuitively, as Weidman recalled: "Doris [and I] never talked about technique, as its coming out of Humphrey-Weidman technique."[42] Nona Schurman noted that Humphrey-Weidman technique was actually two techniques.[43] She suggested that while their techniques were completely different, they worked from the same artistic principles, specifically that all movement in space was a fall and a recovery from a fall.[44] Humphrey and Weidman used the same movement principles, but each approached their classes in a contrasting pedagogical manner. Weidman described Humphrey's teaching method: "Doris used to teach—many times—creatively. By that I mean she would come into class with new ideas which she would to do. She never solidified the technique as I did."[45]

As Weidman began to build his technique into a firm structure, he formulated a logical order for his exercises, thereby insuring sound anatomical training. In a conversation with Schurman about their techniques, she noted that many times Humphrey contributed to the movements and Weidman organized the movements into a form. Weidman explains how his technique was determined: "One summer [1934] José [Limón] and I worked on the technique to make it solid."[46] Schurman recalled that they worked at Weidman's 176-acre farm in Blairstown, New Jersey, seventy miles from New York City. At the end of the summer when they returned to teach at the studio in September, Weidman taught all this new movement material in study form. Weidman referred to these as "study form" or "series" and he described them as "quite beautiful, quite

230

symphonic, it [movement] flows from one thing, evolves into another, modulates from one kind of movement to another."[47] Weidman developed his own movement phrases into "series"; he also formulated many of Humphrey's movement phrases. Weidman remembered how he solidified Humphrey's movement phrases: "Peter Hamilton also helped [me] put a lot of her things together in a series—like her succession bends. Those succession bends are a series lasting about six to eight minutes. They are composed of about sixteen to twenty things and every morning before class she would do one of those things. But I put them into a form."[48]

Weidman had clear technical ideas; he was noticeably prolific in movement invention, and did not need to rely on Humphrey to develop his technical system. "I did not go into the falls," Charles said, "because that was still associated with Doris and that was the basis of her technique."[49] In his book *The Illustrated Dance Technique of José Limón,* Daniel Lewis defines fall: "A fall is the complete release of the muscles as the body, giving into gravity, drops. A fall in any part of the body, as well as the entire body, releases a vast amount of kinetic energy. This energy can be harnessed by catching it in either a recovery or rebound."[50] Charles, rather than Doris, was more interested in developing their techniques. Ernestine Stodelle confirms this point: "Her [Humphrey's] approach was not to establish a technique or to make exercises for purposes of technical training. The Weidman studies by contrast were done always the same."[51] Eleanor King, who danced with Humphrey and Weidman from 1928 to 1935, confirms Stodelle's statement: "With Charles, who was tremendously inspiring and encouraging, we did more vigorous studies . . ."[52] When teaching classes in 1928, Charles was known to give students specific phrases from his dances, as noted by King in her book *Transformations*: "Cleo [Atheneos] and I particularly loved working with Charles' class too, where he gave us strong dramatic twists and thrusts from his *Savonarola,* necessitating a quick backbend drop to the knees. And the insouciant patterns of his Scarlatti dances were delightful."[53] Janet Towner remembers Weidman's pedagogical approach to technical training in his classes during the 1970s:

> The way Charles worked is that he made the technique a dance—studies or series. They did have a sense of a dance and had a real dynamic flow to them. They might start out simply and then progress to something more involved, or they might start out with parts that would keep growing and blending until finally an ultimate part was a sense of a phrase of an entire movement. They were very energetic. We used all of the Humphrey-Weidman principles.[54]

In the Preface to her book *Modern Dance Fundamentals*, Schurman writes that her exercises, described through word descriptions, figures, and Labanotation, are "based solidly on the technical principles I learned while studying with Doris Humphrey and Charles Weidman."[55] Humphrey and Weidman's artistic application of basic principles of body movement—fall and recovery, succession and opposition, metric or foot rhythm, and breath rhythm—were revolutionary.[56] This period of experimentation in technique was exciting indeed, as Schurman affirms when she writes: "Their technique classes, so full of choreographic invention and provocative ideas on many subjects were a joy to take."[57] Clearly, Weidman and Humphrey's affirmative attitude and the basis of their artistic and philosophic approach to dance began in the classroom.

Weidman and Humphrey movement styles cannot be separated from their technique series studied in the classroom. No movement style can be separated from its technical training or technique system. For example, in the classical ballet, the traditional bow (*curtsey* or *révérence*) developed from European court dances. The traditional usage of the terms "ladies and gentlemen" and the etiquette of "ladies before gentlemen," when dancing grand allegro steps in a ballet class, originated from historical dancing in the Renaissance. In a

232

Humphrey or Weidman class the terms men and women are used, not only because of obvious male and female gender differences but, more importantly, because of the rise of social equality during the 1930s. Using the terms women and men suggested the acceptance and promotion of social equality. Moreover, it strengthened a cooperative relationship between men and women, a trait of Humphrey and Weidman movement style. At this time, Humphrey-Weidman was the only modern dance company that had a men's group; others had only women dancers. To use the terms men and women, rather than male and female or ladies and gentlemen, was characteristic of Humphrey-Weidman; equality of social position began in the classroom through their technique.

Humphrey-Weidman technique was superior in its conception because of its customary usage of varied and distinct compositional elements. Acknowledgment of this significant point has been minimized or neglected when referring to Weidman's technique. He established a unique use of the elements and principles of design along with the choreographic device of theme-and-variations that distinguished his technique as part of the revolution of modern dance against the rigid forms of classical ballet.

Class Structure

The form or structure of Weidman technique classes contrasts greatly with Graham technique classes. Weidman began his classes standing, with the body at full height, working the trunk in his *Body Bends Series*, while Graham began her classes sitting on the floor, working the torso in the "contraction and release" exercise. The trunk or torso is used in a clearly contrasting manner in each of these techniques. Graham uses the vertical plane in the "contraction and release" sequence, while Weidman uses the sagittal, frontal, and transverse planes in his *Body Bends Series*. In Weidman's *Body Bends Series*, the rib cage lifts up and moves forward in space towards the audience; the Weidman dancer actively and emotionally goes towards the audience.

In the "contraction and release," the Graham dancer uses an inward and downward contraction in the pelvis, pulling the audience emotionally inward, then sends the body up to "turn around the spine," or rotate on its axis. Dynamically, the Graham technique is mostly bound flow, while the Weidman technique is free flow—rebound to free flow. Additionally, in the Weidman technique, the breath is used to complement the dynamic flow, in contrast to expelling the air as in a Graham contraction. Weidman acknowledged this contrasting trait when he said about his technique: "It's the breath in the movement. It's the breath. And that is where it's completely different from Graham . . ."[58] Weidman's emphasis on the breath is recognizable in his movement material that uses suspension. Daniel Lewis, noted Limón dancer and teacher, defines movement suspension as "a prolonged high point. It is created at the peak of the movement by continuing the movement and delaying the takeover of gravity."[59] Weidman used numerous movement suspensions at the beginning of class in his first exercise, *Body Bends Series*.

Weidman's *Body Bends* are so strenuous that Nona Schurman developed her own short preliminary series based on Humphrey-Weidman principles to literally warm up a dancer's body before performing Weidman's *Body Bends Series*. Schurman's prelude sequence and exercises of Humphrey and Weidman are presented in her book, *Modern Dance Fundamentals*. David Wynn affirms the need for a pre-class warm up, and describes how Weidman's class began in the 1950s: "In class Charles seldom talked. He would call the exercise or series he wanted us to do, start the drum, and watch us with an eagle eye. He always expected his classes to be warmed up and ready to go, and if they weren't it could be difficult, as he plunged right in. We usually started with what we called "the Body Bends" which was really a very taxing series . . . hence the need to warm up beforehand."[60] Weidman created an open and accepting atmosphere at his studio and in his classes, as Margaret O'Sullivan recalled: "When new students came to class they followed along for a few classes and then he would start to give them corrections. He was not at all intimidating, so it made for a relaxed atmosphere."[61]

A Typical Weidman Class

Weidman said, "A dance class should have the shape of a dance."[62] Therefore, his technical training system had contrast and variation. About his classes, O'Sullivan, who danced with Weidman's company during the 1970s, writes: "Classes started promptly at 6:00 p.m. with Charles on the drum. We always started class with either 'body bends' or 'succession bends' and depending on which we started with, it dictated what we would work on for the remainder of class."[63] A typical Weidman class began with the *Body Bends* and moved directly into *Humphrey Succession Bends* or *New Succession Bends* that developed the beautiful Humphrey-Weidman body side bends. His class moved to the *Old Arch* or *New Arch* that developed the arch of the foot for elevation, *Free Kicks* and *Arm Under Leg Extensions* that trained the body for strength and flexibility of the legs. *Floor Stretches*, *Thigh Stretch*, and *Traveling Stretches* trained the body for mastery of the strenuous Weidman floor work. *Modulations* practiced moving from the floor to standing and elevation. *Study in Contrast* was a study in linear and dynamic contrast. *Series of Turns* developed from a simple shift of weight and the *Hop Series* trained a dancer in the Weidman style of elevation.

Weidman's technical studies have a clear physical development with a full dynamic range that produces an excellent dancer who could easily perform other modern dance techniques and styles due to the breadth of Weidman technique. Janet Towner confirms this point when she described a typical class.

235

We usually started out with the body bends which were very energetic including rebound and moved along very quickly into the studies of side successions. He incorporated Humphrey's movement and he said, "Doris used to do this in class but it was never put into a series so I put it into a series." Charles also created a new succession of side bends. His technique included all the successions, rebound movements, breath, fall and recovery. All of these were inside each of the series and that's what made them so rich. But what I loved about them was that you were dancing—it was never technique for technique's sake. He didn't let you fall into getting stuck in technique. It was the expression of dance, so the technique was just part of the process. To keep it alive and vital he made you feel you were dancing. "Let's get on with it, let's dance," Charles would say.[64]

Because Weidman's technique system employs numerous compositional elements, a dancer trained in his technique is keenly aware of dance composition. Humphrey-Weidman teachers will emphasize the compositional elements stressed in Humphrey's *The Art of Making Dances,* such as rhythm, dynamics, motivation, and design. When Deborah Carr reflects on her training with Harriette Ann Gray she says, "as dancers, from a technical point of view, we were taught to pay attention to all of these [compositional elements] and these are incorporated in the studies."[65] This simultaneous training in choreography is unique to this technique system, as Beatrice Seckler recalls: "The movements are unlimited, there is a basic principle but you are free to chose whatever movement is correct for your subject."[66]

The *Body Bend Series* begins simply, but when analyzed, it consists of seven complex sections and each section is a variation on the first theme. Refer to Appendix A for a detailed description of the *Body Bend Series.* In Weidman's notes on *Approaches to Composition,* he explained his *Body Bends Series:*

Approaches to Composition—Exercises
Classes start with a warm up of body bends.
A. Stand in a wide stance with feet square

Hold arms out to sides, slightly forward
Bend forward in 8 counts
Bend sideward to right in 8 counts
Bend sideward to left in 8 counts
Bend backward in 8 counts
Repeat the above body bends in 4 counts
Repeat the above body bends in 2 counts
For the breath the arms swing to right then to left (dropping with gravity and pulling up against it).
B. The bends with the torso twisting to right and then left in 8 counts
C. The scoop and reach bend:
Face the right (arms open) in 2 counts. Scoop the arms over head, bending knees in 2 counts and recover to face front in 2 counts. Repeat to left.
D. Circular bends in 8 counts: Left leg forward, right out to side. Start circle bending the torso to right side; bring arm and torso around to front; then to left side turning feet out; bending both knees equally to a big backbend; and return to normal. Repeat 2 times. Repeat above with right leg forward starting circle to the left.[67]

All of the Weidman technique series are skillfully developed in a similar manner and are physically demanding to perform. Resources for studying Humphrey-Weidman movement style and technique are: *Modern Dance Fundamentals* by Nona Schurman and Sharon Leigh Clark; Schurman's *From Studio to Stage*, videotape; *The Dance Technique of Doris Humphrey* by Ernestine Stodelle; *Charles Weidman, On His Own*, videotape; *Two Masterpieces of Modern Choreography* by Doris Humphrey, videotape; archival films and videotapes held by the Dance Division, The New York Public Library for the Performing Arts; and Labanotation scores are available from the Dance Notation Bureau in New York City and at the Dance Notation Bureau Extension at Ohio State University.

Through this investigation, teachers, students, dancers, critics, and historians will gain a better understanding of the movement style and technique of Charles Weidman. With the eclecticism of today's American modern dance it becomes more difficult to identify individual movement styles because so much

237

movement material from artists of previous decades has been borrowed and blended. It is important to be able to recognize the movement style and training system of one of the most prominent forces in the development of American Modern Dance—Charles Weidman.

Lecture-Demonstration Format

On their own, embarking on a new artistic adventure, Humphrey, Weidman, and Lawrence realized that the key to both artistic and financial success was the development of their school. To interest future students to enroll in their classes, Weidman and Humphrey presented a series of lecture-demonstrations at their studio in 1929. With Lawrence at the piano, Weidman and Humphrey probably danced examples of their new movement vocabulary and perhaps new solo dances. Because their technique was, at this time, evolving, they probably embellished upon techniques drawn from Denishawn classes. The important point is that they created a structured form for their lecture-demonstration. They developed this form for their first group of dancers, and in 1929 presented their lecture-demonstration to 1,000 students at Hunter College.[68]

In January 1931, the first series of modern dance lecture-demonstrations was organized by The New School for Social Research. In the fall, the Roerich Society of New York presented a series of fifteen dance recitals under the direction of Lucille Marsh, in which distinguished dance artists demonstrated and analyzed various types of dance. Some of those who participated were Ruth St. Denis, Martha Graham, Michel Fokine, Mary Wigman, Charles Weidman, Irma Duncan, Doris Humphrey, and Ruth Page.[69] "Classes and lecture-demonstrations were given to educate the public about dance and the general public was hence participating in the creative development of dance," Jano Cohen notes in her Master's thesis *Examination of the W.P.A. in the 1930's*.[70] During the time of the Federal Dance Project (from August 1935 to October 1936) in New York City,

238

there were over three hundred performances, not including Broadway or opera. In *The New York Times* on June 7, 1936, John Martin observed the increase of all types of dance activities. "The general total of recitals, lectures, demonstrations and the like has apparently reached a temporary level at about 350 per season."[71] To support the National Dance Congress, on May 21, 1936, major artists presented a special Demonstration Program in which significant emphasis was placed on the role of dance in education. *"Demonstration on Technique,* Graham and Group; *Educational Demonstration on Dalcroze Eurythmics,* Paul Boepple and Group; *Lecture-Demonstration on Technique and Form,* Doris Humphrey and Group; *Demonstration of Percussion with and without movement,* Franziska Boas and Group; *Demonstration in Dance Method,* Polly Korchien and Group; and *Theme and Variations,* Anita Zahn and Group."[72]

The variety of these demonstrations indicated the importance of the lecture-demonstration to every genre of modern dance. During a tour of the United States in 1936, Hanya Holm presented a lecture-demonstration as part of her program. Not only was it important for artists to communicate to an audience about the aesthetic values inherent in their work, but the public enjoyed these presentations, as was evidenced in Albertina Vitak's review of the Lester Horton Group on February 17, 1939. "Demonstrations of technique and methods are becoming more popular with modern dance groups, and with their audiences."[73] Within his demonstration, Horton describes the "reasons and motivations behind his method in teaching technique and choreographic compositions."[74] Horton's lecture and demonstration were divided into three parts: Technique and Compositional Forms (Studies of Turns and Falls); Dance Construction (symmetrical and asymmetrical structure, motive phrase, studies in contrast); and concluded with performances of his dances.[75]

From 1936 to 1940, Weidman and Humphrey with their company spent January through May touring the United States teaching master classes, conducting lectures, performing technique demonstrations, and giving concerts. Developed from their first lecture-demonstration in 1929, Weidman and Humphrey constructed a refined lecture-demonstration that began with a lesson given by Humphrey on "The Individual Approach to Movement and Choreography." Next, three to six women would perform technique studies that included the front, back, side, and spiral (Schurman's term is spiral, Stodelle's term is circular) falls. After the women, Weidman and three or more men performed compositional studies. These studies showed how simple movements could be shaped into dance by using elements of rhythm, dynamics, design, and gesture. In the second part of their program, the company performed dances from the repertory.[76] During 1935 Weidman presented lecture-demonstrations with his Men's Group in which he explained his approach to dance composition, the methods used in composing, and the difference between what is known as the masculine dance and the feminine dance. Weidman's lecture-demonstration format was similar to Horton's; it was thorough, interesting, and informative as his written notes indicate.

Having had the experience as an instructor of both men and women there seems to me to exist a thin line that separates the sexes. At times the stepping across on either party's part is permissible; however, the dwelling in the opposite's territory becomes offensive. The exercises we do are given to both men and women. The execution after the laws are realized, become personal and as you will see tonight each person will be different.

We believe first and foremost that natural laws of movement must be realized . . . In dealing with dancing and dance composition the further one departs from the natural and the more one distorts the laws the better the dance.

We will begin with an exercise moving under the natural laws of succession and balanced by the natural law of opposition. By natural law of succession I mean the unfolding of one part after another from a center. The center in this case is the pelvic region, however it doesn't always have to be. (Illustration: Pushing Up, *Ringside*)

240

Everything that you have so far seen . . . has had the natural as its basis. Now just how can one distort? You have seen natural motions moving from the center in logical succession. These centers or sources of succession . . . are located in different parts of the body. Now instead of moving these parts naturally they are moved unnaturally—in a more unusual and unexpected manner. The result will depend on a personal characteristic: one's own ability to organize and relate these properly. I may point out that despite the distortion the movements are still successional simply because they succeed one another. I call it a distorted succession. (Illustration: Distorted Succession in Three Planes)

To me one of the most valuable assets in dance composition is the formula of contrast. In painting, this formula is used in the contrast of darks against lights, of cool colors against warm ones, of plain surfaces against highly decorative ones. In movement this is done with contrasting a soft movement against a hard, moving the body or body parts from a closed contracted position to an explosive one, or moving vertically to horizontally. (*Study in Contrast*)

We believe heartily against going to other places or other peoples for dance forms . . . I will now do a dance that although it is what we call modern, has the flavor of another race—Spanish. (*Danzon*)

The next dance deals with pantomime and humor; it shows our approach to pantomime. The same principles that govern the abstract dance govern pantomime such as design, rhythm, balance, and quality. (*Happy Hypocrite*)

In the development of a theme we invent a motif and use it as the backbone of an exercise or composition. We vary it in different planes and rhythms. We extract from it all that is possible then, as best as we can we place and organize our material to form the finished product.

In *Studies in Conflict* you will observe the development of a theme carried still further. These three dances have for their main motif the idea of conflict; at times of a physical nature, at times more of what might be called mental or imaginary. The first dance depicts the struggle of one individual with his own self. The second is a combat between two distinct individuals, or two ideas or two forces. The third dance carries the conflict idea further, where one individual contends with a mass or group. Let me add that althrough the whole has been kept quite impersonal and abstract . . . the contending parties are not individuals, but ideas or forces. You will recognize certain designs and movements repeated and varied performed by one individual or many.[77]

241

Weidman decided to compose a technique demonstration about twenty years later, but in this new approach he would allow the technique to unfold in an uninterrupted fashion. Sylvia Pelt Richards indicated that Weidman's lecture-demonstration *Classroom, Modern Style* was restaged in the summer of 1958 with students in his repertory classes from the New Dance Group Studio. It was also performed at the Henry Street Playhouse on January 11, 1959.[78] Richards describes this lecture-demonstration performance as one that focused on dancing more than lecturing. "The program opened with an informal talk by Charles about modern dance and its beginnings and continued immediately with a demonstration of techniques . . . built upon familiar Weidman principles."[79] Weidman began to shorten his lecture for certain performances until on November 4, 1959, at the YM-YWHA in Philadelphia, Weidman's *Classroom, Modern Style*, "a technical demonstration of Weidman movement style was presented as a work."[80] Roberta Krugman's review dated March 11, 1951, describes *Classroom, Modern Style* as a new work, and Winthrop Palmer's review of Weidman and his Theatre Dance Company's performance on March 10, 1951 in *Dance News* calls it "an entertaining new curtain raiser."[81] In her review, Krugman describes the compositional structure of the work: "A compilation of the exercises done in every Humphrey-Weidman class, organized formally in spacing and floor plan so that the company goes through a typical class without breaks or explanations."[82] Krugman also states that Weidman was on stage, where he accompanied the group of dancers on a drum, along with Freda Miller on the piano. Richards further describes the work's technical details as being a "presentation of technique sequences which Charles had developed and to which he assigned such descriptive names as 'Body Bends,' 'The Old Arch,' 'Series of Hops,' 'Studies in Contrast,' and 'Modulations.'"[83] For nearly a decade Weidman's *Classroom, Modern Style* continued to be performed by his company and students in all types of performance situations. Martin describes *Classroom,*

Modern Style in a review on January 3, 1960. "The Weidman technical demonstration, which opened the Annual Conference on Creative Teaching of Dance to Children at the 'Y,' was a 'humdinger.' The material was very impressive and arranged in an exciting sequence."[84]

The historical importance of reconstructing Nona Schurman's Humphrey-Weidman technique demonstration *From Studio to Stage*, created in 1957 at the New Dance Group Studio in New York City, is its establishment of a link to the historic period of Humphrey-Weidman, from 1935 to 1948. Not only does it create a bridge to this renowned period of Humphrey-Weidman; additionally, it shows the relevance of the lecture-demonstration format to the development of American modern dance. Schurman's technique demonstration uses Humphrey's, Weidman's, and Schurman's technical movements organized in a form that is strictly characteristic of Humphrey-Weidman. *From Studio to Stage* incorporates both Humphrey's and Weidman's technical sequences and movement styles, making it possible to separate the two techniques. More important, *From Studio to Stage* was created after Weidman's technique demonstration *Classroom, Modern Style,* and it elucidates the important fact that the Humphrey-Weidman technique is not only used to develop skillful dancers, but that the technique system *is* the dance.

Chapter Nine

A New Decade

(1938-1948)

Real art can never be escape from life.
In histrionic terms, illusions are not false impressions
nor misconceptions of reality. The world of illusion which
the audience expects from the artist is, in fact, the world of their real selves,
the image of their own world, the translation of their hopes and fears, their joys
and sufferings into the magic of the stage.

Charles Weidman
Random Remarks

With the Second World War brewing in Europe and the fateful bombing
of Pearl Harbor in 1941, Doris, Charles, Pauline, and José continued to work,
although emotionally distracted by the throes of war. As the draft was reinstated,
men dancers were called to serve their country, putting serious strain on company
personnel. Charles Francis Woodford, Doris' sea-faring husband (renamed Leo),
took a new job on a ship with the United Fruit Company transporting bannas from
San Cristobal in the Panama Canal Zone. Leo suggested to Doris that it would be
more practical at this time if she didn't use men in her company.[1]

His advice fell on deaf ears since the company had to continue their tours.
Doris hated leaving her young son and home for extended journeys. But she had
worked so hard for (twenty) years to become a dancer and to have a first-rate
company that she couldn't stop now and deprive Charles or the rest of the
company of their opportunities either.[2] Doris and Charles abandoned performing

their solos; instead, they performed along with their company in large group works such as Weidman's *Suite Atavisms, Opus 51,* and Humphrey's *Square Dances.* The company's New York City season started around Christmas time and continued with performances of concerts and lecture-demonstrations every weekend until April or May unless they were on tour.[3] During summers they usually went to Bennington, but in 1939 the Summer School of Dance was held at Mills College. After the stint at Mills, Doris and Charles would teach at Perry-Mansfield, followed by their summer intensive for teachers at their studio. It was a rigorous schedule of performing, composing, and teaching, all of which was insufficient to pay the bills. The reality of their artistic venture was constant fatigue, lack of sufficient food, and borderline poverty. The rent was months overdue at their Tenth Street apartment and the utilities were turned off. They cooked on sterno by flashlight and candles, and they used the light socket in the hallway to plug in the radio and iron. Living conditions were abject.[4]

For the fall tour, Doris left her young son Humphrey with Charles' father, Grandpa Weidman, in Lincoln, Nebraska.[5] While on tour in 1940, Doris' accidental fall down a flight of stairs would subsequently lead to arthritis of the hip. Shortly after this incident, José left the company due to a misunderstanding with Charles concerning his attention to a new company member, Charles Hamilton Weisner (renamed Peter Hamilton). Pauline tried to convince José and Charles to reconcile but this conflict was never resolved.[6] With the heightened anxiety of this situation, Charles became distant and depressed; on José's departure he began to abuse alcohol. Pauline was concerned about Charles' drinking and said so to Doris, who tried to help. Charles would not draw attention to his emotional pain; instead he kept it hidden inside. In the course of this time, there was much work to be done because the Humphrey-Weidman Company had a splendid opportunity to have its own performing theatre.

Sixteenth-Street Studio

They decided to move from the Eighteenth Street studio to 108 West Sixteenth Street, a larger studio space with a small theatre that they called Studio Theatre. Their company members helped them move into their new studio. Nona Schurman recalls the dancers carrying drums, mirrors, costumes, and sheet music through the streets of New York City to the new Studio Theatre.[7] Their company members were part of an extended family and Doris and Charles expected them to contribute to their artistic efforts just as they had done as company members at Denishawn. Humphrey-Weidman company members were given specific tasks to organize and get the Studio Theatre in working condition.

The Sixteenth Street Studio Theatre was Schurman's home for the next four years. Like other company members she had to work other jobs to earn a living. Leaving her family in Montreal to come to New York City to become a dancer, she needed to earn money to live on her own, and she did so by teaching Humphrey-Weidman technique—many times under her teachers' names.

Some company members, like Beatrice Seckler, didn't have the same financial burdens because she lived with her parents who were extremely supportive of her dancing career. Beatrice was a remarkable dancer and she was known for practicing her technique and rehearsing dances not necessarily in the studio, but...using mental visualization...lying on the couch with her eyes closed in her parents' living room. When anyone entered the house, her mother would whisper, "Shush...Bea's rehearsing." Members of the Humphrey-Weidman Company had different economic situations. Doris had the financial support of her husband, but as a man, Charles had to support himself and his own endeavors.

In the course of moving into the Sixteenth Street Studio Theatre, the dance family members, who had previously lived together, moved into separate living quarters. Limón traveled to California and subsequently performed with May O'Donnell, a noted modern dancer. Pauline decided to leave New York City to visit José and shortly thereafter, to everyone's surprise, José and Pauline were married.

On My Mother's Side

December 26, 1940, marked the first performance of the Humphrey-Weidman Company at their newly acquired Studio Theatre on Sixteenth Street in New York City. The program featured Weidman's *On My Mother's Side* along with sections of Humphrey's *Song of the West*, "The Green Land" and "Desert." Their new Studio Theatre had 150 seats acquired from the Metropolitan Opera, and the stage area was 25 by 50 feet. Folding gray screens served as wings and a light blue curtain was hung as a backdrop. Their audience entered through a foyer decorated with photographs, sculptures, and flowers.[8]

In her review of Weidman's *On My Mother's Side* in *The American Dancer*, Albertina Vitak commented on his fresh, inventive approach. "He has deftly arranged a set of family portraits taken from his own forebearers in Nebraska, a most original and novel idea and a perfect vehicle for him."[9] *On My Mother's Side* consisted of a suite of solos that may be characterized as Weidman's genre of autobiographical dances. "Charles Weidman's dance composition *On My Mother's Side*," writes Louis Horst, "portrays variations on the theme of the family."[10] Using dancers as a chorus to chant verses written by the Humphrey-Weidman company and narrated by a former company member, William Archibald, with a piano score composed by Lionel Nowak, Weidman's solo created tender sketches of members on the maternal side of his family: a lusty young pioneer, Great Grandfather Wolcott; a dignified pioneer, Great Grandfather Hoffman; gentle, blind Grandmother Hoffman; builder Grandfather Hoffman; a dancer, Aunt Jessie; Charles' Mother, Vesta; and Weidman himself.[11] In the concluding section of the work Charles danced himself as a young boy who loved to dance and who was affectionately called Sonny by his family. The chorus chanted:

> Today a fellow likes to dance
> No one knows why
> Maybe because he likes to dance
> No one knows why— [12]

Weidman danced back to his days with the Denishawn Dancers using gestures from their Oriental dances, archaic poses of Shawn's *Gnossienne*, and then he "tries a toe at ballet," Margaret Lloyd wrote. "None of it will do . . . He moves tentatively, then more freely, into reminiscences . . . from the Humphrey-Weidman repertory," as the chorus chants, "Then the modern creed it got him," and declares him as a leader of the modern dance movement.[13] Weidman combined all the elements of theatre art so successfully that he achieved notoriety. Albertina Vitak praised *On My Mother's Side* and Weidman's showmanship. "It is a very clever work, full of highly imaginative, well arranged gestures or passages, but perhaps, it is really Mr. Weidman's eloquent execution of them that tells, rather than the arrangement."[14]

At the Bennington Summer Dance Festival in 1941, Weidman and Humphrey presented *Decade*, a dance overview of the first ten years of their choreographic partnership. Always plagued by the villain, Mr. Business, the work presented excerpts from a decade of their dances in sections titled: "Vision of a New Life," "The Path of Realization," "Kaleidoscope of the Theatre," "Fugue of Confusion," "Dialogue with Mr. Business," and "Departure toward a New Vision." During this time, Humphrey's hip injury caused her continual suffering so Weidman took the Humphrey-Weidman Company out on tour. After the tour, a joint Humphrey-Limón concert of Bach works premiered at the Studio

Theatre, including Limón's stunning solo *Chaconne*. It seemed that Humphrey was being drawn toward an artistic association with Limón.

The draft board classified Limón as I-A; he requested a deferment so he could dance in Humphrey's *G-Major Partita*.[15] Weidman was called in for the draft in March 1942; he was rejected and received 4F status, disqualified perhaps because of age—he was forty-one years old. In April Limón was drafted into the army along with other men dancers. This made dances including men impossible to keep in the repertory. But Weidman and Humphrey continued to create dances. After the premiere of Humphrey's work *Inquest* in March 1944, her lower back and hip injury caused her constant pain and she seriously considered that her injury might force her to retire from the stage.

Inquest was a dramatic work about poverty performed to Norman Lloyd's music. Humphrey uses a narrator who reads a newspaper report of the death through starvation of a cobbler, played by Weidman, and his wife, played by Humphrey.[16] Interestingly, *Inquest* seems to have mimicked their own poverty, but the dance treatment of the subject was universalized through the theatrical idea of "a living newspaper"—the cobbler represented humanity. Their stunning performances in *Inquest* drew large audiences to their Studio Theatre on Sixteenth Street.

The arthritis in Humphrey's hip had radiated to her spine and the pain was unbearable. Her last appearance on stage was her performance in *Inquest* on May 26, at Swarthmore College, culminating in the final appearances of Humphrey and Weidman dancing together as partners.[17] It disheartened her, as Selma Jean Cohen writes in her book, *Doris Humphrey: An Artist First*: "Now that she could no longer perform, the atmosphere of the Studio Theatre depressed her; it felt like an empty shell, and she turned it over to Charles who formed his own school and company there."[18]

Humphrey was depressed by her physical condition. How could she continue her career in dance? How could she create works if she herself couldn't move and explore new movement possibilities? Her situation was gloomy. Lawrence suggested to her that she might create new dances for Limón's small company. She could be Limón's mentor and artistic advisor. Humphrey reluctantly agreed and began a duet for Limón and Beatrice Seckler in *The Story of Mankind,* with music by Norman Lloyd and costumes by Pauline Lawrence. The work had its premiere at the Bennington College Summer School on July 11, 1946. Throughout the late 1940s and early 1950s, Humphrey composed master works for Limón's company. Her new compositions included those for trios, quartets, and large ensembles such as *Lament for Ignacio Sánchez Mejías* (1946), *Day on Earth* (1947), *Night Spell* (1951), *Ritmo Jondo* (1953), and *Ruins and Visions* (1953).

Flickers

Weidman, Katherine Litz, and Peter Hamilton performed nightclub engagements at the Rainbow Room, which put a lighter touch on life through the strain of the war. Weidman's success at the Rainbow Room was due to his inventive skill in creating hilarious nightclub dances. The titles alone conjure up comic images: *Park Avenue Intrigue, War Dance for Wooden Indians, The Professor Visits Harlem,* and *Rumba to the Moon,* to the music of Xavier Cugat.

In 1942 Weidman composed a delightful comedic dance *Flickers* that developed into one of his most well-known works. Humphrey "gave hilarious performances both as the skinny pioneer woman, felling Indians right and left with a rake," writes Selma Jean Cohen, "and as Theda Bara, for whom she stuffed the arms and thighs of her costume to look voluptuous."[19] With a score stylized after a player piano by Lionel Nowak and using *kinetic pantomime*, Weidman composed a fantastic farce on the silent movies. Margaret Lloyd describes

Flickers: "'Hearts Aflame,' based on the old mortgage plot; 'Hearts Courageous,' the time-honored Western; 'Flowers of the Desert,' with Charles in the white burnoose of a Valentino-type sheik coming between Beatrice Seckler and Lee Sherman as a pair of lovers; and 'Wages of Sin,' showing Doris slinking around in a rare impression of Theda Bara."[20]

The original 1941, 1942, and 1943 casts of characters of *Flickers* were as follows. *First Reel, Hearts Aflame*: Ronald, Charles Weidman; Lillums, Katherine Litz; Villain, Lee Sherman; Accomplice, Marie Maginnis; Father, Charles Hamilton (1943-no Accomplice). *Second Reel, Wages of Sin*: She, Doris Humphrey; He, Charles Weidman; Wife, Gloria Garcia; Child, Beatrice Seckler; Party Guests, members of the company. *Third Reel, Flowers of the Desert*: The Girl, Beatrice Seckler; Her Lover, Lee Sherman; and Sheik, Charles Weidman (1943-Sheik, Agnes, Percival). *Fourth Reel, Hearts Courageous* (1941-42): Pioneer Mother, Doris Humphrey; Pioneer Father, Charles Weidman; Children, Katherine Litz, Beatrice Seckler; Neighbor Boy, Charles Hamilton; Squaw, Marie Maginnis; Indian Chief, Lee Sherman; Indians, members of the company. *Fourth Reel, Hearts Courageous* (1943): Broncho Billy, Peter Hamilton; Squaw, Marie Maginnis; Pioneer Mother, Nona Schurman; Pioneer Father, Charles Weidman; Indian Chief, Lee Sherman; Indians, members of the company.[21]

In 1970, Weidman received a grant from the New York State Council on the Arts to restage *Flickers* with his company Barry Barychko, Kathy Eaton, Joanne Edelmann, Trent Gray, Robert Kosinski, Marcia Lesser, Gary McKay, Linda Ravinski, Janet Towner, and Paul Wilson. Costumes were designed by Weidman and executed by Rose Marie Casassa and Janet Towner. The cast was as follows. *First Reel, Hearts Aflame*: Ronald, Robert Kosinski; Lillums, Janet Towner; Villain, Barry Barychko; Father, Trent Gray. *Second Reel, Wages of Sin*: She, Linda Ravinski; He, Charles Weidman; Wife, Marcia Lesser; Child,

Trent Gray; Party Guests, the company. *Third Reel, Flower of the Desert:* Flappers, Joanne Edelmann, Marcia Lesser; Agnes, Janet Towner; Percival, Robert Kosinski; Sheik, Paul Wilson. *Fourth Reel, Hearts Courageous:* Pioneer Mother, Linda Ravinski; Pioneer Father, Charles Weidman; Children, Joanne Edelmann, Marcia Lesser; Bronco Billy, Robert Kosinski; Squaw, Kathy Eaton; Chief Sweet Honey Bear, Barry Barychko; Warriors, Trent Gray, Gary McKay [22]

When Weidman suggested his project for *Flickers* to composer Lionel Nowak in 1941, their discussion centered on the action of the four reels. Weidman told Lionel he would rework Alan Porter's scenario, including the exact time allotted for the action, and send it to him. Here are Weidman's notes that he sent to Lionel:

Reel One "Hearts Aflame"
Characters: Ronald, Lillums, Her Father, Villain, and His Accomplice
30 Seconds of Overture
Note: This first reel is the best example of the early flickers. The action and mime is very fast (two to three times quicker than normal). The jerkey movements show that the reel has been cut several times.
15 Seconds, Scene One
Ronald enters with a suitcase. He has left the city and has come to the country for some fresh air.
20 Seconds, Scene Two
Lillums (a farmer's daughter) is out in a field picking flowers. Ronald comes upon her and asks her for directions. They see each other and fall in love. He asks her if she knows about any available jobs. She says her father could use his help. They "jump off" the scene.
20 Seconds, Scene Three. Outside the farmer's house
Lillums brings Ronald to the house and goes to get her father. Ronald smells the air. Lillums and her father enter. Ronald asks for a job and the father says yes. The father gives Ronald a rake. Father and Lillums go off stage. Ronald rakes and goes offstage (raking). The Villain and his Accomplice come onstage and plot their dirty business and go offstage. Blackout
2 Minutes and 30 Seconds. Outside the farmer's house

Lillums comes skipping onstage with a tray of freshly baked pies (made of thick jello). She puts them on the windowsill to cool. The Villain approaches her and he declares his love for her as his accomplice encourages him. Lillums shuns him but the Villain gets bolder. She runs to get her father. Then the Villain produces their mortgage. Both father and daughter fear the Villain has them in his clutches. Ronald comes onto the scene and seeing the situation he starts a fight with the Villain and Accomplice. There is fighting, pies thrown, etc. During the fight Ronald is pushed over an old tree stump, where he finds a buried bag of gold. He gives it to the Villain and Ronald and Lillums embrace.
15 Seconds of Inerlude music.

Reel Two "Wages of Sin" (Period 1910)
Note: In this reel the dramatic action and mime is distorted to a slow tempo (two or three times slower than normal).
1 Minute, Scene One. Leper Colony
It is night; there is a high fence, where a sign reads Leper Colony. A palm tree protrudes depicting that the scene is somewhere in the South Seas. Out slinks "She" (the vampire). She tries pulling at the base of the fence and finally finds two planks that give (made w/rubber hose). She pulls them apart and squeezes through them and then goes offstage.
1 Minute, Scene Two. Waterfront
A big shipping container (bale) sits on a dock, where a sign reads NEW YORK. A big knife opens the top of the bale; big eyes peer out and a knife slashes down one side. Slipping out of the container "She" (the Vamp) slinks offstage.
1 Minute and 5 Seconds. Scene Three. A party scene on Park Aveue
A party hostess and her guests enjoy a party as the Vamp enters. Then several men including ("He") enter the party. The Vamp sees him, fascinates him, and draws him to her. "He" cannot resist.
45 Seconds, Scene Four. Her Den (leopard skin over her couch, etc.)
"He" comes into her den—"She" seduces him.
35 Seconds, Scene Five. Mother and Child (His)
To the music of "Hearts and Flowers" the mother is crying and the child asks why?
Scene Six. Her Den.
"He" is in her clutches. He feels an itch on his arm, another on his neck, another on his foot, and realizes that he has contacted leprosy. He points at her accusingly and falls down dead. "She" throws a black shroud over him, steps over him, and goes to find another victim.

Reel Three "Flame of the Desert" (Period 1920)
45 Seconds of Introductory music
Characters: The Sheik, Agnes, and Percival
35 Seconds, Scene One. A Street in North Morocco
To the music of "Dardanella" several women are walking across the street.
The Sheik passes through them and they all swoon.
1 Minute, Scene Two. A Party Scene
The entire action is done to a Tango, suspending mime and emotion *à la tango* rhythm. Guests have teacups (which later they rattle emotionally) and a tray of cookies. Agnes is downstage left waiting for Percival. Percival come in, sees Agnes, and they embrace. He looks at his wristwatch, tells her he must leave for a spell and departs. The guests and Agnes feel an ominous "something" and the Sheik enters. He sees Agnes and fascinates her—against her will, but fascinated, she dances a tango with him (to the accompaniment of the guest's nervous clattering of their teacups). The tango ends with the Sheik pulling Agnes offstage. Percival dashes in—sees no Agnes—sees no guests—realizes something has happened. He sees a glass on a stand, picks it up and crushes it. He throws it down into a small basket that is pushed out to receive it and takes it offstage.
50 Seconds, Scene Three. Inside the Sheik's Tent
Agnes is asleep on a couch, while two Harem girls are dozing in front of her. The Sheik enters as the Harem girls *salaam* and the Sheik commands them to leave. Then he pursues Agnes. She runs offstage with the Sheik chasing after her. Percival runs in—sees no one—then sees a sword on the couch. He picks it up and breaks it in two throwing it down into a large basket that is shot out to catch it. In despair Percival goes offstage.
45 Seconds, Scene Four. Outside the Sheik's Tent
Agnes runs in being pursued by the Sheik. He catches her and makes her tango (she is going backwards) toward the proscenium—he dances her up the wall of the proscenium. Percival enters. He sees Agnes with the Sheik he pulls her away from the Sheik. Percival takes the Sheik and throws him up in the air and breaks him in two. A long basket is shot out to catch the Sheik. Agnes and Percival embrace.

Reel Four. "Hearts Couragous" (Period—Pioneer)
Characters: Pioneer Father, Pioneer Mother, Two Children (girls), Bronco Billy, Squaw, and Indians
40 Seconds, Scene One.
Indians squat around an imaginary fire smoking and plotting an attack. They crawl offstage (like bloodhounds) smelling tracks.

30 Seconds, Scene Two. Pioneer Homestead
Pioneer Father is chopping wood, Mother is digging, Children are skipping, and Squaw is shelling peas. In the course of this action Indians sneak in from behind and drag off the Squaw unnoticed by the others. The family discovers the Squaw missing and Bronco Billy rides in to the rescue. They tell him everything that happened and he goes to rescue her. Blackout.
45 Seconds, Scene Three. Pioneer Homestead
All are waiting. The Squaw dashes in points to a direction (miming) the Indians are coming. Bronco Billy rides onto the scene. They all barricade themselves behind present props and drag on props used in previous reels such as Leper fence, NY bales, etc. The Indians are slowly crawling up toward those hiding and fighting from behind the props. Just as the Indians are about to capture the pioneer family, the Pioneer Father throws a sign over the fence reading "Continued Next Week."[23]

With Alan Porter's delightful scenario Weidman and Nowak framed the meter and measures of the various musical selections for each section of the four reels. Their notes on the musical structure for the score of *Flickers* gives an interesting account of how the music connected with the storyline to create such an imaginative, charming piece of theatre; for example "Hearts Aflame" uses a waltz motif for Lillums, a Hearts Aflame dance for Lillums and Ronald, an evil motif for the Villain, a motif for the desperate mortgage plot, and a rousing pie throwing finale. [24]

And Daddy Was a Fireman

With the idea of creating a sequel to *On My Mother's Side*, Weidman premiered *And Daddy Was a Fireman* at Studio Theatre on March 2, 1943, to a musical score of adapted popular airs by Herbert Haufrecht. Perkins Harnley, Weidman's high school friend, designed props and scenery using cutout pieces giving Weidman's dance one-dimensionality similar to cartoons. One of Harnley's set designs used a four-foot square yellow, ornate frame trimmed in red velvet displaying a painting of "Daddy." A fire engine created by dancer Peter Hamilton supported Weidman's conception of a pantomimic tale of his father, Captain C. E. Weidman (pronounced Weedman) of the Lincoln (Nebraska) Fire Department. *And Daddy Was a Fireman* featured several theatrical episodes: a group of chattering townswomen; Peter Hamilton as both the threatening, vicious character of Fire, and the villainous Captain Malone; and the meeting and courtship of Charles' mother Vesta, originally danced by Humphrey. *And Daddy Was a Fireman* spins Weidman's autobiographical tale ending with his father's promotion to the Canal Zone in Panama. Always combining narrative with his dances, Weidman wrote the spoken text that described the theme of Fire:

> Fire, Fire, destructive force
> Demon of want, till it runs
> Its course,
> Despicable, unpredictable, a
> Thing to beware
> But apt at times one needs
> Its glare.[25]

As was characteristic of Weidman's theatre-dance, *And Daddy Was a Fireman* relied heavily on props and costumes. In her article "What Is Choreography?" in *Dance Magazine*, Lucile Marsh notes Weidman's stylistic treatment of props, especially in his portrayal of his father's Herculean adversary, Fire: "In the Weidman work fire was first seen as scarves flicking out from under picnic tables . . . At the end, fire was a real flame from a match."[26] While Weidman worked with Haufrecht on the final score, he had previously discussed the project with Lionel Nowak. Weidman and Nowak had developed a strong collaborative bond while working on the music for *And Daddy Was a Fireman*. Weidman in his usual manner, wrote a letter to Nowak with his scenario for the section he titled Dance No. 2, Engine House No. 1:

257

Dear Lionel-

As the group was giving the last gesture in honor of Daddy, who finally worked his way up to Engine House No. 1, the boys bring on scenery that suggests the interior of Engine House No. 1. The lights go up on the scene with the firemen in a pose like an old fashioned photograph (4 slow counts). Daddy enters. He is very gay and elated that he has a job. Using a rhythm of 5 (accenting 1 & 3), the men turn and greet him in 3 slow counts. Daddy gives a handshake to each man and they finally all face the big fire engine in 8 measures 5s. This fire engine is a large cutout. The next sections use the kinetic pantomime idea. They start pantomimically and then the movement design of their gesture is made into dance movement. The first is polishing things. (Rhythm is almost exactly like that in the big circle of *With My Red Fires*).

Pantomimic theme in 4 measures 4/4

First Dance theme in 4 measures 4/4

Pete jumps high on second fireman's shoulders on 2 counts

Crescendo and a statement of first theme 1 & 2, 3, 4

Roll call of 6 counts (Broad) Hold 2 counts (no music)

Men end in this line up:

Daddy—first in line

Jo

Frank

Pete

2nd Work Rhythm—Pulling a hose

Rhythm of 6 (accents of 1 & 3)

Start a little slow as an introduction 2 measures 6s

Work theme 4 measures 6s

The next can be a ground bass idea if you desire. The men seeing that Daddy's doing so well and they go upstage and rest as Daddy works frantically. This is for 9 measures 6s

Roll call of 6 counts (Hold 2 counts no music)

Jo

Daddy

Frank

Pete

3rd Work theme—Sweeping

Pete gets a broom in 4 counts

Frank gets a broom in 3 counts

Jo gets a broom in 2 counts

Daddy gets a broom in 2 counts
All hold 2 counts
They stand in a line one behind the other on stage right.
Sweeping rhythm of 4 measures 4/4
1 & 2 & 3 & 4 &
They hold looking on 2 measures 4/4. Then they go play checkers.
Daddy works for 12 measures 4/4
Roll call of 6 counts (Hold 2 counts no music)

                    Jo
             Frank
        Daddy
    Pete

Last Work theme—Turning a Wheel
Take wheel in 4 slow counts
Rhythm of 3—Turn it Right 2 counts
Let it snap back on 3rd count
The next is competition. Daddy and Pete (who symbolizes Malone, the old Chief) become like wheels and go spinning around. (Daddy's the best) 8 measures 6/8 [27]

The next year in 1944, Weidman commissioned Lukas Foss to compose the score for a new work called *The Heart Remembers*. The work was not in the comedic genre as Weidman had been occupied in *And Daddy Was a Fireman* and *Flickers*; it was a solemn work with religious overtones, perhaps a precursor to his later works *Song of Solomon* and *Rose of Sharon*. The work, which was performed in April 1944, portrayed the circumstances involving love and friendship. Foss's musical score shows the fourteen sections and content of Weidman's *The Heart Remembers*:

Introduction, Girls enter; *Andantino*, Boys enter; Tragic Lyrical Girl's Solo (Rose of Sharon); *Allegro*, Solomon's Entrance; *Andante*, Solo of Wooing; *Andantino*, Behind Words; Solomon's Solo Dance; Wedding Dance (Oriental in flavor); Love Duet; Solomon's Retreat; "At night on my bed"; "I chase you I am sick of love"; Invocation to Bring Back Beloved; and "I found him whom my soul loveth." [28]

A House Divided

During 1945 Weidman composed several theatre works for his Dance Company—using narration he called them Theatre Dance.[29] One of his most noteworthy works, *A House Divided* was an earnest dramatic portrait of Abraham Lincoln, the sixteenth President of the United States. *A House Divided* shows Weidman's concern for the social injustice and tragedy of war. The United States had been fighting four devasting years in World War II. As an artist whose credo was to elevate dance from entertainment to art, Weidman portrayed topical issues in his works. Margaret Lloyd confirms this when she writes: "In the midst of war he is making a conscious plea for unity . . ."[30] With music composed by Lionel Nowak, *A House Divided* was first performed at the Humphrey-Weidman Studio-Theatre on June 24, 1945. Weidman played the role of Abraham Lincoln. Other performers included Peter Harris, Albert Manny, Paul Wilson, Ann Dunbar, Betty Osgood, Pat Shafer, Barbara Thomas, Jane Thompson, Nadine Gae, Saida Gerrard, and Peter Hamilton.[31]

Employing his theatrical skills to create the conflicting factions of the Civil War, Weidman sensitively presents episodes or scenes in which the exaltation of the human spirit triumphs over adversity. Using actor Peter Harris to speak the thoughts of Lincoln, the work begins with the solemn ritual of Lincoln's funeral. This formal historic beginning portrays a small group of men and women mourning at a grave marked by a large cross and covered with a black shroud. The narrator enters carrying a wreath as he announces the death of President Lincoln. He places the wreath on the grave as the women clasp their hands in a dance of lamentation using sequences of Weidman techniques. Others enter wearing dark blue costumes and repeat these thematic modulation slides to the floor and recoveries.[32] As the cross is removed, the figure of Lincoln enters in a black frock coat; slowly he moves toward the group in blue as a group wearing gray costumes enter. Representing the conflict between the North and South,

Lincoln faces these two opposing groups as they violently rush toward each other. In another scene Weidman shows his plea for an end to prejudice and hatred by portraying several Negro slaves being beaten by their cruel overseer. The final scene shows the killing of a slave girl by her master and the reactions of an intolerant, wealthy Southern lady. The work ends with Lincoln's gesture of care as he carries the girl's body to her home. Beating drums unite the North with the South as the narrator proclaims, "A house divided against itself cannot stand."[33]

Fables of Our Time

Weidman was awarded a Simon Guggenheim Fellowship in 1947 to produce *Fables of Our Time*, a suite of four dances based on the stories of James Thurber. Regarding his collaborative relationship with James Thurber, Weidman wrote:

> Although I and my name have been associated with that of James Thurber for many years as a successful interpreter of his works, I have only met him twice. Our collaboration has been through correspondence. With the translation of his wonderful works into my medium [sic]—a combination of narration, mime, and dance, I have always aimed at keeping my dances pure Thurber. When I felt I had an idea that could be better expressed, say in movement, I would write him to get his permission. He was always cooperative and would let me change what I had asked. One instance was in the Fable "The Owl Who Was God." In his story the dumb Owl leads all the beasts and birds down a highway and an enormous truck mows them down. If my medium [sic] was the movies then I could have done it his way . . . So, I piled my set of boxes into a suggestion of a mountain and all the animals and birds, including the Owl, were destroyed by falling off a high precipice. Thurber's reply to this change was he had always believed "winged creatures could fly," and added, "Such was the power of the dance."
>
> Doris Humphrey shared my enthusiasm for James Thurber. She also thought his works were wonderful stage and dance material. Her ballet "The Race of Life" was the first Thurber work we did. Doris was the Mother, José Limón the Father, and I the Child.
>
> I believe that it was Doris who suggested that I do "Fables for Our Time." The four Fables I picked were "The Unicorn in the Garden," "The

Shrike and The Chipmunks," "The Owl Who Was God," and "The Little Girl and the Wolf." I have never been afraid of humor . . . so I made the last Fable slapstick humor. I portrayed both the Little Girl and the Wolf. The late Margaret Lloyd, the dance critic of the *Christian Science Monitor*, threw up her hands and cried bad taste. She was writing her now famous *Borzoi Book of Modern Dance* so instead of having her reactions recorded, I replaced the "Little Girl and the Wolf" with the "Courtship of Arthur and Al" as "The Beavers." In obtaining permission to use these, Thurber's written reply permitted me to use them. It also contained a bit of pure Thurber: "In order that my attorneys won't lose their minds, it is understood that if you make an unheard of amount of money that I receive a sizable percentage."

"The Unicorn in the Garden" was in the recent Broadway production of the "Thurber Carnival." A friend of mine in Detroit, who has a T.V. station and interviewed famous people who passed through that city, talked with James Thurber. He told her that he preferred my version to the one that was in the show. The reason was (besides the wonderful words spoken by the narrator) I have two other mediums [sic]—mime and dance. By using these three elements it can take me into that imaginative and almost spiritual world that Thurber is capable of creating, as a title of one of his books suggests: It is "My World & Welcome To It."[34]

The hilarious *Fables of Our Time* had its world premiere at Jacob's Pillow Dance Festival on July 10, 1947, with Freda Miller as the composer and accompanist, and was narrated in a "crisp, sophisticated fashion by Jack Ferris," writes Doris Hering.[35] Walter Terry's review of *Fables of Our Time* states: "The audience laughed loud and long over 'The Unicorn in the Garden,' 'The Shrike and the Chipmunks,' 'The Little Girl and the Wolf,' and 'The Owl Who Was God' and gave every indication of relishing the results of a Guggenheim award."[36] About Weidman's performance in "The Shrike and the Chipmunks," Hering's review notes: "Who can resist the airy grace of his hands as he plays at being a chipmunk arranging his acorns? Who can keep from laughing at the reluctant sag of his body and the gently distasteful expression on his face as he is led by his little chipmunk wife (the inimitable Betty Osgood) into the bright sunlight—or his plopping, bowlegged gait as the old reprobate owl?[37]

Weidman spent 1947 and 1948 touring the United States and Canada with his Theatre Dance Company, presenting concerts, lecture-demonstrations, and conducting master classes. In addition, Weidman held the post of choreographer and ballet master for the New York City Center Opera. *Dance Magazine* lists Weidman as one of the four ranking opera choreographers in America, along with George Balanchine, Ruth Page, and Antony Tudor. Since his youth in Lincoln, Nebraska, due to his performing experiences with Madame de Vilmar, Weidman admired voice and song, saying: "I like opera as a medium for dance much better than musical comedy. Opera is a distorted form that goes into voice and I like to use dance movement in the same manner."[38] Maybe Weidman's concert dances were influenced by his work in the opera as well. Many of his later works were composed to vocal or choral music, such as *A Song for You, The Christmas Oratorio, The Easter Oratorio*, and *Saint Matthew Passion*. His Bach dance works use a full chorus with voices supporting the strength of the movements that Weidman placed in counterpoint or contrapuntal form, as seen in these dances. The use of a large group of dancers forms a dynamic counterpart to the chorus, highlighting Weidman's skillfully crafted works for large ensembles. These works exhibit Weidman's fascination with transformation through the German libretto. These passion plays of Christ are mostly in abstract form; only a few sections rely on Weidman's pantomime skills. Weidman's work in the opera served him well in his search for clarity within his dance compositions and performances.

263

Chapter Ten

Living His Own Dreams

(1930-1960)

I have always believed that the audience and the performer are indivisible.
Both artist and audience enter the house—although through different doors—from
the same street. They have both seen the same headlines, left the same world of
reality behind them. And while the artist puts on his makeup, the audience leaves
its everyday disillusionment in the checkroom.

Charles Weidman
Random Remarks

The tenets of Charles Weidman's dance creations has remained constant
throughtout his career: "Their intent, concerned with human values and the
experience of our times . . . carried by the fullest emotional impact the artist can
muster."[1] This fundamental artistic credo dominated his concert works and was
about to transform the dance on the Broadway stage. Weidman's first experience
in choreographing for the Broadway theatre was when Norman Bel Geddes, one
of the most innovative theatre directors and designers of the 1920s and 1930s,
invited Weidman and Humphrey to compose the incidental dances and a
concluding bacchanal for his production of *Lysistrata*.

Broadway, The Big Apple

One evening Mr. Bel Geddes and his staff came to the Humphrey-
Weidman studio at Nine East Fifty-Ninth Street to watch class and select twelve

women and six men dancers for their production. The selected dancers were Jerome Andrews, Cleo Atheneos, Ernestine Henoch, Letitia Ide, Eleanor King, Charles Laskey, José Limón, and others. Being in their first Broadway show was exciting, but the rehearsals were long, physically draining, and unremitting—with no rehearsal salary.

Lysistrata, a comedy in two acts adapted from Aristophanes' play by Gilbert Seldes, opened at the Walnut Theatre in Philadelphia on April 28, 1930. It then moved to Broadway to the Forty-Fourth Street Theatre on January 5, 1931. The set consisted of a massive spiral staircase leading up to the Acropolis comprising fifty steps of various shapes, widths, and depths. When transferring the dance from the studio to the stage, the first rehearsal on Bel Geddes' set proved difficult. "Our carefully rehearsed bacchanal was a bedlam of disorder, that resulted in many injuries as we dashed madly up and down this treacherous construction," Humphrey-Weidman dancer Helen Savery wrote.[2]

After Humphrey and Weidman adapted their choreography for the set, the dance created a spectacular visual effect. In his review in *The New York Times*, Brooks Atkinson declared: "Norman Bel Geddes . . . has designed a magnificent production, imaginative, free, sculptural and colorful, and the concluding bacchanal, when viewed from the rear of the auditorium, is a memorable flow of color and motion."[3] *Lysistrata* was a tremendous success and ran for almost a full year.

While Weidman and Humphrey were dancing with Denishawn on their Asian Tour, the musical revue *Americana* opened at the Belmont Theatre on July 26, 1926. With book and lyrics by J. P. McEvoy, music by Con Conrad and Henry Souvaine, *Americana* ran for 128 performances. Two years later, a second *Americana* opened on October 30, 1928—a total disaster, this lasted only twelve performances.[4]

To bolster the morale of the American people, suffering from the emotional distress of the Depression, J. P. McEvoy conceived a sequel to his first patriotic review called *New Americana*, sometimes referred to as *Americana*. Produced by Lee Shubert at his Shubert Theatre, *New Americana* opened on October 5, 1932. It proved to be a "pioneer among revues," wrote David Ewen, "in that it included in its program formal ballet with performances by the Weidman and Humphrey Dancers."[5]

By the end of May, contracts were signed for all fourteen women in Humphrey's group as well as for Weidman and two men to perform previously conceived concert dances in *New Americana*: Weidman's *Piccoli Soldati*, Humphrey's *Water Study*, Weidman's *Ringside*, "a stylized prizefight," and Humphrey's *The Shakers*, "a Shaker meeting."[6]

While attending the Juilliard School of Music, Bernard Herrmann and Weidman became friends. When Weidman was working on *New Americana* he suggested Herrmann could compose a ballet. Herrmann called his work *Marche Militaire*, although Weidman named his choreographed ballet *Amour à la Militaire*. *Amour à la Militaire* was one of the show's standout numbers and was danced by Cleo Atheneos, Sylvia Manning (replaced in the tenth week by Dorothy Lathrop), José Limón, and Weidman.[7] *New Americana* marked the Broadway début of the Modern Dance. In his review in *The New York Times*, Atkinson confirmed this point when he wrote:

> No other commercial revue has gone quite so far with its dancing. There are the usual tap-dance turns and several beguiling chorus numbers. But with the Charles Weidman and Doris Humphrey dancers the musical revue begins to acquire plastic ideas. To the tune of "Satan's Little Lamb" they dance a fantastic number in the best vein of the modern stage. But Charles Weidman's lithographic portrait of a Madison Square bout [*Ringside*] has a descriptive rhythm that gives the dance a new prestige in the theatre, and the ballet waves sweeping across a beach [*Water Study*] is breathlessly

lovely. Amid all its confusion of humorous ideas "Americana" has set a pioneer's standard with its choreography.[8]

John Martin's review stressed how these two modern dance choreographers had affected the ordinary person in the audience when he concluded: "The dances staged by Doris Humphrey and Charles Weidman in 'Americana' . . . have opened a new field to the dance, and a new field to the revue; and in doing so have opened even the most optimistic, as well as the most skeptical eyes to the appeal of good dancing to the ordinary audience . . . Indeed, the dancing runs away with the show."[9] Martin observed that Weidman's success was due not so much to his ability to transfer his compositions to the Broadway stage, as to his facility in creating new dances for the Broadway theatre: "Given the best song in the revue, 'Satan's Little Lamb,' he has staged a jazz ensemble which is not only extraordinarily effective as a revue dance but is a first-rate composition as well."[10] Weidman, in his choreography for *New Americana*, employed various dance types such as tribal-based and vernacular, both considered roots of jazz dance as a theatrical form. He was successful in using social dance in *New Americana* as Martin's review noted: "In his amusing polka to 'Whistling for a Kiss,' . . . there are glimpses of that delicious mood which made 'The Happy Hypocrite' a delight.'"[11]

Another historic first used in the revue *New Americana* was the collaboration of the song-writing team of Harold Arlen and Johnny Mercer. The song remembered most often is "Brother Can You Spare a Dime?" with lyrics by E. Y. Harburg and Jay Gorney, "a major hit in 1932-33, a kind of theme song for the Depression," David Ewen wrote.[12] Even with its innovations *New Americana* had shortcomings as Gerald Bordman concluded in his review: "The comedy was weak or old hat or both. Skits made fun of movie moguls and breadline racketeers. But modern dance was apparently either too somber or too advanced for Broadway's pleasure-seekers and Americana's comedy too lame. The show survived less than ten weeks."[13]

While *Americana* was still running on Broadway, Weidman was engrossed in creating his most ambitious project—making a full-length dance drama of Voltaire's *Candide*. He adapted Voltaire's story, conceived the costumes, commissioned the composers, devised a vocal score for the dancers that alternated with the music, and began a rehearsal schedule more demanding than the company members had ever experienced before.[14] By this time, Humphrey had married Charles Francis Woodford, a sea captain she had met on a vacation cruise, and was pregnant; therefore the company was turned over to Weidman for his new project.

Late-night rehearsals for *Candide* began at the Eighteenth Street studio after every show of *Americana* at the Shubert Theatre. Helen Savery who, after graduating from Barnard College, studied at the Humphrey-Weidman studio and danced in *Lysistrata* and *Americana*, wrote about the rigors of Weidman's rehearsals for *Candide*:

> Night after night we rode the subway from the theatre where *Americana* was playing down to the studio, where we struggled with his vague, complicated, and often impromptu choreography. Because he had rehearsed the principal dancers—Eleanor King, José Limón, Katherine Manning—during the day, no doubt he was as exhausted as we were. By 3:00 a.m. this fatigue caused several emotional crises.[15]

The rehearsal situation was difficult and tedious since Weidman was creating *Candide* without music, using only counts, because the score was in the process of being composed. The rehearsal schedule for leading dancers Limón, King, and Manning was every day, including Sundays, throughout the entire winter until the opening at the Booth Theatre on May 15, 1933.[16] These *Candide* rehearsals were a true test of endurance, persistence, patience, and commitment for Weidman and the entire company. In her article, "Dancing in the Depression," Savery remembers the fierce dedication of the Humphrey-Weidman dancers:

> The young modern dancers of the early thirties were an amazingly dedicated and hard-working group. There was little or no drifting from one school to another. We were loyal to our chosen leaders and almost fiercely dedicated to their special dance technique and creativity. We were keenly aware that we were blazing new trails for Modern Dance, excessively scornful of the classical ballet tradition. We accepted without protest the necessity for part-time jobs to support ourselves, and we felt lucky to be paid ten dollars for a performance.[17]

With music composed by and arranged by Genevieve Pitot and John Coleman, Ian Wolfe adapted the text of *Candide* "into rhymed couplets to be spoken by a narrator."[18] Weidman conceived of an innovative stage device that anticipated contemporary trends where the dancers contribute to the dramatic action with their own voices. Eleanor King describes the dancer's roles. "In *Candide*, in the Eldorado scene, the dancers chanted nonsense syllables: 'Za zee zum za zee.' In the rape scene by the Bulgarian soldiers the men shouted, 'War, that is our business; rape that is our job!' and we girls, tossed into the air, used our own voices in screaming protest."[19]

Michael Myerberg, who assisted in the management of *New Americana*, was impressed with Weidman's *Candide*, a project that predated Leonard Bernstein's 1956 opera. With Myerberg's encouragement, J. J. Shubert agreed to collaborate on the production of *Candide* by providing a one-week run at his Booth Theatre. For Weidman this was a dream come true because at this time modern dance choreographers could only afford to do one performance on a Sunday afternoon or evening.

The entire Humphrey-Weidman organization rallied to do their best work for this special occasion. Weidman summoned Humphrey from her family's cottage in Vermont to supervise dress rehearsals. Pauline Lawrence designed the costumes and Perkins Harnley designed the theatre posters.

The plot of Voltaire's *Candide* follows the wanderings of the principal character Candide, who is left unprotected through a series of miserable exploits. Weidman danced the leading role of the hero (Candide) and Eleanor King played the hero's lover, Cunégonde. William Matons danced Candide's optimistic tutor, Dr. Pangloss, and Limón played the narrator, a type of master-of-ceremonies, among other roles. Charles used gray wooden boxes to create the stage set that became garden wall, fortress walls, tables, chairs, or beds that were pushed into place by the dancers.[20] In Weidman's *Candide*, dance action, music, and narrative happened simultaneously. The narrator was Richard Abbott,"who spoke through a huge mask of Voltaire which was suspended at the side of the stage," Lillian Moore writes.[21] *Candide* was a dance drama in two acts, four scenes and an interlude. Each scene in the dance drama began with a vision as follows: Scene One, "Vision: Conflict between Pessimism and Optomism"; Scene Two, "Vision: (The Church) Praise and Supplication"; Scene Three, "Vision: Travel and Promenade"; and Scene Four, 'Vision: Fate Intervenes."[22]

The opening-night performance was successful and the cast was jubilant at the audience's enthusiastic response. In the newspapers the next day, the show received mixed reviews. Some examples: "this version of Voltaire's romance should run for many weeks"; "Voltaire must have looked down from heaven and chuckled"; "impressive dancing"; "an interesting experiment"; "recommended to those who want to see Mr. Weidman dance and do not mind Voltaire's words reduced to a syllable"; and "it missed the point of Voltaire's *Candide* completely."

After a full house on opening night, the week's audience attendance dwindled due to unseasonably hot weather and spring thunderstorms. Weidman felt as if the ill fortune of Candide was seeping into his real world. Everyone involved with the production believed that the critics killed the show. It was a financial failure. After production costs were paid, the box office had no money left to pay the dancers. Charles had to borrow money to travel to his farm in New Jersey that he, José, and Pauline had recently purchased with their savings from *New Americana*. It was a bitter disappointment for everyone.

As an innovator of Broadway theatre dance, Weidman was subject to criticism from dance, theatre, and music reviewers who evaluated his art and publicized its faults. Fortunately, he had another chance to redeem his original *Candide* when, in 1936, the Federal Dance Project produced his revised *Candide*.

The failure of *Candide* did not seem to hinder the judgment of Broadway producers, when after the great success of *New Americana*, Charles found himself rehearsing for Irving Berlin's *As Thousands Cheer*. Charles was "good-natured and easy going," Limón wrote. "Producers loved him. Besides, they wanted what he had. It was fresh and new. It would sell. Best of all, they could get him—and his dancers—for a song."[23]

As Thousands Cheer was a topical revue of newspaper sketches and dances with satirical allusions to current events. Directed by Hassard Short and produced by Sam H. Harris, it opened at the Music Box Theatre on September 30, 1933. The cast included Marilyn Miller, Clifton Webb, Helen Broderick, and Ethel Waters.[24] The different scenes showed sections of a daily newspaper with front-page news, the society page, and the comics. Short used an innovative way to project the "newspaper headlines across the proscenium before each number."[25] The cast impersonated movie stars and political leaders with the aid of lifelike masks of these characters. Helen Broderick portrayed Herbert Hoover and the Statue of Liberty.

Charles may have been influenced to compose his topical dance *Lynchtown* in 1936 because he witnessed the reactions of audiences to one deeply distressing episode in *As Thousands Cheer*. Early in Act II, a news item flashed onto the stage and read: "Unknown Negro Lynched by Frenzied Mob." In his *New Complete Book of the American Musical Theatre*, David Ewen described this powerful scene. "What followed was Ethel Waters singing 'Supper Time,' a ballade telling of a colored woman getting supper ready for her husband, who had just been lynched."[26] After her portrayal of "Supper Time," Ethel Waters received successive ovations and stopped the show. Charles learned the poignant theatricality of this subject and the artistry of Ethel Waters.

In *As Thousands Cheer*, Weidman composed his best dance numbers with Limón (who had been promoted to Weidman's assistant), Letitia Ide, and other Weidman dancers who were featured in his dances "Heat Wave," "Revolt in Cuba," "The Lonely Heart's Column," "Not for All the Rice in China," and Irving Berlin's greatest song "Easter Parade." Weidman's effectively staged production number of "Easter Parade" ended Act I. In his book, *New Complete Book of the American Musical Theatre*, David Ewen describes the number: "The people parading in their Easter finery down Fifth Avenue were all brown (to simulate the color of the rotogravure sections then found in the Sunday papers). They suddenly became motionless, frozen into an immobile position, as Marilyn Miller and Clifton Webb sang 'Easter Parade.'"[27] Weidman was delighted by the favorable outcome of his dances for this Broadway show. *As Thousands Cheer* was "a triumph, running a year," or 400 performances, and "making a handsome profit, a rarity during depression days," before closing on September 8, 1934.[28]

At this time, the Humphrey-Weidman Company was dancing in two Broadway shows simultaneously: *As Thousands Cheer* and *The School for Husbands*, the Theatre Guild's version of Molière's comedy. It opened at the Empire Theatre on October 16, 1933, and closed on January 20, 1934. Weidman

273

and Humphrey were contracted to perform and choreograph a ballet *The Dream of Sganarelle*. Humphrey danced the roles of Columbine and Shepherdess, while Weidman performed the roles of Harlequin and the Dancing Master.

These Broadway producers offered Weidman and Humphrey an opportunity that most Broadway choreographers didn't have available to them at the time. When they were contracted to create dances for a Broadway show, their company was hired too. It was an extraordinary situation for them to work with dancers trained in their personal movement styles and techniques. A central challenge for any Broadway choreographer is developing the necessary stylistic unity with dancers trained in various techniques and styles. Humphrey and Weidman remedied this situation, thus attaining successful results on the Broadway stage.

Their company was employed in two Broadway theatre productions during 1933-34. This was the first time in the history of the American musical theatre this occurred and would not be replicated until the late twentieth century when Tywla Tharp was contracted for *Singin' in the Rain* at the Gershwin Theatre in 1985. Tharp's reasons for taking the contract for the Broadway revival were similar to Humphrey and Weidman's financial and creative motives:

> A revival of *Singin' in the Rain* had been running for years in London to capacity crowds, and its New York cousin looked like a shoo-in. With any luck I would be able to park my company in the show for several seasons, providing not only an alternative to our frantic touring but also, once the show was running smoothly, the opportunity to rehearse new dances during the afternoons. We could start a school to develop understudies and road companies. In my quixotic world, Broadway would subsidize art. More immediately, we could be free from the long-term financial worries, and the opening-night benefit would clear out our *Catherine Wheel* deficit. That was the plan.[29]

The School for Husbands employed Humphrey and Weidman along with their dancers Cleo Atheneos, Ernestine Henoch, Ada Korvin, Eleanor King, Katherine Manning, Hyla Rubin, Marcus Blechman, George Bockman, Kenneth Bostock, Jack Cole, and Francis Reed. Once they began rehearsals in the theatre the dancers' contract was $30 a week; after January 1934 their salary was raised to $40 a week.[30] The Broadway production was directed by Lawrence Langer, with music by Edmond W. Richett, and was a new version of Molière's *The School for Husbands* that had its premiere in 1661 at the Académie de la Danse in Paris under the patronage of King Louis XIV. Mr. Langner inserted the ballet interlude between the two acts of the play to reflect Molière's tendency to introduce ballets in his later works.[31] The situation of the play revolves around old man Sganarelle (Osgood Perkins), who wants to marry a young woman, Isabella (June Walker). In a dream, Sganarelle asks guidance from the spirits of Solomon, Socrates, two Egyptians, and a Dancing Master. With their help he receives permission from Isabelle's father to marry, and they perform a wedding pavanne with other couples. As soon as Sganarelle dances with his bride, played by Humphrey, "the music quickens to a fast contradance. The dancing master enters and dances away the bride," writes Eleanor King.[32] In his review of *School for Husbands* in *The American Dancer*, Joseph Arnold notes Humphrey and Weidman's mastery of French baroque dance:

> The chief dancing number in the *School for Husbands* is a ballet, lasting about 25 minutes, which was adapted, so the program stated, from *Le Marriage Forcé*, originally danced in 1664 by Louis XIV and his court. It is, in the transformation effected by Weidman and Miss Humphrey, a burlesque satire. The ballet successfully preserves both the stiltedness and wantonness of the French court dances."[33]

As Thousands Cheer and *The School for Husbands* couldn't be more stylistically antithetical, bringing attention to the versatility of the Humphrey-

275

Weidman partnership. Joseph Arnold declared: "Charles Weidman is a complete dancer. He is an imaginative and sensitive artist, and he is an interpreter of the dance art."[34] Martin's review in *The New York Times* observed their artistry: "Miss Humphrey is as captivating as the great Isabella herself, and there is more Molière in one move and gesture of Charles Weidman than hours of spoken text."[35]

Before the start of the first summer dance intensive at Bennington College, Weidman was contracted by Robert Alton to compose the dances for an original Broadway musical revue, *Life Begins at 8:40*. David Freedman conceived the book, Ira Gershwin and E. Y. Harburg wrote the lyrics, and Harold Arlen composed the music. *Life Begins at 8:40*, directed by John Murray Anderson and Philip Loeb, actually began nightly at 8:40 p.m. at the Winter Garden Theatre.[36]

The show opened on August 27, 1934, and was a success. Weidman's strongly choreographed musical numbers featured Bert Lahr, with several distinctive dance numbers. Weidman was now at the pinnacle of his Broadway career, as recognized in Arnold's review of *Life Begins at 8:40*: "This writer has steadfastly held that Charles Weidman is the best male dancer in this country: 'He has always been impressed by his authentic feeling for the true dance, as he has always been repelled by the synthetic exhibitions of the poseurs who have largely taken possession of the New York concert stage.'"[37]

In the biggest dance number, "Shoein' the Mare," "the rage for Cuban dance was spoofed at . . ."[38] Weidman was a perfect choice to conceptualize "Shoein' the Mare," featuring Ester Junger and the Weidman Dancers: Regina Beck, George Bockman, Geri Chopin, Aline Davis, Darley Fuller, Ilse Gronau, Mary Howard, Ethel Medsker, Betty Schlaffer, Josephine Schwartz, Tom Draper, William Gerrard, and Michael Logan.[39] Weidman capitalized on various Cuban dances but particularly used the Rumba, to which he added his own stylistic arms and compositional structure. Weidman appears to have added his own distinctive

276

features of what was considered jazz dancing. Arnold's review in *The American Dancer* took notice: "strutting becomes a unique trademark of the show. The most conspicuous feature of his numbers is a spasmodic jerking of the torso, which . . . is the bond he thinks should unite serious dancing with the jazz of a Broadway revue."[40]

Life Begins at 8:40 paid off its entire production costs in just ten weeks. The revue cost over $130,000 to produce. Its weekly gross was estimated at $40,000, with operating costs about $23,000—leaving a handsome profit. The show ran for seven months (237 performances) and closed on March 16, 1935. Immediately, a touring company with Letitia Ide replacing Ester Junger performed *Life Begins at 8:40* in Pittsburgh, Philadelphia, Washington D.C., and Chicago until May 1935.[41]

As Weidman was performing his dance adaptation of *Candide* as part of the Federal Dance Project at the Nora Bayes Theatre, he was contracted to create the choreography for a new musical comedy as part of the Federal Theatre Project *I'd Rather Be Right*. He collaborated with the greatest figures of the Broadway stage including the show's star, George M. Cohan. About the show and Cohan's performance George Bordman wrote, "It was a great role . . . for the great showman. He could be brash, vital, chauvinistic, and preachy."[42] *I'd Rather Be Right* was written by George S. Kaufman and Moss Hart, with lyrics by Lorenz Hart and music composed by Richard Rodgers. Directed by George S. Kaufman, *I'd Rather Be Right* "was a warm-hearted jab at the Roosevelt adminstration."[43]

Weidman collaborated on some numbers with Ned McGurn, but Weidman's artistry was noticed when touches of vaudeville were interspersed throughout the show. Weidman's modern dances used in the scene "American Couple" did not impress *The New York Times* critic Brooks Atkins, who wrote: "There are some varied dances for tapping and twirling, including one tedious bit of documentation entitled 'American Couple.'"[44] *I'd Rather Be Right* had its

277

premiere on November 2, 1937, at the Alvin Theatre. The show enjoyed a nine-month run with great box-office business because the only other musical playing on Broadway was another Rodgers and Hart show, *Babes in Arms*.[45]

In the fall of 1942, Charles was given a contract to choreograph a new Broadway revue with dancer John Wray. With book and lyrics by John Lund, music by Lee Wainer, and directed by Lawrence Hurdle, *New Faces of 1943* opened at the Ritz Theatre on December 22, 1942. The show was compiled of thirty-three sketches commenting on all facets of American life. Some of the sketches were "The Assembly Line," "Richard Crudnut's Charm School," "Land of Rockefellera," "Shoes," "Back to Bundling," and "Musical Chairs."[46] *New Faces of 1943* ran for ninety-four performances closing on March 13, 1943.

During performances Weidman was contracted to create the choreography for the Broadway show *Star Dust*. A comedy produced and directed by Michael Myerberg, *Star Dust* opened on September 7, 1943, in Philadelphia. Walter Kerr, author of *Star Dust*, was chair of the Drama Department at Catholic University in Washington, D.C., where the show was first produced and directed by Kerr.[47] Many critics considered the poor direction and inadequate acting reasons for *Star Dust's* early demise in Baltimore on September 25, 1943.

Weidman went directly into rehearsals for *Marching with Johnny*, a musical revue produced by the National Congress of Industrial Organization's War Productions. The show opened on November 22, 1943, in Newark, New Jersey, and it was scheduled for an eight-week run at the City Center of Music and Art. Weidman was choreographic supervisor and staged the dances with Dan Eckley. Through the show's fervent patriotism, the C.I.O. production pointed to labor's part in the war effort.[48] The show never made it to Broadway; it closed on December 25, 1943, in Philadelphia, meanwhile Weidman was in final rehearsals.

Weidman and Lauretta Jefferson created the dances for the musical comedy *Jackpot,* starring Nanette Fabray. Written by Guy Bolton, Sidney

Sheldon, and Den Roberts, with lyrics and music by Howard Dietz and Vernon Duke, and directed by Roy Hargrave, *Jackpot* was produced by Vinton Freedley at the Alvin Theatre on January 13, 1944. In his review in the *New York Herald Tribune*, Howard Barnes explained the plot of the show: "The idea of the piece is amusing and topical enough to have inspired a better frame work for the songs and dances. A pretty defense worker permits herself to be the prize in a war-bond selling campaign, and is promptly won by three marines."[49]

Jackpot's first-act finale called "Grist for De Mille" was Weidman's parody on *Oklahoma!* Weidman used leading dancers Don Liberto, Billie Worth, and Althea Elder, along with Peter Hamilton, Florence Lessing, and Flower Hujer. In his review in the *New York Daily News,* John Chapman wrote about Weidman's clever ballet idea:

> Last night's audience sat on its hands most of the time and when it applauded it did so perfunctorily and out of a sense of duty. Once it did get up a little steam over a ballet which closed the first act, titled "Grist for De Mille' and staged by Charles Weidman.
> This is a burlesque of such Agnes De Mille numbers as are to be found in "Oklahoma" and "One Touch of Venus," in which Miss Wickes explains that things aren't the same in musical comedy since the ballet came to Shubert Alley. The idea and the way Mr. Weidman had worked it out are genuinely humorous, but unfortunately Mr. Weidman hasn't dancers good enough to get the most out of it. If you're going to top De Mille you must have the best dancers.[50]

Weidman collaborated with Humphrey in 1944 on a new Broadway musical comedy called *Sing Out, Sweet Land!* a salute to American folk and popular music written by Elie Siegmeister. Walter Kerr wrote the book and Lawrence Langner and Theresa Helburn directed the show with additional staging by Leon Leonidoff. Presented by the Theatre Guild, the show opened amid a snowstorm on December 27, 1944, at the International Theatre in New York.

279

The four dances choreographed by Weidman and Humphrey featured dancers Peter Hamilton, Irene Hawthorn, and Ethel Mann (Reed) with a group of twenty dancers.[51] After an enthusiastic performance on opening night, the Broadway show *Sing Out, Sweet Land!* received varied reviews from the critics. In *The New York Times*, Lewis Nichols noted the show's plot: "Since the songs had to be connected in some fashion, Mr. Kerr chose the figure of one Barnaby Goodchild, [Alfred Drake] a vocal Paul Bunyan, who sings and dances and wanders through America."[52] A rave review in the *New York Daily News* written by John Chapman showed his enthusiasm for *Sing Out, Sweet Land*:

> Just wonderful, a calvacade of American songs . . . spotted through this series of words and music are dances and production numbers and I can't tell which I like best. I thought the Illinois Wilderness scene . . . was grand—but then came the Oregon Trail scene and Foster's "Oh, Susannah," after that was a Mississippi River scene in which Jack McCauley, Alma Kaye and Mr. [Burl] Ives sang and acted "Frankie and Johnny" in such a fashion which had me hugging myself for joy.[53]

Contrarily, the *New York Post* reviewer, Wilella Waldorf, wrote: "One or two of the dancing numbers staged by Doris Humphrey and Charles Weidman are pleasantly amusing, but for the most part they, too, partake of the slightly stale quality of the entire production."[54] Even with differing critical reviews, *Sing Out, Sweet Land!* played to large audiences for three months before closing on March 24, 1945.

Weidman's next Broadway show was a musical comedy based on the story of *Cinderella* by Perrault. *If The Shoe Fits* opened at the New Century Theatre on December 5, 1946. Written by June Carroll and Robert Duke, with lyrics by June Carroll, music by David Raksin, and produced by Leonard Sillman, *If The Shoe Fits* presented a large cast of characters. The show was lengthy, with a prologue, two acts, and thirteen scenes, but Weidman was in his element as a master of wit and comedy. With seventeen dancers in the Corps de Ballet (nine women and seven men), Weidman choreographed about seven dance numbers including "Start the Ball Rollin," "Night After Night," "With a Wave of My Hand," and "If the Shoe Fits."[55] Unfortunately, the lighthearted show closed after only twenty performances on December 21, 1946.

In collaboration with Humphrey, Weidman finalized his work with leading dancers Josephine Keene and Helene Ellis for the Broadway production of *The Barrier*. Considered to be a hybrid form of musical drama and opera, the show traveled to Ann Arbor, Michigan, on June 3, 1950, where Weidman directed the dances and performed a leading dance part.[56] In his article, "Broadway Callboard" in *Dance News*, Arthur Todd expressed how much in demand Weidman was as a topnotch choreographer:

> Charles Weidman will stage the dance sequences for the Langston Hughes--Jan Meyerowitz musical drama *The Barrier* produced by Daniel Meyerberg. Due for its tryouts at Woodstock, N.Y. the week of September 3, it will come to N.Y. shortly afterwards. Present plans call for Weidman to play a featured roll in the production. If so, he will have to relinquish it soon after the Broadway premiere because of prior commitment to stage the dances for both the NY and Chicago fall engagement for the N.Y. City Opera Company.[57]

The Barrier, a musical drama, opened at the Broadhurst Theatre on November 2, 1950. Produced by Michael Myerberg and Joel Spector, the action of the show takes place on a hot summer day in a rural Georgia community.[58] Based on his play *Mulatto*, Langston Hughes wrote the book and lyrics and Jan Meyerowitz composed the music. Using movement to portray the development of their relationship, the exposition of this complex story involves the two main characters Col. Thomas Norwood (Lawrence Tibbett) and his Negro housekeeper, Cora Lewis (Muriel Rahn). In their youth, their roles were danced by Josephine

Keene and Marc Breaux, who danced in *Kiss Me, Kate,* and with Weidman's Company as a principal dancer. Unfortunately, after four performances, *The Barrier* closed on November 4, 1950.[59] Twenty days later, the successful Frank Loesser musical *Guys and Dolls* opened at the Forty-Sixth Street Theatre (with choreography by Michael Kidd), and ran for three years on Broadway.

After a six-year hiatus Weidman created the dances for *The Littlest Revue,* which opened off-Broadway at the Phoenix Theatre on May 22, 1956. A stellar cast included Tammy Grimes, Odgen Nash, and Joel Grey. Weidman received numerous congratulatory telegrams during the run of the show:

> Western Union Telegram, May 22, 1956
> To Charles Weidman
> Phoenix Theatre
> "Brilliant is the word Charles for what you have done—Thanks to you I am a very happy author—All the Best   Ogden"[60]

> Western Union Telegram, May 22, 1956
> To Charles Weidman
> Phoenix Theatre
> "We wish you the best of luck tonight—knock em dead—May the Littlest Revue be the Biggest Success." Marvin Gordon and Bill Hooks[61]

> Western Union Telegram, June 9, 1956
> To Charles Weidman
> Phoenix Theatre
> "We will be watching. I wrote to everyone. God bless you and good luck." John and LaVone[62]

After the success of *The Littlest Revue* Weidman collaborated with Ray Harrison on his last Broadway show. *Portofino* was an original musical comedy that opened at the Adelphi Theatre on Friday, February 21, 1958. With book and lyrics by Richard Ney, music by Louis Bellson and Will Irwin, and direction by Karl Genus, the action takes places on a piazza in Portofino, Italy. *Portofino* consists of a prologue, two acts, and three scenes. Using sixteen dancers (eight women and eight men), Weidman and Harrison choreographed witty musical numbers such as "Dance Of The Whirling Wimpus," "Guido's Tango," "Bacchanale," and "Kitty Car Ballet."[63] Weidman received this congratulatory telegram on the opening night of *Portofino*:

> Western Union Telegram, February 21, 1958
> To Charles Weidman
> Adelphi Theatre
> "Let Critics Fall Where They May—I Cast My Laurels At Your Feet."
> Good Luck—Ernie[64]

New York City Center Opera Company

In June 1950, Charles Weidman received the prestigious *Dance Magazine Award* for his outstanding choreography and unique performing talent. He received rave reviews for his dances and stage direction in the New York City Opera productions of *The Love for Three Oranges* and *The Dybbuk* in New York City. Weidman, as resident choreographer and ballet master, often commuted to Chicago, where the New York City Opera was in residence. "Expressive dance and pantomimic movement have been Weidman's forte for two decades, it is those facets that should make his operatic work valued and interesting," Ann Barzel wrote.[65]

The New York City Opera's production of *The Love for Three Oranges* was an "amazingly successful production," wrote Nik Krevitsky in his review in *Dance Observer*. Krevitsky continued to credit Weidman for the success of the opera, noting that the entire production "becomes a movement drama in which all the singers move as dancers, and it becomes difficult to differentiate the actual dance sequences from the rest of the proceedings."[66] In an interview with Ann

Barzel, Weidman explained that his approach to staging opera scenes was to creatively coordinate both singers and the dancers by "blending their movements and gestures in a similar style. The dancing should not be a divertissement, but part of the dramatic whole—belonging to the plot of the opera and growing out of the singing."[67] In an interview with Authur Todd, Weidman maintained that his success with opera was fundamentally rooted in the opera's libretto:

> I consider one of my most successful opera dances the one in *Traviata*, where I base the dance on the words of the young bullfighter who wants to marry the girl but first must kill the bulls to win her. Similarly, though my dances for *Aida* are spectacular, they are also according to the libretto. The company dances in front of Amneris, with their backs to the audience, because it is a dance of entertainment to her.[68]

Some might consider that Weidman made a drastic departure from traditional opera by changing the size of the dance ensemble and through his innovative use of stage space. During the 1950s, an average opera company used two to three dozen dancers, but Weidman's basic dancing group was four girls and four boys and this number was doubled for *Aida* and *The Love for Three Oranges*.[69]

In Chicago, Weidman worked with Ruth Page, a noted ballet choreographer, and her dancers through the Chicago Dance Council. He also created a solo, *Medea* for the renowned ballerina Mia Slavenska, which premiered at the Jacob's Pillow Summer Dance Festival in Lee, Massachusetts. When Weidman created the dance sequences for the Broadway musical drama *The Barrier*, he was also artist-in-residence at the American Dance Festival at Connecticut College. Charles taught classes at his school (a January 1953 intensive) to more than thirty students, among these were Richard Englund, Paul Taylor, and Deborah Zall.[70] He gave master classes and lecture-demonstrations nationally, managed his school and company, composed new works—most notably James Thurber's *The War Between Men and Women* in eleven kinetic pantomime scenes—and rehearsed and performed with his Theatre Dance Company. At fifty years of age, Weidman's artistic energy, vitality, and noteworthy contributions could not be denied.

Forced Transition

The closing of the Sixteenth Street Studio Theatre in October 1951 began a sorrowful undercurrent that tugged at Weidman until 1960. Since inflating real estate prices made it impossible for him to maintain the Studio Theatre, he moved to a small, dismal space at West Fifty-Fifth Street. With this move Weidman made a total break from his artistic partnership with Doris Humphrey. This separation began a transition that would be full of obstacles.

Emotionally injured by Humphrey's decision to nurture José Limón's artistic career, Weidman was a master at hiding his anguish behind a carefree manner. Why didn't Humphrey continue the Humphrey-Weidman School and Company? Why didn't she compose new works for a company trained in the Humphrey-Weidman style and technique, thus supporting and promoting Weidman's career? Answers to these questions are haunting. This, I believe, is the root of Weidman's neglect and subsequent lack of the recognition he deserves for his dance.

Some say that Pauline Lawrence pestered Humphrey to promote Limón's career. Some dance scholars think Humphrey and Limón were ideologically aligned, but others say that philosophically and artistically it was Weidman and Humphrey who were two sides of the same coin.[71] Humphrey complained about how Weidman over-commercialized his art by choreographing Broadway shows. Whenever she pressured him to compose more concert dances, Weidman declined offers to work on Broadway and his income was greatly reduced as a result. Of course, such action limited his opportunities for the future. Seemingly, Weidman always tried to please both Humphrey and Lawrence, each of whom tended to be domineering. Many times Humphrey and Lawrence would argue about pragmatic and philosophic matters, and Weidman would just retreat. Over time, the irreconcilable riff with Limón over his attentions to a new, younger dancer (Peter Hamilton) brought Weidman much sadness. Weidman had never worked on his own—alone—and didn't want to. He needed the support of, and was highly inspired by, women artists such as St. Denis, Graham, Humphrey, Lawrence, Ronny Johannson, Tamiris, Vivian Fine, Freda Miller, Barbara Morgan, Ruth Page, among others.

Humphrey allied herself with Limón and Lawrence, and everyone moved into separate apartments. Weidman's artistic family left him—he was truly alone. During the 1950s, while Weidman struggled to maintain his artistic career, Humphrey and Limón were enjoying success on the concert stage and in their newly developed positions on the prestigious faculty in the Juilliard School of Music's Dance Program.

In 1950, hesitating on his Broadway show *The Barrier,* Weidman asked Humphrey for help. This situation seems more than a plea for artistic assistance. Charles found his way to connect with Doris the only way he knew how…he faltered—and wanted her to pull him through. He desperately wanted things to be as they were. He wavered emotionally, escaping through alcohol dependency. While Humphrey and Limón departed on a European tour, Weidman suffered from depression, and became reclusive.

Weidman was not invited to teach at the American Dance Festival from 1948-50, but in August 1951 he danced in the premiere performance of Pauline Koner's *Amorous Adventure* in the American Dance Festival at Connecticut College. Weidman also premiered a new solo, *A Song for You* to Portuguese songs by Elsie Houston, a Brazilian soprano. He had hoped to collaborate with Houston before her death in 1946, and this solo was a tribute to her memory. Perhaps this solo was also an expression of Weidman's loss for his partnership with Humphrey. In her review, Winthrop Palmer observed that the suite of dances "seemed to be about a man possessed with a woman's voice."[72] Was the man dependent upon the woman for love and support? Palmer's account in this section of *A Song for You* describes gestures of reaching out and a realization of emptiness, giving one an image of loss as "Weidman is slowly drawn into a circle of ghastly yellow light and opens and closes his hands in contact with nothing at all . . ."[73] Doris Hering's review reaffirms this idea of loss of love: "And in the tender posturings of the last dance, which was obviously a love song, one saw with alarm hints of a style of decorative plastique that placed Mr. Weidman squarely back into his Denishawn origin—odd place for him to be at this late date."[74]

Hering finds it "odd" that Weidman tenderly presents his Denishawn roots. Perhaps in *A Song for You* he is remembering the beginning of his partnership and love for Humphrey that were inexplicably tied to Denishawn. It seems a natural inclination for a person to reflect on fond memories of the past when the present and future are dim. *A Song for You* indicates Weidman's yearning for the past. His life was not as full now due to the loss of his artistic alliance with Humphrey, Limón, and Lawrence. At the same time, his assistant Peter Hamilton left—breaking out on his own with another company.

Unfortunately, financial peril brought another painful loss. Weidman had to dissolve his company for a short time, but in December 1953 he settled into a handsome new studio at 934 Eighth Avenue. There he composed James Thurber's *The War Between Men and Women*. The work had its first performance on April 25, 1954, at the 92nd Street Y. *The War Between Men and Women* used fifteen dancers and was choreographed in eleven scenes. Weidman played the role of the Man opposite Lila Lewis, who danced the Woman. Weidman also composed *Saudades* to the music of Milhaud for Nadine Gae. Using Tchaikovsky's "Symphonie Pathétique" for musical background, Weidman

287

composed *Air Gaie,* which opened the program "with light fresh style," Louise
Guthman wrote in the *Dance Observer.*[75]

Weidman was invited to maintain residence in the Los Angeles area
during 1956-57. He lived at the Hollywood Inn while teaching at several studios,
including Perry's Studio in Hollywood, and he was on the faculty at Idyllwild
Arts Academy Summer School of Dance. At this time, Weidman began a
teaching tour that forced him to rebound and depend on himself.

Due to lack of money Weidman was living at the Woodward Hotel on
Broadway and Fifty-Fifth Street in New York City, where he painfully survived
the pathos of Doris Humphrey's death on December 29, 1958. In a tribute to
Humphrey, Weidman decided to choreograph one of her unfinished projects
based on a book by James Thurber and E. B. White, *Is Sex Necessary? Or Why
You Feel the Way You Do.* Immediately he set about to get permission for the
project from Thurber and White. They both agreed without reservation, so
Charles decided to stage the dance in a 1959 summer workshop at Portland State
College in Portland, Oregon. Using a great deal of pantomime, the form
Weidman used in *Is Sex Necessary? Or Why You Feel the Way You Do* is that of
an illustrated lecture, alternating between slides on a screen, and live scenes, most
of which are set in rhythmic action to music.

Returning to New York City, Weidman assembled a company of dancers
and created *Classroom, Modern Style,* a technique demonstration, and *Further
Fables for Our Time* which included the Thurber fables "The Clothes Moth and
the Luna Moth," "The Tigress and Her Mate," "The Rose, the Fountain and the
Dove," "Oliver and the Other Ostriches," and "What Happened to Charles"?
Weidman also restaged *Is Sex Necessary? Or Why You Feel the Way You Do* and
The War Between Men and Women. These were shown in a performance at the
Henry Street Theatre on February 12-14, 1960. At the age of sixty, Weidman
began a new decade with renewed dedication and strength of purpose.

Chapter Eleven

Expression of Two Arts
(1960-1970)

I have always been impatient with the *art pour l'artist*.
Clarity and understandability has remained the basis of my dance creations.

Charles Weidman
Random Remarks

Ruth L. Murray, Chair of the Department of Physical Education for Women, invited Weidman to teach at Wayne State University in a three-day residency culminating with his performance in the Adventure Series Concert.[1] In 1960, while at Wayne State, Weidman met a young art student, Mikhail Santaro, who asked permission to sketch in Weidman's class. Teaching that summer in the Connecticut College American Dance Festival, Weidman arranged for Mikhail Santaro to be in residence. In a letter to George R. Kernodle, Director of Theatre at the University of Arkansas, regarding a residency there, Weidman wrote: "I am somewhat associated with a young brilliant artist—Mikhail Santaro—he joined me this summer in New London, Conn—was artist-in-residence in the big Summer dance school there . . ."[2]

Weidman's residency in the American Dance Festival that summer marked his re-entry into the professional dance scene, establishing him, as it did in 1934 at Bennington College, as a prime mover in American modern dance. After this residency, Weidman was invited to teach at a prestigious summer dance camp where Santaro accompanied him. In the same letter to Kernodle, Weidman wrote: "Then he [Santaro] went with me to Interlochen, Michigan, where at a ten-day workshop session did costumes and sets. He also has done the same thing at Wayne (Detroit) where I first met him. He is not primarily a costume and set designer but a painter."[3]

Studio Theatre

By the end of the summer, they decided to establish a studio and theatre where they might each follow their separate careers and collaborate on joint projects. They found a second-floor loft in a building just off Sixth Street in the florist district in New York City. They converted this loft, at 102 West Twenty-Ninth Street, into a small dance studio, a thirty-seat theatre, storage space for costumes and props, and a living area for Weidman. The Studio Theatre represented a considerable investment, since the entire second floor of the building had to be surveyed and building plans of all floors, including the cellar, had to be approved. They hired architect Irving G. Kay to proceed with the renovation plans.[4] Second-floor occupancy was limited to seventy-four persons, and no apartment use on this floor was permitted (although Charles did live at the studio in a small apartment). They named it the Expression of Two Arts Studio and Theatre, and it became a home where Weidman taught and the two men presented programs of Weidman's dances, Santaro's lectures or demonstrations of painting and calligraphy, and eventually combined their arts.

While the studio theatre and apartment were being renovated, Weidman departed on his annual teaching tour of colleges and universities, where he taught his technique and restaged his dances. In this studio, for the next fifteen years, Weidman trained dancers and taught his Dance Teachers' Summer Workshop which, in 1970, consisted of one and a half hour technique classes and half-hour notation classes, for just $35 for seven sessions.[5] He kept his classes affordable

290

and lived simply; the rent of the loft was $150 monthly, but in September 1974 the rent was increased to $325 monthly.[6] Part of the renovation was Weidman's specifications for the floor in his studio, as Margaret O'Sullivan remembers:

> Charles was very proud of the floor he had installed on 29th Street. I think he said it was white birch, which had wonderful buoyancy and had a plastic runner around the dressing area leading to the studio. When it was time to go across the floor, he would be simultaneously smoking his cigarette, rolling up the runner, and beating the drum without missing a beat! It always amazed us.[7]

Weidman and Santaro's collaboration was based on similar artistic views; their works stressed clarity of form and used the principle of rebound. Santaro's artistic statement described his work as a type of kinetic sculpture. "Mikhail Santaro is a sculptor working in . . . wire and wood. He has created a striking new form of sculpture . . . 'Spring Action' sculpture . . . a form that springs into artistic action. Yet it curves to an infinite inner serenity."[8] Weidman based his dance technique on rebound, a springing action with a dynamic shift of energy.

One of their first dances, *To Make a Form - To Give It Life,* to Corelli's Twelve Chamber Trio Sonatas, Opus 4, combined dance and painting in an innovative manner, as did their next work, *Calligraphy of the Dance.* While Weidman danced, Santaro painted his motions in an interactive way. In a review of their performance in Chicago, Ann Barzel describes Santaro's performance: "Santaro, a personable Russian-Japanese, and a painter with dance training gave a daub-talk on his own. He talked, he ran, he dove to the floor—all ending in inspired smears on his canvas."[9]

Weidman and Santaro shared an admiration for the traditional Asian arts such as Japanese Kabuki theatre and Chinese opera. Weidman composed a duet with Santaro in 1964 called *A Chinese Actor Prepares for the Role of the God of*

291

War. Using Igor Stravinsky's music entitled Symphony of Wild Instruments, Weidman wrote the following program note regarding the work:

Notes on *"A Chinese Actor Prepares For The Role of the God of War"*

The audience will see the role of "The Actor Preparing for a Part," which is the nature of the dance to be performed.

Suddenly a man appears. He falls to one knee and outstretches one arm pointing up to Heaven, the other arm pointing down to the Earth.

Large sheets of paper moving like mountains and winds are brought in and are given to the man. These depict the man's sacred preparation to receive his ritual robes. The papers glide to the floor, and long wooden poles are divided between the players. In a moment, the players move the poles in circles churning up the voices of the dead. In the next moment, the poles are swords battling against an evil enemy.

The players gather the papers and crush them into bodies. Paper pushed into a loop at the end of a pole becomes a God Head, a symbol of war and mass dead. One player demonstrates his appetite for killing by swinging a pole and smashing the paper. This player sacrifices himself in the face of the God Head and his body is covered with the paper. The player of the God of War dances off into the Heavens.

This is one explanation for the papers and the poles, but a number of explanations might apply; it is up to the audience's interpretation. The papers and poles are devices meant to transform the stage space into a field of action for dance. They become symbols and transcend the movement and the music.[10]

When Weidman and Santaro went on tours and taught master classes and performed their works, they had technical specifications for their classes and concerts. Before arriving at a location or site, they would send their requirements and a publicity packet in advance to each sponsor, as follows:

For his lecture performance, Mr. Santaro prefers to have two suspended boards, 4 feet by 5 feet, with ten sheets of white paper on each. One board hanging left center stage, one upstage center. If this is not possible, easels must be provided.

In "Saints, Sinners and Scriabin" Mr. Weidman requires a secure standing wall, 5 feet by 5 feet, upstage left. For the solo "In the Beginning," seven battens or hooks must be overhead as per the diagram. The stage set consists of a continuous clothesline (which will be supplied) and must be strong, exactly as according to the diagram. A small mobile will also be supplied.

Lighting requirements: In "Saints, Sinners and Scriabin" there will be 22 blackouts and 21 light changes.[11] [Weidman choreographed and danced twenty-two diverse solos, which exhibited his expertise in dramatic characterization.]

Saints, Sinners and Scriabin   Recorded by Gina Bachauer
(From the Suite of 24 Preludes, Opus 11, by Scriabin)
Choreographed and Danced by Charles Weidman

No. 1	in C Major (played)
No. 2	Themes of Destruction
No. 3	in G Major—Whirligig
No. 4	Sad Garden
No. 5	Voices Heard
No. 6	Dillinger
No. 7	in A Major—Cirro-Cumulus
No. 8	Seraphic Sermon
No. 9	Undecided Prophet
No. 10	in C Sharp Major—Red Balloon
No. 11	Mohammed's Mountain
No. 12	in D Minor—Bullroarer
No. 13	Thoughts Beneath a Tree
No. 14	in G Flat Major—Elms
No. 15	Savanarola
No. 16	Saint Francis

(Short Intermission)

No. 17	Rasputin
No. 18	in A Flat Major—qu Quoi
No. 19	Theme About a Chair
No. 20 & 21	For the Saints' Ecstatic Promenades
No. 22	For Some Remorse
No. 23	The End[12]

Theatre Dance Company

With vigor, Weidman continued to be artist-in-residence at colleges and universities throughout the United States and Canada. He taught aspiring dancers his technique and restaged such noted works as *Fables for Our Time*, *Lynchtown*, and his technique demonstration *Classroom, Modern Style*. He also taught intensive courses at his studio in December and June, thereby attracting young and talented dancers to his movement style, technique, and choreography. It was through this influx of young dancers that Weidman developed his new company and composed his most beautiful formalist dances, most notably *The Christmas Oratorio* (1961), *Brahms Waltzes* (1967), *The Easter Oratorio* (1967), *In the Beginning* (1972), and *Saint Matthew Passion* (1973).

The Yuletide spirit was celebrated in December 1961 with Weidman's new production of Johann Sebastian Bach's *The Christmas Oratorio*, which included sets and lighting by Mikhail Santaro. The program notes state: "The story of Christmas is told through Dance and Dramatic sequences; through the theme of moving forms and sets."[13] In an oratorio, the musical composition consists of arias, recitatives, duets, trios, and choruses sung to orchestral accompaniment. In this first performance the cast included Weidman, Lauretta Abbot, Harry Bell, Lorna Benedict, Elaine Burdick, Roy Fentress, Clyde Gore, Jewell Jacobs, Ed Kalata, Carol Korty, Hilbert Rapp, Max Shufer, and Dot Virden.[14] On December 27, 1966, Charles, with the members of his company, Barry Barychko, Joanne Edelmann, Trent Gray, Jerianne Heimendinger, Dennis Kocjan, Robert Kosinski, Marcia Lesser, Julie Maloney, Linda Ravinsky, Janet Towner, and Paul Wilson, performed in *The Christmas Oratorio* at two First Unitarian Churchs in Manhattan. In December 1969 they performed Bach's *Oratorio* at the Cathedral of St. John The Divine. The program was as follows:

294

Bach's Christmas Oratorio

Act I
"Praise, joy and gladness be blended in one"
The Company
"And Joseph went up also from Galilee"
Robert Kosinski
"Behold the bridegroom, love divine . . . thy hope is from on high"
Evangelist: Linda Ravinsky
"How can I best admire thee?"
Joanne Edelmann, Julie Maloney, Janet Towner
"Because there was no room for Him at the Inn"
Prophetess: Linda Ravinsky
Joseph & Mary: Robert Kosinski, Julie Maloney
"Sovereign Lord and King Almighty"
(Prophecies depicting important events in the life of Christ)
Charles Weidman and the Company
Baptism of Christ
Expulsion of the Moneychangers
The Raising of Lazarus
The Kiss of Judas
The Crucifixion
The Descent from the Cross
The Entombment
The Resurrection
Christ Figure: Robert Kosinski
"And the angel said, 'Be not afraid'"
"Slumber Beloved, enjoy Thy sweet rest"
Madonna: Janet Towner
"Glory to God in the highest"
The Company

Intermission

Act II
"And so in dying Thou alone shall be my dearest love"
Man: Charles Weidman
Echo Air: Janet Towner
"Jesu, my delight and pastor"
Charles Weidman and Janet Towner
"Let me but live to tell my story"

Linda Ravinsky and Robert Kosinski
Joanne Edelmann, Marcia Lesser, Julie Malony
Barry Barychko, Dennis Kocjan, Robert Kosinski, Paul Wilson
Janet Towner—after and in memory of Marjory Carey
Jerianne Heimendinger, Marcia Lesser
"Jesu, guide my every action"
(Dance of Compassion) The Company
Quartet and Finale
Charles Weidman and the Company[15]

In the Beginning, a suite of solo dances that Weidman composed in 1962, was his recollection of the dance styles of the great artists of the twentieth century: Ruth St. Denis, Harald Kreutzberg, La Argentina, Doris Humphrey, Martha Graham, Helen Tamiris, and Charles Weidman. In this suite Charles performed twelve solos, including two of his early solos, *Japanese Actor* and *Submerged Cathedral*—the only dance he performed exactly as it was originally created.[16] Weidman's program notes for *In the Beginning* state that it was "autobiographical and, quite fitting to Debussy, an impressionist suite dealing with the beginnings of American Modern Dance (around 1929) . . . The set designed by Mr. Santaro puts the suite into fantasy."[17] Weidman composed the suite using Claude Debussy's First Book of Preludes played by Albert Ferber. Weidman's program notes for *In The Beginning* show his propensity for dramatic characterization and revisit some of his earlier works.

In the Beginning
1. Opening
2. Sails—An impression of a Kabuki actor-dancer whose exit from the stage is like that of a beautiful sail-ship going out to sea.
3. The Wind on the Plain
4. One Who Walks in a Garden—An impression of Helen Tamiris
5. Study—And at times suggesting Harold Kreutzberg
6. Steps In The Snow—An impression of Doris Humphrey

296

7. Study
8. The Maid with the Flaxen Hair—An impression of Martha Graham
9. Impressions—"Danza," "Revenge with Music," "Argentina"
10. The Submerged Cathedral
11. Study—Kinetic Pantomime
12. Minstrels And Closing[18]

Weidman's impression of Martha Graham was taken directly from her dance *Maid with the Flaxen Hair,* composed to the Claude Debussy's, Preludes for Piano, Book I, No. 8, and performed at the Forty-Eighth Street Theatre in New York on April 18, 1926.[19] Weidman was a master of stylization and had a remarkable kinetic memory. A penchant for composing dances in honor of the great artists with whom he worked and by whom he was influenced dominated his later creative works.

The Fifteenth Anniversary Season of the American Dance Festival was celebrated July 9 through August 19, 1962, at Connecticut College in New London, Connecticut. Charles Weidman and his Theatre Dance Company shared *Five Saturday Evenings* of performances with the following dance artists: Erick Hawkins, Alvin Ailey Dance Theatre, Katherine Litz, Pearl Lang and Company, Glen Tetley, Paul Draper, Ruth Currier and Dance Company, Lucas Hoving and Company, Paul Taylor Dance Company, and Daniel Nagrin.[20] Weidman and his company, Andre Bernard, Marjorie Carey, Elizabeth Farley, Clyde Gore, Max Shufer, and Dot Virden, performed *Three Thurber Fables* accompanied by George McGeary, pianist. Weidman selected the following fables for their prose or verse and their poignant moral conclusions: "The Clothes Moth and the Luna Moth," "The Tigress and Her Mate," and "The Unicorn in the Garden."[21]

Much had been accomplished in the three years through Weidman and Santaro's joint venture at the Expression of Two Arts Studio Theatre at 102 West Twenty-Ninth Street. They had toured their duet concerts at colleges, as well as teaching master classes; Weidman had composed new solos and group works for his small company; Santaro had the opportunity to design sets and lighting, and to continue creating his visual art. Throughout July 1963, they continued their artistic collaboration by presenting *A Conception of Honegger's King David.* Weidman's company was lauded by the critics for *King David:* "with a stunning performance by Dot Virden in the title role this should go on your 'must see' list," Harold Garton wrote in *Back Stage*.[22] The text for *King David* was written by Andre Morax and narrated by Andre Bernard. David's dance lament featured Dot Virden and Lazar Dano interchanging the role of David. The translation of Morax's libretto of David's lament reads:

> O had I wings like a dove
> Then I would fly away and be at rest
> Save in the tomb alone is there no comfort.[23]

In her review in *Back Stage*, Jennie Schulman writes of David's lament: "Dot Virden, supported in simultaneous movements by Lazar Dano, maintained the spellbinding illusion of the soul taking leave of the tormented body, supported by an invisible arch-angel."[24] Virden also gave a stunning interpretation of the Witch of Endor and, at the conclusion of the work Virden exchanged roles with Dano, who danced David opposite her as matriarch of the women before the ark of the covent. In her review, Schulman proclaimed: "The word star has been despoiled . . . in our times, but in the original and truest sense of the word, Dot Virden is a star dancer."[25] A supporting cast included Marjorie Carey, Allison Koprowski, Ingrid Snerdley, and Max Shufer. Weidman's ingenious conception of Honegger's *King David*, accompanied by sets and lighting by Santaro, prompted Schulman's review in *Back Stage* to note their extraordinary collaborative partnership:

This duo again indicates that totally new concepts of theatre can be conceived despite limitations of space and a sparseness of "materialistic stuff." Weidman, who has been around longer than most people in the modern dance field, is still at his creative peak as a choreographer and the fantastic effects Santaro can come up with out of scraps of material, papier-mâché and wire are totally symbolic of the artist's ability never to recognize any blocks the world may place in his way.[26]

The School of Speech at Northwestern University in Evanston, Illinois, presented *An Evening of Magic*, An Expression of Two Arts with Charles Weidman and his Theatre Dance Company on February 19, 1964. Weidman, Santaro, Andre Bernard as narrator, Marjorie Carey, Lazar Dano, Max Shufer, and Dot Virden performed a full-length concert. The program began with a duet by Weidman and Santaro, *To Make a Form - To Give It Life*, to the music of Corelli. The second work was *Jacob's Marriage,* with script and music by Johann Kuhnau and narrated by Andre Bernard. The program note states: "*Jacob's Marriage* is Kuhnau's Biblical Sonata No. 3. This tape is by Colin Tilney, playing on a Tschudi harpsichord."[27] Weidman danced the role of Jacob, Marjorie Carey danced Rachael, Dot Virden danced Leah, and Max Shufer played Labon. After intermission the company danced *Fables for Our Time* and concluded the program with *Brahms Waltzes, Opus 39.*

In 1966, when Weidman's position as resident choreographer and ballet master for the New York City Center Opera was not renewed and no new offers came for Broadway shows, financial burdens forced Weidman to sell his farm in New Jersey. The selling of his farm was another heartbreak; it ended twenty years of memories of fond friends, Doris, Pauline and José.

Weidman received a grant from the National Council on the Arts in 1969 to compose a new work with a selected ensemble of dancers who rehearsed with him during six weeks. He invited these nine dancers to be a part of the project: Carol Geneve-Sevilla, Maya Doray, Mary Ann Mee, Martin Morginsky, Beatriz-

Maria Prada, Donna Rizzo, Max Shufer, Dot Virden, and Charles Wilson.[28]   Max Shufer had been dancing with Weidman for many years, and Maya Doray was also Weidman's administrative assistant. Weidman invited Dot, Carol Geneve, Mary Ann, and Donna to New York for six weeks of rehearsals. Mary Ann and Donna had graduated from Stephens College and studied with Harriette Ann Gray. Carol Geneve's mother had a studio in California, where Weidman taught when he was on the West coast.[29] The performances of Weidman's works with lighting designs by Santaro took place on June 12-14, 1969 at the Expression of Two Arts Studio Theatre at 102 West Twenty-Ninth Street, New York City. The program began with the Opening Dance to Bach's *The Christmas Oratorio*. The featured work, made possible by the National Council on the Arts, took the title of the grant's identification number, A69-I-123:

A 69-I-123	
1. Opening The Company	
Mother and Child	Beatriz-Maria Prada, Donna Rizzo
The Happy Inciter	Dot Virden
Something Discovered	Charles Weidman
2. Gusanos de Maguey	Carol Geneve-Sevilla, Dot Virden
(Worm of the Maguey)	Conceived and forms by Santaro
3. Rhythm of Eleven	The Company
Short Variations	Donna Rizzo, Carol Geneve-Sevilla
	Dot Virden, Charles Wilson[30]

After intermission, the program concluded with a longer work, *Of and Out of This World* to the music of Camille Saint-Saens. Weidman created a whimsical work in thirteen sections as follows:

Of and Out of This World	Saint-Saens
Dedicated to James Thurber	
Opening	Charles Weidman and the Company

Pantomime	Charles Wilson, Dot Virden, Donna Rizzo
Women in Bed	Maya Doray
Delsartian Exponent	Charles Weidman, Beatriz-Maria Prada
Cock-Eyed Waltz	Dot Virden, Carol Geneve-Sevilla, Max Shufer, Charles Wilson
The Bloodhound and the Bug	Charles Weidman
The Rose, The Fountain and the Dove	Beatriz-Maria Prada, Maya Doray, Mary Ann Mee, Max Shufer, Charles Wilson
Women in Bed	Maya Doray or Mary Ann Mee, Max Shufer
The Recessive Knee	Beatriz-Maria, Carol Geneve-Sevilla, Charles Wilson
The Moth and the Star	Charles Weidman, Charles Wilson
Bustling Ladies	Mary Ann Mee, Carol Geneve-Sevilla, Donna Rizzo, Beatriz-Maria Prada
Duo on a Piano	Max Shufer, Charles Wilson
Cartoons	Charles Weidman and the Company[31]

It is interesting to note that within *Of and Out of This World*, Weidman employs signature choreographic motifs: an opening dance; kinetic pantomime; Delsartian principles; and themes about women. It is fascinating that, with each new decade in Charles Weidman's life, there was a new beginning, venture, or phase always marked by transition and a renewal or transformation. He was born in a new decade in 1901; he joined the Denishawn School and Company in 1920; he created a partnership and alliance with Doris Humphrey and Pauline Lawrence in 1928; when Humphrey retired from dancing, he was on his own in 1948; Humphrey died in 1958; Weidman established the Expression of Two Arts Theatre with Mikhail Santaro in 1960; and Santaro departed with his family to China in 1970, leaving Weidman once again, on his own, to reinvent himself.

During the late 1960s until 1975, Weidman and his newly formed company performed every weekend at the Expression of Two Arts Theatre, including Christmas, New Year's, Fourth of July, and Hanukkah. The important thing to Weidman was that his works were being performed. But dance tastes were changing and young New York choreographers were rebelling against traditional aesthetic values in technique and choreography. Chance choreography, music collage, minimal pedestrian movement, and contact improvisation had radically changed the style of American modern dance and performers' expectations of audience members.

Weidman was the object of a review in *Dance Magazine* by Marcia Marks in 1967 that had a negative air, insinuating that his company's performance was nostalgic, and questioning whether the "remnants of a successful career [should] be exposed to the public or kept graciously in a studio for fond admirers only."[32] Marks disliked almost the entire program, declaring that *The Easter Oratorio* "is an ambitious undertaking—too ambitious," that *Brahms Waltzes* were too long, and that *Dialogue Situation Two* was "a conglomeration of episodes that fail to make any clear impression."[33] It now became apparent that Weidman's work was not that interesting to the younger generation of critics.

The changing aesthetics of modern dance were certainly a factor in Weidman's lack of recognition. He was not visible on the forefront of avant-garde and postmodernism, as was Merce Cunningham and James Waring. He had not received the financial support to continue working, as had Martha Graham. Weidman did not enjoy the facilities to properly present his beautiful abstract dances, as had José Limón, Alvin Ailey, Paul Taylor, Alwin Nikolais, or Murray Louis. It seemed obvious that Weidman's contributions to American Modern Dance far outweighed the above illustrious moderns, but when Weidman finally reached his pinnacle as an artist, the decade had given way to novel ideas representing a sharp departure from tradition.

Perhaps Weidman's use of gesture and *kinetic pantomime* influenced the postmoderns. Anna Halprin studied with Humphrey-Weidman until 1945, when she moved to the West Coast. In Weidman's works "an atmosphere of nonchalance, a deceptive appearance of improvisation" may have set the stage for Halprin's creative work in California during the 1960s.[34] While Weidman was employing traditional principles in composition such as theme-and-variations form and creating his most beautifully structured works based on Humphrey-Weidman technique, younger dance artists, with support from critics, were departing as radically as possible from established choreographic form by rejecting dance technique and using improvised performances. If only Weidman had lived five more years to see a new decade and the gradual return to the incorporation of classic modern values in dance, he might have held more significance for the younger generation. Fortunately, prominent contemporary choreographers and teachers such as Deborah Carr, Garth Fagan, Bill T. Jones, Daniel Lewis (Limón), Carla Maxwell (Limón), Norwood Pennewell (Fagan), Jennifer Scanlon (Limón), Paul Taylor, Janet Towner, Nina Watt (Limón), David Wynn, (and perhaps Murray Lewis, Mark Morris, and Doug Varone) were impressed by Humphrey-Weidman techniques and compositional traits; therefore, Weidman has indirectly influenced a younger generation. Weidman was not only a guiding force to modern American dance, but he also steered the dance in musical theatre (Jack Cole, Bob Fosse, Gene Kelly, and Jerome Robbins), jazz dance, ballet, and opera (New York City Center Opera) into new directions. Weidman had pioneered for the art of dance to which his life was dedicated. Charles Weidman's quest to evolve a form of dance indigenous to contemporary America had been achieved.

Chapter Twelve

Coming Full Circle
(1970-1975)

A dancer's career might be called a *quest*—always seeking
to say new things, and to say them in new ways.

Charles Weidman

Fifteen year-old Charles Weidman believed he was destined to become a
dancer. Twenty-three years later, by 1938, he had created his most significant
works such as *Quest, Atavisms, This Passion,* and *Opus 51;* his illustrious career
had been established. For the next three decades, Weidman, undaunted by
financial or personal obstacles, continued his journey through American dance
questing to attain his artistic vision.[1] The last fifteen years of his life were spent
creating the art of dance at the Expression of Two Arts Studio Theatre.

During the early 1970s Charles, or Chas as he called himself, was fully
involved in artistic projects: teaching, restaging dances, composing new works,
notating his dances, and maintaining his company's performance schedule at his
Studio Theatre. His company performed at 7:30 p.m. every Sunday evening,
including holidays; performances were more like a family gathering, he and his
company performed for standing-room-only crowds on some Sundays, or to no
one—Charles was then the audience for his company, and they for him. He and
his dancers also performed production tasks such as publicity, programs, and
ticket sales. Since audience members walked into the performing space, tacked to
the door on a small index card Charles wrote: "Doors Open At 7:15 p.m. Please

Do Not Ring Bell After 7:30 p.m."[2] Charles greeted members of the audience and introduced his dances with his witty style. After performances, the company and audience were invited into Charles' tiny livingroom, just on the other side of his loft studio theatre, for a small reception. From May 16, 1971 to July 6, 1975 many notable dance professionals attended his performances and signed his guest book including Suzanne Sheldon, Zena Rommett, Shirley Manasevit, Betsy Carden, Joyce Trisler Woodford, Peter Hamilton, Walter Terry, Don McDonagh, Shela Xoregos, along with hundreds of dance enthusiasts.[3] "No other dance artist or dance company offered performances in New York City every single week of the year, year after year. Charles was unique in this, and also way ahead of what became a popular trend: to present dance performances in a loft setting," Janet Towner writes.[4]

Weidman's dance repertory appealed to people of all ages; his company performed for audiences in unique settings. During June 1971, performances were arranged through the Hospital Audience, Inc. for Weidman's Theatre Dance Company to perform in area hospitals such as Brooklyn State, King's Park State, and Pilgrim State.[5] Weidman's company performed in May at the 92nd Street Y and performed as part of the New York Dance Festival at the Delacorte Theatre in September 1972; however, regional touring was a sizable part of their schedule.[6]

Charles maintained a busy schedule; he worked tiredlessly to secure work for himself and his company. His correspondence seeking to aquire performing or teaching engagements for himself or his company ranged through studios, schools, colleges, churches, hospitals, regional ballet companies, summer camps, professional orchestras, and theatres. Charles restaged *Lynchtown* with the Repertory Dancers, directed by Shirley Ubell in Hackensack, New Jersey; in 1973, he was artist-in-residence at the University of Calgary in Alberta, Canada; and Frank Hatch of the Department of Dance at California State University, Fullerton, engaged Charles to restage sections of *New Dance* for their students.[7]

In 1973, Charles became a Professor of Dance in the Department of Health and Physical Education at Brooklyn College, one of the institutions in the City University of New York system, where he taught "Movement for Acting" and "Humphrey-Weidman Technique." At this same time, Charles consulted with legal and financial counsel Richard Carlson for the incorporation of the Charles Weidman School of Modern Dance as a tax-exempt organization with a board of directors.

Works Preserved in Dance Notation

From 1971 to 1974, Charles had substantial correspondence with the Dance Notation Bureau regarding the Labanotation scores for his works. In a letter from Muriel Topaz, dated November 24, 1971, she asked his permission to include *Brahms Waltzes No. 1* in "a collection of reading materials to be used in conjunction with the teaching of Labanotation. Included in this collection will be short movement phrases from repertoire and classroom technique phrases of master teachers."[8] Charles did not sign the clearance form; instead he wrote a letter to Topaz on November 26 and gave his permission to use this waltz, but asked these questions: "I do not read Notation; however, the arm description in the left looks more like [waltz] No. 5 not No. 1." He questioned the fast 6/4 and was concerned about the "use of weight," which shows his determination to clarify the stylistic Humphrey-Weidman elements reflected in the score.[9]

Weidman received small royalties paid twice yearly by the Dance Notation Bureau for restaging his dance works - $25.00 for the first performance and $10.00 per performance thereafter.[10] Many colleges performed Weidman's works from Labanotation scores through the Dance Notation Bureau: Temple University performed *Traditions* in December 1972; Mount Holyoke College performed *Brahms Waltzes* in November 1973; Iowa State University performed *Brahms Waltzes* in 1973; there were also repeat performances by Temple

University of *Traditions*, by Mount Holyoke College of *Brahms Waltzes*, and by the State University of New York at Potsdam of *Brahms Waltzes* in April 1974.[11]

In concert with the Dance Notation Bureau, Charles decided to stage his works for college dancers himself. He received a letter from Maria Grandy in early February 1974, confirming his arrangements for setting *Brahms Waltzes* at SUNY Potsdam. His fee would be $400 plus transportation, room and board. Rehearsals were scheduled for February 20 and 21—from noon to 4:00 p.m. and from 6:00 to 10:00 p.m. "After you leave, our Recontructor Miss Airi Hynninen will remain to continue the rehearsals," Grandy wrote.[12] Having Weidman stage his work, then having a reconstructor rehearse the work was an ideal situation.

Through the years, Weidman's dancers, along with countless numbers of college dancers, have enjoyed performing *Brahms Waltzes*, Weidman's classic tribute to his former partner occurs in the following program note: "Dedicated to Doris Humphrey because it was the kind of movement she loved and could dance so beautifully."[13] *Brahms Waltzes* is noted for its structural clarity, charm, and wit. Charles aptly titled the sixteen waltzes as follows:

1. Opening based on two themes
2. Soft side extensions and modulations
3. Movement that stretches like a rubber band
4. Ponytail
5. Arms using a questions and answer idea (hitch hiker)
6. Tee-hinny (turn while seated on the floor)
7. Luscious falls
8. Soft leaps
9. Hands
10. Fast turns
11. From a Chinese four-square walk
12. Eyes (kinetic pantomime)
13. Dramatic falls
14. Second part of thirteen
15. The well-known waltz
16. Ending (bows) [14]

Weidman used Gina Bachauer's recording of Johannes Brahms' Liebeslieder Waltzes, Opus 39; however, live piano accompaniment supports the breath rhythm inherent in the work more fully than taped music and is preferable.

Saint Matthew Passion

Weidman and his company danced his oratorio works *The Christmas Oratorio, The Easter Oratorio,* and *Saint Matthew Passion* in various performance venues, including churches and theatres. When Charles originally composed three parts of *Saint Matthew Passion* in December 1968, he danced these three sections with David Hebel. The notes in the program state:

> Behold, my Saviour now is taken,
> Moon and Stars,
> Have for grief the night forsaken.
>
> Open, oh fathomless pit,
> all thy terrors.
>
> They lead Him hence;
> with cords they bind Him.[15]

Weidman's company danced two performances of *Saint Matthew Passion* in June 1973; one performance took place at the Expression of Two Arts Studio Theatre, another at the Spencer Memorial Church in Brooklyn. Ellen Stodolsky's review in *Dance Magazine* noted Weidman's masterful choreography: "This is a flowing dance chronicle of Christ's passion, crucifixion and resurrection, a ritualistic dance of devotion. Each section of the Bach work is narrated by actor Dennis Kear with dignified strength, while the dancers further illuminate the momentous events."[16] Since Weidman's death, only excerpts from the original full evening's work have been restaged for small companies and college dance

ensembles. The four sections of *Saint Matthew Passion* performed by the
Geneseo Dance Ensemble used these program notes:

I
The Opening
II
"Break and die, thou dearest heart . . .
A child which thou has trained,
Now a serpent has become . . ."
III
"His gracious promise doth the soul uplift."
IV
The Closing [17]

Stodolsky remarks, "[Saint Matthew] Passion is primarily composed of large-
group, unison movement—swirling bodies in long skirts, arms raised to Heaven,
curve and dip in limpid phrases."[18] In dancing these four dances from the
original, I recognize that unison movement is used only to emphasize the strength
of the group through unity; otherwise in these dances Weidman makes great use
of contrapuntal patterns and theme-and-variations form. Moreover, the use of
contrast is recognizably inherent in the theme of the work, as was noted by
Stodolsky's review: "When the tension mounts, as when His followers learn that
Christ is to be crucified, the movement takes on a rougher, less fluid character.
Small, flattened, archaic-looking jumps creep in; airy attitude turns strain against
down-thrusting arms."[19] In the Closing Dance, which recognizes Christ's
resurrection, Weidman uses a strong diagonal focus from upstage right to
downstage left. The large ensemble holds this directional focus throughout unless
they dance a circle, which momentarily unifies the group between diagonal
phrases. Many forward leg extensions with flexed feet and forward-thrusting
arms make this section difficult to perform. Further, the contrapuntal

310

(counterpointed) phrasing of movement sequences emphasizes the swirling action that Stodolsky notes in her review. The final image of the work unified the group in a large circle; with chests lifted to Heaven, the dancer's circle moves clockwise using forced-arch walks; an exaltation of the spirit.

Visualization, or From a Farm in New Jersey

In the spring of 1974, Charles applied for a grant from the National Endowment for the Arts to choreograph a new work to a commissioned score. Disappointed when his application was denied, he decided to continue with his project and create his dance to an existing score, Concerto No. 4 in C Minor, Opus 44 by Camille Saint Saens. Charles worked quickly to complete the twenty-four minute work, *Visualization, or From a Farm in New Jersey,* since Janet Towner, who was dancing the leading role, had already made her travel reservations to visit her family in early August.[20] Instead of postponing the rehearsals until Janet returned to New York, Charles decided to premiere the work before she left and then continue to perform it during their fall season—that left only six weeks to rehearse and produce the work Towner thought. She was amazed when in only two weeks Charles had completed the work for its first performance on July 14, 1974, one week before his seventy-third birthday.

Part One, *On the Farm,* an eleven-minute solo, was a remarkable dance biography of Ruth St. Denis, which used scenes of her childhood on her family's farm in Sommerville, New Jersey, and highlighted her famous career in five sections: On the Farm; Realization—the Ripple; Revelation—the Yogi; A Piece of Material from the Clothes Line; and *The Incense.*[21] Charles, through his vivid verbal descriptions and his own exquisite performance, had an uncanny ability to communicate to his dancers the exact gestures, movements, and motivations he desired of them. This was his process when rehearsing with Janet Towner; she

311

was transformed into Ruth St. Denis as a "young girl who is filled with the joy and energy of unharnessed physical movement," Towner writes. "The imagery of nature and youthful exuberance came through the gestures and the spontaneous freedom of expression which Weidman urged me during rehearsal by his enthusiastic reactions—even his laughter."[22] In his review Walter Terry acknowledged Towner's artistry:

> Janet Towner . . . is superb as [Ruth] Dennis-St. Denis, not only in the ebullient childhood explorations but as the great star. Without resembling St. Denis in any way physically, she has, through Weidman's guidance, captured to an uncanny degree many of the characteristics, inner as well as overt, of the dance world's fabled "Miss Ruth."[23]

As the solo progressed Towner revealed the core of St. Denis' movement ideas and spirituality through joyous child's play, cartwheeling, falling to the ground, restful contemplation, stretching upward one arm into a rippling motion, and her use of fabric from a clothesline, which transformed into a sari and then into her famous dance, *The Incense*.[24] In his review Walter Terry declared Weidman's genius: "Mr. Weidman, in his choreography, has created in purely dance terms the incredible evolution of a dance genius, Ruth St. Denis, and here, in Part I of this biography, his own choreographic concept of this evolution is surely a work of genius."[25]

Part Two, *The Glory That Was Denishawn*, was a thirteen-minute exposition of twelve dances from the Denishawn repertory performed by nine dancers: Visualizations; *Valse Caprice, Scarf Dance* (Doris Humphrey); *Gnossienne* (Ted Shawn); *Greek Veil Plastique* (Ruth St. Denis); *Crapshooter* (Weidman); *Danse Américaine* (Weidman); *Sunrise* (Humphrey); *Serenata Morisca* (Martha Graham); Orientalia; *Nautch* (St. Denis); *Dance of Siva* and *Japanese Spear Dance* (Shawn); and *The Garden of Karma* (St. Denis and Shawn).[26] Janet Towner also danced Humphrey in her *Scarf Dance*; Barry

Barychko danced Ted Shawn; Martha Karess danced Humphrey in *Sunrise*; Scott Volk portrayed Charles Weidman; Rebecca Kelly danced as Martha Graham; Deborah Carr and Joanne Kaczynsky danced as Scarf and Nautch Dancers; and Roger Robichaud portrayed Robert Gorham.[27] Through the rehearsal process Towner recognized how Weidman's powerful ability could "transport you . . . [through] his own performance . . . With a twinge of an eyebrow, a tilt of the chin, a flicker of changing focus, Charles could transport you and reveal to you . . . his vision . . ."[28]

To Carry On

Charles was involved in numerous important projects to preserve his legacy. Herbert Kummel, executive director of the Dance Notation Bureau, wrote Charles a letter dated August 15, 1972, regarding his interest in creating a film on the roots of Humphrey-Weidman dance, with a focus on style. If Charles could provide him with an outline, a list of specific choreographic sections to be included in the film, legal terms and agreements, and select an artistic staff, money could be raised by the Dance Notation Bureau to produce the film.[29] Charles always replied to letters promptly—usually within two days, and always sent hand-written letters. (For his files he made carbon copies, using the back of programs or workshop posters. He, along with Martha Graham, thought not using both sides of a sheet of paper was wasteful.) In his reply to Kummel on August 17, 1972, Charles wrote:

> I had a meeting with four of the Humphrey-Weidman dancers and teachers. These four spanned the Humphrey-Weidman period from 1928 to 1948: Ernestine Stodelle, who was in the first group; Beatrice Seckler ("New Dance" Period) 1936; Nona Schurman, 1941; and Barbara Doeffer (Thomas), who was in Doris' last work "Inquest." Ernestine and Nona will send in their ideas for scripts or scenarios. As you probably know, Ernestine writes beautifully so maybe what she sends could be used as part

of a narrative script. I would like to see this project develop into fantasy contrasted by extremely dramatic dancing and also to include zany Weidman humor.[30]

For the next year, plans for the film progressed as the Bureau raised funds to support the project. Meanwhile, Charles and his dancers were teaching and performing in Canada at the University of Toronto, York University, Ryerson Polytechnical Institute, and the Toronto Public Libraries. The highlight of the summer came on June 3, 1973, when Charles received an honorary degree from Jersey City College in New Jersey. Teaching, rehearsing, and performing continued at his Studio Theatre, and in 1974, Charles received a grant from the New York Foundation for the Arts to compose a new work with a commissioned score and to restage *Opus 51, Flickers,* and *Atavisms,* with the expectation that these works would be filmed or videotaped. While on a January tour, Charles and his company gave a lecture-demonstration and master class at Arkansas State University, arranged by Mrs. Alta Burns of the Department of Health, Physical Education and Recreation. In April Charles was scheduled to be guest artist at the Instituto Nacional de Bellas Artes in Mexico City, and he had a signed contract with the Baltimore Symphony to perform with his company, to give a lecture, and a master class that would be filmed on July 22, 1974, his seventy-third birthday.

Because of the interest of Professor Betsy Carden, plans were made with the Television Center at Brooklyn College to videotape Weidman's recent work *Visualizations, or From a Farm in New Jersey* on February 25, 1975. Directed by Judy Rose, Walter Terry introduced the video, which featured Janet Towner as Ruth St. Denis and Barry Barychko as Ted Shawn. "I will narrate, announcing the roles, including those of Martha as she 'slashes through' *Serenata Morisca,* Doris in *Sunrise,* and yours truly in *Crapshooter,*" Weidman wrote.[31]

Weidman received many honorary positions in 1975. In a letter dated March 19, 1975, from the José Limón Dance Foundation, Charles was invited to

Limón's first independent Broadway season. The next day he received a letter from Ruth Currier, Artistic Director, who invited him to serve on the Limón Company Artistic Advisory Board of Directors. In his reply letter on March 22, Charles accepted the position as an advisory board member; however, he could not attend the scheduled meeting on April 15 because Alvin Ailey started his season that night and Ailey had invited him to attend as a special guest. Ailey dedicated his season to Weidman in tribute to his significant contributions to dance in America.[32] In a letter dated May 19, 1975, Renee Morgan, Assistant to Alvin Ailey, wrote: "Mr. Ailey has asked me to convey again, his appreciation of your contributions to the study and art of dance and also to send his many thanks for your participation in our most recent City Center Season."[33]

Charles received a letter dated May 15, 1975 from Anita Warburg, Secretary, Committee for the Dance Collections, inviting him to be a Charter Member of the International Dance Committee of the Conseil International de la Dance (C. I. D. D.), that UNESCO had added to its roster of nongovernmental organizations. The purpose of the committee was to preserve all forms of choreography and to organize the preservation and classification of this art form. Honorary Members included: Jerome Robbins, Lew Christensen, Alwin Nikolais, Merce Cunningham, Alvin Ailey, Arthur Mitchell, Eliot Feld, Lincoln Kirstein, Agnes de Mille, Martha Graham, Ruth Page, Alexandra Danilova, Twyla Tharp, Lucia Chase, Robert Joffrey, Hanya Holm, and Bella Lewitzsky. Weidman accepts the invitation to serve on May 18, 1975.[34]

Weidman had been invited by Bari Rolf, program coordinator of the American Bicentennial Mime Festival at the School of Drama at the University of Washington, to perform *A Letter to Mrs. Bixby - A Lincoln Portrait* at the Festival on July 11-25, 1976, in Albuquerque, New Mexico. On February 10, 1975 Charles received a contract from Mrs. Stanley North to teach in the dance program at Beaupre Summer Performing Arts Center for Girls.

When Charles wasn't traveling across the United States and Canada teaching and sharing his art with young dancers, he was developing the dancers in his company into artists by spending hours in classes and rehearsals. In his tiny studio, only fifteen by twenty-two feet—even less when twenty-five seats were arranged for an audience, his company danced in one of the most difficult performing situations, with the audience up-front and personal. Why did most of his dancers work with him for so many years? Janet Towner believed this stemmed from his philosophy of life that she recalls he wrote about in his ninth-grade essay, *My Vocation*.

> The Spartan circumstance in which Charles was living and working, considering his stature as a modern dance pioneer, were poignant to me. However, he behaved as though he were living and working in a palace. His captivating presence and energy were contagious; I soon knew that I had entered Charles Weidman's palace which was filled with the riches of his compassionate and joyful understanding of life.[35]

Coming Full Circle

One of Charles Weidman's earliest calls to action was during his first month at the Denishawn School. He quickly rehearsed, was rushed out to Tacoma, Washington, replaced injured Robert Gorham in the leading role in *Xochitl* opposite Martha Graham, and made his début as a dancer. And what a splendid début it was; he received a rave review in the Tacoma newspaper—alas in the name of Robert Gorham. Still, Weidman and Gorham became fast friends.

Weidman's next challenge, bestowed upon him by Shawn, was the comic *Danse Américaine*. According to Shawn, Weidman preferred to dance romantic and tragic themes; this caused disagreements between them while in rehearsal for the comic pantomime. But after Weidman's first performance of *Danse Américaine*, Shawn explained, "the audience clapped insistently for an encore, and in an about-face, he claimed that he had been in favor of the number all along."[36] With the subsequent success of *The Crapshooter* Weidman's hesitation developed into his signature style *kinetic pantomime*, making him a leading comic interpreter of his time.

Weidman's next journey was taken with his mentor, Doris Humphrey, who became his partner and collaborator. Together with artists Pauline Lawrence and José Limón, Weidman's search to develop his own movement style, technique, and choreography would traverse a rocky but wonderful path for twenty years. Doris didn't have as difficult a time with choreography as Charles did. She had been composing dances before Denishawn and had been experimenting with new movement possibilities guided by St. Denis. Charles was lost—he decided to go to Ronny Johansson for help but was discouraged by Doris, who suggested that he rely on himself—so he did. And for their first joint concert Charles composed several works, the most enduring of which was *Submerged Cathedral* or *Cathédrale Engloutie*.

During their twenty years of working together, Weidman and Humphrey developed a lasting dance technique based on shared movement principles and revolutionized the art of choreography in the twentieth century in such works as *Rudepoema, Duo-Drama, New Dance,* and *Theatre Piece*. In an interview in 1972, Walter Sorell asked Charles if he and Doris had discussed at great length the concepts of the master works they created together. Charles replied:

> Not at all, we were attuned to one another in such a way that we could choreograph on the spot. I lost Doris three times, and three times the loss was painful, even though it was different. In 1938 I lost her love (but she always told me, art is the only thing that matters, so I stayed on, and we continued to work and dance together). In 1948 I lost my partner in her (when arthritis crippled her). In 1958 we all lost her.[37]

317

Charles Weidman profoundly loved Doris Humphrey. Together they created a castle of thoughts and ideas symbolically presented through Charles' continued performance of *Submerged Cathedral*.

Throughout his life, Weidman's unfaltering strength of purpose gave him the power to persevere against emotional and financial obstacles. Endless financial perils that began during the Depression plagued his professional career. It was, perhaps, these factors from which he rebounded: stress caused by the emotional strain of the Spanish Civil War and Second World War; loss of his parents and sister; his addiction to alcohol; loss of his beloved partner, Doris Humphrey; and loss of his cherished friends, Jack Cole, Eleanor Frampton, Pauline Lawrence, José Limón, and Helen Tamiris. Through these struggles he created his most beautifully formal and zany comedic works. Not one of Weidman's dancers interviewed for this manuscript ever mentioned these burdens. Instead they reflected upon Charles' energy, warmth, humor, wit, and endless capacity for inventive movement. His mind was continually and actively engaged in his dancer's quest. American philosopher Susanne Langer put it this way: "A mind that is oriented, no matter by what conscious or unconscious symbols, in material and social realities, can function freely and confidently even under great pressure of circumstance and in the face of hard problems."[38]

Charles' intellect was rooted in a historic knowledge of the past, giving him a deep understanding of the present. The ideas Weidman presented in his works were simple—the polarity of the fall-rebound and the strength of the human spirit to conquer adversity. All of Weidman's works show these artistic beliefs. His program note for *Submerged Cathedral* states: "Legend has it that off the coast of Brittany periodically a cathedral rises out of the water. The ringing of the bells and the chanting of the monks are heard—silence when the cathedral sinks back into the sea."[39]

318

Throughout my research many events in Charles Weidman's career appeared to be more than coincidental. Few artists keep their first works; however, Weidman continued to perform *Submerged Cathedral* exactly as it was created. *Submerged Cathedral* symbolized through movement the basic ritual of a life purposefully oriented. Claude Debussy's music surges to heights of affirmation and then slowly, gradually swirling, spirals downward. This work could be Weidman's counterpart to Humphrey's *Two Ecstatic Themes*, with its sharp ascending motions and circling, descending movements. Perhaps it was Weidman's reflection on his life through "movement visualization" to Debussy's music.

How appropriate it was for Weidman to begin and end his independent career with a work that symbolized the strength of the human spirit as represented in the cathedral rising from the depths of the sea and the inevitable force of the sea submerging it again—a ritual of nature—and of life.

Chapter Thirteen

Legacy and Witnesses

MY VOCATION
BY
CHARLES WEIDMAN
(Ninth-Grade Essay, The Bancroft School)

"He who cherishes a beautiful vision, a lofty ideal in his heart will some day realize it," says James Allen. Columbus cherished a vision of another world and he discovered it. Copernicus fostered the vision of a multiplicity of worlds and a wider universe and he revealed it. Buddha beheld the vision of a spiritual world of stainless beauty and perfect peace and he entered into it, and I five years ago cherished the vision of my future occupation or profession.

As long ago as I can remember I have cherished the vision of becoming an artist and thought that my talents reached for that profession only. But as time passed and almost before I realized it I had found myself studying upon a vocation which had developed from my art and for which I have greater talent. Lincoln hasn't any school in which I can prepare for this profession thoroughly. My time has been and will be spent until my departure from Lincoln, in libraries, museums, and art galleries, where I can increase my knowledge upon the vocation and where I shall do all that is in my power to learn as much as possible so that I will have a general survey of the art when I enter the [Denishawn] school.

My aims are not to become rich (although the majority of the people who have specialized in this art are very wealthy) but are to succeed in making my thoughts and ideas come true. I do not intend to live in the castle of the other fellow who worked hard to make it as many people of this and all other occupations do, but to succeed as Farrar (Geraldine Farrar), and that is though my hard work and efforts to build my own palace of my own thoughts and ideas so that I can live in it in peace and comfort and not be a parasite in name or reality.

The art, which I intend to call mine someday, is one of the oldest and according to many authorities the most refined of all occupations and arts. In many instances it has made the sick well, the unhappy happy, the unfit fit, and Uncle Sam would not have his "Spartan Army" today if it was not for it. Beautiful it is, but many people have not recognized its true value especially the Americans. They do not know that the feeble minded is so because they do not practice it, the blind likewise, that the crippled could be nursed back to health again by it, and that the drunkard would be no more if he practiced it.[1]

RANDOM REMARKS

BY

CHARLES WEIDMAN

I have always believed that the audience and the performer are indivisible. Both artist and audience enter the house—although through different doors—from the same street. They have both seen the same headlines, left the same world of reality behind them. And while the artist puts on his makeup, the audience leaves its everyday disillusionment in the checkroom.

Real art can never be escape from life. In histrionic terms, illusions are not false impressions nor misconceptions of reality. The world of illusion which the audience expects from the artist is, in fact, the world of their real selves, the image of their own world, the translation of their hopes and fears, their joys and sufferings into the magic of the stage.

The artist must not run away from himself, from his "center of being." He is the bearer of a message, and it is his responsibility to tell it—in whatever medium it may be—intelligibly, forcefully and with his utmost artistic ability. He may sometimes fail in the delivery of his message, but he must never fail in his purpose.

It is often said of the modern dance that it is not easily understood, that its silent language of movement is so intricate as to veil its meaning. But since any dance presentation lives only while it is being performed and since it can hardly be preserved for later in files and books, it would utterly fail to accomplish its task or even to justify its existence could it not clearly convey its message. Only poets, musicians, painters or sculptors can dare challenge their contemporaries with their media of art and yield to the judgement of posterity. The dancer can do

323

this as little as can the actor or singer. *L'art pour l'art* is for him the death sentence expressed by his own feeble attempt to convince his audience.

I have always been impatient with *art pour l'artist*. Clarity and understandability has remained the basis of my dance creations. Their intent, concerned with human values and the experience of our times, must be carried by the fullest emotional impact the artist can muster. Then, with the conception of the idea, the intelligibility of its message and the emotional intensity of presentation, the artist's primordial task is fulfilled and—however his artistic deliverance may be judged—his sincerity cannot be doubted.

Some may say that I am going too far when I desire to make my dance creations as easily understandable as a movie. But this may explain why more and more I have come to believe in the pantomimic dance drama. The word "pantomime" does not mean to me the presentation of a dumb show, as most dictionaries define it, or the mere telling of a story or action without the use of explanatory words. To me it is the transport of an idea into movement, the animation of the feeling behind the idea, an animation in which suddenly all commas and periods, all silent moments of an unwritten play become a reality in movement. Moreover, it may be likened to that emotional sequence of a growing world of images which we may experience when listening to a symphony, full of logical continuity and expressiveness where words might seem feeble and music inadequate.

I may be prejudiced in favor of the pantomimic dance, because I have found that my gift as a dancer is essentially tied up with my dramatic talent as an actor, or—let us better say—as a mime. The modern mime must be a modern dancer, and as such his entire body must be alive. This cannot be acquired by emotional experience, only by hard physical training. It may be best called bodily awareness. In order to test this bodily awareness in one of my dance compositions, I went so far as to exclude the face, i.e., the facial expression, completely from the pantomimic presentation.

Any idea being projected produces its specific movement and gesture pattern which is, in itself, purely abstract. Though, basically, pantomime is not mere storytelling, a story may be, and usually is, achieved by what is done. But to attain such ends, the means must be determined by strict form, since form alone leads to artistry.

In seeking to reach my audience and to convey my message in the easiest understandable manner, I often chose the channels of humor. There are various kinds of humor, but first and foremost it must be said that, whenever a humorous element is required, it can come only from the performer himself and must be projected by him.

In the beginning I employed the most obvious humor, the sadistic type of humor, the effect of which is almost guaranteed with every audience. However, with time, I was continually looking for a broader expression of what I wanted to achieve, and I attempted to abstract the essense of any emotion projected through movement. Here is an example. Instead of being frantic as, let us say, a minstrel would be when a bucket of water is thrown over him, I tried to convey the same idea without impersonating a minstrel and with no bucket of water causing the emotion. This attempt finally crystallized into a dance called *Kinetic Pantomime*. In this composition I so juggled, reversed and distorted cause and effect, impulse and reaction that a kaleidoscopic effect was created without once resorting to any literary representation.

It has been a long and arduous way from this comedy pantomime to Thurber's *Fables for Our Time*. But my basic approach to subject matter, though it has widened and developed, has never changed. Content and form are equally important to my choreographic pantomimes. I have never believed that artistry can be achieved without adhering to strict form, nor that the heart of the public can be reached, if the artist is blind to the life that surrounds him or tries to shut himself off from it by escaping into mere fantasy and romance. Art demands that we be a part of life and merge with it. Art and life are as indivisible an entity as the artist and his audience.[2]

REMEMBERING CHARLES WEIDMAN
BY
JANET TOWNER

Through some sort of miraculous good fortune I stumbled into the world of Charles Weidman in 1969, six years before his death. Having no concrete idea of what I was looking for in my own development as a dancer, knowing only that I had loved to dance since the age of nine and had found myself gravitating toward some involvement in it, I arrived in New York with my former husband.

I saw an advertisement for secretarial work in exchange for dance classes with Charles Weidman in *The Village Voice*, and so, the next afternoon I went to his Expression of Two Arts Theatre at 102 West Twenty-Ninth Street. I found the address led me to a rather dilapidated building, just off Sixth Avenue, in the middle of the florist district. I climbed the stairs to the second floor, knocked on the door, and was greeted by Charles and his administrative assistant, Maya Doray. After introductions, Charles exited down a narrow hallway, while Maya gave me some work filing papers.

I soon discovered that the narrow hallway where Charles had exited after greeting me the first day I met him led to his one-room living quarters in the back of the loft. The hallway was flanked on one side by a closet piled to the ceiling with costumes (some dating from the 1930s). On the other side was a small bathroom with a sink, shower, and a mirror (around which we dancers crowded to apply makeup for the Sunday performances).

Everything about the space Charles lived and worked in was humble, small, simple, and pared down to day-to-day living necessities. Charles' personal living space was a room about twenty feet by fifteen feet, which served as a livingroom, office, kitchen, and bathroom. During the week, except to answer the phone for Charles when he was teaching or in rehearsal, we never entered his living space, but on Sundays it was our dressing room. From the moment we arrived for afternoon rehearsal we entered it freely. For our Sunday performances Charles always prepared a snack for us, usually his guacamole and crackers—and there was the teakettle on the stove for making tea or instant coffee. Between our rehearsal and performance we gathered in Charles' livingroom where many times he launched into a story about Doris (Humphrey), or Martha (Graham), or Miss Ruth (St. Denis), or some other dance luminary. He seemed to know just when we needed something to tickle our funny bone or inspire us.

I remember my first class with Charles. I was immediately swept into the energy of his dance class, the rhythmic guidance of his fine drumming, and the excitement of the movement. I remember that it all felt so exciting; the movement fit my own feelings about life and my sense was that something vital and deeply meaningful had happened in that first class. I performed with Charles almost every Sunday evening for the next six and one-half years. I became a principal dancer in his company, his teaching assistant, and secretary.

During the years I knew Charles, he wanted to make his dance ideas accessible to everyone. In his classes he presented the Humphrey-Weidman technique at a swift pace; he taught the ideas of the movement principles, which led to the expression of something bigger—his dances were based on these ideas. In his classes his drumming urged our movements towards the expression of its dynamics. Before we began a series Charles would beat out the rhythm of the movement as an introduction so we knew exactly which technical series we were about to do. He always commented on the movement quality: "give it breath," or in a suspending movement, "delight in delay." Many of Charles' other comments related to our projection and intention when we were performing the movements: "space in the face," or "desire to get somewhere." He was fully involved with his classes and his own intensity seemed to infuse his students with energy and concentration. His classes were serious undertakings, but there was time for spontaneous humor and laughter as well. "Not yet a poem," he might quip as a student struggled with a difficult movement. There was a strong link between our one-hour technique class and the repertory rehearsals that followed. Everything we worked on in the technique class developed into a vehicle for the expression of a specific Weidman choreographic phrase. All of the dance elements and movement qualities we studied in his technique classes were reflected in an actual emotional content within his choreography.

Charles was always in the present, but his works manifested a continuum of past and present. The Sunday evening performances included many of his works from the past alive with the enduring ideas from the original recreated with us in the present. We performed works from the 1930s through the 1970s such as *Lynchtown,* with its pointed social comment, the opening dance from *Opus 51,* with its lyric beauty, *Bargain Counter, Fables for Our Time, Brahms Waltzes, The Christmas Oratorio, The Easter Oratorio, Saint Matthew Passion,* and his last work *Visualizations, or From a Farm in New Jersey.* There were other works in his mind, I know. He was never at a loss for ideas to transform into movement, only at a loss for the time in which to express them. Circumstances never stopped his creative work. I always sensed in Charles the urgency to get his ideas translated into a dance form, which would carry them on; maybe that is why he always worked so fast—he had so much to say.

329

I know that my life would be much less meaningful and joyful had I not known and worked with Charles Weidman. His depth of spirit, love of life, his vitality, and ability to make us laugh at ourselves, were characteristics he personified as an artist, teacher and human being. I learned so much about art and life from him—and about myself. "You always have to have hope," he once said, and surely he never gave up hope. In his last letter he wrote to me only a few days before his death he pondered: "I have always expected miracles and I have always been rewarded . . ." He closed that letter as he closed all of his letters, "Carry On. As ever, Charles."

Janet Towner, June 2005

IMPRESSIONS OF CHARLES WEIDMAN
BY
DEBORAH CARR

The first time I saw Charles Weidman was in the summer of 1972 at the American Dance Festival at Connecticut College. I was a student, a year away from graduating from Stephens College with my BFA in Dance. Charles had reconstructed Doris Humphrey's *New Dance* and his own *Flickers* for a temporary company that had been assembled to perform and preserve some of the masterworks of modern dance. Although I discovered later that he was very down-to-earth and approachable, I was too shy to introduce myself, even though I was a student of Harriette Ann Gray, one of his favorite dancers and his assistant in the late 1930s.

I had been interested in Charles, Doris, and José Limón since my high school days in Kansas City where I had the good fortune to meet José and take a master class. Very early on, I fell in love with the Humphrey-Weidman technique as well as the beautiful choreographic philosophy. I was fortunate in being allowed to study and perform with the college students at the University of Missouri at Kansas City while still a teenager in the late 1960s. It was there that I first experienced the work of Doris Humphrey, learning *Brandenburg Concerto* from labanotator Ray Cook. That experience led me to choose Stephens College upon finishing high school, where I could study with Harriette Ann Gray, a brilliant teacher and beautiful dancer from the Humphrey-Weidman Company. After that summer of 1972, I was determined to meet Charles and learn as much as I could from him. Immediately after graduating from Stephens College in 1973, I headed for New York City and straight for the Weidman studio.

Charles was not at all what I expected. I had steeled myself for a very severe New York professional. Instead, I was greeted by a kind and dedicated teacher with an unquenchable sense of humor. His highly physical style of movement suited me both technically and temperamentally. I began performing with his small company and rehearsing in his cramped studio. I will always remember my early years in New York with great fondness. Every day began with the anticipation of the new movement I would learn from Charles or the stories he would tell. He was one of those rare individuals who provide inspiration to last a lifetime.

Times were difficult. Charles had little money and I had even less upon which to survive. The dancers of the Humphrey-Weidman Company, many of whom I came to consider my second family, reminded me of the difficulties all the early dance pioneers had to overcome during the Depression. I often remarked to Beatrice Seckler, who became my mentor after Charles' death in 1975, that I didn't see how things were much better for artists in the post-Depression years. Charles did his best to help all the young dancers that came to him. He gave us some very practical advice such as: " Save your per diem money when on tour by allowing people to take you out to dinner. That way, you would have money to buy food when you came home to New York." For a period of time, I lived on a loaf of bread and a jar of peanut butter with an occasional apple thrown in. Charles began making soup for me to take home and supplement my skimpy meals. Although I have always been grateful for help from people who had plenty to spare, I learned at a young age to feel blessed by the generosity of those who had little to spare and yet were always willing to share what they had. Another bit of advice was to never to allow a lack of money to keep you from taking class. As a result, he allowed many students to take class and run up a tab. Sometimes they could pay later, and sometimes he let them work off their debts by running lights or helping with mailings, etc. I think it might be difficult to find such generosity today, but dance was less a business and more of a calling to these early modern dancers.

Charles was an artist who totally lacked pretension or arrogance. He had finished teaching a lovely section of the *Saint Matthew Passion* and I excitedly told him how beautiful I thought it was. When he looked surprised and asked me if I really thought it was good, I felt humbled that an artist of his stature would even be interested in the opinion of a then twenty-one year old dancer. The first piece I performed with Charles was his *Christmas Oratorio*. It was a beautiful full evening's work with group sections very reminiscent of Doris Humphrey's group pieces from the late 1930s. During rehearsals, I developed the bad habit of looking around the room to see what dancers were doing in other parts. Charles became annoyed and asked me if I couldn't remember what I was supposed to do. I explained that I wanted to see how the dance was put together. He frowned and told me I was too young to be a choreographer and to pay attention to my dancing. Several weeks later, I came into rehearsal to see two chairs put out in front of the performing space and the other dancers smiling conspiratorially. Charles asked me if I felt comfortable with my parts. When I said that I did, he instructed me to take a seat and began rehearsal. As he ran through the piece, he kindly explained to me his thoughts on the choreography and how he had structured the work. He always had the time for anyone who wanted to learn.

Over the years, I have met many people who knew Charles or studied with him. Invariably they will say first how much they loved him, and then what a wonderful artist he was. Time spent with Charles was usually fun. His infectious sense of humor could turn around even the most difficult day. Occasionally, he would take on little projects for the betterment of his dancers. At one point, having decided that I was entirely too shy, he made up his mind to "socialize" me. I believe this decision was the result of my tagging along constantly to pick his brain. He said I was always at his heels like a little puppy and I needed to learn to talk to people other than him. After the next Sunday studio performance, I was to sit down with a member of the audience at his post-performance wine and cheese gathering and have a discussion. I began to panic and told him that I didn't really like "regular" people. He had that already figured out and had chosen a victim with whom I might feel comfortable. Betty Jones's mother was to be in the audience, and I was to talk with her. He gently hinted that perhaps I was a little socially retarded and that this was an important step in my personal development. I had studied with Betty a bit and thought she was very nice, so I concluded that perhaps this would be possible. What would we talk about? Charles was getting frustrated with me but suggested that I talk about José and the films that I had been viewing at Lincoln Center. As it turned out, Betty's mother was lovely and we had a nice conversation. Charles, however, viewed his experiment as being only partially successful as I was right back at his heels the next weekend and chattering in his ear.

I was not fortunate enough to know Charles at the height of his performing career, but I was much richer for having been able to witness his incredible talent even when he was no longer in his prime. Much has been said about his remarkable face and his ability to change from one character to another in a matter of seconds. When he was reconstructing a solo he was about to video and I was curious about it, I asked him if I could watch him rehearse. I was not disappointed since he was always gracious and eager to share his talent with dancers. In *Saints, Sinners, and Scriabin*, he portrayed a number of different characters such as Savonarola, Rasputin, and Dillinger. In contrast, there is a very tender and beautiful section where he faced upstage for a moment and when he

334

turned around to the audience, he was transformed into St. Francis. In the group works that I performed with him, he became a variety of animals in Thurber's *Fables for Our Time* and Abraham Lincoln in *A House Divided.* I have never, in my many years in the modern dance field, met his equal as a performer, nor have I met his equal as a choreographer for sheer versatility. He created beautiful pure dance works such as *Brahms Waltzes,* and dramatic works with social comment like *Lynchtown.* Dancing with him was fulfilling on many different levels.

After Charles died in 1975, I spent the next twenty-five years as the Artistic Director of my own company that performed my works and many of his, along with an occasional piece by Doris Humphrey. At the present time, I am teaching at my alma mater, Stephens College. I am heartened by the knowledge that Charles still has much to say to the current younger generation as they respond with great enthusiasm to his technique and humanistic approach to art, which many years before had also become my own. Charles and the Humphrey-Weidman Company adopted me as a young dancer to pass on their timeless philosophy of art. I took away not only the great experience of working with these amazing people but acquired the obligation and pleasure to share it with others down the road.

Deborah Carr, May 2005

CELEBRATING CHARLES WEIDMAN
BY
JONETTE LANCOS

On April 30, 1989, in front of a building that housed the José Limón Studio at 38 West 19th Street, I said goodbye to my friend, Niki Harris, and with several others entered the building and walked to the elevator. There I was delighted to see Ray Cook, who had reconstructed Doris Humphrey's *The Shakers* for the Wilkes-Barre Ballet, of which I had served as assistant director.

As the elevator opened onto the bright foyer on the ninth floor, Louise Allen checked my name and I received a program. As I entered the studio I noticed a warm, friendly atmosphere. Members of the upcoming panel were chatting while dancers and technicians were preparing for the performance. Audience members were socializing and some were meeting new friends.

Alwin Nikolais conversed with Marian Horosko, Marcia Siegel talked with Deborah Jowitt, Betsy Carden set up a display of Charles Weidman tee-shirts for purchase, Pauline Tish and Letitia Ide engaged in an animated dialogue while Phyllis Lamhut sailed into the studio and warmly greeted Nik (Alwin Nikolais) and others. Deborah Carr and Beatrice Seckler discussed details concerning the performance, technicians checked sound levels, and positioned a video camera to tape the occasion. Within ten minutes the audience was complete and chatting loudly when Miriam Cooper, President of the Charles Weidman School of Modern Dance, Incorporated, asked everyone to take their seats so that the panel discussion, *The Influences of Charles Weidman*, could begin. The panel members were Eleanor King, Alwin Nikolais, Betty Osgood, Bill Hooks, Nadine Gae,

337

David Wynn, and moderator Marian Horosko. They all took their seats at two long tables in the center of the studio.

Horosko cordially introduced the panelists and began the discussion with a brief introduction about Charles Weidman's youth and training at Denishawn. She proceeded to read a gracious message from Martha Graham, who fondly remembered working with Charles at Denishawn. Graham recalled Charles and her sister, Georgia, performing in *Boston Fancy* that "stopped the show every time, even in New Delhi! Charles Weidman was my friend and as a deeply sensitive artist gave to me many gentle and performing moments during my life at Denishawn." Martha Graham sent her thanks to all those attending the benefit, "for your devotion to Charles."

After enthusiastic applause, as an introduction to the panelists, Horosko described the creative periods of Charles Weidman's career. While listening to the panel, I gleaned a panoramic view of Weidman's career from Denishawn to Bennington College, the glorious Humphrey-Weidman-Lawrence alliance to the Charles Weidman Company, and Weidman's vital contribution to the musical theatre. The panel did not comment on Weidman's later period at the Expression of Two Arts Theatre with Mikhail Santaro, his tenure with the New York City Opera, or Weidman's offering of master classes in more than one hundred colleges and universities across the United States. The panelists remembered Weidman's technique and his classes, marveled at his performing ability and witty personality, but omitted comment on Weidman's choreographic expertise and his superb use of form and musicality.

Eleanor King made her debut in 1928 with the original Humphrey-Weidman Company. King spoke of her experiences: "Charles was warm and stimulating. I

338

think everyone always loved working with Charles. With Charles we had characterization and theatre . . . but the lovely thing was the combination of austere Doris with her cool detachment and the warm-hearted Charles; it was the most wonderful combination. I feel I was very blessed to work with Charles—very, very, very blessed."

Alwin Nikolais recalled his experiences with "the big four" (Weidman, Humphrey, Graham, and Holm) at Bennington College (1937-1939). Nikolais stated that Weidman was known for his comic flair on stage but he was also very funny in daily life remembering, "it was such hilarity and such a contrast, I don't remember Charles ever being unfunny." Nikolais continued to relate many witty stories about Weidman, and then settled into philosophical meditation: "I think that Charles, Doris, Martha, and Hanya had this passion, it wasn't just passion for exhibitionism, it was passion for an art and it's much different, much different. I look at the kids today who have no passion for the art. They have passion for exhibitionism; they have passion for dancing—but where can we get that wonderful dynamic thing that created this dance which was so important to the United States and which seems to be forgotten?" Nikolais recalled, "this extraordinary passion that Charles had—and also remember, he was surrounded by a matriarchal society and he managed to become a jewel among them. It was with Charles that I decided to become a dancer."

After hearty applause for Alwin Nikolais, Horosko reads a message from Ernestine Stodelle, who was a member of the Doris Humphrey Concert Group and the Humphrey-Weidman Company from 1929 to 1935. Stodelle's concluding statement: "As a former member of the Humphrey-Weidman family, I join you in saluting Charles Weidman and also his partner Doris Humphrey and Pauline Lawrence—combined, their influence on my life was nothing less than profound."

339

Horosko continued. "There was a wonderful period on 16th Street . . . there were performances every single week. There were people learning how to dance, learning the repertoire, and learning this Weidman technique." With this statement Horosko introduced Betty Osgood. Osgood was a member of the Humphrey-Weidman Company and the Charles Weidman Company who received rave reviews for her role as a chipmunk in *Fables of Our Time*. She taught the Weidman technique at the 16th Street studio. Osgood remembered:

"I wanted to study with Charles and I had this privilege. The teaching was just different for both Doris and Charles. You learned from the dances or excerpts from the dances, and Charles and José made up a technical study that we used to learn turns and falls but you really learned by doing the dances. The vocabulary of movement was different for every dance. While talking about Charles, a wonderful man, I thought of the principles he had. He kept dancing, that's all he knew how to do. Through thick and thin he kept doing what he was able to do. He always said, 'Have faith.' One day the bill collector was coming and he quickly ran into the class and started the Body Bends. The bill collector said, 'Where's Mr. Weidman?' Nobody answered. 'Have faith,' and the money would come. I learned from him that it's all right to be sentimental, but it's not all right to sentimentalize. He used to say, 'such and such a person was a darling,' and he meant it—that he could express this love—and that's what we all had for him."

"Following the world's best chipmunk is a very hard act!" remarked Bill Hooks. As a student at the University of North Carolina and an avid member of the Dance Club, Hooks had his first meeting with the Charles Weidman Company while watching a performance from the wings. Mr. Hooks remembered: "Suddenly someone grabbed me during *Lynchtown* and said: 'We need a body! Lie down and play dead.' I did, and I was dragged across the stage in *Lynchtown* and that was my first encounter with Charles Weidman." After completing college, Hooks came to the 16th Street studio. Hooks continues: "Now you've heard a lot about how free and how loose and how wonderful the Humphrey-Weidman technique was . . . there was a very specific First Series of Turns, Second Series of Turns,

340

and variations thereof, First Series of Jumps, Leaps, and so forth. As well as all of these wonderful pieces from the repertory, because no class was ever given that didn't end with doing a study from a real dance which had been a piece of the Humphrey-Weidman repertory for years." Weidman choreographed for the opera, Broadway, nightclub, and the concert stage. Hooks remarked, "It was all dance. It was all part of the same thing and it all had this incredible edge of excitement about it and he swept everybody along with him. It was an incredible place to be."

Nadine Gae, a member of the Charles Weidman Dance Theatre in the 1940s, remembered Weidman as a distinguished performer. Gae recalled watching Charles during a performance of *On My Mother's Side*. "I realized what a marvelous performer this man was," Gae remarked. "I really had never seen anyone do as little and hold your attention so well. It was a wonderful lesson to me. He would just lift an eyebrow or do a little hand movement and you were just held."

David Wynn, a member of the Charles Weidman Dance Theatre and the José Limón Dance Company, reaffirmed the enthusiasm and encouragement that propelled Weidman's classes. Wynn recalled Weidman as a performer. "*In Fables of Our Time*, the Unicorn in the Garden section, someone had to hold the fence in place offstage. "I did that," Mr. Wynn remarked. "Charles would come over and lean on that fence and watch the unicorn . . . the intensity of that performance, the absolute poise and professionalism when he did this trivial, wonderful, funny, little piece—it fascinated me like nothing that I've seen since, except possibly, being on stage with José Limón. They both had it here (touching his heart). My whole professional career began at Charles' studio. I had studied dance in college and a little before that, but it was not the same thing at all. I realized that this was the real thing, that this man had it—he had it here (touching his heart), and he was giving it to me."

The sincere emotions expressed by each panelist were visually restated by a presentation of Mr. Weidman's works that included a wide range of forms. Carol Mezzacappa and Craig Gabrian in Concert performed the affirmative, bright *Brahms Waltzes* (excerpts) and the witty *Bargain Counter*; Mino Nicholas and Dawn DeAngelo performed the abstract representation of social equality between man and woman in *Duo-Drama*; and Deborah Carr's Theatre Dance Ensemble performed the clarity of form and joyous celebration in *Christmas Oratorio* (excerpts). As these works embraced me. I remembered Mr. Wynn saying, "This man had it—he had it here (touching his heart), and he was giving it to me."

Jonette Lancos, 1989

PERFORMING WITH CHARLES WEIDMAN
BY
MARGARET O'SULLIVAN

Charles is recognized as being one of the pioneers of dance in America. He had a direct influence on those whose names are recognized around the world including Gene Kelly, Bob Fosse, Jack Cole, and Alvin Ailey, to name just a few. For those who had the luck and good fortune to work and perform with him, his genius is indisputable. I was one of those lucky ones. I could go on and extol his brilliance as a choreographer, teacher, and performer; however, I will leave that to the famous. In addition to all that talent, Charles had a delightful, mischievous, little-boy-quality and we never knew when it might appear.

I was performing with Charles when he had his studio on West 29th Street just off 6th Avenue. In addition to outside performances, we were expected to perform every Sunday of the year. The same program would run for about six or seven weeks. Needless to say, this was an invaluable experience for us as performers. We had been doing *Bargain Counter* for several weeks and were all feeling very comfortable with the piece in which Charles had danced as the floorwalker. There is a section in the piece where the lady shoppers fall on top of Charles and we each had our specific counts and steps when we were to get up. I was the first one that was to move but found that someone had a tight grip on my leg—Charles! Myra and Selby were also in his clutches. What could we do but improvise?

After the Sunday performances, we would always go to the back to Charles' living quarters to have some Rhinegarten. There was Charles with that

343

mischievous little smile saying he thought we were getting a bit stale. He loved it. Another time Charles was commissioned to do a reconstruction of Doris Humphrey's *New Dance*. This was especially exciting for all of us young dancers as many of the famous original cast (Beatrice Seckler, Edith Orcutt, Miriam Cooper, Letitia Ide) was coming to work with us. Needless to say, there was some "disagreement" among the ladies on certain sections. One day we were adoringly sitting on the floor listening to them "discuss" when Charles appeared from his living quarters. We were facing Charles, but their backs were to him and they didn't know he was there. With that wonderfully malleable face, he started mimicking each of them, knowing we were desperately trying not to burst into laughter. He was thoroughly enjoying our predicament. These rehearsals went on for a few Saturdays and not much progress was being made with the reconstruction as the ladies' disagreements continued, until Charles walked into the studio one day and announced, "The spirit of Doris just came to me and said it should be this way," and he proceeded to take charge. That's when the work started to take shape.

Charles had the ability to find humor in most anything and this made working with him so pleasant. He would give corrections and sometimes become annoyed with us but was never intimidating. That atmosphere made for a perfect learning environment for all of us.

Margaret O'Sullivan, June 2005

344

WEIDMAN IMPRESSIONS

BY

ROBERT B. KOSINSKI

Do you know why Alvin Ailey dedicated his 1975 season to Charles?

I don't know why Ailey dedicated his 1975 season to Charles, but I witnessed a meeting between the two choreographers at the Delacorte Theater in Central Park during a late summer dance festival there called the New York Dance Festival. Charles and the company were at the Delacorte in the early 1970s participating in the festival in a series of dress rehearsals for a performance that also included other dance companies. I remember sitting near the stage, which was open—no proscenium arch, back wall, or wings—watching Patricia McBride and Jean-Pierre Bonnefous perform a pas de deux from one of Balanchine's ballets. Her earring flew off and landed in front of me; I have always regretted returning it to her.

After the New York City Ballet had finished rehearsing, we were waiting to take the stage, when from one corner Alvin Ailey quickly came out and warmly greeted Charles. Charles, in turn, happily greeted Ailey. It was as if they had known each other for years, but hadn't seen each other in a long time. They launched into an animated conversation; I didn't eavesdrop because I was young and stupid. It was clear to me that the two men shared a close friendship. Perhaps it was because they were major choreographers and dancers in the canon of American modern dance, or shared mutual friends, or traveled in the same social circles—I don't know for sure, but I was fascinated by how they seemed to be so easy and free together and how happy they were to see each other. I do remember that during that Delacorte Festival Charles and I performed *The Moth and the Star.* I was the young, energetic moth and he was the older, but no less ardent moth; in the studio I danced both roles. (I think it may have been one of his last performances outside the studio before he died.)

During a West coast tour in 1972 we were at Reed College, in Portland, Oregon, where Charles and I performed *Traditions* together. I can't remember who started and who finished, but the idea of the atavistic theme of the dance was obvious to the audience. His warm-up consisted of five or six *demi-pliés;* he then was ready to go on stage. I remember when the company was rehearsing for the premiere of his *Saint Matthew Passion* (Bach). We worked through the winter and it was very cold. Charles always impressed me because whenever we were going to learn a new section of the work, he always had the steps and sequence ready for us. I had worked for other choreographers and they always requested that the dancers try different moves or dance sequences, kind of like choreography as you go along. But Charles always had everything ready for his dancers. We never did movement, steps, or sequences over and over again, trying different things. He demanded perfect execution, which we didn't always deliver, but we didn't waste time trying different looks.

Charles was a demanding choreographer and teacher and he could be at times very cruel and insulting, yet his students and company members were devoted to him. When I was taking classes and in the company I remember several times when students and company performers were ridiculed, and cried as a result. Charles could easily upset people with his caustic comments, but he included anybody who showed up regularly for classes in the company, and we performed for fifty weeks a year every Sunday night in his studio on 29th Street in Manhattan.

Robert B. Kosinski, June 2005

REMEMBERING CHARLES WEIDMAN
BY
M. ROSALIND PIERSON

The making of any of us, be it artist, doctor, lawyer, is, I suspect, closely dependent on those who give us what we need at the moments we are receptive and ready for their gifts. At least this is how I measure my journey.

I was twenty-two and barely a year out of Bennington College, when I joined the Dancer's Theatre Company, directed by Martin Morginsky. I was quickly assigned to a couple of roles in Charles Weidman's *Flickers,* because one of the dancers was leaving the company. Shortly thereafter, the cast met at Weidman's studio, which was above a ribbon store on 28th Street in New York's millinery district, where Weidman coached us in our *Flickers* roles and began teaching us *Brahms Waltzes.* We later learned that Weidman had agreed to give *Brahms Waltzes* to Morginsky in exchange for the company members' participation in his *Christmas Oratorio* that December.

My early teachers had engendered in me a healthy respect for dance history and its makers, so I met Mr. Weidman with a sense of awe, despite his cramped and dingy quarters. From the moment he began to teach the *Brahms Waltzes*, I felt a bond, a refreshing reference to my Virginia Tanner roots, and an affinity with the vocabulary, its subtle nuance and its clarity. I loved these short dance gems, relished their musicality, delighted in the play they allowed, and the dynamic range they demanded. Charles must have sensed my delight, for one evening at the end of rehearsal, he pulled me aside and told me that he was casting me as the "Red Angel" in *The Christmas Oratorio,* a role I was later to learn filled much of the hour-and-a-half dance.

347

One afternoon, shortly thereafter, I climbed above the ribbons to learn my solo—or so I thought. Upon my arrival, Charles shooed three or four cats into his living quarters behind the studio, walked to the tape recorder, turned on some music, and went to the back. I assumed I was to count out the section so that I knew its shape and phrasing, so I carefully noted the counts and phrases on a piece of paper, and then went to fetch the master. Weidman looked a bit surprised at my appearance and asked if I had finished. When I told him that I had counted out the music, he stuttered and muttered in his impatient, but decidedly Weidman way, "Well, go do your dance. Go do your dance!" Somewhat bewildered, but definitely energized, I hurried back to the studio and frantically began to shape a seven-minute solo.

Two or three times during my allotted two hours, Charles peered at me from the back and asked if I had finished. My heart raced, my adrenaline pumped, and when he demanded a look, I traveled a seven-minute journey with no recollection of the contents of its passage. Charles grumbled about a few things and inserted a movement here or a pause there, then sent me home. I don't believe that solo was ever remotely the same in any of the performances, but I do know that I was never given time to worry about it.

Charles appeared to live quietly in his back room, with his innumerable cats, but he lived at the speed of light in rehearsal. It was as if his muse cracked a whip we could not hear, driving him to insist his dancers read an unseen script. Fortunately, among the cast, there were some veterans who knew the dancing words and could convey them to the tyros! Charles knew the steps, knew every nuance. In fact, he drove you mad with knowing when you could not grasp his thought, but he was never mean—driven, yes, impatient, yes, but always generous with praise when what he expected was accomplished.

Weidman was a curious mix of wit and dedication. One of my favorite memories is of a his *Christmas Oratorio* rehearsal that was interrupted by a frantic banging on the door: "Mr. Weidman, Mr. Weidman, the building is on fire!" Charles, unfazed, continued the run. The banging grew more and more frantic and Charles finally went to the door and said, "Please, we only have a few more minutes!" (We were still running the last section.) At this point, several firemen rushed through the door carrying a very large hose. One proceeded to the window, which opened on an airshaft, and sent a stream of water into the shaft. Two other firemen surveyed the scene, one pausing before a painting, which appeared to be puzzling him. Charles watched this fireman for some time, then drew close and waited for an opportunity to interact. The young man finally found words: "I think I understand this; I have one question. What does this mean?" He pointed to a check mark in an abstract painting. Charles, with only a tiny twinkle in his eye, responded, "Why that's an accent!" The fireman paused, pondered for a moment, then exclaimed, "Oh, I see!" I, with the rest of the dancers, muffled the giggles that would have embarrassed the young fireman, who really did want to understand. But once the Fire Department had dragged their hoses out the door, we had not a second to explode into laughter because Charles was at the tape recorder, ready to work again.

The short run of *The Christmas Oratorio* was a special time for me as a dancer. Bach's music and Weidman's interpretation of it sent me flying into seemingly boundless space even though the studio was really very small. One section of the work, in particular, touched me deeply. In it I, perched atop a pile of the famous Humphrey-Weidman boxes, hovered above Charles as he danced the premonitory solo depicting Christ's suffering. My slow gestures were designed to support and lift the figure below me. In that duet, I truly felt as if threads of light streamed from my hands, gently binding me to this gentle man, who seemed to know my soul.

After one of the performances, a woman asked me what kind of makeup I had used, because I seemed to "glow." Charles, who was close by and had

349

overheard, was quick to respond, "Why that isn't makeup—she does glow!" Such high praise from such an important figure has been a cherished and sustaining gift.

The following spring, I was among the group of dancers who performed with Charles in London, England, and Oslo, Norway. Much of this trip was sad and filled with unpleasant occurrences. But rather than dwell upon the darker aspects of Weidman's life and career, I prefer to honor his gentleness, his unmatchable wit, his unique musicality, his ability to tap the deepest, richest part of a dancer and set her free to shine.

M. Rosalind Pierson

WORKING WITH CHARLES WEIDMAN

BY

DOT VIRDEN MURPHY

Fall 1961

From an ad in *Back Stage* or *Show Business*, "Charles Weidman will hold auditions for dancers." I went, took the class and was accepted. I attended two classes a week and we rehearsed after class. Charles was at that time giving weekend performances with Mikhail Santaro. We began working on a piece from his repertory about people walking in patterns and hurrying from here to there. I cannot remember the name. He was not pleased with the progress of the work and wanted to begin the Bach, so we stopped. *The Christmas Oratorio* had its first performances that December 1961.

January 1962—Spring

During this time we worked on an odd piece in which Marjorie Carey, myself, and another woman portrayed three licentious women. Lazaro (Lazar Dano), a Cuban dancer, showed up at this time and was also in the piece. Charles continued his weekend performances in which this piece and others were shown. Sometime during that time he created a work about an old priest to Debussy's *Submerged Cathedral*. This could have been an old piece or a new one based on an old theme. He created a humorous piece to Mozart Flute Concertos (available on video) about the Hero, Heroine, and Villain, using a piece of cloth to skillfully suggest each character. He created a St. Francis solo and other dances called *Saints, Sinners and Scriabin* to music by that composer. Not knowing the dances

351

Charles created before I came, or knowing very much about him, it all seemed new to me.

<u>Summer, 1962</u>

Charles taught a month-long workshop, three or four days a week, at his studio. During this time we learned the Doris Humphrey successional study; this greatly helped us better understand the movements in *Brahms Waltzes,* which we had been learning all year in class. We also learned many other studies from Humphrey-Weidman technique. That summer we performed the complete *Brahms* Waltzes. Charles performed with us. I think it was this summer that Charles was invited to perform three of the Thurber "Fables" at the American Dance Festival in Connecticut. I performed with Charles. We were nervous that he might start drinking, but he was superb in performance, and I remember I never saw him drink again.

<u>Winter, 1962</u>

I am sure that *The Christmas Oratorio* was performed again. I do not think I was in it, but I remember going to see it and wishing I were!

<u>Spring, 1963</u>

I sporadically went to the studio, danced for a while, and left for a month or two. I had a small son and lived alone. Charles once or twice a year set up teaching tours and would go out on the road for a month or so. He had connections with private teachers, schools, and colleges. This is the way he could pay the bills on the studio. That spring he approached me and said, "Where have you been? I have been waiting for you to come so I can choreograph *King David* for you." Max Shufer, who was also in it, was with Charles longer than anyone and was very loyal to him. Charles created all the sets, props, and costumes for

352

King David. I remember my mother sent me some old ruffles off my tester bed. These got dyed and refashioned into the ghost of Samuel, one of the puppets used in the piece. For a month I went to the studio. Charles taught class, rehearsed us, and worked on costumes. He made metallic collars and headpieces out of copper sheet, musical instruments out of aluminum pie pans. *David and Goliath* was created around an earlier piece Charles had danced. A figure of paper cutout became the soul of David in despair. Small copper wings on arms and ankles became Lazar's, "Dove" who lifts David up in "O, for wings of a Dove." Huge netting covered the dancers glorifying "God before the Ark of the Covenant." Garland dancers take leave of the earth as in a Chagall painting. (This image is straight from Charles). The finale is an incredible turning dance. Three dancers (Lazar, Marjorie, and myself) enter with slow walking and turning movements. The three of us danced in unison, descending to the floor and rising again, never ceasing this turning movement. As it builds to a crescendo, the other dancers enter, picking up the walking and turning movement. This builds to a grand climax of joyful movement, and slowly all dancers descend to their knees with arms reaching above their heads in a prayer gesture as the music softly closes. One incredible thing about performing in *King David* was the huge amount of props that we consistently used throughout. Also, Charles used the narration just as it was in the music spoken by Andre Bernard.

February 19, 1964

We performed at Northwestern University, where we also performed at a large high school in Evanston, Illinois. Charles performed brilliantly and was in great form. The Theatre Department that had invited us loved him. The Kuhnau piece *Jacob's Marriage* was folksy, very funny and, as always, musically a delight to dance. Back at the studio the weekend performances continued but not every week. I remember working on *War Between Men and Women* but it was not performed at this time. I left the City in the fall of 1964 but stayed in touch with Charles. I went to Texas Women's University in Denton for two summers (at this time I was living in Mississippi, 1965 and 1966). Charles set *Bargain Counter* on us; he was superb as the floor manager and stole the show, of course. We also did *The Easter Oratorio* that he had created in New York. We performed these pieces in concert at the University, opening with *Classroom, Modern Style,* accompanied by Charles on the drum.

Fall, 1969

I moved to New Orleans and worked with the New World Dance Company. I set the opening to *The Christmas Oratorio* and also performed in it. The next spring we invited Charles to come to New Orleans for a week to give master classes and to set *The Easter Oratorio*. We performed this piece at Dillard University and at the Jewish Community Center. Charles began the program with *Classroom, Modern Style* and one of his solos to Mozart. We ended the program with *The Easter Oratorio*. I remember the dancers wondering how we would get it all together in one week. Charles showed us how to make beautiful crepe skirts for the Bach and we we up late into the night making those skirts! This was my last time to dance with Charles, but we stayed in touch over the years.

I did participate in a class he conducted in San Francisco in the spring of 1973, where the performance included *A House Divided*. I never performed in this piece but remember it as brilliant theatre, with Charles performing. I also attended a performance in his studio in New York sometime after that, but did not see him again before his death. About his classes, the studio, favorite dances, and what I learned, I will put this all together by saying that dancing with Charles was a joy. His musicality and phrasing, when dancing Brahms or Bach, made one feel as if he and these great composers conspired to create such beauty. Charles

354

teased and would not let you take yourself too seriously. He was never malicious or mean, but he could get frustrated and push to "get it right." He was humble and created magic at the 102 West 29th Street studio. Out of nothing he brought joy. Although his life was not easy, he looked beyond the insensitive things that pull one down to inspire the sublime. His classes were about dancing not just technique. On cue his drum beat the rhythm and you flew across the floor. He was challenging and fun. In his choreography he would arrive at the technique through images such as Joy! Joy! Joy! as the dancers burst across the floor in a circling path to announce the coming of the Nativity in *The Christmas Oratorio*. I was so fortunate to have studied and danced with Charles. Choosing a favorite dance is impossible; every experience was inspiring and life-affirming.

Dot Virden Murphy, July 2005

DANCING WITH CHARLES WEIDMAN
BY
DEBORAH JOWITT

I was studying at the New Dance Group around 1955, when Charles Weidman came to teach some classes. I'd begun my modern dance training with Harriette Ann Gray, a former member of the Humphrey-Weidman Company, and loved the big swings and forthright exercises he gave us. He asked Stanley Berke, Barbara Kirschner, and me to appear in a series of performances he was presenting—once a week as I remember—in the Carnegie Hall studio run by Viola Essen.

We three were the youngest members of the group he assembled to dance *The War Between Men and Women* (he'd premiered it in 1954 at the 92nd Street Y) and his silent film spoof, *Flickers*. Charles performed in both (Barbara and I were the gamboling nymphs the henpecked husband dreamed of in *War*, and maybe a couple of flappers in *Flickers*). I recall him vividly as a Rudoph Valentino sheik, walking Flower Hujer as a Theda-Bara vamp backward up the wall in their ardent tango. He also created a new addition to his Thurber *Fables for Our Time*, a touching piece for Stanley and himself as the young, flame-eager moth and his older self. The other dancers, including his onetime lover and Humphrey-Weidman colleague Peter Hamilton, must all have been well over 40—the men willing but slightly sardonic, the women docile and soft-bodied. I think some of us began the evening with a technique demonstration.

I loved Charles; he was kind and patient and always cheerful. His glory days were over. He had been evicted a few years before from the Studio Theater in 16th Street where so many Humphrey-Weidman dances had been rehearsed and performed; his finances were shaky. On the other hand, he had conquered his alcoholism and was determined to keep working.

One performance stands out in my mind. Doris Humphrey had come to see our show, dressed in tailored elegance. She arrived early, using her cane to haul herself up the stairs that led from the lower office and dressing room area to the studio. We performed in very basic lights, all controlled by one switch at the end of a cord that hung off a bar near the piano bench where Freda Miller sat. Freda accompanied everything but *War* (we danced that to a lo-fi recording of Tchaikovsky's *Symphonie Pathétique*).

That night, whoever handled that little switch was too ill to show up (if it was Freda, what did we do—dance to tapes?). The audience was due to arrive shortly. Charles, slightly embarrassed but not at all put out, asked Doris if she would run the lights. She agreed and limped to the chair nearest the piano. While we stood by in respectful amazement, Charles coached his former partner, the woman we all knew to be one of the great choreographers of the 20th century, through our paltry light cues. How courageous both she and Charles both seemed to me that night, how fervently we danced for them, and how much I wanted Doris to see that Charles was not to be pitied, that he was still an artist, and that in a shabby studio for an audience of maybe 50 people, he could still create theatrical magic.

Deborah Jowitt, March 2006

EPILOGUE

When Charles Weidman died in 1975, his will designated that his estate be divided between fifteen legatees. Until these fifteen legatees had agreed on the stipulations set forth by Weidman's will, authorization of monies, approval of rights for performances of his repertoire, and the collection of royalties rested with the Public Administrator for the State of New York. By 1988, the transfer of monies from Mr. Weidman's various bank accounts into one account, and the disbursement of these monies to the fifteen legatees had been completed. Charles Wilson, who danced with Charles Weidman, was appointed Administrator for the Estate. Late in 1989, Wilson distributed most of the estate to the fifteen legatees, who in turn, donated their bequests to the Charles Weidman Dance Foundation.

Rest In Peace, Dear Charles

For those of you who do not know,
Charles Weidman is buried in the Garden of the Apostles,
Kensico Cemetery on Lakeview Avenue in Valhalla, New York.
He was buried on July 21, 1978.
The Board of Directors of the Charles Weidman
School of Modern Dance Incorporated placed a headstone on his grave in
February 1983 with an inscription written by Janet Towner:
Charles Edward Weidman
July 22, 1901—July 15, 1975
Dancer, Choreographer, and Beloved Humanist

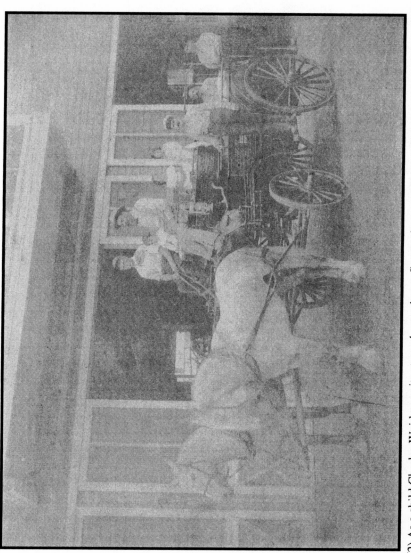

(2) As a child Charles Weidman sits atop a horse-drawn fire truck, ca. 1905. Charles Edward Weidman, Sr. was Fire Chief of the Lincoln (Nebraska) Fire Department. Photograph reproduced through the courtesy of the Jerome Robbins Dance Division, The New York Public Library, Astor, Lenox, and Tilden Foundations.

(3) Young Charles Weidman performing a Russian dance in his first recital ca.
1919. With no formal dance training he created nine dances and his costumes.
Eleanor Frampton was impressed with his creativity and offered him a scholarship
to her dance school. Photograph reproduced through the courtesy of the Jerome
Robbins Dance Division, The New York Public Library, Astor, Lenox, and Tilden
Foundations.

(4) Charles Weidman, ca. 1921
Photograph by Sissman Studio. Reproduced through the courtesy of the Jerome Robbins Dance Division, The New York Public Library, Astor, Lenox, and Tilden Foundations.

(5) Ruth St. Denis in *Burmese Solo*, ca. 1923. Photograph by Nickolas Muray, © Nickolas Muray Photo Archives.Reproduced through the courtesy of the Jerome Robbins Dance Division, The New York Public Library, Astor, Lenox, and Tilden Foundations.

(6) Charles Weidman dances his Romantic solo *Pierrot Forlorn*, ca. 1921. Photograph by George Bockman. Reproduced through the courtesy of the Jerome Robbins Dance Division, The New York Public Library, Astor, Lenox, and Tilden Foundations.

(7) Charles Weidman dances with Martha Graham in *Arabic Duet*, ca. 1921. For the first three years of their careers with the Denishawn Dancers, Weidman and Graham were partners. Photograph reproduced through the courtesy of the Jerome Robbins Dance Division, The New York Public Library, Astor, Lenox, and Tilden Foundations.

(8) Charles Weidman dances with Paul Mathis, Lenore Scheffer, and Ted Shawn in Shawn's *Siamese Ballet,* ca. 1922. Photograph by Nickolas Muray, © Nickolas Muray Photo Archives. Reproduced through the courtesy of the Jerome Robbins Dance Division, The New York Public Library, Astor, Lenox, and Tilden Foundations.

(9) Charles Weidman with Doris Humphrey and the Denishawn Dancers in
Sonata Tragica, Humphrey's first programmed credit for choreography, ca. 1923.
Other dancers are Louise Brooks, Lenore Sadowska, Anne Douglas, Lenore
Scheffer, Georgia Graham and Lenore Hardy. Photograph by White Studio.
Reproduced through the courtesy of the Jerome Robbins Dance Division, The
New York Public Library, Astor, Lenox, and Tilden Foundations.

(10) Charles Weidman partners Anne Douglas with Ted Shawn and Georgia Graham in Shawn's *Sevillanos,* ca. 1923. Photograph by Maurice Goldberg. Reproduced through the courtesy of the Jerome Robbins Dance Division, The New York Public Library, Astor, Lenox, and Tilden Foundations.

(11) Charles Weidman in costume and makeup for the popular Kabuki dance drama *Momiji Gari*, ca. 1926. Photograph reproduced through the courtesy of the Jerome Robbins Dance Division, The New York Public Library, Astor, Lenox, and Tilden Foundations.

(12) America's fascination with Asia is the focus in *Sun Bathers in Sunny Florida*, ca. 1930. Unidentified photographer. George Eastman House.

(13) Charles Weidman dances with Martha Graham in a Neighborhood Playhouse production of *A Pagan Poem*, ca. 1930. Photograph by Nickolas Muray, © Nickolas Muray Photo Archives. Reproduced through the courtesy of the Jerome Robbins Dance Division, The New York Public Library, Astor, Lenox, and Tilden Foundations.

(14) Charles Weidman dances in *A Pagan Poem*, ca. 1930. Photograph by Nickolas Muray, © Nickolas Muray Photo Archives. Reproduced through the courtesy of the Jerome Robbins Dance Division, The New York Public Library, Astor, Lenox, and Tilden Foundations.

(15) Charles Weidman, ca. 1930
Photograph reproduced through the courtesy of the Jerome Robbins Dance
Division, The New York Public Library, Astor, Lenox, and Tilden Foundations.

(16) Pauline Lawrence Limón, ca. 1930   Photograph by Marcus Blechman
Reproduced through the courtesy of the Jerome Robbins Dance Division,
The New York Public Library, Astor, Lenox, and Tilden Foundations.

(17) Charles Weidman in *Danse Profane,* ca. 1930
Photograph by Helen Hewett. Reproduced through the courtesy of the Jerome
Robbins Dance Division, The New York Public Library, Astor, Lenox, and Tilden
Foundations.

(18) Charles Weidman dances with José Limón in *Dance on a Spanish Theme*, ca. 1932. Photograph reproduced through the courtesy of the Jerome Robbins Dance Division, The New York Public Library, Astor, Lenox, and Tilden Foundations.

(19) Charles Weidman dances with Cleo Atheneos, Katherine Manning, and Ernestine Henoch (Stodelle) in *Candide,* ca. 1933.   Photograph by Edward Moeller.   Reproduced through the courtesy of the Jerome Robbins Dance Division, The New York Public Library, Astor, Lenox, and Tilden Foundations.

(20) Charles Weidman with José Limón, and George Bockman in *Traditions*, ca. 1935 Photograph by Barbara Morgan, © Willard and Barbara Morgan Archives Reproduced through the courtesy of the Jerome Robbins Dance Division, The New York Public Library, Astor, Lenox, and Tilden Foundations.

(21) Charles Weidman with José Limón and George Bockman in *Traditions*, ca. 1935. Photograph reproduced through the courtesy of the Jerome Robbins Dance Division, The New York Public Library, Astor, Lenox, and Tilden Foundations.

(22) Charles Weidman and Doris Humphrey in *New Dance*, ca. 1935. Photograph reproduced through the courtesy of the Jerome Robbins Dance Division, The New York Public Library, Astor, Lenox, and Tilden Foundations.

(23) Charles Weidman dances the role of the Floorwalker in *Bargain Counter*, ca. 1936. Photograph reproduced through the courtesy of the Jerome Robbins Dance Division, The New York Public Library, Astor, Lenox, and Tilden Foundations.

(24) The Humphrey-Weidman Company in Charles Weidman's *Lynchtown*, ca. 1936. Photograph by Barbara Morgan, © Willard and Barbara Morgan Archives.

(25) Doris Humphrey (center), Charles Weidman (right), Nona Schurman (left), Beatrice Seckler (left) in Humphrey's *The Shakers*, ca. 1938 Photograph by Barbara Morgan, © Willard and Barbara Morgan Archives.

(26) Beatrice Seckler in Doris Humphrey's *The Shakers*, ca. 1938. Photograph by Barbara Morgan, © Willard and Barbara Morgan Archives.

(27) Charles Weidman dances with the Humphrey-Weidman Company in *Opus 51*, ca. 1938. Photograph by Barbara Morgan, © Willard and Barbara Morgan Archives.

(28) Charles Weidman uses his stylish arms and expansive stage space while dancing with the Humphrey-Weidman Company in *Opus 51*, ca. 1938. Photograph by Barbara Morgan, © Willard and Barbara Morgan Archives.

(29) The Humphrey-Weidman Company uses Weidman's *kinetic pantomime* in *Opus 51*, ca. 1938. Photograph by Barbara Morgan, © Willard and Barbara Morgan Archives.

(30) Charles Weidman in *Traditions*, ca. 1940. Photograph reproduced through the courtesy of the Jerome Robbins Dance Division, The New York Public Library, Astor, Lenox, and Tilden Foundations.

(31) Nona Schurman in a stylistic Humphrey-Weidman jump in her *Running Laughter*, ca. 1942. Photograph by Gerda Peterich, courtesy of Nona Schurman.

(32) Charles Weidman dances with Doris Humphrey and their company, ca. 1940. Photograph reproduced through the courtesy of the Jerome Robbins Dance Division, The New York Public Library, Astor, Lenox, and Tilden Foundations.

(33) Charles Weidman in *On My Mother's Side*, ca. 1940. Photograph by Barbara Morgan. Reproduced through the courtesy of the Jerome Robbins Dance Division, The New York Public Library, Astor, Lenox, and Tilden Foundations.

(34) Charles Weidman and his Theatre Dance Company in *And Daddy Was a Fireman*, ca. 1943 Photograph by Gerda Peterich. Reproduced through the courtesy of the Jerome Robbins Dance Division, The New York Public Library, Astor, Lenox, and Tilden Foundations.

(35) Charles Weidman as Abraham Lincoln in *A House Divided*, ca. 1945
Photograph by Gerda Peterich. Reproduced through the courtesy of the Jerome
Robbins Dance Division, The New York Public Library, Astor, Lenox, and Tilden
Foundations.

(36) Charles Weidman and Doris Humphrey, ca. 1945 Photograph by Gerda Peterich. Reproduced through the courtesy of the Jerome Robbins Dance Division, The New York Public Library, Astor, Lenox, and Tilden Foundations.

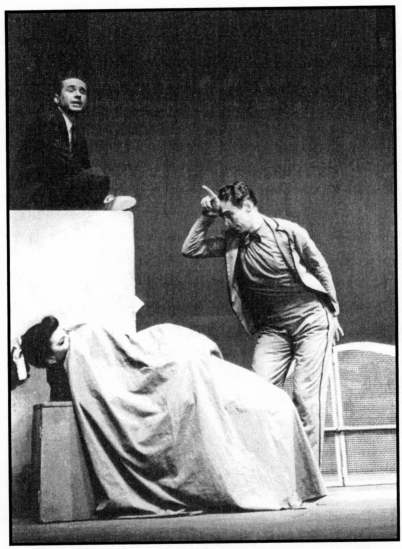

(37) Charles Weidman with Felisa Conde and narrator Jack Ferris in "The Unicorn in the Garden" from *Fables of Our Time*, ca. 1947 Photograph by Gerda Peterich. Reproduced through the courtesy of the Jerome Robbins Dance Division, The New York Public Library, Astor, Lenox, and Tilden Foundations.

(38) Charles Weidman, teaching portrait with drum, ca. 1960
Photograph reproduced through the courtesy of the Jerome Robbins Dance
Division, The New York Public Library, Astor, Lenox, and Tilden Foundations.

(39) Charles Weidman teaches *kinetic pantomime* to college students, ca. 1960. Photograph reproduced through the courtesy of the Jerome Robbins Dance Division, The New York Public Library, Astor, Lenox, and Tilden Foundations.

(40) Charles Weidman receives flowers as recipient of The Dance Heritage Award, ca. 1972. Photograph by George H. Meyer. Reproduced through the courtesy of the Jerome Robbins Dance Division, The New York Public Library, Astor, Lenox, and Tilden Foundations.

(41) Charles Weidman, with James Mullen, becomes a Doctor of Humane Letters at Jersey City State College, ca. 1972. Photograph by Jersey Pictures, Inc. Reproduced through the courtesy of the Jerome Robbins Dance Division, The New York Public Library, Astor, Lenox, and Tilden Foundations.

APPENDIX A

WEIDMAN'S BODY BENDS SERIES

The *Body Bend Series* begins simply but, when analyzed, consists of seven complex sections, A - G. Each section is a variation of the first theme, A.

Part One: A. Uses the directions front, right, left, and back; it deals purely in linear space. Performed with a bounce on the "one" of each count and a rebound on the "and" between the count. The meter is 4/4 Andante, metronome 70. The time aspect of this section uses a concept of shortening the phrase length from 8 counts (repeated once) to 4 counts (repeated once) to 2 counts (repeated twice) to 1 count (repeated four times). This establishes the concept of rebound and breath rhythm, along with metric rhythm. Usually in class this is performed in two-group form, or call and response. Refer to Appendix B for further clarification.

To begin: start with legs separated, directly under hips, feet forward. Bend the body forward with a flat back, arms side; recover vertical. Bend body right with left arm placed high (above head), right hand on front of left thigh; recover vertical. Bend body left, with right arm placed high (above head), left hand on front of right thigh; recover vertical. Turn out legs and bend knees, palms of hands on back of thighs, bend body back; recover vertical.

Part Two: B. Establishes a shift of weight with a fall into recovery and suspension. Stand on the right leg, using the arms to right, side middle, drop the arms placed low, shift the weight center (count 1), pull the arms up to left, side middle while shifting the weight to the left (count 2). Repeat left. Alternate eight times, total.

Part Three: C. Establishes a fall and recovery into a suspension with a change of direction. The arms are used as in B but the body twists to forward diagonal right with inhale of breath and suspension (count 1 and); hold suspension (count 2); body drops forward to the right thigh (count and 3); rebound to standing (count 4). Repeat left. Alternate eight times.

Part Four: D. Establishes a change of front and a change of direction with a body bend. Pivot on the heel of the right foot to face side into a profile position. This archaic design uses fall/recovery and rebound into a suspension into a back direction. The arms are used as in B and as impulse to pivot body to right (count 1 and); hold suspension count 2; body arches back (count and 3); rebound to suspension (count 4). Repeat left. Alternate eight times.

Part Five: E. A variation of D but changing the dynamic quality to legato, and the meter to 9/8. Rotate on the heel of the right foot into a profile archaic position, simultaneously open arms to side (count 1, 2, 3); arms move above head, palms facing side middle or outward (count and); arms curve diagonal back, passing through low to forward middle as the legs bend and the body bends back (count 1, 2, 3 and); return to starting position, moving the arms placed low and side (count 1, 2, 3, and). Repeat left. Alternate four times.

Part Six: F. Varies the metric rhythm and tempo by performing E in three beats. Rotating on the heel of the right foot into a profile archaic position, simultaneously arms open to side (count "and"); arms move above head, palms facing side middle or outward (count 1); arms curve diagonal back, passing through low to forward middle as the legs bend and the body bends back (count

362

and 2); return to starting position, arms placed low and side (count and 3). Repeat left. Alternate four times.

Part Seven: G. Uses a spatial variation of a circle and alternates from a linear design to a three-dimensional curve; connecting the lines gives a 3/4 circle. Bending the body in four directions using a transverse plane, the dynamics remain smooth throughout this part. Starting in a wide fourth position parallel: left forward, right foot back (slightly outwardly rotated), back of left hand in small of back, right arm side. Bend body to the right (count 1); rotate body with a flat back to forward right diagonal (count 2); move to forward direction (count 3); move to left forward diagonal (count 4); rotate on ball left foot, bend knees, rotate body to side bend left (count 5); circle body into back arch (count 6); stretch knees, right arm to place high in using succession, pushing the heel of the hand upwards, recover the body to vertical (count 7); open right arm side, rotate on heel of left foot to parallel (count 8). Repeat right. Transition: circle right foot in and open to fourth position parallel. Repeat left, twice.

APPENDIX B

Weidman's Dance Technique in Figure Drawings

Figure Drawings by
Thomas MacPherson

Dancers
Heather Acomb
Jonette Lancos
Christine Loria
Jacqueline McCausland
Laura Mosscrop
Chukwuma Obasi

Body Circle   Part 1

Body Circle   Part 2

Body Circle   Part 3

Body Circle   Part 4

369

Body Circle   Part 5

Succession Down   Part 1

Succession Down   Part 2

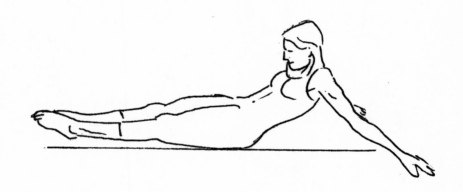

Succession Down   Part 3

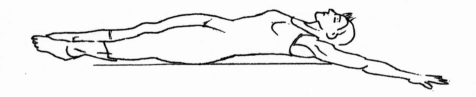

Succession Down   Part 4

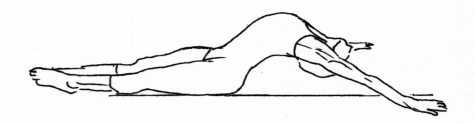

Succession Up   Part 1

375

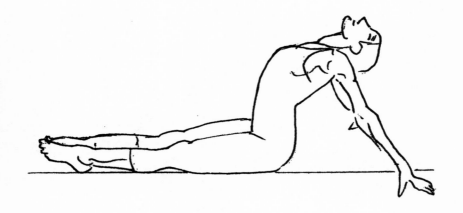

Succession Up   Part 2

Succession Up   Part 3

377

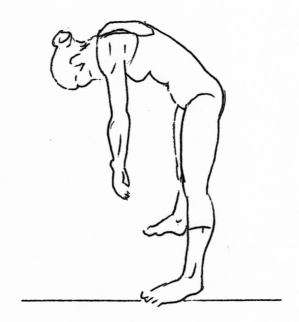

Succession Forward   Part 1

Succession Forward   Part 2

Succession Backward

380

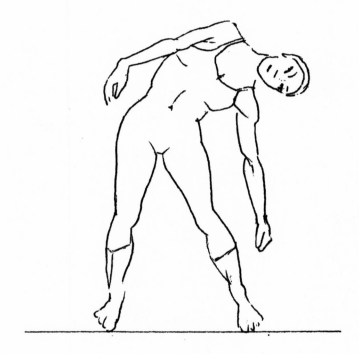

Succession Sideward

381

Opposition

Parallelism or Archaic

383

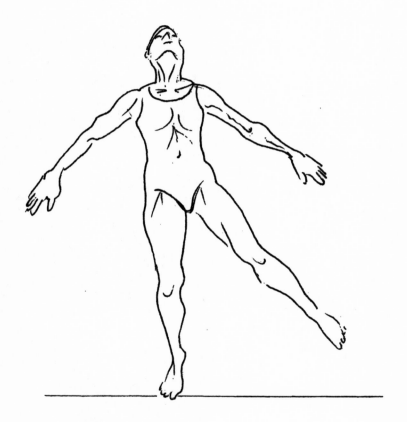

Suspension Position for Flat Turn

Suspension   Balance on One Leg

385

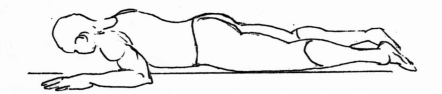

Push-Up to Hip Lift   Part 1

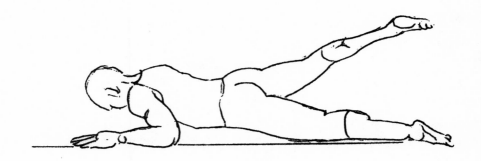

Push-Up to Hip Lift   Part 2

387

Push-Up to Hip Lift   Part 3

388

Push-Up to Hip Lift   Part 4

Push-Up to Hip Lift   Part 5
(Illustration uses left leg)

390

Push-Up to Hip Lift   Part 6

391

Push-Up to Standing   Part 7

392

Modulation Slide   Part 1

393

Modulation Slide   Part 2

394

Modulation Slide   Part 3

395

Modulation Slide   Part 4

Modulation Slide   Part 5

Body Bends   Part One   Begin on Two Feet

398

Body Bends   Part One   Bend Body Forward

Body Bends   Part One   Rebound Vertical

400

Body Bends   Part One
Bend Body Sideward to Right

401

Body Bends   Part One   Rebound Vertical
Repeat Body Bend Sideward to Left,
then Rebound Vertical

Body Bends   Part One   Bend Body Backward

403

Body Bends   Part One   Rebound Vertical

Body Bends   Part Two   Start on Two Feet

405

Body Bends   Part Two   Shift of Weight to Right

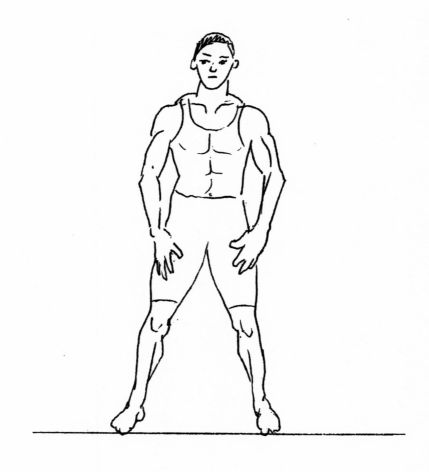

Body Bends   Part Two   Center Weight, Drop Arms

Body Bends   Part Two   Shift of Weight to Left

Body Bends   Part Three
Twist Forward Diagonal to Right

409

Body Bends   Part Three   Succession Forward Diagonal

Body Bends   Part Three
Rebound Forward Diagonal
Repeat to Left. Alternate Right and Left Eight Times

411

Body Bends   Part Four (Back View)
Pivot on Ball of Foot, Rotate Hips, Face Side

Body Bends   Part Four (Back View)   Bend Backward

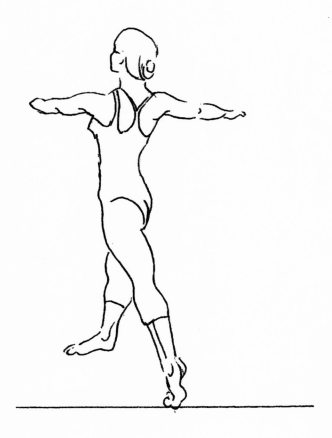

Body Bends   Part Four (Back View)   Rebound

414

Body Bends   Part Four (Front View)
Pivot on Ball of Foot, Rotate Hips, Face Side

415

Body Bends   Part Four (Front View)   Bend Backward

Body Bends   Part Four (Front View)   Rebound

417

Body Bends   Part Five & Six (Count 1)

418

Body Bends   Part Five & Six
Pivot on Heel of Foot, Rotate Hips, Face Side, Arms Side

Body Bends   Part Five & Six
Arms Placed High (Palms Face Out)

Body Bends   Part Five & Six
Arms Back Diagonal, Bend Knees and Lift Chest

421

Body Bends   Part Five & Six
Circle Arms, Cross Arms Over Lifted Chest

Body Bends   Part Five & Six
Pivot on Heel of Foot, Rotate Hips, Face Front, Arms Side

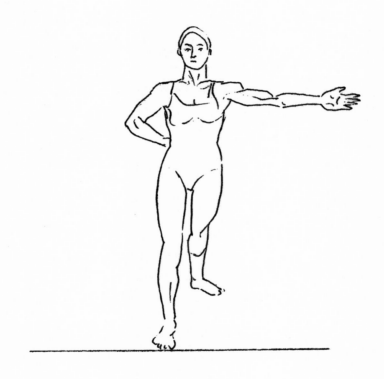

**Body Bends   Part Seven   Begin: Circle Left Foot Forward,
Left Hand on Back, Right Arm Side**

Body Bends   Part Seven   Bend Sideward to Right

425

Body Bends   Part Seven   Flat Back Forward Diagonal Right Through Forward, to Flat Back Forward Diagonal Left

426

**Body Bends   Part Seven   Bend Sideward to Left,
Pivot on Heel of Foot to Rotate Hip**

Body Bends   Part Seven   Bend Backward

428

**Body Bends   Part Seven   Suspend Vertical
Push with Heel of Hand, Stretch Arm Up**

429

Body Bends   Part Seven   Repeat Left
Circle Right Foot Forward, Right Hand on Back
Left Arm Side

430

Knee Fall   Start with Legs Forward

431

Knee Fall   Succession Back

432

Knee Fall   Succession Back, Push To Knees

433

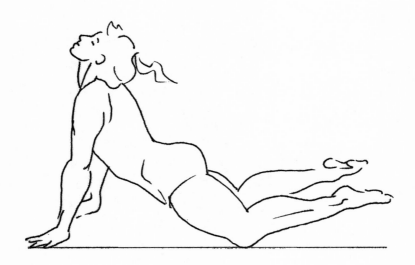

Knee Fall   Fall Forward to Hands

434

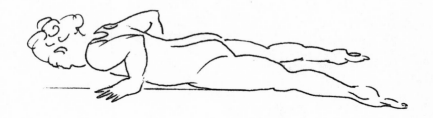

Knee Fall   Prone

435

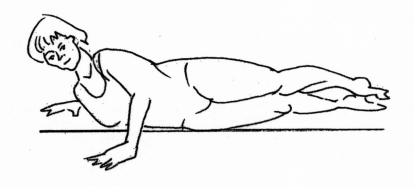

Knee Fall   Roll to Right

Knee Fall   End with Legs Forward   Repeat

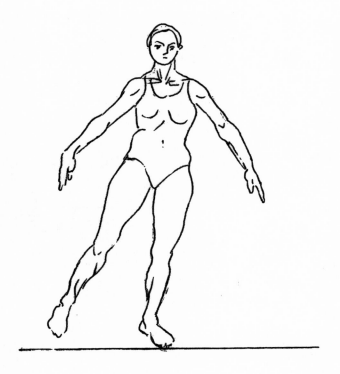

Side Crossing   Part 1

438

Side Crossing   Part 2

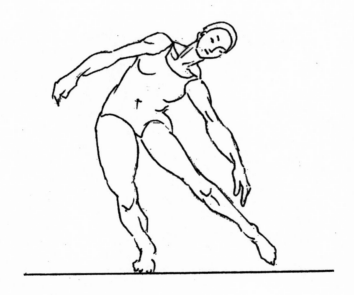

Side Crossing   Part 3

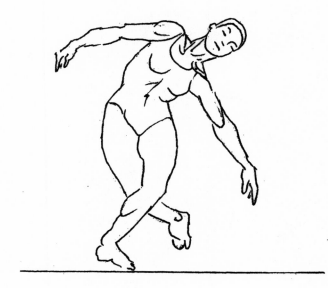

Side Crossing   Part 4

Doris Humphrey's Spiral Fall   Part 1

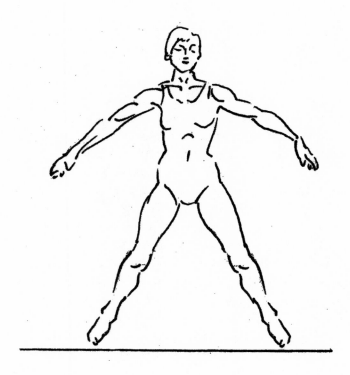

Doris Humphrey's Spiral Fall   Part 2

Doris Humphrey's Spiral Fall   Part 3

Doris Humphrey's Spiral Fall   Part 4   (Front View)

445

Doris Humphrey's Spiral Fall   Part 5

Doris Humphrey's Spiral Fall   Part 6

Doris Humphrey's Spiral Fall   Part 7

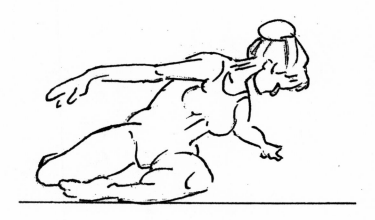

Doris Humphrey's Spiral Fall   Part 8

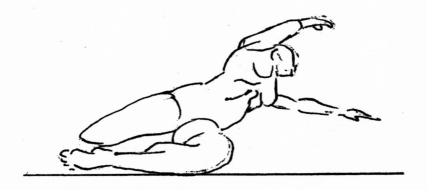

Doris Humphrey's Spiral Fall   Part 9

450

Doris Humphrey's Spiral Fall   Part 10

451

Doris Humphrey's Spiral Fall   Part 11

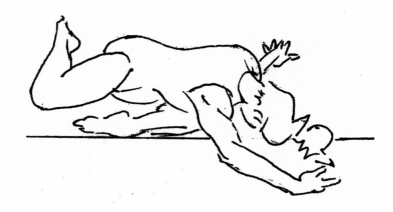

Doris Humphrey's Spiral Fall   Part 12
Retrace Parts 11 Through 1

453

APPENDIX C

DANCE CHRONOLOGY

CONCERT WORKS COMPOSED BY CHARLES WEIDMAN

<u>1919</u>
February 18, Bancroft School Auditorium, Lincoln, Nebraska
Russian (Crakon)
Aztec (Grieg)
Greek (Liszt)
Spanish (Moszkowski)
Impressions of Ruth St. Denis (Joyce)
Egyptian (Tschaikowsky)
East Indian (Cai)
Javanese (Maloof)
American Indian (Herbert)

<u>1920</u>
Eleanor Frampton's School Recital, Temple Theatre, Lincoln, Nebraska
Aztec Dance
Spanish Dance
Hari-Kari

<u>1928</u>
Brooklyn Little Theatre, March 24
Americanisms ("Prelude," "Ringside," "Cowboys")
Cathédrale Engloutie (Debussy)
Gershwin Preludes (Gershwin)
Japanese Actor (Horst)
Juggler (Borodin)
Minstrels (Debussy)
Passion [Savonarola] *Compassion* [St. Francis] (Satie)
Pathetic Study (Scriabin, with Humphrey)
Pierrot (Scott)
Scriabin Study (Scriabin)

455

1928
Guild Theatre, New York, April 7
Jesu, Joy of Man's Desiring (Bach)
Rhythmic Patterns of Java
Singhalese Drum Dance
Israel (Ernest Bloch's *Israel Symphony*)
(Concept by Irene Lewisohn, choreographed with Humphrey and Graham,
Neighborhood Playhouse)

1929
Nuages et Fêtes
On the Steppes of Central Asia
Leprechaun
Ein Heldenleben (Richard Strauss)
(Concept by Irene Lewisohn, Weidman with Graham, Manhattan Opera House)
Rumanian Rhapsody No. 1
Etude No. 2

1930
January 5, Maxine Elliot's Theatre
A Salutation to the Depths (Rudhyar, with Humphrey)
Air on a Ground Bass (Purcell, with Humphrey)
Choreographic Waltz (Ravel, with Humphrey)
Marionette Theatre (Prokofieff)
The Tumbler of Our Lady (Respighi)
Two Studies (Scriabin, No. 2 co-choreographed with Humphrey)

January 9, Maxine Elliot's Theatre
Three Studies (Honegger, "Diffidence," "Annoyance," "Rage")
Scherzo (Borodin)
The Conspirator (Honegger)
La Valse (Ravel, with Humphrey, Jan. 11, Maxine Elliot's Th.)
A Pagan Poem (Charles Martin Loeffler)
(Concept by Irene Lewisohn, Weidman with Graham, Mecca Temple)

1931
Commedia (*Burlesca,* Bossi, Feb. 4, Craig Th.)
Danse Profane (Debussy, Feb. 4, Craig Th.)
La Puerto del Vino
Music of the Troubadours (co-choreographed with Blanche Talmud)

456

1931

The Happy Hypocrite (February 7, Craig Th.)
Piccoli Soldati (*The Little Soldiers*, August 18)
Steel and Stone (Henry Cowell, Feb. 7, Craig Th.)
Gymnòpédie
Nocturne (*Notturno*, August 18)
String Quartet (Ernest Bloch)
(Concept by Irene Lewisohn, with Humphrey, Apr. 23, Library of Congress)

1932
Danza
Dance of Sport and *Dance of Work*
(Henry Cowell, co-choreographed with José Limón and William Matons)
Studies in Conflict (Dane Rudhyar, arranged by Vivian Fine))
Prologue to Saga
Danzon

1933
Candide (Booth Theatre, New York, May 5)
L'Amour à la Militaire (*Piccoli Soldati*)
Suite in F (with Humphrey)
Farandole from the opera *Carmen*

1934
Alcina Suite (Handel)
(with Humphrey, "Introduction," "Pomosa et Allegro," "Pantomime," "Minuet")
Kinetic Pantomime (Colin McPhee)
Three Mazurkas (Alexander Tansman, with Humphrey, July 27, Bennington)
Memorials: To the Trivial, To the Connubial, To the Colossal (Jerome Moross)
Affirmations (Vivian Fine, Nov. 17, Washington Irving High School)
The Christmas Oratorio (J. S. Bach, with Humphrey)

1935
Duo-Drama (Roy Harris, with Humphrey, Jan. 6, Guild Th.)
Rudepoema (Villa-Lobos, with Humphrey, April 15)
American Saga
New Dance (Wallingford Riegger, with Humphrey, Bennington, August 3)
Traditions (Lehman Engel, October 12)
"Stock Exchange" from *Atavisms* (Dec. 15, Carnegie Hall)

457

1936

Quest: A Choreographic Pantomime (Norman Lloyd, Bennington, August 13)
Atavisms ("Bargain Counter," "Stock Exchange," "Lynchtown")
Promenade
Theatre Piece (Wallingford Riegger, with Humphrey, Guild Th., Jan. 19)

1937

May 6 to July 4, Nora Bayes Theatre, New York
Candide (Wallingford Riegger and Genevieve Pitot)

1938

This Passion (Norman Lloyd, Guild Theatre, New York, January 23)
Studies in Technique for Men
Opus 51 (Vivian Fine, Vermont State Armory, Bennington, August 6)

1940

On My Mother's Side (Lionel Nowak, Vassar College, January 20)

1941

Decade: A Biography of Modern Dance from 1930 to 1940 (Aaron Copland)
(Co-choreographed with Humphrey, Aug. 9, Vermont State Armory)
War Dance for Wooden Indians (Rainbow Room)
The Professor Visits Harlem (Rainbow Room)
The Happy Farmer (co-choreographed with Peter Hamilton)
Portraits of Famous Dancers

1942

Flickers (Lionel Nowak, Humphrey-Weidman Studio Theatre)
Theatrical Dances ("Snow Fall," "Penguin," choreographed with Lee Sherman)

1943

And Daddy Was a Fireman (Herbert Haufrechet, Mar. 2, Studio Theatre)
The Dancing Master
Rumba to the Moon (Xavier Cugat, Rainbow Room)
La Comparsa
Park Avenue Intrigue (Rainbow Room)
Song of Songs
Imitations and Satires

458

1944
The Heart Remembers (Lukas Foss)
Dialogue

1945
Three Antique Dances
A House Divided (Lionel Nowak, June 24, Humphrey-Weidman Studio Theatre)
David and Goliath (Johann Kuhnau)

1947
Fables for Our Time (Freda Miller, July 10, Jacob's Pillow Dance Festival)

1948
Panamic Suite
Box Plastique

1949
Rose of Sharon
Song of Solomon

1950
Medea (Solo for Mia Slavenska, Jacob's Pillow Dance Festival)
Dance of the Streets

1951
A Song For You (Portuguese songs, Jacob's Pillow Dance Festival)

1954
Air Gaie (Tchaikovsky, April 25, 92nd Street Y)
Saudades (Milhaud, April 25, 92nd Street Y)
The War Between Men and Women (April 25, 92nd Street Y)
Penelope Pursued

1957
Volpone

1959
Memorial Program in Honor of Doris Humphrey
Classroom, Modern Style (Freda Miller, Technique demonstration)
Is Sex Necessary? Or Why You Feel the Way You Do
(Concept by Humphrey, Portland State College, Portland, Oregon)

1960
Five Further Fables (Feb. 12, Henry Street Th.)

1961
Brahms Waltzes (Johannes Brahms, Liebeslieder Waltzes, opus 39)
Saints, Sinners and Scriabin (Scriabin, Suite of 24 Preludes, opus 11)
The Christmas Oratorio (Bach)
To Make a Form - To Give It Life
(Corelli, with Mikhail Santaro, Expression of Two Arts Studio Theatre)
Calligraphy of the Dance (with Santaro, Expression of Two Arts Studio Th.)

1962
In the Beginning (Debussy, July, Expression of Two Arts Studio Th.)

1963
King David (Honegger, July 11, Expression of Two Arts Studio Th.)
Danse Russe
Dialogue and Situation

1964
Suite Intriga (Mozart, Expression of Two Arts Studio Th.)
Study (Samuel Barber, Expression of Two Arts Studio Th.)
A Chinese Actor Prepares for the Role of the God of War
(Stravinsky, with Santaro, Expression of Two Arts Studio Th.)
Jacob's Marriage (Johann Kuhnau)

1965
A Letter to Mrs. Bixby - A Lincoln Portrait
Diabelli Variations (Beethoven, Expression of Two Arts Th.)

1967
The Easter Oratorio (Bach, Expression of Two Arts Th.)
Dialogue Situation Two

1969
A 69-I-123 (June 12, Expression of Two Arts Th.)
Of and Out of This World (Saint-Saens, June 12, Expression of Two Arts Th.)

<u>1973</u>
Saint Matthew Passion (Bach, Expression of Two Arts Th.)

<u>1974</u>
Visualizations, or From a Farm in New Jersey
(Camille Saint-Saens, July 14, Expression of Two Arts Th.)

DANCE CHRONOLOGY

BROADWAY MUSICALS, PLAYS, OPERAS

COMPOSED BY CHARLES WEIDMAN

<u>1930</u>
Lysistrata (Broadway play with Doris Humphrey, Jan. 5, Forty-Fourth St. Th.)

<u>1931</u>
Hamlet (players sequence only)

<u>1932</u>
Americana (Broadway musical with Humphrey, October 5, Shubert Th.)

<u>1933</u>
Candide (John Coleman and Genevieve Pitot, May 15, Booth Th.)
As Thousands Cheer (Broadway musical, Sept. 30, Music Box Th.)
The School for Husbands (Broadway play, Oct. 16, Empire Th.)

<u>1934</u>
Life Begins at 8:40 (Broadway musical, Aug. 27, Winter Garden Th.)

<u>1935</u>
Iphigenia in Aulis (opera, co-choreographed with Humphrey, Feb. 23)

<u>1937</u>
I'd Rather Be Right (Broadway musical, Nov. 2, Alvin Th.)
Candide (Riegger and Pitot, Federal Dance Project, May 6, Nora Bayes Th.)

<u>1939</u>
The Race of Life (Original danced musical, Jan. 30)
To the Dance (Original danced musical, Jan. 30)

1942
New Faces of 1943 (Broadway musical, Dec. 22, Ritz Th.)

1943
Star Dust (Broadway musical, Sept. 7, Philadelphia)
Marching with Johnny (Broadway musical, Nov. 22, Newark, NJ)
Spoon River Anthology

1944
Jackpot (Broadway musical, Jan. 13, Alvin Th.)
The New Moon (Broadway musical)
Sing Out, Sweet Land! (Broadway musical, Nov. 13, International Th.)
The Merry Widow (opera)

1946
If the Shoe Fits (Broadway musical, Dec. 5, New Century Th.)

1948
Benefit: Spanish Refugee Appeal
(Performed with Martha Graham, Jan. 25, Ziegfeld Th.)
Der Rosenkavlier (New York City Opera)
Turandot (New York City Opera)
La Traviata (New York City Opera)
Carmen (New York City Opera)
Die Meistersinger (New York City Opera)

1950
The Barrier (Broadway musical, Nov. 2, Broadhurst Th.)
The Love For Three Oranges (New York City Opera)
The Four Ruffians (New York City Opera)
The Dybbuk (New York City Opera)
Aida (New York City Opera)

1956
The Littlest Revue (off-Broadway musical, May 22, Phoenix Th.)
Waiting for Godot (Broadway play)

1958
Portofino (Broadway musical, with Ray Harrison, Feb. 21, Adelphi Th.)

APPENDIX D

Selected Phrases from the Labanotation Score

Charles Weidman's

"Lynchtown" (1936)

Music: Lynchtown, Lehman Engel (1936)
Arranged from the surviving parts by Robert Coleridge in
1984. Performed by Susan Chess on a K2000 synthesizer in
2006 as a companion to the revised score.

Notation: Els Grelinger (1986)
Based on the 1960 score by
Lucy Venable and Ann McKinley

Editor of the 2006 Dance and Music Edition: Odette Blum
With reference to the 1960 score and a silent film of
"Lynchtown" performed by Weidman's repertory class at
Connecticut College in 1960.

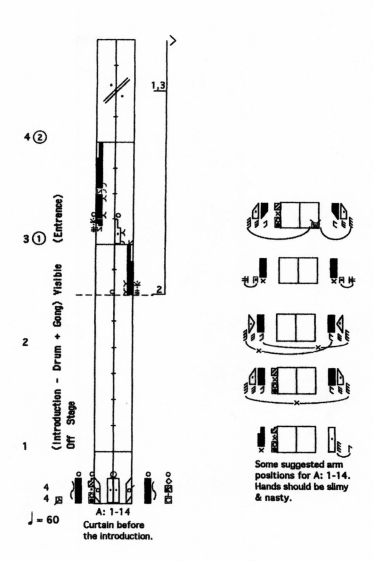

Some suggested arm
positions for A: 1-14.
Hands should be slimy
& nasty.

A: 1-14
Curtain before
the introduction.

Women's Entrance

465

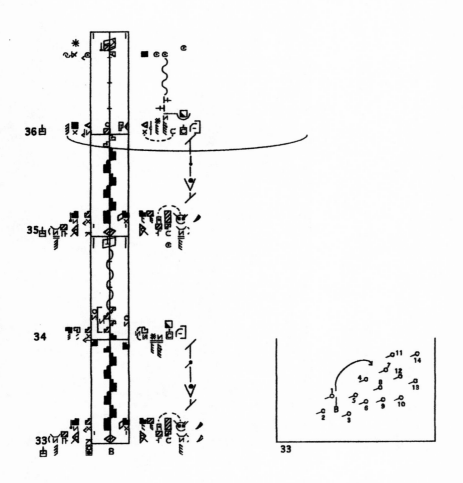

36

35

34

33

33

B

Incitor's Theme "B"

466

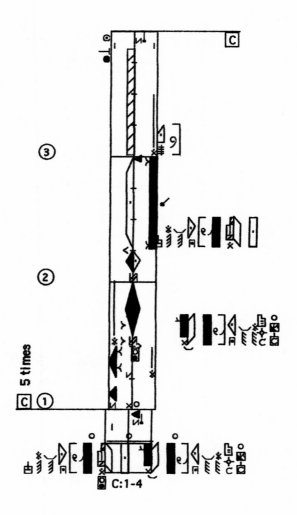

Men's Entrance "C"

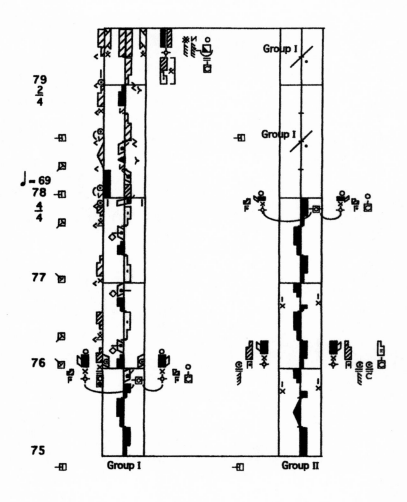

Group I and II   "Tearing" Gesture with Jump

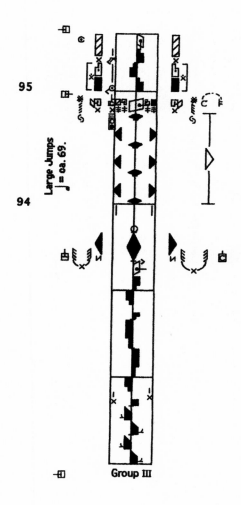

Group III   "Large Jump" Theme

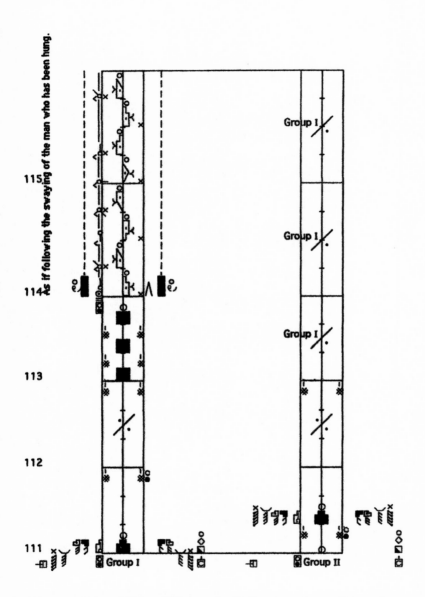

Group I and II   "Popcorn" Jumps into Swaying

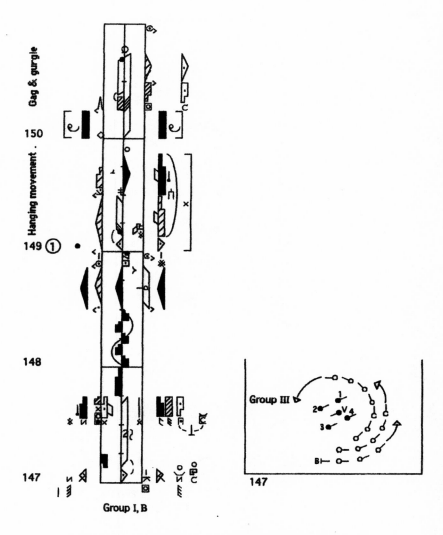

Gag & gurgle

Hanging movement .

150

149 ①

148

147

Group I, B

Group III

1
2
V 4
3
B

147

Group I   "Turn and Runs" in Circle

471

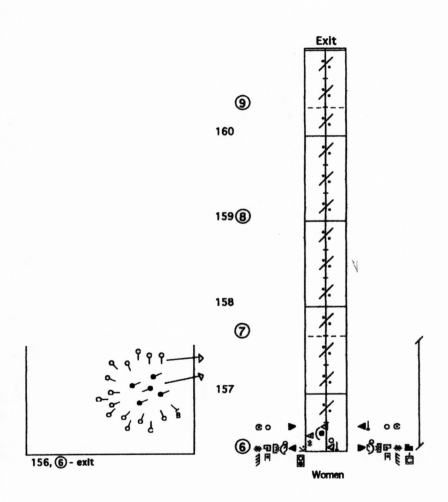

Exit

9

160

159 8

158

7

157

156, 6 - exit

6

Women

Women's Exit

NOTES

Introduction   Journey to Weidman

1. Nona Schurman was born on November 6, 1909, in Nova Scotia, Canada, and was brought up near Montreal. She studied music as a child, starting piano at age five, and changing to cello. After high school graduation she spent two years in Lausanne, Switzerland, where she continued her study of the cello, adding voice, Dalcroze Eurhythmics, and study of the French language that included philology. Returning to Montreal, she continued her musical studies at McGill Conservatory of Music and also studied Drama (Play Direction and Writing). It was at McGill that she became interested in Modern Dance. She began her serious dance training in New York with Hanya Holm, but then began to study with Doris Humphrey and Charles Weidman, appearing with them at their Studio Theatre. She became one of their principal teachers and company members by 1939 and represented Humphrey and Weidman at Bennington College, Mills College, and New York University. She joined the staff of the YMHA and New Dance Group in 1939. She appeared with her performing group in her own choreography at the Dance Center of the 92nd Street Y in New York and at the Studio Theatre. She was on the production staff of the Roxy Theatre in New York and she directed and choreographed Otto Lueing's opera *Evangeline* for the Columbia Opera Workshop. She created the role of Clorinda in the Monteverdi opera *Il Combatimento de Tancredi e Clorinda* at Tanglewood. She appeared in the Broadway musical *Shootin' Star* and served with U.S.O. during World War II. For many years she was director of the Young Concert Dancers of the New Dance Group Studio. Always interested in Dance Notation, her dance *Hebrides Suite* was one of the first dances to be notated in Labanotation and to receive a copyright from the Library of Congress in Washington, D.C. Interested in furthering the dance, she has given much time to dance organizations. She has served on the Board of Directors of the New Dance Group Studio, the Dance Notation Bureau, Dance Films, Inc., and has been Convention Chair for the National Dance Guild. She was a member of the Doris Humphrey Fund Committee and she has served on the Board of Directors of the Charles Weidman School of Modern Dance, Inc. Besides teaching at her own studio, the New Dance Group Studio, YM & YWHA, she has taught at Connecticut College, High School of the Performing Arts, High School for Music and Art, Juilliard School of Music, Teachers College of Columbia University, Barnard College, New York University School of Education. After leaving New York City, she has taught at the State Dance School in Stockholm, Sweden, was Artist-in-Residence at Illinois

State University, Guest Artist at the North Carolina School of the Arts, State University College at Geneseo (where she received the Chancellor's Award for Excellence in Teaching), Guest Teacher at Stephens College, and Guest Teacher at the Cornish Institute. In 1972 the Macmillan Company published her *Modern Dance Fundamentals* that illustrates the Humphrey-Weidman technique through Labanotation, word descriptions, and the human figure. She was Artistic Director of the video *Charles Weidman: On His Own.* Miss Schurman resides in Geneseo, New York.

    2. Deborah Carr is a graduate of Stephens College, where she studied with Harriette Ann Gray, soloist with the Humphrey-Weidman Company. After graduation, Ms. Carr moved to New York and joined Charles Weidman's Theatre Dance Company. In 1976, she established her own company that performed original works by Ms. Carr and maintained many dances from the classic repertory of Charles Weidman and Doris Humphrey. Deborah Carr's Theatre Dance Ensemble was a respected company that was invited to perform in prestigious dance festivals such as the American Dance Festival, the Riverside Dance Festival, the Early Years of Modern Dance Festival at Purchase College, and the New Dance Group Retrospective. In addition to Charles Weidman, Ms. Carr has worked with other Humphrey-Weidman dancers including Ernestine Stodelle, Beatrice Seckler, Peter Hamilton, George Bockman, and Nona Schurman. She has studied Limón technique with Ruth Currier and Betty Jones and has performed with Limón dancers Carla Maxwell, Gary Masters, and Fred Mathews. Ms. Carr has many years of teaching experience on both the college and professional levels. She has been on the faculty of St. Joseph's College and City College in New York and has taught as a guest artist at universities throughout the country. In the United States, she has set repertory on a variety of professional companies and has also taught in England and Ireland. Recently, she taught for the professional studies program at the Limón Institute and coached the Limón Company on Doris Humphrey's "New Dance." She joined the Stephens faculty as Guest Artist for the fall semester of 2003 and became a full-time faculty member in 2004/2005.

    3. *From Studio to Stage* is an original Humphrey-Weidman technique demonstration choreographed by Nona Schurman in 1957 at the New Dance Group Studio in New York City. The work was composed using eight dancers, four women and four men. In 1990, Jonette Lancos and Nona Schurman restaged *From Studio to Stage* for the Geneseo Dance Ensemble. A videotape of this reconstruction is in the archives of the José Limón Foundation.

    4. Beatrice Seckler (1910-2002) was born in Brooklyn, New York. She trained at the Neighborhood Playhouse and she studied with Michio Ito. She then studied and performed with the Humphrey-Weidman Company from 1935 to 1944, where she created roles in *The Shakers, New Dance, Lynchtown, Theatre*

Piece, and *Flickers.* She performed with the José Limón Trio in 1945 and with the Charles Weidman Theatre Dance Company. Later, she danced as guest artist with the companies of Sophie Maslow and Anna Sokolow. She created roles in Sokolow's *Lyric Suite* (1954), and *Rooms* (1955), as the original performer of the solo "Escape." She performed as soloist with the New York City Dance Theatre in 1949 and served as artistic director of the Dancers' Theatre Company, a repertory group founded in 1964. She was Artistic Advisor to Deborah Carr's Theatre Dance Ensemble and was Artistic Director of the video *Charles Weidman: On His Own.*

5. Janet Towner received the 2000 Distinguished Alumnus Award from the School of Music and Department of Dance at the University of Oregon in recognition of "significant achievement in the preservation and continuation of America's dance legacy." A native Oregonian, Towner attended the University of Oregon initially as an English major, but she continued to dance in the developing program founded by Dr. Frances Dougherty. Towner spent a year of study at the Vienna Academy of Music and Dance and in 1969 moved to New York City to begin a seven-year association with dance pioneer Charles Weidman. She was a student, teaching assistant, and principal dancer in his company. In 1974 she was the vehicle for his choreographic vision of *Ruth St. Denis* and subsequently became the assistant director of the Charles Weidman Foundation upon his death in 1975. Towner's activities for the Weidman Foundation took her to many universities as well as dance companies—teaching, coaching, and directing dances from Weidman's diverse repertory. In 1990, Towner received a Master's degree in dance from the University of Oregon, completing her curriculum with a thesis documenting the creation of Weidman's last work—that danced vision of *Ruth St. Denis.* Through her teaching, directing, and writing, she has contributed to a video documentary sponsored by the Weidman Foundation. She served as director of "Dance as Social Criticism" (a videotape funded by the Oregon Committee for the Humanities). Towner has linked the present generation of American dance students and artists to Charles Weidman's American dance legacy.

6. José Limón (1908-1972) was born in Culiacán, Mexico, on January 12, 1908. When he was seven years of age his family moved to Arizona and later to Los Angeles, CA. In 1928, after a year at UCLA as an art major, Limón moved to New York City to continue his art studies. It was here that he saw his first dance program by German expressionists Harald Kreutzberg and Yvonne Georgi. Limón discovered the expressive power of dance after seeing a performance of *Angel of Last Judgment* by Kreutzberg. He began his dance training with Charles Weidman and Doris Humphrey in 1929. By 1932, he had become Weidman's assistant in technique classes and performed in Broadway shows choreographed by Weidman. He performed with the Humphrey-Weidman Company from 1929

to 1945. He married Pauline Lawrence in 1941. Then in 1946 he founded his own dance company with Doris Humphrey as his artistic advisor and choreographer. Over the next twenty-five years, he built his company into one of America's important modern dance institutions. Many of his works have become classics, such as *The Moor's Pavane, There is a Time,* and *Missa Brevis.* He was a key faculty member in Juilliard School's Dance Division beginning in 1953, and he also directed Lincoln Center's American Dance Theatre in 1964-65. In recognition of his achievements, Limón was honored with two *Dance Magazine* Awards, the Capezio Award, and honorary doctorates from four universities. In the fall of 1996, he was the subject of a major exhibition at the New York Public Library for the Performing Arts, The Heroes of José Limón. In July 1997, he was inducted into the Hall of Fame at the National Museum of Dance in Saratoga Springs, NY. His autobiographical writings were edited by Lynn Garofola and published in 1999 by Wesleyan University Press as *An Unfinished Memoir.*

From Weidman to Contemporary Dance

7. "Charles Weidman School of Modern Dance Newsletter" (Vol. 9, No.1, Fall 1995): 8.
8. Henriette Bassoe, "Flights Beyond the Horizon with Charles Weidman," *The American Dancer* (March 1941): 32.
9. *Charles Weidman Papers, Special Collections,* The New York Public Library for the Performing Arts (MGZMD 99, Box 5, Folder 79).
10. Ibid.
11. Jonette Lancos, "Celebrating Charles Weidman, Panel Discussion." Tape recording, José Limón Studio, 38 West Nineteenth Street, New York City, 30 April 1989.
12. Lillie F. Rosen, "Talking With Paul Taylor," *Dance Scope* 13 (Winter/Spring 1979): 84.
13. Janet Lynn Roseman, *Dance Masters: Interviews with Legends of Dance* (New York: Routledge, 2001): 85.
14. Bill T. Jones, Letter to Author, April 25, 2005.

Chapter One   A Vocation

1. Janet Towner, interview by author. Tape recording, Durham, NC, June 11, 1989.
2. *Charles Weidman Papers, Special Collections,* The New York Public Library for the Performing Arts (MGZMD 99, Box 5, Folder 87).

3. David Wynn, "Three Years with Charles Weidman," *Dance Perspectives* (1980) 60: 14.

4. Jonette Lancos, "Celebrating Charles Weidman, Panel Discussion," (April 30, 1989): tape recording.

5. *Charles Weidman Papers, Special Collections*, The New York Public Library for the Performing Arts (MGZMD 99, Box 5, Folder 89).

6. Beatrice Seckler, interview by author. Tape recording, New York, New York, March 19, 1989.

7. José Limón, *An Unfinished Memoir* (Hanover, NH: Wesleyan University Press of New England, 1998; Middletown, CT: Wesleyan University Press, paperback, 2001), 23.

8. Janet Towner, interview by author. Tape recording, Durham, NC, June 11, 1989.

9. Nona Schurman and Sharon Leigh Clark, *Modern Dance Fundamentals* (New York: Macmillan Company, 1972), 26.

10. Deborah Carr, interview by author. Tape recording, New York, New York, March 19, 1989.

11. Janet Towner, "Charles Weidman's Choreographic Process in the Creation of *Visualization, or From a Farm in New Jersey*," (M.S. thesis, University of Oregon, 1990), 82.

12. Nona Schurman, personal notes, May 2005.

13. David Wynn, "Three Years with Charles Weidman," *Dance Perspectives* (1980) 60: 22.

14. Nona Schurman and Sharon Leigh Clark, *Modern Dance Fundamentals* (New York: Macmillan Company, 1972), xx, xxii.

15. Janet Towner, interview by author. Tape recording, Durham, NC, June 11, 1989.

16. Ibid.

17. David Wynn, "Three Years with Charles Weidman," *Dance Perspectives* (1980) 60: 25.

18. Deborah Carr, interview by author. Tape recording, New York, New York, March 19, 1989.

19. Internet Broadway Database, "Charles Weidman on Broadway," http://www.ibdb.com/person.asp?ID=4812.

20. José Limón, *An Unfinished Memoir*, 39.

21. *Dance Magazine,* December 1951, 2.

22. Arthur Todd, "The Opera Enigma: and What Four Choreographers Have Done About It," *Dance Magazine*, April 1951, 22.

23. Ibid.

24. *Charles Weidman Papers, Special Collections*, The New York Public Library (MGZMD 99, Box 5, Folder 79).

25. José Limón, "Dance for Men in the Schools," *Journal of Health, Physical Education and Recreation* (Vol. 11: 3, March 1940): 148, 189-90.

26. Winthrop Palmer, *Theatrical Dancing in America,* 2d ed. Revised (Cranbury, NJ: A. S. Barnes and Company, 1978), 101.

27. Margaret Lloyd, *The Borzoi Book of Modern Dance* (New York: Alfred A. Knopf, 1949; reprint, Pennington, NJ: Princeton Book Co., 1987), 91.

28. Marcia B. Siegel, *Days on Earth* (New Haven, CT & London: Yale University Press, 1987), 137.

29. *Dance: Four Pioneers* (WNET/13, 1965), filmstrip.

30. José Limón, *An Unfinished Memoir*, 66, 67.

31. Lillian Moore, *Artists of the Dance* (Brooklyn, NY: Dance Horizons, 1969), 296.

32. John Martin, *America Dancing* (New York: Dodge Publishing Company, 1936; reprint, Brooklyn, NY; Dance Horizons, 1968), 239 (page reference is to reprint edition).

33. Winthrop Palmer, *Theatrical Dancing in America,* 103.

34. Olga Maynard, *American Modern Dancers: The Pioneers* (Boston: Little, Brown and Company, 1965), 136.

35. José Limón, *An Unfinished Memoir*, 36.

36. Ibid., 39.

37. Sylvia Pelt Richards, "A Biography of Charles Weidman with Emphasis upon His Professional Career and His Contributions to the Field of Dance," (Ph. D. diss. , Texas Woman's University, 1971), 70.

38. Don McDonagh, *The Complete Guide to Modern Dance* (Garden City, NY: Doubleday & Company, 1976), 114.

39. Ibid.

40. *Time Magazine*, "Chipmunk at Jacob's Pillow," July 28, 1927, 54.

41. Walter Terry, "Moderns in Review," *Dance News*, September 1947, 41.

42. Doris Hering, "Concert Series in Review," *Dance Magazine*, April 1960, 26.

43. Jack Anderson, *Art without Boundaries* (Iowa City, IA: University of Iowa Press, 1997), 183.

44. http://www.dancenotation.org

45. *Dance News*, January 1950, 10.

46. Elinor Rogosin, *The Dance Makers* (New York: Walker and Company, 1980), 24.

47. Walter Sorell, "Weidman Returns to the Lexington 'Y' May 4," *Dance News*, May 1972, 1-2.

48. *Charles Weidman Papers* (MGZMD 99, Box 5, Folder 79).

49. Sylvia Pelt Richards, "A Biography of Charles Weidman," 316.

50. *Charles Weidman Papers* (MGZMD 99, Box 2, Folder 35).

51. Sylvia Pelt Richards, "A Biography of Charles Weidman," 329.

52. Ibid., 333.

53. Ibid., 335-38.

54. Fernau Hall, "Charles Weidman at the Commonwealth Substitute, *Ballet Today*, May 1965, 15.

55. Sylvia Pelt Richards, "A Biography of Charles Weidman," 341-43.

56. Margaret O'Sullivan, letter to author, July 6, 2005.

57. Joan Levy Bernstein, "Dancing with Doris Humphrey," *Dance News*, November 1978, 13, 16.

58. Janet Towner, "Charles Weidman's Choreographic Process," 34.

59. *Dance Magazine*, June 1950, 36.

60. "Awards Presented to Five Modern Choreographers," *Dance Observer*, (vol: 21-26, 1954-1959, January 1959): 7.

61. *Charles Weidman Papers* (MGZMD 99, Box 5, Folder 89).

62. *Charles Weidman Papers* (Clippings, MGZR).

63. Elinor Rogosin, *The Dance Makers*, 16.

64. Jennifer Dunning, "Honoring the Life and Work of a Modern Dance Pioneer," *The New York Times*, June 30, 1985, 5,10.

65. *Dance: Four Pioneers* (WNET/13, 1965) filmstrip.

66. Margaret Lloyd, *The Borzoi Book of Modern Dance,* 89.

67. John Martin, *America Dancing,* 240.

68. Winthrop Palmer, *Theatrical Dancing in America,* 105.

69. Jennifer Dunning, "Honoring the Life and Work of a Modern Dance Pioneer," 5.

70. Ibid.

71. Ninth Annual Scripps Award Program, American Dance Festival, Duke University, June 1989.

72. Deborah Jowitt, *Time and the Dancing Image*, (Berkeley and Los Angeles, CA: University of California Press, 1988), 157.

73. Obituaries, *Variety*, June 23, 1975.

74. Jennifer Dunning, "Honoring the Life and Work of a Modern Dance Pioneer," 10.

Chapter Two   Early Years

1. Walt Whitman, *Leaves of Grass* (New York: Random House; Modern Library original edition), 1891-92, 119.

2. Robert A. Carter, *Buffalo Bill Cody: The Man Behind The Legend* (New York: John Wiley & Sons, 2000), 128.

3. Edward Humphrey, ed. *The Webster Family Encyclopedia* (Webster Publishing Company, 1984), s.v. "Nebraska," by Marvin F. Kivett.

4. Edward Humphrey, ed. *The Webster Family Encyclopedia* (Webster Publishing Company, 1984), s.v. "Cowboys" by Joe B. Frantz.

5. Roy W. Robbins, *Our Landed Heritage. The Public Domain 1776-1936* (New Jersey: Princeton University Press), 1942.

6. Edward Humphrey, ed. *The Webster Family Encyclopedia* (Webster Publishing Company, 1984), s.v. "Homesteading" by Paul W. Gates.

7. Federal Writers' Project of the Works Progress Administration for the State of Nebraska, *Nebraska: A Guide to the Cornhusker State* (Nebraska: Stratford Press, 1939; reprint St. Clair Shores, Michigan: Scholarly Press, 1976), 101-103.

8. Ibid., 4.

9. Roy W. Robbins, *Our Landed Heritage. The Public Domain 1776-1936*, 326.

10. Edward Humphrey, ed. *The Webster Family Encyclopedia* (Webster Publishing Company, 1984), s.v. "Frontier in American History" by Ray A. Billington.

11. Margaret Lloyd, *The Borzoi Book of Modern Dance* (New York: Alfred A. Knopf, 1949; reprint, Pennington, NJ: Princeton Book Co., 1987), 90.

12. Roy W. Robbins, *Our Landed Heritage. The Public Domain 1776-1936*, 326.

13. Edward Humphrey, ed. *The Webster Family Encyclopedia* (Webster Publishing Company, 1984), s.v. "Frontier in American History" by Ray A. Billington.

14. Roy W. Robbins, *Our Landed Heritage. The Public Domain 1776-1936*, 301.

15. Ibid., 331.

16. *Nebraska State Journal*, July 12, 1901.

17. *Nebraska State Journal*, July 13, 1901.

18. *Nebraska State Journal*, July 22, 1901.

19. *Charles Weidman Papers, Special Collections*, The New York Public Library (MGZMD 99, Box 5, Folder 84).

20. Margaret Lloyd, *The Borzoi Book of Modern Dance,* 81.

21. *Nebraska State Journal*, July 24, 1901.

22. Sylvia Pelt Richards, "A Biography of Charles Weidman with Emphasis upon His Professional Career and His Contributions to the Field of Dance," (Ph. D. diss., Texas Woman's University, 1971), 55.

23. In the book *Nature and Treatment of Stuttering: New Directions*, Richard F. Curlee and Gerald M. Siegel suggest a genetic disorder, (perhaps an aunt or uncle or grandparent stuttered) as well as environmental factors may cause

a child to stutter. There are also neurological disorders and psychological disorders that may cause childhood stuttering.

24. Dr. Linda House, Interview with Melissa Heald, September 20, 2004.

25. Shirley D. Manasevit, "A Last Interview with Charles Weidman," *Dance Scope* 10 (Fall/Winter 1975-76): 33.

26. Janet Towner, "Charles Weidman's Choreographic Process in the Creation of *Visualization, or From a Farm in New Jersey*," (M.S. thesis, University of Oregon, 1990), 23.

27. As a way to reduce his stuttering Weidman could have used several methods, such as speaking slowly and diaphragmatic breathing. In 1940, his cursive notes for speaking during lecture demonstrations stated, "speak slowly," "slower," and "slowly" written in big, black, block print.

28. Margaret O'Sullivan, letter to author, July 6, 2005.

29. Nona Schurman, telephone conversation with author, September 24, 2004.

30. Deborah Carr, letter to author, June 16, 2005.

31. Dr. Linda House, Interview with Melissa Heald, September 20, 2004.

32. Federal Writers' Project, *Nebraska: A Guide to the Cornhusker State,* 114-16.

33. Ibid.

34. Ibid., 182.

35. Ibid., 187.

36. Ibid., 184.

37. *Charles Weidman Papers* (MGZMD 99, Box 5, Folder 79).

38. Sylvia Pelt Richards, "A Biography of Charles Weidman," 54.

39. Margaret Lloyd, *The Borzoi Book of Modern Dance,* 110.

40. Ibid.

41. Edward Humphrey, ed. *The Webster Family Encyclopedia* (Webster Publishing Company, 1984), s.v. "Roller Skating" by Alvin M. Levy.

42. Sylvia Pelt Richards, "A Biography of Charles Weidman," 57.

43. Edward Humphrey, ed. *The Webster Family Encyclopedia* (Webster Publishing Company, 1984), s.v. "Needlework" by Cornelia Wagenvoord

44. Sylvia Pelt Richards, "A Biography of Charles Weidman," 55.

45. Ibid., 54.

46. Ibid., 55.

47. *Charles Weidman Papers* (MGZMD 99, Box 9, Folder 113).

48. Sylvia Pelt Richards, "A Biography of Charles Weidman," 54.

49. Ibid., 55.

50. Ibid.

51. Ibid., 56.

52. Edward Humphrey, ed. *The Webster Family Encyclopedia* (Webster Publishing Company, 1984), s.v. "Panama Canal Zone" by Walter A. Payne.

53. Edward Humphrey, ed. *The Webster Family Encyclopedia* (Webster Publishing Company, 1984), s.v. "Panama" by Paul D. Simkins.

54. Sylvia Pelt Richards, "A Biography of Charles Weidman," 56.

55. Ibid., 57.

56. Ibid.

57. *Charles Weidman Papers* (MGZMD 99, Box 5, Folder 79).

58. Sylvia Pelt Richards, "A Biography of Charles Weidman," 58, 59.

59. Current speech fluency theory concludes that a boy who stutters may be anxious because of distance from his mother. Speech problems may become more pronounced following a violent encounter, such as being frightened by a dog, or being thrown in a lake.

60. Sylvia Pelt Richards, "A Biography of Charles Weidman," 59.

61. *Charles Weidman Papers* (MGZMD 99, Box 5, Folder 84).

62. Shirley D. Manasevit, "A Last Interview with Charles Weidman," 34.

63. Federal Writers' Project, *Nebraska: A Guide to the Cornhusker State,* 123.

64. Elinor Rogosin, *The Dance Makers* (New York: Walker and Company, 1980), 15.

65. Federal Writers' Project, *Nebraska: A Guide to the Cornhusker State,* 189.

66. Elinor Rogosin, *The Dance Makers,* 15.

67. Shirley D. Manasevit, "A Last Interview with Charles Weidman," 34.

68. Ibid.

69. Walter Terry, *Miss Ruth* (New York: Dodd, Mead & Company, 1969), 94.

70. Marcia B. Siegel, *Days on Earth* (New Haven, CT & London: Yale University Press, 1987), 2.

71. Suzanne Shelton, *Divine Dancer: A Biography of Ruth St. Denis* (New York: Doubleday & Company, 1981), 110.

72. Ibid., 111.

73. Marcia B. Siegel, *Days on Earth,* 2.

74. Suzanne Shelton, *Divine Dancer: A Biography of Ruth St. Denis,* 112.

75. Ruth St. Denis, *An Unfinished Life* (New York: Harper & Brothers Publishers, 1939; copyright renewed 1967, HarperCollins Publishers), 157.

76. Walter Terry, *Miss Ruth,* 94.

77. Ruth St. Denis, *An Unfinished Life,* 158.

78. Ibid.

79. Christina L. Schlundt, *The Professional Appearances of Ruth St. Denis & Ted Shawn, 1906-1932* (New York: The New York Public Library, 1962), 80.

80. Sylvia Pelt Richards, "A Biography of Charles Weidman," 76.

81. Shirley D. Manasevit, "A Last Interview with Charles Weidman," 34.

82. Suzanne Shelton, *Divine Dancer: A Biography of Ruth St. Denis,* 134.

83. Elinor Rogosin, *The Dance Makers,* 15.

84. Suzanne Shelton, *Divine Dancer: A Biography of Ruth St. Denis,* 134.

85. Ibid.

86. Don McDonagh, *Martha Graham: A Biography* (New York: Praeger Publishers, 1973), 23.

87. Christina L. Schlundt, *The Professional Appearances of Ruth St. Denis & Ted Shawn, 1906-1932,* 28, 29.

88. Suzanne Shelton, *Divine Dancer: A Biography of Ruth St. Denis,* 134.

89. Sylvia Pelt Richards, "A Biography of Charles Weidman," 60.

90. John Martin, *America Dancing* (New York: Dodge Publishing Company, 1936; reprint, Brooklyn, N.Y.; Dance Horizons, 1968), 227 (page reference is to reprint edition).

91. Sylvia Pelt Richards, "A Biography of Charles Weidman," 70.

92. Shirley D. Manasevit "A Last Interview with Charles Weidman," 35.

93. Sylvia Pelt Richards, "A Biography of Charles Weidman," 64.

94. Shirley D. Manasevit, "A Last Interview with Charles Weidman," 35.

95. Sylvia Pelt Richards, "A Biography of Charles Weidman," 64.

96. Ibid.

97. Janet Mansfield Soares, *Louis Horst: Musician in a Dancer's World* (Durham and London: Duke University Press, 1992), 16.

98. Christina L. Schlundt, *The Professional Appearances of Ruth St. Denis & Ted Shawn, 1906-1932,* 99.

99. Sylvia Pelt Richards, "A Biography of Charles Weidman," 70.

100. Ibid., 87.

101. Eleanor King, *Transformations* (Brooklyn, NY: Dance Horizons, 1978), 300.

102. Elinor Rogosin, *The Dance Makers,* 35.

103. Shirley D. Manasevit, "A Last Interview with Charles Weidman," 34.

104. Sylvia Pelt Richards, "A Biography of Charles Weidman," 71.

105. Eleanor King, *Transformations,* 106.

106. Sylvia Pelt Richards, "A Biography of Charles Weidman," 86.

107. Ibid., 74, 75.
108. Eleanor King, *Transformations,* 301.
109. Sylvia Pelt Richards, "A Biography of Charles Weidman," 77.
110. Ibid., 78.
111. Ibid., 79, 80.
112. Ibid., 79.
113. *Charles Weidman Papers* (MGZEA 99, #334).
114. http://www.clevelandartprize.org/dance_1964.htm
115. Ibid.
116. Eleanor King, *Transformations,* 300.
117. Shirley D. Manasevit, "A Last Interview with Charles Weidman,"
35.
118. Ibid., 35, 36.
119. Sylvia Pelt Richards, "A Biography of Charles Weidman," 87.
120. Ibid.
121. Ibid., 88.
122. Ibid.
123. Shirley D. Manasevit, "A Last Interview with Charles Weidman,"
32.

Chapter Three   The Global Influence

1. Elinor Rogosin, *The Dance Makers* (New York: Walker and
Company, 1980), 16.
2. Douglas Gilbert, *American Vaudeville* (New York: Dover
Publications, Inc., 1940), 52.
3. Bob Thomas, *Astaire: The Man, the Dancer* (New York: St. Martin's
Press, 1984), 18.
4. Douglas Gilbert, *American Vaudeville,* 5.
5. Print Exhibition of Historic New York City, New York Public Library,
Bryant Park. Niblo's Garden was built at the corner of Broadway and Prince
Street in 1823 by Irish impresario William Niblo. Purchasing Columbia Garden,
Niblo added the San Souci Theatre, a saloon and hotel to the landscaped grounds
that opened in 1829. The theatre where *The Black Crook* played seated 3,000
spectators. European dancers introduced the polka there in 1844.
6. Bernard Sobel, *A Pictorial History of Vaudeville* (New York: The
Citadel Press, 1961), 22.
7. Douglas Gilbert, *American Vaudeville,* 3.
8. Ibid., 247.
9. Ibid.

10. Bernard Sobel, *A Pictorial History of Vaudeville*, 222.

11. Ruth St. Denis, *An Unfinished Life* (New York: Harper & Brothers Publishers, 1939; copyright © renewed 1967 HarperCollins), 70.

12. Ibid., 58.

13. Ibid.

14. Jean Morrison Brown, Editor, *The Visions of Modern Dance* (Pennington, NJ: Princeton Book Company, 1979), 7.

15. Winthrop Palmer, *Theatrical Dancing in America,* Second Edition, Revised, (Cranbury, NJ: A. S. Barnes and Company, 1978), 24.

16. Richard Nelson Current and Marcia Ewing Current, *Loie Fuller: Goddess of Light* (Boston: Northeastern University Press, 1997), 150, 151.

17. Walter Terry, and Jack Rennert, *100 Years of Dance Posters* (New York: Universe Books, 1975), 6.

18. Ruth St. Denis, *An Unfinished Life,* 40.

19. Richard Nelson Current and Marcia Ewing Current, *Loie Fuller: Goddess of Light,* 144.

20. Ibid.

21. Jules Heller, *Printmaking Today* (New York: Holt, Rinehart and Winston, Inc., 1972), 136.

22. Carl Shanahan, interview by author, June 10, 2004, New York, New York.

23. Ibid.

24. Richard Lane, *Images from the Floating World: The Japanese Print* (New York: Tabard Press, 1978), 21.

25. Ibid., 11.

26. Public Broadcasting System, *Japan: Memoirs of a Secret Empire,* May 26, 2004. Videocassette.

27. Jules Heller, *Printmaking Today* (New York: Holt, Rinehart and Winston, Inc., 1972), 135.

28. Natsu Nakajima, interview by author, May 1-3, 1989, Brockport, "Butoh Residency: Japanese Avant-Garde Dance/Theatre," SUNY Brockport, New York.

29. Ann Yonemura, *Yokohama: Prints from Nineteenth-Century Japan.* (Washington, D.C.: Smithsonian Institution, 1990), 41.

30. Nicole Coolidge Rousmaniere, "The accessioning of Japanese art in early nineteenth-century America: Ukiyo-e prints in the Peabody Essex Museum, Salem," *Apollo: The International Magazine of the Arts* (March 1997: Volume 145, Issue 421), 24.

31. Public Broadcasting System, *Japan: Memoirs of a Secret Empire,* May 26, 2004. Videocassette.

32. Ann Yonemura, *Yokohama: Prints from Nineteenth-Century Japan*, 22.

33. Ibid., 15.

34. Colta Feller Ives, *The Great Wave: The Influence of Japanese Woodcuts on French Prints* (New York: The Metropolitan Museum of Art, 1974), 14.

35. Ibid., 8.

36. Clay Lancaster, "The First Japanese Dance Performed in America," *Dance Magazine*, January 1956, 45.

37. Colta Feller Ives, *The Great Wave: The Influence of Japanese Woodcuts on French Prints*, 37.

38. Martha Graham, *Blood Memory* (New York: Doubleday Publishers, 1991), 178.

39. Library of Congress Exhibition *The Floating World of Ukiyo-e: Shadows, Dreams and Substance*, <http/www.LibraryofCongress.com> (June 2, 2004).

40. Frank Lloyd Wright, *The Japanese Print: An Interpretation* (New York: Horizon Press, 1967), 19.

41. Carl Shanahan, interview by author, June 10, 2004, New York, New York.

42. Frank Lloyd Wright, *The Japanese Print: An Interpretation* (New York: Horizon Press, 1967), 81.

43. Paul Love, "How to Look at Dancing," *The New Republic* 93, December 29, 1937, 223.

44. Colta Feller Ives, *The Great Wave: The Influence of Japanese Woodcuts on French Prints*, 89.

45. Jane Sherman, *Denishawn: The Enduring Influence* (Boston: Twayne Publishers, 1983), 52-53. For a detailed description of Ruth St. Denis' dance *Valse à la Loie,* refer to Sherman's *Denishawn: The Enduring Influence* and *The Drama of Denishawn.*

46. Martha Graham, *Blood Memory* (New York: Doubleday Publishers, 1991), 92.

47. Charles Weidman, *Oral History Interview by Marian Horosko, 1966-67* (New York: Dance Collections, New York Public Library).

48. Helen Caldwell, *Michio Ito* (Berkeley and Los Angeles: University of California Press, 1977), ix.

49. Ibid., ix.

50. Ibid., 50.

51. Ibid., 17.

52. Robert Abrams, ed., *Performance Review Saeko Ichinohe Dance Company* <http/www.exploredance.com/saeko041304.html> (June 2, 2004).

53. Ibid.

54. Edward Humphrey, ed. *The Webster Family Encyclopedia* (Webster Publishing Company Ltd., 1984), s.v. "Loti, Pierre," by Charles G. Hill.

55. Colta Feller Ives, *The Great Wave: The Influence of Japanese Woodcuts on French Prints*, 96.

56. Samm Sinclair Baker and Natalie Baker, *Family Treasury of Art* (New York: Galahad Books, 1981), 138.

57. Walter Terry and Jack Rennert, *100 Years of Dance Posters* (New York: Universe Books, 1975), 5.

58. Ibid., 58.

59. Angna Enters, "Notes on Dance Form," *The Dance Magazine*, December 1930, 5.

60. Dahesh Museum of Art, Exhibition Panel, New York, New York.

61. Roger Shattuck, *The Banquet Years* (New York: Vintage Books; Toronto: Random House of Canada, Revised Edition, 1968), 17.

62. Elizabeth Kendall, *Where She Danced* (New York: Alfred A. Knopf Inc., 1979) 83.

63. Nickolas Muray, "Nickolas Muray Looks at the Dance," *Dance Magazine*, May 1928, 38.

64. Helen Caldwell, *Michio Ito* (Berkeley and Los Angeles: University of California Press, 1977), 20.

65. Theodore E. Johnston, *Hands to Work and Hearts to God* (Brunswick, Maine: Bowdoin College Museum of Art, 1969) 1.

66. Notes to *The Shakers*, Labanotation Score (New York: The Dance Notation Bureau)

67. Edward Humphrey, ed. *The Webster Family Encyclopedia* (Webster Publishing Company, Ltd., 1984), s.v. "Ralph Waldo Emerson," by Lewis Leary.

68. Ibid.

69. Edward Humphrey, ed. *The Webster Family Encyclopedia* (Webster Publishing Company, Ltd., 1984), s.v. "Walt Whitman," by James E. Miller, Jr.

70. Ibid.

71. Ted Shawn, *Dance We Must* (Pittsfield, Mass.: The Eagle Printing and Binding Company, 1950), 113.

72. Edward Humphrey, ed. *The Webster Family Encyclopedia* (Webster Publishing Company, Ltd., 1984), s.v. "Walt Whitman" by James E. Miller, Jr.

73. Ted Shawn, *Dance We Must,* 113.

74. Ruth St. Denis, *An Unfinished Life* (New York: Harper & Brothers Publishers, 1939; copyright © renewed 1967 HarperCollins), 73.

75. Deborah Jowitt, *Time And The Dancing Image* (Berkeley and Los Angeles, CA: University of California Press, 1989), 128.

76. Jane Sherman, *The Drama of Denishawn Dance* (Middletown, CT: Wesleyan University Press, 1979), 45.

77. Ibid., 33.

78. Ibid., 134.

79. Doris Humphrey, *The Shakers*, reconstruction by Ray Cook, 1975, Wilkes-Barre Ballet Theatre, Wilkes-Barre, Pa.

80. *Charles Weidman Papers, Special Collections*, The New York Public Library (MGZMD 99, Box 5, Folder 87).

Chapter Four   Dancing with Denishawn

1. Ruth St. Denis, *An Unfinished Life* (New York: Harper & Brothers Publishers, 1939; copyright © renewed 1967 HarperCollins), 329.

2. Shirley D. Manasevit, "A Last Interview with Charles Weidman." *Dance Scope* 10 (Fall/Winter 1975-76): 36.

3. Janet Mansfield Soares, *Louis Horst: Musician in a Dancer's World* (Durham, NC and London: Duke University Press, 1992), jacket cover.

4. Shirley D. Manasevit, "A Last Interview with Charles Weidman," 36.

5. *Charles Weidman Papers, Special Collections*, The New York Public Library (MGZMD 99, Box 5, Folder 79).

6. José Limón, *An Unfinished Memoir* (Hanover, NH: Wesleyan University Press of New England, 1998; Middletown, CT: Wesleyan University Press, paperback, 2001), 23.

7. Ruth St. Denis, *An Unfinished Life,* 3,7.

8. Ibid., 2.

9. Ibid., 3.

10. Ted Shawn, *Every Little Movement* (Pittsfield, Mass.: The Eagle Printing and Binding Company, 1954), 18.

11. Ruth St. Denis, *An Unfinished Life,* 8.

12. Ted Shawn, *Every Little Movement,* 22, 28, 50, 51.

13. Ruth St. Denis, *An Unfinished Life,* 16.

14. Walter Terry, *Miss Ruth* (New York: Dodd, Mead & Company, 1969), 9.

15. Ted Shawn, *Every Little Movement,* 82.

16. Walter Terry, *How to Look at Dance* (New York: William Marrow and Company, 1982), 82.

17. Ted Shawn, *Every Little Movement,* 74.

18. Jane Sherman, *The Drama of Denishawn Dance* (Middletown, CT.: Wesleyan University Press, 1979), 112.

19. Ted Shawn, *One Thousand and One Night Stands* (Garden City, NY: Doubleday & Company, 1906), 156.

20. Ted Shawn, *Every Little Movement,* 34-36.

21. Ibid., 35.

22. Ibid.

23. Charles Weidman, "Interviews by Marian Horosko," 1966-67, Dance Collections, Phonotape.

24. Ibid.

25. Ted Shawn, *Every Little Movement,* 34-36.

26. Ibid., 66.

27. Ibid., 74.

28. Jane Sherman and Barton Mumaw, *Barton Mumaw, Dancer* (Brooklyn, New York: Dance Horizons, 1986), 278.

29. Jane Sherman, *The Drama of Denishawn Dance* (Middletown, CT: Wesleyan University Press, 1979), 64.

30. Ted Shawn, *Every Little Movement,* 75.

31. Jane Sherman, *The Drama of Denishawn Dance,* 84.

32. Charles Weidman, "Popular Sports Steps," *Dance Lovers' Magazine,* June 1925, Vol. 4, No. 2, 23-24, 63.

33. Jane Sherman, *The Drama of Denishawn Dance,* 112.

34. Ibid., 112, 113.

35. Ted Shawn, *Every Little Movement,* 63.

36. Ibid.

37. Elizabeth Kendall, *Where She Danced* (New York: Alfred A. Knopf, Inc., 1979), 164.

38. Jane Sherman and Barton Mumaw, *Barton Mumaw, Dancer,* 315.

39. Nona Schurman, interview by author, March 1988.

40. Jacqulyn Buglisi, Class observation, Alvin Ailey School, New York, New York, May 23, 2005.

41. Noa Belling, *The Yoga Handbook* (United Kingdom: New Holland Publishers, 2000), 60.

42. Ted Shawn, *One Thousand and One Night Stands,* 56.

43. Susanne K. Langer, *Problems of Art* (New York: Charles Scribner's and Sons, 1957), 96, 106.

44. Nona Schurman, interview by author, July 13, 1989.

45. Jane Sherman, *Denishawn: The Enduring Influence,* 16, 17.

46. Ruth St. Denis and Ted Shawn, "Denishawn Dancing Technique," Ruth St. Denis Paper, 1915; Folders 361-374, Dance Collection, New York Public Library.

47. Jane Sherman, *Denishawn: The Enduring Influence,* 18, 19.

48. Jane Sherman, *The Drama of Denishawn Dance,* 15.

49. St. Denis and Shawn, "Denishawn Dancing Technique," The New York Public Library, Folder 364.

50. Nona Schurman and Sharon Leigh Clark, *Modern Dance Fundamentals* (New York: Macmillan Company, 1972), 43.

51. Ernestine Stodelle, *The Dance Technique of Doris Humphrey*, 40, 44, 63.

52. Ruth St. Denis and Ted Shawn, "Denishawn Dancing Technique," Folder 364.

53. Sherman and Mumaw, *Barton Mumaw, Dancer*, 315.

54. Ernestine Stodelle, *The Dance Technique of Doris Humphrey*, 68, 69.

55. Nona Schurman and Sharon Leigh Clark, *Modern Dance Fundamentals*, 35-41.

56. Ibid., 38, 39.

57. Ernestine Stodelle, *The Dance Technique of Doris Humphrey*, 54.

58. St. Denis and Shawn, "Denishawn Dancing Technique," Folder 364.

59. Ernestine Stodelle, *The Dance Technique of Doris Humphrey*, 103-167.

60. Nona Schurman and Sharon Leigh Clark, *Modern Dance Fundamentals*, 114-128.

61. Ibid., 59, 60.

62. Ernestine Stodelle, *The Dance Technique of Doris Humphrey*, 119-120.

63. St. Denis and Shawn, "Denishawn Dancing Technique," Folder 365.

64. *Charles Weidman Papers* (MGZMD 99, Box 5, Folder 79).

65. Ibid.

66. Louis Horst and Carroll Russell, *Modern Dance Forms* 2nd ed., (Pennington, NJ: Princeton Book Company, 1987), 52.

67. Ibid.

68. Ibid., 59, 60.

69. José Limón, *An Unfinished Memoir* (Hanover, NH: Wesleyan University Press of New England, 1998; Middletown, CT: Wesleyan University Press, paperback, 2001), 147.

70. Louis Horst and Carroll Russell, *Modern Dance Forms*, 63.

71. Deborah Carr, interview by author, 19 March 1989.

72. Louis Horst and Carroll Russell, *Modern Dance Forms* 2nd ed., 74.

73. Ibid., 70.

74. Ibid., 69.

75. Ruth St. Denis, "Music Visualization." *The Denishawn Magazine*. Vol. 1, No. 3 (1925): 1.

76. Ruth St. Denis, *An Unfinished Life,* 215.

77. Ibid.

78. Ibid.

79. Ibid., 214.

80. Ted Shawn, *Every Little Movement*, 88.

81. Christina L. Schlundt, *The Professional Appearances of Ruth St. Denis & Ted Shawn, 1906-1932* (New York: The New York Public Library, 1962), 49, 51.

82. Jane Sherman, *Denishawn: The Enduring Influence*, 50.

83. Christina L. Schlundt, *The Professional Appearances of Ruth St. Denis & Ted Shawn, 1906-1932*, 49, 51.

84. Doris Humphrey, "New Dance: An Unfinished Autobiography," *Dance Perspectives* 25 (Spring 1966): 55.

85. Ibid.

86. Selma Jean Cohen, *Doris Humphrey: An Artist First* (Middletown, CT: Wesleyan University Press, 1972), 35.

87. Doris Humphrey, "New Dance: An Unfinished Autobiography," 55, 56.

88. Suzanne Shelton, *Divine Dancer: A Biography of Ruth St. Denis* (New York: Doubleday & Company, 1981), 187.

89. Ruth St. Denis, *An Unfinished Life*, 260.

90. Ibid.

91. Christina L. Schlundt, *The Professional Appearances of Ruth St. Denis & Ted Shawn, 1906-1932*, 55, 56.

92. Jane Sherman, *Denishawn: The Enduring Influence*, 7.

93. Suzanne Shelton, *Divine Dancer: A Biography of Ruth St. Denis*, 191.

94. Jane Sherman, *The Drama of Denishawn Dance*, 151.

95. Ibid.

96. Ted Shawn, *One Thousand and One Night Stands*, 202, 203.

97. Jane Sherman, *Soaring* (Middletown, CT: Wesleyan University Press, 1976), 62.

98. Ted Shawn, *One Thousand and One Night Stands*, 201.

99. Jane Sherman, *Soaring*, 171.

100. Ibid.

101. Ted Shawn, *One Thousand and One Night Stands*, 188.

102. Jane Sherman, *Soaring*, 101.

103. Ted Shawn, *One Thousand and One Night Stands*, 169.

104. Jane Sherman, *Soaring*, 150.

105. Ted Shawn, *One Thousand and One Night Stands*, 200.

106. Christina L. Schlundt, *The Professional Appearances of Ruth St. Denis & Ted Shawn, 1906-1932*, 58.

107. Jane Sherman, *Soaring*, 155.

108. Ibid., 191.

Chapter Five   Dancing with Martha Graham

1. Ted Shawn, *One Thousand and One Night Stands* (Garden City, New York: Doubleday & Company, 1960), 152.

2. Don McDonagh, *Martha Graham: A Biography* (New York: Praeger Publishers, 1973), 23.

3. Ruth St. Denis, *An Unfinished Life* (New York: Harper & Brothers Publishers, 1939; copyright © renewed 1967 HarperCollins), 206, 207.

4. Janet Mansfield Soares, *Louis Horst: Musician in a Dancer's World* (Durham and London: Duke University Press, 1992), 20.

5. Ted Shawn, *One Thousand and One Night Stands*, 91.

6. Ibid., 91, 92.

7. Ibid.

8. Ibid., 93.

9. Jane Sherman, *The Drama of Denishawn Dance* (Middletown, CT: Wesleyan University Press, 1979), 60.

10. Selma Jean Cohen, *Doris Humphrey: An Artist First* (Middletown, CT: Wesleyan University Press, 1972), 35.

11. Jane Sherman, *The Drama of Denishawn Dance*, 59.

12. Christina L. Schlundt, *The Professional Appearances of Ruth St. Denis & Ted Shawn, 1906-1932* (New York: The New York Public Library, 1962), 45-60.

13. Martha Graham, *Blood Memory* (New York: Doubleday Publishers, 1991), 77.

14. Jane Sherman, *The Drama of Denishawn Dance*, 60.

15. Ibid., 61.

16. Ted Shawn, *One Thousand and One Night Stands*, 93.

17. Ibid.

18. Don McDonagh, *Martha Graham: A Biography*, 27.

19. Martha Graham, *Blood Memory* (New York: Doubleday Publishers, 1991), 79.

20. Don McDonagh, *Martha Graham: A Biography*, 28.

21. John Martin, *America Dancing* (New York: Dodge Publishing Company, 1936; reprint, Brooklyn, N.Y.; Dance Horizons, 1968), 229 (page reference is to reprint edition).

22. Don McDonagh, *Martha Graham: A Biography*, 28.

23. Ibid.

24. Agnes de Mille, *Martha: The Life and Work of Martha Graham* (New York: Random House, 1991), 55.

25. Martha Graham, *Blood Memory*, 66, 67.

26. Ibid.

27. Christina L. Schlundt, *The Professional Appearances of Ruth St. Denis & Ted Shawn, 1906-1932*, 38, 39.

28. Ibid., 39.

29. Ibid., 38, 39.

30. Ted Shawn, *One Thousand and One Night Stands*, 94.

31. Ibid., 101.

32. Agnes de Mille, *Martha: The Life and Work of Martha Graham*, 65.

33. Christina L. Schlundt, *The Professional Appearances of Ruth St. Denis & Ted Shawn, 1906-1932*, 41.

34. Ted Shawn, *One Thousand and One Night Stands*, 106, 107.

35. Martha Graham, *Blood Memory*, 87.

36. Ibid.

37. Ibid.

38. Ted Shawn, *One Thousand and One Night Stands*, 116.

39. Christina L. Schlundt, *The Professional Appearances of Ruth St. Denis & Ted Shawn, 1906-1932*, 41-45.

40. Ted Shawn, *One Thousand and One Night Stands*, 134, 135.

41. Martha Graham, *Blood Memory*, 91.

42. Ibid.

43. Agnes de Mille, *Martha: The Life and Work of Martha Graham*, 69.

44. Helen Caldwell, *Michio Ito* (Berkeley and Los Angles: University of California Press, 1977), 45.

45. Martha Graham, *Blood Memory*, 103.

46. Eleanor King, *Transformations* (Brooklyn, NY: Dance Horizons, 1978), 8.

47. Selma Jean Cohen, *Doris Humphrey: An Artist First* (Middletown, CT: Wesleyan University Press, 1972), 79.

48. Alice Lewisohn Crowley, *The Neighborhood Playhouse* (New York: Theatre Arts Books, 1959), xix.

49. Ibid., xix, xx.

50. Ibid., 14.

51. Ibid., 20.

52. Ibid., 42, 43.

53. Ibid., 86, 87.

54. Ibid., 189.

55. Agnes de Mille, *Martha: The Life and Work of Martha Graham*, 114.

56. http//search.eb.com/women/articles/Bernstein_Aline.html

57 Alice Lewisohn Crowley, *The Neighborhood Playhouse*, 237.

58. Ibid., 240.

59. Agnes de Mille, *Martha, The Life and Work of Martha Graham,* 123.

60. Ibid.

61. Alice Lewisohn Crowley, *The Neighborhood Playhouse,* 240, 241.

62. Ibid., 241.

63. Richard Strauss, *Ein Heldenleben*, produced by David Mottley, New York Philharmonic, compact disc MK37756, CBS Records, 1983.

64. Bryan Gilliam, *The Life of Richard Strauss* (Cambridge, UK: Cambridge University Press, 1999), 69.

65. Ibid., 62.

66. Ibid., 68.

67. Alice Lewisohn Crowley, *The Neighborhood Playhouse,* 235.

68. Agnes de Mille, *Martha, The Life and Work of Martha Graham,* 124.

69. Ellen Knight, *Charles Martin Loeffler: A Life Apart in American Music* (Urbana, IL: University of Illinois Press, 1993), 125.

70. Ibid., 124.

71. Ibid.

72. Agnes de Mille, *Martha: The Life and Work of Martha Graham,* 124.

73. Ibid.

74. Ibid.

75. Ibid.

76. José Limón, "Dance for Men in the Schools," *Journal of Health, Physical Education and Recreation* Vol. 11: 3, March 1940: 148.

Chapter Six   The Humphrey-Weidman Alliance

1. Marcia B. Siegel, *Days on Earth* (New Haven, CT & London: Yale University Press, 1987), 106, 107.

2. Eleanor King, *Transformations* (Brooklyn, NY: Dance Horizons, 1978), 1.

3. Ibid., 4.

4. Lillian Moore, *Artists of the Dance* (Brooklyn, NY: Dance Horizons, 1938, reprint 1969), 291.

5. Eleanor King, *Transformations,* 6.

6. Deborah Jowitt, *Time and the Dancing Image* (Berkeley and Los Angeles, CA: University of California Press, 1989), 137.

7. Jane Sherman, *Denishawn: The Enduring Influence* (Boston: Twayne Publishers, 1983), 98.

8. Ibid., 138.

9. Marcia Siegel, *Days on Earth*, 38.

10. Deborah Carr, interview by author, March 19, 1989.

11. Ibid.

12. Beatrice Seckler, interview by author, March 19, 1989.

13. Ruth St. Denis, *An Unfinished Life* (New York: Harper & Brothers Publishers, 1939; copyright © renewed 1967 HarperCollins), 325.

14. Ibid., 326.

15. Ibid., 325.

16. Jane Sherman, *Denishawn: The Enduring Influence*, 17, 18.

17. Ruth St. Denis, *An Unfinished Life*, 321.

18. Sylvia Pelt Richards, "A Biography of Charles Weidman with Emphasis upon His Professional Career and His Contribution to the Field of Dance," (Ph.D. diss., Texas Woman's University, 1971), 140.

19. Charles Weidman, Interview by Marian Horosko, 1966, 1967. Oral History, Dance Collections, New York Public Library, New York, New York.

20. Selma Jean Cohen, *Doris Humphrey: An Artist First* (Middletown, CT: Wesleyan University Press, 1972), 77.

21. Doris Humphrey, "New Dance: An Unfinished Autobiography," *Dance Perspectives* 25 (Spring 1966): 74.

22. Ibid., 74, 75.

23. Ibid., 76.

24. Shirley D. Manasevit, "A Last Interview with Charles Weidman." *Dance Scope* 10 (Fall/Winter 1975-76): 39.

25. Ruth St. Denis, *An Unfinished Life*, 322.

26. Selma Jean Cohen, *Doris Humphrey: An Artist First*, 82.

27. Ibid., 82, 83.

28. Margaret Lloyd, *The Borzoi Book of Modern Dance* (New York: Alfred A. Knopf, 1949; reprint, Pennington, NJ: Princeton Book Co., 1987), 83.

29. Jane Sherman, *Denishawn: The Enduring Influence*, 100.

30. Jane Sherman, *Soaring* (Middletown, CT: Wesleyan University Press, 1976), 11.

31. Ibid., 15.

32. Margaret Lloyd, *The Borzoi Book of Modern Dance*, 83.

33. José Limón, *An Unfinished Memoir* (Hanover, NH: Wesleyan University Press of New England, 1998; Middletown, CT: Wesleyan University Press, paperback, 2001), 84.

34. Eleanor King, *Transformations*, 13.

35. Ibid., 29.

36. Lillian Moore, *Artists of the Dance*, 290.

37. Eleanor King, *Transformations*, 39.

38. Lillian Moore, *Artists of the Dance*, 291.

39. José Limón, *An Unfinished Memoir*, 19.

40. Kathleen Cannell, "Weidman Conducts a Master Class," *The Christian Science Monitor*, 6 May 1950, 5.

41. Ibid.

42. Ibid.

43. Susannah Newman, telephone conversation, June 1988.

44. Selma Jean Cohen, *Doris Humphrey: An Artist First*, 90.

45. José Limón, *An Unfinished Memoir*, 28, 29.

46. Christina L. Schlundt, *Tamiris: A Chronicle of Her Dance Career, 1927-1955* (New York: The New York Public Library, Astor, Lenox and Tilden Foundations, 1972), 18, 19.

47. Ibid., 20, 21.

48. Lois Balcom, "Review of the Month," *Dance Observer*, April 1942.

49. Eleanor King, *Transformations*, 44.

50. Winthrop Palmer, *Theatrical Dancing in America*, 2nd ed., Revised, (Cranbury, NJ: A. S. Barnes and Company, 1978), 101.

51. Eleanor King, *Transformations*, 75.

52. Ibid., 75, 76.

53. Ibid., 53.

54. Deborah Jowitt, *Time and the Dancing Image*, 166.

55. José Limón, *An Unfinished Memoir*, 58.

56. Ibid., 163.

57. Ibid., 158.

58. Ibid., 58.

59. John Martin, *America Dancing* (New York: Dodge Publishing Company, 1936; reprint, Brooklyn, NY: Dance Horizons, 1969), 233, 234 (page references are to reprint edition).

60. Deborah Jowitt, *Time and the Dancing Image*, 165.

61. José Limón, *An Unfinished Memoir*, 58.

62. Deborah Carr, telephone conversation, October 12, 1990.

63. Lillian Moore, *Artists of The Dance*, 295.

64. Weidman, Interview by Marian Horosko.

65. Ibid.

66. Eleanor King, *Transformations*, 87.

67. Nona Schurman, interview by author, June 23, 1988.

68. Gus Giordano, *Jazz Dance Class: Beginning Thru Advanced* (Pennington, NJ: Princeton Books, 1992), xvii.

69. Ibid., 59.

70. Ibid., 62.

71. Jane Sherman, *The Drama of Denishawn Dance* (Middletown, CT: Wesleyan University Press, 1979), 146.

72. Ruth St. Denis, *An Unfinished Life*, 221.

73. John Martin, *America Dancing*, 236, 237.

74. Walter Sorell, ed., *The Dance Has Many Faces,* Third Edition. (Chicago IL: a cappella books, an imprint of Chicago Review Press, 1992) 266-267.

75. Jane Sherman, *Denishawn: The Enduring Influence*, 97.

76. Don McDonagh, *The Complete Guide to Modern Dance* (Garden City, NY: Doubleday & Company, 1976), 113.

77. Ibid., 112, 113.

78. Marcia Siegel, *Days on Earth*, 160.

79. Helen Dzhermolinska, "Blueprint for a Ballet," *Dance Magazine*, April 1951, 42, 43.

80. Frederic L. Orme, "Charles Weidman: The Master Mime," *The American Dancer*, December 1938, 11.

81. Ibid., 34.

82. Seckler, interview by author, March 19, 1989.

83. Ibid.

84. Selma Jean Cohen, *Doris Humphrey: An Artist First,* 98.

85. Ibid., 100.

86. Ibid., 123.

87. Ibid., 128.

88. Ibid., 131, 132.

89. José Limón, *An Unfinished Memoir,* 162.

90. Henry Gilford, Dance Reviews, *The Dance Observer*, May 1936, 16.

91. Ibid.

92. Ibid.

93. José Limón, *An Unfinished Memoir,* 51.

94. Henry Gilford, Dance Reviews, *The Dance Observer*, May 1936, 16

95. José Limón, *An Unfinished Memoir,* 51.

96. Ibid.

97. Selma Jean Cohen, *Doris Humphrey: An Artist First,* 136.

98. Ibid.

99. José Limón, *An Unfinished Memoir,* 54.

100. Marcia Siegel, *Days on Earth*, 154.

101. José Limón, *An Unfinished Memoir,* 54.

102. Eleanor King, *Transformations,* 221.

103. Nona Schurman, manuscript notes, May 5, 2005.

104. José Limón, *An Unfinished Memoir,* 77.

105. Margaret Lloyd, *The Borzoi Book of Modern Dance,* 95.

106. José Limón, *An Unfinished Memoir,* 66.

107. Ibid., 67.

108. Ibid., 108.

109. Ibid., 67.
110. Margaret Lloyd, *The Borzoi Book of Modern Dance,* 97.
111. Lois Balcom, "Reviews of the Month," *Dance Observer*, February 1942, 23, 24, 51.
112. Margaret Lloyd, *The Borzoi Book of Modern Dance,* 107.
113. José Limón, *An Unfinished Memoir,* 71.
114. Ibid.
115. Ibid.
116. Ibid.
117. Ibid.
118. Ibid.
119. Ibid., 72.
120. Lois Balcom, "Reviews of the Month," *Dance Observer*, 51.
121. Marcia Siegel, *Days on Earth,* 167.
122. Charles Weidman, Interview by Marian Horosko.
123. Ibid.
124. Ernestine Stodell, *The Dance Technique of Doris Humphrey* (Pennington, NJ: Princeton Book Company, 1978), 19.
125. Jack Anderson, "Spare Worlds Rich in Suggestions," *The New York Times*, May 24, 2005, 5.
126. Bill T. Jones, *"Falling and Catching: Dancing through the Other Door,"* Unpublished Lecture notes, February 4, 2000.
127. Charles Weidman, Interview by Marian Horosko.
128. Ernestine Stodelle, *The Dance Technique of Doris Humphrey* (Pennington, NJ: Princeton Book Company, 1978), 20.
129. Nona Schurman and Sharon Leigh Clark, *Modern Dance Fundamentals* (New York: The Macmillan Company, 1972), 35.
130. Elinor Rogosin, *The Dance Makers* (New York: Walker and Company, 1980), 23, 24.

Chapter Seven   Democracy and Patriotism

1. Walt Whitman, *Leaves of Grass* (New York: Random House; The Modern Library, original edition, 1891-2), 3.
2. Walter Sorell, ed., *The Dance Has Many Faces*, Third Edition. (Chicago IL: a cappella books, an imprint of Chicago Review Press, 1992), 203.
3. Sondra Horton Fraleigh, *Dance and the Lived Body: A Descriptive Aesthetics* (Pittsburgh: University of Pittsburgh Press, 1987), 43-48.
4. John Martin, *The Modern Dance* (Brooklyn, NY: Dance Horizons, 1966), 13.

5. Frank Meister, "The Esthetics of Art," *American Photography* 39, October 1945, 35.

6. Margaret Gage, "A Study in American Modernism," *Theatre Arts Monthly*, March 1930, 198.

7. Fraleigh, *Dance and the Lived Body*, xxxiii.

8. John Martin, *Book of the Dance* (New York: Tudor Publishing Company, 1963), 142.

9. *Dance: Four Pioneers* (WNET/13, 1965) filmstrip.

10. John Martin, *Book of the Dance,* 138.

11. Judith Lynne Hanna, "Patterns of Dominance," *The Drama Review 31* (Spring 1987): 30.

12. Wladyslaw Taterkiewicz, "The Great Theory of Beauty and Its Decline," *The Journal of Aesthetics and Art Criticism 31* (Winter 1972): 167.

13. Wilfried A. Hofmann, "Of Beauty and the Dance: Towards an Aesthetics of Ballet," *Dance Perspectives 55* (Autumn 1973): 18.

14. Taterkiewicz, "The Great Theory of Beauty and Its Decline," 173-74.

15. Ibid., 174.

16. Ibid., 177.

17. Gage, "A Study in American Modernism," 230.

18. Hans Wiener, "The New Dance and Its Influence on the Modern Stage," *The Drama Magazine 19*, November 1928, 39.

19. Elinor Rogosin, *The Dance Makers* (New York: Walker and Company, 1980), 16.

20. John Martin, *Book of the Dance,* 138.

21. Julia L. Foulkes, *Modern Bodies: Dance and American Modernism from Martha Graham to Alvin Ailey* (Chapel Hill, NC: University of North Carolina Press, 2002), 132.

22. *Charles Weidman Papers, Special Collections*, The New York Public Library (MGZMD 99, Box 5, Folder 79).

23. John Martin, *America Dancing* (New York: Dodge Publishing Company, 1936; reprint, Brooklyn, NY: Dance Horizons, 1968), 76 (page reference is to reprint edition).

24. Olga Maynard, *American Modern Dancers: The Pioneers* (Boston: Little Brown and Company, 1965), 8.

25. Lucile Marsh, "Modern Dance Art," *The Drama Magazine 17*, April 1929, 197.

26. Sondra Horton Fraleigh, *Dance and the Lived Body: A Descriptive Aesthetics*, xxxii.

27. Ibid, xxxiii.

28. Edward W. Mathews, "Applied Modernism," *The School Arts Magazine*, May 1931, 570.

29. Ralph Adams Cram, "The Limits of Modernism in Arts," *Art and Decoration* 20, January 1924, 12.

30. José Limón, *An Unfinished Memoir* (Hanover, NH: Wesleyan University Press of New England, 1998; Middletown, CT: Wesleyan University Press, paperback, 2001), 38.

31. Ibid., 36.

32. Daniel J. Boorstin, "Can patriotism be legislated?" *U. S. News & World Report*, February 13, 1989, 26.

33. Tony Buttitta and Barry Witham, *Uncle Sam Presents: A Memoir of the Federal Theatre 1935-1939* (Philadelphia: University of Pennsylvania Press, 1982), 14.

34. Ibid., 50.

35. Marcia B. Siegel, *Days on Earth* (New Haven, CT & London: Yale University Press, 1987), 171.

36. Julia L. Foulkes, *Modern Bodies: Dance and American Modernism from Martha Graham to Alvin Ailey,* 140.

37. Lillian Moore, *Artists of The Dance* (Brooklyn, NY: Dance Horizons, 1938, reprint 1969), 294.

38. Olga Maynard, *American Modern Dancers: The Pioneers*, 100, 101.

39. Elsa Findlay, "Concert Dancers Organize," *The American Dancer*, February 1931, 13.

40. *Humphrey-Weidman Group Programs*. Dance Collections MGZB vol. 11, 15 December 1934, 1935 season, New York Public Library.

41. *Humphrey-Weidman Group Programs*, "Men in the Dance," MGZB vol. 11, May 1935, Dance Collections, New York Public Library.

42. José Limón, *An Unfinished Memoir*, 58.

43. Ibid.

44. Ibid., 59.

45. Ibid., 59.

46. John Martin, *America Dancing*, 237.

47. "Traditions," *Deborah Carr Theatre Dance Ensemble*, produced and directed by Deborah Carr and Beatrice Seckler, videocassette. Private collection.

48. Henry Gilford, "Dance Reviews," *The Dance Observer*, May 1936, 16.

49. John Martin, "Weidman's 'Affirmations' Prove to be More Strength Than Name of Number Implies," *The New York Times*, January 7, 1935, 8.

50. Joseph Arnold, "Dance Events Reviewed," *The American Dancer*, February 1935, 26.

51. John Martin, "Weidman's 'Affirmations' Prove," 7.

52. Henry Gilford, Dance Reviews, *The Dance Observer*, 16

53. Joseph Arnold, "Dance Events Reviewed," 26.

54. Ibid.

55. Ibid.

56. Nona Schurman, conversation with author, April 1989.

57. Joseph Arnold, "Dance Events Reviewed," 26.

58. Henry Gilford, "Dance Reviews," *The Dance Observer*, 161, 17.

59. Joseph Arnold, "Dance Events Reviewed," 26.

60. Margaret Lloyd, *The Borzoi Book of Modern Dance* (New York: Alfred A. Knopf, 1949; reprint, Pennington, NJ: Princeton Book Co., 1987), 82.

61. "New Dance," *1978 American Dance Festival*, Restaged by Charles Weidman, produced at American Dance Festival, Dance Horizons Video, distributed by Princeton Book Company, 1989.

62. Christina L. Schlundt, *Tamiris: A Chronicle of Her Dance Career, 1927-1955* (New York: The New York Public Library, Astor, Lenox and Tilden Foundations, 1972), 18, 19.

63. Ibid., 53.

64. Martha Graham Dance Company Program, "Sketches From Chronicle," New York Season, City Center, New York, NY, May 2005.

65. Ibid.

66. Harry Cable, "The Soldier's Forum," *Dance Magazine*, July 1942, 6.

67. Margaret Lloyd, *The Borzoi Book of Modern Dance*, 101.

68. Sylvia Pelt Richards, "A Biography of Charles Weidman with Emphasis upon His Professional Career and His Contribution to the Field of Dance," (Ph.D. diss., Texas Woman's University, 1971), 196-98.

69. Lillian Moore, *Artists of the Dance*, 296.

70. José Limón, *An Unfinished Memoir*, 76.

71. Margaret Lloyd, *The Borzoi Book of Modern Dance*, 101.

72. José Limón, *An Unfinished Memoir*, 77.

73. Margaret Lloyd, *The Borzoi Book of Modern Dance*, 101, 102.

74. Ibid., 102.

75. Joseph Arnold, "Dance Events Reviewed," 26.

76. *Humphrey-Weidman Group Program*, vol. 13, 1937.

77. Margaret Lloyd, *The Borzoi Book of Modern Dance*, 102.

78. Ibid., 103.

79. *Charles Weidman Papers* (MGZMD 99, Box 7, Folder 99).

80. Margaret Lloyd, *The Borzoi Book of Modern Dance*, 103.

81. Christina L. Schlundt, *Tamiris, A Chronicle of Her Dance Career*, 34.

82. Henry Gilford, "Dance Reviews," *The Dance Observer*, April 1936, 6.

83. Walter Terry, *How to Look at Dance* (New York: William Morrow and Company, 1982), 88.

84. Walter Terry, *The New York Times*, June 30, 1985.

85. *Charles Weidman Papers* (MGZMD 99, Box 7, Folder 100).

86. José Limón, *An Unfinished Memoir,* 87.

87. Margaret Lloyd, *The Borzoi Book of Modern Dance*, 109.

88. Ibid.

89. Ibid.

90. Ibid.

91. Ibid.

92. H. W. Janson, *History of Art* (Englewood Cliffs, NJ: Prentice Hall Publishers, 1966), 529 .

93. José Limón, *An Unfinished Memoir,* 89.

94. Selma Jean Cohen, *Doris Humphrey: An Artist First* (Middletown, CT: Wesleyan University Press, 1972), 155.

95. Ibid., 155, 156.

Chapter 8   Shaping a Movement Style and Technique

1. Lillie F. Rosen, *American Dance Guild Newsletter* vol. 9, no. 7, (November-December, 1974): 14.

2. Joseph H. Mazo, *Prime Movers* (New York: William Morrow and Company, 1977), 140.

3. Webster's New Universal Unabridged Dictionary, 2nd ed. (New York: Simon & Schuster, 1983), 1, 810.

4. Ray Cook, *A Handbook for the Dance Director* (New York: Dance Notation Bureau, 1977), 35.

5. Ibid., 37.

6. Sondra Horton Fraleigh, *Dance and the Lived Body: A Descriptive Aesthetics* (Pittsburgh: University of Pittsburgh Press, 1987), 6.

7. Ray Cook, *A Handbook for the Dance Director,* 37.

8. George Jackson, "About Balanchine," *The Dance Has Many Faces*, Walter Sorell, ed., (New York: a capella books, 1992), 161.

9. Nona Schurman, interview by author, June 20, 1988.

10. Ibid.

11. Selma Jean Cohen, *Doris Humphrey: An Artist First* (Middletown, CT: Wesleyan University Press, 1972), 119.

12. Ibid.

13. Ernestine Stodelle, *The Dance Technique of Doris Humphrey* (Pennington, NJ: Princeton Book Company, 1978), 17.

14. Elizabeth Kendall, "Talking with Katherine Litz," *Dance Scope* 8 (Spring/Summer, 1974); 11.

15. Nona Schurman, "Notes on Humphrey-Weidman Demonstration," Personal Archives.

16. Ibid.

17. Ibid.

18. Nona Schurman, interview by author, June 20, 1988.

19. Ibid.

20. Ibid.

21. Beatrice Seckler, interview by author, March 19, 1989.

22. Deborah Carr, interview by author, March 19, 1989.

23. Ibid.

24. Charles Weidman, Interview by Marian Horosko, Dance Collections, New York Public Library.

25. Nona Schurman, interview by author, June 20, 1988.

26. Nona Schurman, studio session with author, July 13, 1989.

27. Louis Horst and Carroll Russell, *Modern Dance Forms*, 2nd ed., Dance Horizons (Pennington, NJ: Princeton Book Company, 1987), 57-59.

28. Ibid., 61.

29. Ibid.

30. Ibid., 78.

31. Ibid., 70.

32. Ibid., 74.

33. Charles Fowler, *Music: Its Role and Importance in Our Lives.* Teacher's Annotated Edition (New York: Glencoe/McGraw Hill), 617.

34. Louis Horst and Carroll Russell, *Modern Dance Forms*, 23.

35. Henriette Bassoe, "Flights beyond the Horizon with Charles Weidman," *The American Dancer*, 32 March 1941, 32.

36. Ibid.

37. Don McDonagh, *The Complete Guide to Modern Dance* (Garden City, NY: Doubleday & Company, 1976), 112.

38. Webster's New Universal Unabridged Dictionary, 2nd ed. (New York: Simon & Schuster, 1983), 1, 872.

39. Sondra Horton Fraleigh, *Dance and the Lived Body: A Descriptive Aesthetics* (Pittsburgh: University of Pittsburgh Press, 1987), 105.

40. Edith Stephen, "Modern Dance—A Technique or Philosophy," *The Dance Observer,* January 1955, 12.

41. Charles Weidman, Interview by Marian Horosko.

42. David Wynn, "Three Years with Charles Weidman," *Dance Perspectives 60,* (1980), 23.

43. Nona Schurman, "Notes on Humphrey-Weidman Demonstration."

44. Ibid.

45. David Wynn, "Three Years with Charles Weidman," 23.

503

46. Ibid.

47. Charles Weidman, Interview by Marian Horosko

48. David Wynn, "Three Years with Charles Weidman," 23.

49. Charles Weidman, Interview by Marian Horosko.

50. Daniel Lewis, *The Illustrated Dance Technique of José Limón* (New York: Harper & Row, Publishers, 1984), 43.

51. Ernestine Stodell, "Humphrey-Weidman: Their Theory of Movement," *Focus on Dance 11* (1962): 21.

52. Eleanor King, "The Influence of Doris Humphrey," *Focus on Dance 5* (1969): 7.

53. Eleanor King, *Transformations* (Brooklyn, NY: Dance Horizons, 1978), 17.

54. Janet Towner, interview by author. Tape recording, Durham, NC, June 11, 1989.

55. Nona Schurman and Sharon Leigh Clark, *Modern Dance Fundamentals*, 26.

56. Ibid.

57. Ibid.

58. Charles Weidman, Interview by Marian Horosko.

59. Daniel Lewis, *The Illustrated Dance Technique of José Limón,* 44.

60. David Wynn, "Three Years with Charles Weidman," 24.

61. Margaret O'Sullivan, letter to author, April 26, 2005.

62. Nona Schurman, manuscript notes to author, May 2005.

63. Margaret O'Sullivan, letter to author, April 26, 2005.

64. Janet Towner, interview by author, June 11, 1989.

65. Deborah Carr, interview by author, March 19, 1989.

66. Beatrice Seckler, interview by author, March 19, 1989.

67. *Charles Weidman Papers, Special Collections*, The New York Public Library (MGZMD 99, Box 8, Folder 112).

68. Marcia B. Siegel, *Days on Earth* (New Haven, CT & London: Yale University Press, 1987), 111.

69. Lucille Marsh, *The American Dancer*, July 1931, 39.

70. Jano Cohen, "Creativity in Dance and Government Funding: An Examination of the W.P.A. in the 1930s," *Graduate Dance Review* 1, Temple University, 45.

71. John Martin, *The New York Times*, June 7, 1936.

72. Christina L. Schlundt, *Tamiris: A Chronicle of Her Dance Career, 1927-1955* (New York: The New York Public Library, Astor, Lenox and Tilden Foundations, 1972), 50.

73. Albertina Vitak, "Dance Events Reviewed," *The American Dancer*, May 1939, 38.

74. Ibid.

75. Ibid.

76. Marcia B. Siegel, *Days on Earth*, 166, 167.

77. *Charles Weidman Papers* (MGZMD 99, Box 5, Folder 86).

78. Sylvia Pelt Richards, "A Biography of Charles Weidman with Emphasis upon His Professional Career and His Contribution to the Field of Dance," (Ph.D. diss., Texas Woman's University, 1971), 282.

79. Ibid., 283.

80. Ibid., 285.

81. Winthrop Palmer, "The Season in Review," *Dance News*, April 1951, 8.

82. Roberta Krugman, "Charles Weidman and Company, March 11, 1951 at YM-YWHA," *The Dance Observer, 61*.

83. Sylvia Pelt Richards, "A Biography of Charles Weidman," 286.

84. John Martin, "Dance Reviews," *The New York Times*, January 3, 1960, 2.

Chapter Nine   A New Decade

1. Selma Jean Cohen, *Doris Humphrey: An Artist First* (Middletown, CT: Wesleyan University Press, 1972), 163.

2. Ibid., 152

3. Nona Schurman, manuscript notes, May 2005.

4. Selma Jean Cohen, *Doris Humphrey: An Artist First,* 163.

5. Ibid.

6. Ibid., 162.

7. Nona Schurman, manuscript notes, May 2005.

8. Selma Jean Cohen, *Doris Humphrey: An Artist First,* 164-65.

9. Albertina Vitak, "Dance Events Reviewed," *The American Dancer*, May 1940, 36.

10. Louis Horst and Carroll Russell, *Modern Dance Forms*, 2nd ed., Dance Horizons (Princeton, NJ: Princeton Book Company, 1987), 25.

11. Margaret Lloyd, *The Borzoi Book of Modern Dance* (New York: Alfred A. Knopf, 1949; reprint, Pennington, NJ: Princeton Book Co., 1987), 110-113.

12. Ibid., 113.

13. Ibid.

14. Albertina Vitak, "Dance Events Reviewed," *The American Dancer*, February 1941, 19.

15. Selma Jean Cohen, *Doris Humphrey: An Artist First,* 173.

16. Ibid., 181, 182.

17. Ibid., 182.

18. Ibid., 185.

19. Ibid., 172.

20. Margaret Lloyd, *The Borzoi Book of Modern Dance,* 118.

21. *Charles Weidman Papers, Special Collections,* The New York Public Library (MGZMD 99, Box 7, Folder 104).

22. Ibid.

23. Ibid.

24. Ibid.

25. *Charles Weidman Papers* (MGZMD 99, Box 9, Folder 113).

26. Lucile Marsh, "What is Choreography?" *Dance Magazine,* October 1943, 4-5.

27. *Charles Weidman Papers* (MGZMD 99, Box 9, Folder 113).

28. *Charles Weidman Papers* (MGZMD 99, Box 7, Folder 106).

29. *Charles Weidman Papers* (MGZMD 99, Box 5, Folder 79).

30. Margaret Lloyd, *The Borzoi Book of Modern Dance,* 122.

31. Don McDonagh, *The Complete Guide to Modern Dance* (Garden City, NY: Doubleday & Company, 1976), 115.

32. Ibid.

33. Ibid., 116.

34. *Charles Weidman Papers* (MGZMD 99, Box 5, Folder 87).

35. Doris Hering, "The Season in Review," *Dance Magazine,* May 1953, 12.

36. Walter Terry, "Moderns in Review," *Dance News,* September 1947, 4.

37. Doris Hering, "The Season in Review," *Dance Magazine,* May 1953, 12.

37. Arthur Todd, "The Opera Ballet Enigma: and What Four Choreographers Have Done About It," *Dance Magazine,* April 1951, 37.

Chapter Ten   Living His Own Dreams

1. Charles Weidman, "Random Remarks," Walter Sorell, ed. *The Dance Has Many Faces* (Cleveland and New York: The World Publishing Company, 1951), 29.

2. Helen Savery, "Dancing in the Depression," *Dance Chronicle,* 1984-85 (vol. 7, no. 3): 284, 285.

3. Brooks Atkinson, *The New York Times Theatre Reviews,* June 1930, 20: 1.

4. David Ewen, *New Complete Book of American Musical Theatre* (New York: Holt, Rinehart and Winston, 1958), 7.

5. Ibid., 8.

6. Gerald Bordman, *American Musical Theatre: A Chronicle* (New York: Oxford University Press, 1978), 479.

7. (http//www.uib.no/herrmann/articles/phototours/newyork/page4.html), 10/27/2004.

8. Brooks Atkinson, *The New York Times Theatre Reviews*, June 1932, 19: 3.

9. John Martin, *The New York Times Theatre Reviews*, October 1932, IX: 11: 2.

10. Ibid.

11. Ibid

12. David Ewen, *New Complete Book of American Musical Theatre*, 8.

13. Gerald Bordman, *American Musical Theatre*, 479.

14. Helen Savery, "Dancing in the Depression," 290.

15. Ibid.

16. Eleanor King, *Transformations* (Brooklyn, NY: Dance Horizons, 1978), 137.

17. Helen Savery, "Dancing in the Depression," 291.

18. Eleanor King, *Transformations*, 137.

19. Ibid.

20. Ibid., 138.

21. Lillian Moore, *Artists of the Dance* (Brooklyn, NY: Dance Horizons, 1938, reprint 1969), 293.

22. Edwin Bronner, *Encyclopedia of American Musical Theatre 1900-1975* (South Brunswick, NJ: A. S. Barnes Company, 1980), 694, 695.

23. José Limón, *An Unfinished Memoir* (Hanover, NH: Wesleyan University Press of New England, 1998; Middletown, CT: Wesleyan University Press, paperback, 2001), 49.

24. David Ewen, *New Complete Book of American Musical Theatre*, 26.

25. Ibid.

26. Ibid.

27. Ibid.

28. Gerald Bordman, *American Musical Theatre*, 484.

29. Twaya Tharp, *Push Comes to Shove* (New York: Bantam Books, 1992), 288.

30. George Bockman, Scrapbook 1933-35, MGZRS 79-3924, Dance Collections, New York Public Library for the Performing Arts.

31. Eleanor King, *Transformations*, 162.

32. Ibid.

507

33. Joseph Arnold, "Dance Events Reviewed," *The American Dancer,* November 1933, 7.

34. Ibid.

35. George Bockman, Scrapbook 1933-35, MGZRS 79-3924.

36. David Ewen, *New Complete Book of American Musical Theatre,* 301.

37. Joseph Arnold, "Dance Events Reviewed," *The American Dancer,* October 1934, 8.

38. David Ewen, *New Complete Book of American Musical Theatre,* 302.

39. George Bockman, Scrapbook 1933-35, MGZRS 79-3924.

40. Joseph Arnold, "Dance Events Reviewed," *The American Dancer,* October 1934, 8.

41. George Bockman, Scrapbook 1933-35, MGZRS 79-3924.

42. Gerald Bordman, *American Musical Theatre,* 505-06.

43. Ibid.

44. Brooks Atkinson, *The New York Times Theatre Reviews*, November 1937, 28: 2.

45. Gerald Bordman, *American Musical Theatre,* 505-06.

46. Edwin Bronner, *Encyclopedia of American Musical Theatre 1900-1975*, 858-59.

47. Leonard William Torbert, *Broadway Bound: A Guide to Shows That Died Aborning* (Lanham, MD: The Scarecrow Press, 1983), 440.

48. Ibid.

49. Howard Barnes, "Tunes Without Comedy," *New York Herald Tribune,* January 14, 1944, New York Theatre Critic's Reviews (Vol. V, No. 24, 1944): 284.

50. John Chapman, "Musical 'Jackpot' Makes All Motions But Doesn't Deliver," *New York Daily News*, January 14, 1944, New York Theatre Critic's Reviews (Vol. V, No. 24, 1944): 284.

51. Selma Jean Cohen, *Doris Humphrey: An Artist First* (Middletown, CT: Wesleyan University Press, 1972), 288.

52. Lewis Nichols, "Sing Out, Sweet Land!" *New York Times,* December 28, 1944, New York Theatre Critic's Reviews (Vol. V, No. 24, 1944): 48-50.

53. John Chapman, "SOSL!"—and Sing Hey for Another Musical Delight," *New York Daily News*, December 28, 1944, New York Theatre Critic's Reviews (Vol. V, No. 24, 1944): 48-50.

54. Wilella Waldorf, 'Sing Out, Sweet Land!' A Salute to Folk Music," *New York Post*, December 28, 1944, New York Theatre Critic's Reviews (vol. V, no. 24, 1944): 48-50.

55. Edwin Bronner, *Encyclopedia of American Musical Theatre 1900-1975*, 922, 923.

56. "Via the grapevine," *Dance Magazine*, July 1950, 7.

57. Arthur Todd, "Broadway Callboard," *Dance News*, August 1950, 8.

58. Daniel Blum ed., *Theatre World, Season 1950-51* (New York: Greenberg Publishers, 1951), 38.

59. Ibid.

60. *Charles Weidman Papers, Special Collections*, The New York Public Library (MGZMD 99, Box 2, Folder 18).

61. Ibid.

62. Ibid.

63. Daniel Blum, ed., *Theatre World, Season 1957-58* (Philadelphia: Chilton Company, 1958), 69, 70.

64. *Charles Weidman Papers* (MGZMD 99, Box 2, Folder 18).

65. Ann Barzel, "Charles Weidman—Opera Ballet Master," *Dance Observer*, November 1949, 131.

66. Nik Krevitsky, "Charles Weidman and New York City Opera Company," *Dance Observer*, January 1950), 13.

67. Ann Barzel, "Charles Weidman—Opera Ballet Master," 131.

68. Arthur Todd, "The Opera Ballet Enigma, *Dance Magazine*, April 1951, 37.

69. Ibid.

70. *Charles Weidman Papers* (MGZMD 99, Box 9, Folder 118).

71. Nona Schurman, manuscript notes, May 2005.

72. Winthrop Palmer, "The Season in Review," *Dance News*, October 1951, 5.

73. Ibid.

74. Doris Hering, "Outlook from New London, 1951," *Dance Magazine*, October 1951, 49.

75. Louise Guthman, "Charles Weidman and Theatre Dance Company," *Dance Observer*, June-July 1954, 85.

Chapter Eleven   The Expression of Two Arts Studio Theatre

1. *Charles Weidman Papers* (MGZMD 99, Box 5, Folder 77).

2. *Charles Weidman Papers* (MGZMD 99, Box 3, Folder 48).

3. Ibid.

4. *Charles Weidman Papers* (MGZMD 99, Box 2, Folder 19).

5. Ibid.

6. Ibid.

7. Margaret O'Sullivan, letter to author, April 26, 2005.

8. *Charles Weidman Papers* (MGZMD 99, Box 1, Folder 5).

9. Ann Barzel, "Chicago's American," MGMB, Charles Weidman Clippings, Dance Collections, New York Public Library for the Performing Arts.

10. *Charles Weidman Papers* (MGZMD 99, Box 5, Folder 87).

11. *Charles Weidman Papers* (MGZMD 99, Box 2, Folder 19).

12. Ibid.

13. Program, Dot Virden Murphy Collection, New Orleans, Louisiana.

14. Ibid.

15. *Charles Weidman Papers* (MGZMD 99, Box 2, Folder 25).

16. Sylvia Pelt Richards, "A Biography of Charles Weidman with Emphasis upon His Professional Career and His Contributions to the Field of Dance," (Ph. D. diss., Texas Woman's University, 1971), 324.

17. *Charles Weidman Papers* (MGZMD 99, Box 2, Folder 35).

18. Ibid.

19. Don McDonagh, *Martha Graham: A Biography* (New York: Praeger Publishers, 1973), 304.

20. Program, Dot Virden Murphy Collection, New Orleans, Louisiana.

21. Ibid.

22. Harold Garton, "World of Dance," *Back Stage*, July 26, 1963, 4.

23. Program, Dot Virden Murphy Collection, New Orleans, Louisiana.

24. Jennie Schulman, "Dance Events," *Back Stage*, July 26, 1963.

25. Ibid.

26. Ibid.

27. Program, Dot Virden Murphy Collection, New Orleans, Louisiana.

28. Ibid.

29. Dot Virden Murphy, letter to author, July 12, 2005.

30. Program, Dot Virden Murphy Collection, New Orleans, Louisiana.

31. Ibid.

32. Marcia Marks, "Charles Weidman and Theatre Dance Company, The Village Theatre, June 1967," *Dance Magazine*, August 1967, 32.

33. Ibid

34. Margaret Lloyd, *The Borzoi Book of Modern Dance* (New York: Alfred A. Knopf, 1949; reprint, Pennington, NJ: Princeton Book Co., 1987), 92.

Chapter Twelve   Coming Full Circle: *Submerged Cathedral*

1. Frederic L. Orme, " Charles Weidman: The Master Theme," *The American Dancer*, December 1938, 34.

2. *Charles Weidman Papers, Special Collections*, The New York Public Library (MGZMD 99, Box 1, Folder 14).

3. *Charles Weidman Papers* (MGZMD 99, Box 1, Folder 17).

4. Janet Towner, "Charles Weidman's Choreographic Process in the Creation of *Visualization, or From a Farm in New Jersey,*" (M.S. thesis, University of Oregon, 1990), 25.

5. *Charles Weidman Papers* (MGZMD 99, Box 3, Folder 40).

6. Ibid.

7. *Charles Weidman Papers* (MGZMD 99, Box 1, Folder 11).

8. *Charles Weidman Papers* (MGZMD 99, Box 2, Folder 32).

9. Ibid.

10. Ibid.

11. Ibid.

12. Ibid.

13. Program, Geneseo Dance Ensemble, May 1988.

14. Ibid.

15. Program, Charles Weidman and David Hebel, December 6, 1968. Dance Collections, The New York Public Library, MGMB.

16. Ellen Stodolsky, "Charles Weidman and the Theatre Dance Company Spenser Memorial Church, Brooklyn; Expression of Two Arts Theatre, NYC, June 14, 1973; June 24, 1973," *Dance Magazine*, September 1973.

17. Program, Geneseo Dance Ensemble, April 2000.

18. Ellen Stodolsky, "Charles Weidman and the Theatre Dance Company."

19. Ibid.

20. Janet Towner, "Charles Weidman's Choreographic Process in the Creation of *Visualization, or From a Farm in New Jersey,*" 31.

21. Ibid., 33.

22. Ibid., 73.

23. Walter Terry, "Dancing is where you find it; everywhere," *Saturday Review*, April 1975, 52.

24. Janet Towner, "Charles Weidman's Choreographic Process in the Creation of *Visualization, or From a Farm in New Jersey,*" 72.

25. Walter Terry, "Dancing is where you find it; everywhere," 52.

26. Janet Towner, "Charles Weidman's Choreographic Process in the Creation of *Visualization, or From a Farm in New Jersey,*" 92.

27. Ibid.

28. Ibid., 45.

29. *Charles Weidman Papers* (MGZMD 99, Box 2, Folder 32).

30. Ibid.

31. *Charles Weidman Papers* (MGZMD 99, Box 1, Folder 5).

32. *Charles Weidman Papers* (MGZMD 99, Box 3, Folders 46, 47).

33. *Charles Weidman Papers* (MGZMD 99, Box 1, Folder 1).

34. *Charles Weidman Papers* (MGZMD 99, Box 2, Folder 25).

35. Janet Towner, "Charles Weidman's Choreographic Process in the Creation of *Visualization, or From a Farm in New Jersey*," 25, 26.

36. Ted Shawn, *One Thousand and One Night Stands* (Garden City, NY: Doubleday & Company, 1960), 156.

37. Walter Sorell, "Weidman Returns to Lexington 'Y' May 4," *Dance News*, May 1972, 1, 2.

38. Susanne K. Langer, *Philosophy in a New Key* (Cambridge, MA: Harvard University Press, 1942); reprint, New York: The New American Library, 1948), 243 (page reference is to reprint edition).

39. *Charles Weidman Papers* (MGZMD 99, Box 2, Folder 28).

Chapter Thirteen   Legacy and Witnesses

1. Janet Towner Collection, Portland, Oregon.

2. Walter Sorell, editor, *The Dance Has Many Faces*, Third Edition (Chicago, IL: a cappella books, an imprint of Chicago Review Press, 1992), 28-30.

BIBLIOGRAPHY

Abrams, Robert, ed. *Performance Review Saeko Ichinohe Dance Company.* <http/www.exploredance.com/saeko041304.html> (2 June 2004).

Adler, Diane. "An Interview with José Limón." *Dance Magazine.* July 1953, 37.

Anderson, Jack. *Art Without Boundaries.* Iowa City, IA: University of Iowa Press, 1997.

Arnold, Joseph. "Dance Events Reviewed." *The American Dancer,* July 1933, 7.

_____. "Dance Events Reviewed." *The American Dancer,* November 1933, 7.

_____. "Dance Events Reviewed." *The American Dancer,* October 1934, 8.

_____. "Dance Events Reviewed." *The American Dancer,* May 1934, 8.

_____. "Dance Events Reviewed." *The American Dancer,* February 1935, 11, 26.

_____. "Dance Events Reviewed." *The American Dancer,* March 1936, 12.

Anderson, Jack. "Charles Weidman: Still Pioneering." *Dance Magazine,* September 1964, 32-43.

Andrews, Edward Deming. *The People Called Shakers.* New York: Dover Publications, 1963.

Armitage, Merle and Virginia Stewart. *Modern Dance.* Brooklyn, NY: Dance Horizons, 1970.

Ashihara, Eiryo. *The Japanese Dance.* Tokyo, Japan: Japan Travel Bureau, Inc., 1964.

Atkinson, Brooks. *The New York Times Theatre Reviews.* June 1930.

Au, Susan, *Ballet & Modern Dance.* London: Thames and Hudson, 1988.

Baker, Samm S. and Natalie Baker. *Family Treasury of Art.* New York: Galahad Books, 1981.

Balcom, Lois. "Reviews of the Month." *Dance Observer,* February 1942, 23-24.

_____. "Reviews of the Month." *Dance Observer,* 50-51.

Barnett, Mary. "From Studio to Stage." *Labanotation,* Juilliard School of Music, 1962.

Barnes, Howard. "Tunes Without Comedy." *New York Herald Tribune,* New York Theatre Critic's Reviews, Vol. V, No. 24, January 14, 1944.

Barzel, Ann. "Charles Weidman - Opera Ballet Master." *Dance Observer,* November 1949, 131.

_____. "Chicago's American." MGZMB, Charles Weidman Clipping. Dance Collections, New York Public Library for the Performing Arts.

Bassoe, Henriette. "Flights Beyond the Horizon with Charles Weidman." *The American Dancer*, March 1941, 9, 32.

Beatty, John W. "The Modern Art Movement." *The North American Review* 219, February 1924, 251-64.

Beiswanger, George. "Music for The Modern Dance." *Theatre Arts Monthly* 18, March 1934, 184-91.

_____. "The Dance and Today's Needs." *Theatre Arts Monthly* 30, March 1935, 439-450.

Belling, Noa. *The Yoga Handbook*. United Kingdom: New Holland Publishers, 2000.

Bernstein, Joan Levy. "Dancing with Doris Humphrey." *Dance News*, November 1978, 1, 3, 16.

Bie, Oscar. "Mid-European Expressionism." *Arts and Decoration* 13, June, 25, 1920, 88-89.

Blum, Daniel, ed. *Theatre World, Season 1950-51*. New York: Greenberg Publishers, 1951.

_____. *Theatre World, Season 1957-58*. Philadelphia: Chilton Company, 1958.

Bockman, George. *Scrapbook 1933-35*. MGZRS 79-3924, Dance Collections, New York Public Library for the Performing Arts.

Boorstin, Daniel J. "Can Patriotism be legislated?" *U.S. News & World Report*, February 13, 1989, 26.

Bordman, Gerald. *American Musical Theatre: A Chronicle*. New York: Oxford University Press, 1978.

Borroff, Edith and Marjory Irvin. *Music in Perspective*, New York: Harcourt Brace Jovanovich, Inc., 1976.

Brockway, Merrill and Judy Kinberg. *Dance in America: Trailblazers of Modern Dance*. WNET/13, 1977. Videocassette.

Bronner, Edwin. *Encyclopedia of American Musical Theatre 1900-1975*. South Brunswick, NJ: A. S. Barnes Company, 1980.

Brown, Jean Morrison, ed. *The Vision of Modern Dance*. Princeton, NJ: Princeton Book Company, 1979.

Buglisi, Jacqulyn. *Class Observation*. Alvin Ailey School. New York, NY May 23, 2005.

Butler, Gervase. "Choreographics." *Dance Observer*, February 1942, 27.

Buttitta, Tony and Barry Witham. *Uncle Sam Presents: A Memoir of the Federal Theatre 1935-1939*. Philadelphia: The University Press, 1982.

Cable, Harry. "The Soldier's Forum." *Dance Magazine*, July 1942, 6.

Cahn, Isabelle. *Gauguin*. New York: Arch Cape Press, 1990.

Caldwell, Helen. *Michio Ito*. Berkeley and Los Angeles: University of California Press, 1977.

Campbell, Jack K. *Colonel Francis W. Parker: The Children's Crusader*. New York: Teachers College Press, 1967.

Cannell, Kathleen. "Weidman Conducts a Master Class." *The Christian Science Monitor*, 6 May 1950, 5.

Carr, Deborah. Studio Session, February 1991.

_____. Telephone Conversation, October 12, 1990.

_____. Interview by author, March 19, 1989, New York, NY, Tape Recording.

_____. Interview by author, April 17, 2001, Geneseo, New York.

_____. *Deborah Carr Theatre Dance Ensemble*. Produced and directed by Deborah Carr and Beatrice Seckler. 30 min. Videocassette. Private Collection.

_____. Studio Sessions. February 1988, February 1987, October 1986, October 1985, February 1983.

Carter, Robert A. *Buffalo Bill Cody: The Man Behind The Legend*. New York: John Wiley & Sons, 2000.

Chapman, John. "Musical 'Jackpot' Makes All Motions But Doesn't Deliver," *New York Daily News*, New York Theatre Critic's Reviews, Vol. V, No. 24, January 14, 1944: 284.

_____. "SOSL!"—and Sing Hey for Another Musical Delight," *New York Daily News*, New York Theatre Critic's Reviews, Vol. V, No. 24, December 28, 1944: 48-50.

Chujoy, Anatole. "Dance in Review." *Dance News*, November 1948, 8.

_____. "Dance in Review." *Dance News*, June 1949, 6.

_____. "Dance Notation Proves Successful." *Dance News*, January 1950, 10.

_____. "Dance in Review." *Dance News*, April 1950, 9.

Cohen, Jano. "Creativity in Dance and Government Funding: An Examination of the W.P.A. in the 1930's." *Graduate Review* 1, Temple University.

Cohen, Selma Jean. *Doris Humphrey: An Artist First*. Middletown, CT: Wesleyan University Press, 1972.

Cohen-Stratyner, Barbara Naomi. *A Biographical Dictionary of Dance*. London: Schimer Books, a division of Collier Macmillan Publishers, 1982.

Cook, Ray. *A Handbook for the Dance Director*. New York: Dance Notation Bureau, 1977.

Copeland, Roger and Marshall Cohen, eds. *What is Dance?* New York: Oxford University Press, Inc., 1983.

Cram, Ralph Adams. "The Limits of Modernism in Art." *Art and Decoration*, January 20, 1924, 11-13.

515

Curlee, Richard F. and Gerald M. Siegel. *Nature and Treatment of Stuttering: New Directions*. Second Edition. Needham Heights, MA: Allyn & Bacon, 1997.

Current, Richard Nelson and Marcia Ewing Current. *Loie Fuller: Goddess of Light*. Boston: Northeastern University Press, 1997.

Crowley, Alice Lewisohn. *The Neighborhood Playhouse*. New York: Theatre Arts Books, 1959.

Dahesh Museum of Art, Exhibition Panel, New York, New York.

Dance: Four Pioneers. WNET 13, filmstrip, 1965.

Dance Magazine. "Via the grapevine," January 1950, 49.

_____. "Dance Magazine Awards of the Year in Performance and Choreography." June 1950, 36.

_____. "Via the grapevine." July 1950, 7.

_____. "News from studio and school." October 1950, 50.

_____. "Via the grapevine." January 1951, 10, 11.

_____. "Via the grapevine." December 1951, 2.

_____. "Via the grapevine." July 1951, 6.

_____. "Via the grapevine." November 1951, 1.

_____. "News of Dance and Dancers." February 1953, 3.

_____. "News of Dance and Dancers." March 1953, 3.

_____. "News of Dance and Dancers." August 1953, 4.

_____. "News of Dance and Dancers." December 1953.

_____. "Obituaries Charles Weidman. September 1975, 10, 11.

Dance News. "Weidman Booking Nearly Complete." November 1946, 1.

_____. "Weidman and Company at YMHA." December 1946, 1.

_____. "Weidman at American U." June-August 1947, 7.

_____. "Weidman, Gopal at N.Y. Jubilee." September 1948, 4.

_____. "Charles Weidman begins US Tour." February 1949, 1.

_____. "Shurman, Gentry Offer Joint Show." May 1949, 1.

_____. "Y Schedules 16 Events." July 1949, 1.

_____. "School Activities." October 1949, 15.

_____. "Weidman Selects Chicago Dancers." December 1949, 8.

_____. "Dance on Campus," April 1950, 11.

_____. "Dance Theatre in Last Show." May 1950, 1.

_____. "DEA Names Teachers." June 1950, 10.

_____. "Brooklyn Museum -- New Series." September 1950, 2.

_____. "Wigman Unable to Cross to America." July 1951, 3.

_____. "Dance Festival Begins Aug. 16." August 1951, 1.

_____. "School Activities." February 1951, 10.

_____. "Y Dance Dept. Forms New Group." December 1952, 2.

_____. "Chicagoings." December 1952, 9.

Dance Observer. "Review." April 1942, 24, 51.

_____. "Awards Presented to Five Modern Choreographers." January 1959, 7.

_____. "Choreographics." October 1961, 126.

_____. "College Correspondence." December 1961, 153.

Dance Techniques and Studies. New York: Dance Notation Bureau, 1950.

De Mille, Agnes. *Martha: The Life and Work of Martha Graham*: New York: Random House, 1991.

Dunkley, K. Wright. "Modern Dance Techniques for the Male Dancer." M.S. thesis, University of Utah, 1961.

Dunning, Jennifer. "Recalling the Spirit of Doris Humphrey." *The New York Times*, March 11, 1989, 17.

_____. "Honoring the Life and Work of a Modern Dance Pioneer." *The New York Times*, June 30, 1985.

Dzhermolinska, Helen. "Blueprint for a Ballet." *Dance Magazine*, April 1951, 14, 15, 42, 43.

Engel, Lehman. *This Bright Day.* New York: Macmillan Publishing Co., 1974

Enters, Angna. "Notes on Dance Form." *The Drama Magazine* 21, December 1930, 5-8.

Ewen, David. *New Complete Book of American Musical Theatre.* New York: Holt, Rinehart and Winston, 1958.

Federal Writers' Project of the Works Progress Administration for the State of Nebraska. *Nebraska: A Guide to the Cornhusker State.* Nebraska: Stratford Press, 1939; reprint St. Clair Shores, Michigan: Scholarly Press, 1976.

Findlay, Elsa. "Concert Dancers Organize." *The American Dancer*, February 1931, 13, 34.

Fine,Vivian. "Composers/Choreographer." *Dance Perspectives* 16 (1963): 8-10.

Flage, Percy. "Attitudes, Arabesques." *Dance News*, November 1949, 4.

Foulkes, Julia L. *Modern Bodies: Dance and American Modernism from Martha Graham to Alvin Ailey.* Chapel Hill, NC: The University of North Carolina Press, 2002.

Fowler, Charles and University of Maryland. *Music: Its Role and Importance in Our Lives.* Teacher's Annotated Edition. New York: Glencoe/McGraw Hill, 2000.

Fraleigh, Sondra Horton. *Dance and the Lived Body: A Descriptive Aesthetics.* Pittsburgh: University of Pittsburgh Press, 1987.

Gage, Margaret. "A Study in American Modernism." *Theatre Arts Monthly*, March 1930, 229-232.

Garton, Harold. "World of Dance." *Back Stage*, July 26, 1963, 4.

Gilbert, Douglas. *American Vaudeville*. New York: Dover Publications, Inc., 1940.

Gilford, Henry. "Dance Reviews." *The Dance Observer*, May 1936, 16-17.

Gilliam, Bryan. *The Life of Richard Strauss*. Cambridge, United Kingdom: Cambridge University Press, 1999.

Giordano, Gus. *Jazz Dance Class: Beginning Thru Advanced*. Pennington, NJ: Princeton Books, 1992.

Gottfried, Martin. *Broadway Musicals*. New York: Abradale Press, 1979.

Graham, Martha. *Blood Memory*. New York: Doubleday Publishers, 1991.

_____. *Dance Company Program*. "Sketches From Chronicle." New York Season. City Center Theatre, May 2005.

Gruen, John. *Menotti: A Biography*. New York: Macmillan Publishing Company, 1978.

Guest, Hutchinson, Ann. *Labanotation or Kinetography Laban*. 3rd. ed. New York: Theatre Arts Books, 1977.

_____. "A Labanotator at the Hawaii Conference." *Dance Research Journal* 13 (Fall 1980): 45-50.

Guthman, Louise. "Charles Weidman and Theatre Dance Company." *Dance Observer*, June-July 1954, 85.

Hall, Fernau. "Charles Weidman at the Commonwealth Substitute, *Ballet Today*, May 1965.

Hanna, Judith Lynn. "Patterns of Dominance." *The Drama Review* 31, (Spring 1987): 22-47.

Heller, Jules. *Printmaking Today*. New York: Holt, Rinehart and Winston, Inc., 1972.

Hering, Doris. "N.Y. City Dance Theatre." *Dance Magazine*, February 1950, 42, 43.

_____. "The first season of the N.Y. City Dance Theatre." *Dance Magazine*, February 1950, 10, 11.

_____. "The Concert Season in Review." *Dance Magazine*, July 1951, 30.

_____. "Outlook from New London." *Dance Magazine*, October 1951, 10, 11, 47-50.

_____. "The Season in Review." *Dance Magazine*, May 1953, 12.

_____. "Reviews." *Dance Magazine*, April, 1960, 26.

Himelstein, Morgan Y. *Drama Was a Weapon. The Left-Wing Theatre in New York, 1929-1941*. New Brunswick, NJ: Rutgers University Press, 1963.

Hirsch, Foster. *Kurt Weill On Stage: From Berlin to Broadway*. New York: Alfred A. Knopf, 2002.

Hofmann, Wilfried A. "Of Beauty and the Dance: Towards an Aesthetics of Ballet." *Dance Perspectives* 55 (Autumn 1973): 15-27.

Horst, Louis and Carroll Russell. *Modern Dance Forms*. 2nd ed. Dance Horizons. Princeton, N.J.: Princeton Book Company, 1987.

House, Linda Dr. Interview with Melissa Heald, September 20, 2004.

Humphrey, Doris. *The Art of Making Dances*. New York: Grove Press, Inc., 1959.

_____. "New Dance: An Unfinished Autobiography." *Dance Perspectives* 25 (Spring 1966): 2-81.

Humphrey-Weidman Group Programs. Dance Collections. New York Public Library, MGZB vol. 11.

http://www.dancenotation.org

http//www.uib.no/herrmann/articles/phototours/newyork/page4.html

Ichitaro, Kondo. *The Fifty-Three Stages of the Tokaido by Hiroshige*. Honolulu: East-West Center Press, 1965.

Internet Broadway Database, "Charles Weidman on Broadway." http://www.ibdb.com/person.asp?ID=4812.

Ives, Colta Feller. *The Great Wave: The Influence of Japanese Woodcuts on French Prints*. New York: The Metropolitan Museum of Art, 1974.

Imel, Carmen. "Freda Miller." *Encores for Dance*. AAHPER Publication. (1968-77): 65.

Jackson, Naomi M. *Converging Movements: Modern Dance and Jewish Culture at the 92nd Street Y*. Hanover, NH & London: Wesleyan University Press, 2000.

Janson, H.W. *History of Art*. Engelwood Cliffs, NJ: Prentice Hall Publishers, 1966.

Johnston, Theodore E. *Hands to Work And Hearts To God*. Brunswick, Maine: Bowdoin College Museum of Art, 1969.

Jones, Bill T. Letter to Author, April 25, 2005.

_____. "Falling and Catching: Dancing through the Other Door." Unpublished Lecture Notes, February 4, 2000.

Jowitt, Deborah. *Time and The Dancing Image*. Berkeley and Los Angeles, CA: University of California Press, 1989.

_____. "Roots: Foundations of American Modern Dance." *Village Voice*, November 16, 1988, 84.

Kendall, Elizabeth. *Where She Danced*. New York: Alfred A. Knopf, 1979.

_____. "Talking with Katherine Litz." *Dance Scope 8* (Spring/Summer 1974): 7-17.

King, Eleanor. *Transformations*. Brooklyn, NY: Dance Horizons, 1978.

_____. "The Influence of Doris Humphrey." *Focus on Dance V* (1969): 6-9.

Knight, Ellen. *Charles Martin Loeffler: A Life Apart in American Music*. Urbana, IL: University of Illinois Press, 1993.

Kraus, Richard and Sarah Alberti Chapman. *History of the Dance in Art and Education.* Englewood Cliffs, NJ: Prentice-Hall, 1981.

Krevitsky, Nik. "Eve Gentry & Nona Schurman." *Dance Observer*, June-July 1949, 85.

_____. "Charles Weidman and NY City Opera Company." *Dance Observer*, January 1950, 13.

Kriegsman, Sali Ann. *Modern Dance in America: The Bennington Years.* Boston, MA: G.K. Hall & Co., 1981.

_____. "Interview with a Maverick Modern: Pauline Koner." *Dance Scope 13* (Summer 1979): 36-53.

Krugman, Roberta. "Charles Weidman and Company." *Dance Observer*, April 1951, 61.

Lancaster, Clay. "The First Japanese Dance Performed in America." *Dance Magazine*, January 1956, 45.

Lancos, Jonette. *Celebrating Charles Weidman.* Panel Discussion. José Limón Studio, New York, New York, April 30, 1989.

_____. "The Movement Style and Technique of Charles Weidman." M.A. thesis, State University of New York at Brockport, 1991.

_____. "Pulse of Africa." M.F.A. Creative thesis, State University of New York at Brockport, 1996.

Lane, Richard. *Images from the Floating World: The Japanese Print.* New York: Tabard Press, 1978.

Langer, Susanne K. *Philosophy in a New Key.* Cambridge, MA: Harvard University Press, 1942; reprint, New York: The New American Library, 1948.

_____. *Problems of Art.* New York: Charles Scribner's & Sons, 1957.

Lewis, Daniel. *The Illustrated Dance Technique of José Limón.* New York: Harper & Row, Publishers, 1984.

Lewis, Julinda. "New York City," *Dance Magazine*, April 1984, 50, 52

Limón José. *An Unfinished Memoir.* Hanover, NH: Wesleyan University Press of New England, 1998; Middletown, CT: Wesleyan University Press, paperback, 2001.

_____. "Dance for Men in the Schools," *Journal of Health, Physical Education and Recreation* (vol. 11: 3, (March 1940): 148, 189-90.

Library of Congress Online Exhibition, *The Floating World of Ukiyo-e: Shadows, Dreams and Substance.* <http/www.Library of Congress. com> (June 2, 2004).

Lloyd, Margaret. *The Borzoi Book of Modern Dance.* New York: Alfred A. Knopf, 1949; reprint, Pennington, NJ: Princeton Book Co., 1987.

Love, Paul. "How to Look at Dancing." *The New Republic* 93, December 29, 1937, 222-4.

Manasevit, Shirley D. "A Last Interview with Charles Weidman." *Dance Scope* 10 (Fall/Winter 1975-76): 32-50.

Marks, Marcia. "Charles Weidman and Theatre Dance Company." *Dance Magazine*, August 1967, 32, 33.

Marsh, Lucille. "Modern Dance Art." *The Drama Magazine 17* (April 1927): 196-8.

_____. "When Is a Dance Not a Dance?" *The American Dancer*, January 1935, 10, 28, 31.

_____. "What Is Choreography?" *Dance Magazine*, October 1943, 4, 5.

Martin, John. *The Modern Dance*. Brooklyn, NY: Dance Horizons, 1966.

_____. *Book of the Dance*. New York: Tudor Publishing Company, 1963.

_____. *America Dancing*. New York: Dodge Publishing Company, 1936; reprint, Brooklyn, New York: Dance Horizons, 1968.

_____. "Dance Reviews." *The New York Times*, January 3, 1960, 2.

_____. "The Dance Soviet Style." *The New York Times*, January 6, 1935, 8.

_____. "Weidman's 'Affirmations' Prove to Be More Strength Than Name of Number Implies." *The New York Times*, January 6, 1935, 8.

_____. "Humphrey Dances Show Distinction." *The New York Times*, January 7, 1935, 4.

_____. *New York Times Theatre Reviews*, June 1930.

Mathews DeHart, Jane. *The Federal Theatre, 1935-1939: Plays, Relief, and Politics*. New Jersey: Princeton University Press, 1967.

Mathews, Edward W. "Applied Modernism." *The School Arts Magazine*, May 1931, 570-2.

Matida, Kasyo. *Odori (Japanese Dance)*. Tokyo, Japan: Board of Tourist Industry, 1938.

Maynard, Olga. *American Modern Dancers: The Pioneers*. Boston: Little, Brown and Company, 1965.

Mazo, Joseph H. *Prime Movers*. New York: William Morrow and Company, Inc., 1977.

McDonagh, Don. *The Complete Guide to Modern Dance*. Garden City, New York: Doubleday & Company, Inc., 1976.

_____. *Martha Graham: A Biography*. New York: Praeger Publishers, 1973.

Meister, Frank. "The Esthetics of Art." *American Photography* 39 (October 1945): 35.

Moore, Lillian. *Artists of the Dance*. Brooklyn, NY: Dance Horizons, 1938, reprint 1969.

Muray, Nickolas. "Nickolas Muray Looks at the Dance." *Dance Magazine*, May 1928.

Murphy, Dorothy Virden. Private Collection. New Orleans, LA.

_____. Letter to author. July 12, 2005.

Nakajima, Natsu. Interview by author. "Butoh Residency: Japanese Avante-Garde Dance/Theatre." S.U.N.Y. Brockport, May 1-3, 1989.

Nebraska State Journal. July 12-13, 1901, July 22, 1901, July 24, 1901.

Newman, Susannah. Telephone conversation with author, June 1988.

"New Dance," 1978 American Dance Festival, restaged by Charles Weidman, produced at *American Dance Festival*, Dance Horizons Video, distributed by Princeton Book Company, 1989.

New York Theatre Critics' Reviews. NY: Critics' Theatre Reviews, vol. v, no. 24, 1944.

Nichols, Lewis. "Sing Out, Sweet Land!" *The New York Times,* New York Theatre Critics' Reviews, vol. v, no. 24, December 28, 1944: 48-50.

Orme, Frederic L. "Charles Weidman: The Master Mime." *The American Dancer*, December 1938, 11, 34.

O'Sullivan, Margaret. Letter to author. July 6, 2005.

The Outlook. "Pure Form an Emotional Experience." May 7, 1934, 12, 13.

Palmer, Winthrop and Anatole Chujoy, eds. *Dance News Annual* 1953, "Theatre Dance in My Time" by Leo Lerman. New York: Alfred A. Knopf, Inc., 1953.

Palmer, Winthrop. *Theatrical Dancing in America*. Cranbury, New Jersey: A. S. Barnes and Company, Inc., Second Edition, 1978.

_____. "The Season in Review." *Dance News*, April 1951, 8.

_____. "Dance in Review." *Dance News*, May 1951, 9.

_____. "The Season in Review." *Dance News*, October 1952, 5.

Pease, Esther E. "Epilogue - A Conversation with Louis Horst.' *Impulse*, 1965, 3-7.

Phelps, Mary. "Charles Weidman and his Dance Theatre Company." *Dance Observer*, June-July 1948, 73.

Pickering, Ruth. "The Dance. Doris Humphrey and Others." *The Nation 127* (November 1928): 580.

Piercy, Caroline B. *The Shaker Cook Book: Not by Bread Alone*. New York: Crown Publishers, 1953.

Prickett, Stacey. "Reviewing on the Left: The Dance Criticism of Edna Ocko." *Journal of the Society of Dance History Scholars,* vol. v, no. 1. (Spring 1994): 65-103.

Print Exhibition of Historic New York City. New York Public Library, Bryant
    Park.
Public Broadcasting System. *Japan: Memoirs of a Secret Empire.* May 26,
    2004. Videocassette.
Quinlan, Laurel. "The Early Years Remembered." *Dance Research Journal 14*
    (1981-1982): 86, 87.
Reiter, Susan. "Dance in Review." *Dance News*, November 1981, 8.
Richards, Sylvia Pelt. "A Biography of Charles Weidman with Emphasis upon
    His Professional Career and His Contributions to the Field of Dance."
    Ph.D. diss., Texas Woman's University, 1971.
Robbins, Roy W. *Our Landed Heritage. The Public Domain 1776-1936.* (New
    Jersey: Princeton University Press), 1942.
Rogosin, Elinor. *The Dance Makers.* New York: Walker and Company, 1980.
Rosen, Lillie F. *American Dance Guild Newsletter*, vol. 9, no. 7, November-
    December, 1974.
Roseman, Janet Lynn. *Dancer Masters: Interviews with Legends of Dance.*
    New York: Routledge, 2001.
Rousmaniere, Nicole Coolidge. "The accessioning of Japanese art in early
    nineteenth-century America: Ukiyo-e prints in the Peabody Essex
    Museum, Salem." *Apollo, The International Magazine of the Arts* (March
    1997): volume 145, issue 421, 23-29.
Savery, Helen. "Dancing in the Depression." *Dance Chronicle* (1984-85) vol. 7,
    no. 3.
Schlundt, Christina L. *The Professional Appearances of Ruth St. Denis & Ted
    Shawn 1906-1932.* New York: The New York Public Library, 1962.
_____. *The Professional Appearances of Ted Shawn & His Men
    Dancers 1933-1940.* New York: The New York Public Library, Astor,
    Lenox and Tilden Foundations, 1967.
_____. *Tamiris: A Chronicle of Her Dance Career 1927-
    1955.* New York: The New York Public Library, Astor, Lenox and
    Tilden Foundations, 1972.
_____. "The Choreographer of Soaring: The Documentary
    Evidence." *Dance Chronicle 4* (1983): 363-373.
Schulman, Jeanne. "Dance Events." *Back Stage*, July 26, 1963.
Schurman, Nona. "Notes on Humphrey-Weidman Demonstration." Geneseo,
    New York. Personal Archives.
_____. Interview by author, June 20-23, 1988, Geneseo, New York.
_____. Interview by author, Spring 1989, Geneseo, New York.
_____. Interview by author, March 1988, Geneseo, New York.
_____. Studio session with author, July 13, 1989, Geneseo, New
    York. Video recording.

Schurman, Nona and Sharon Leigh Clark. *Modern Dance Fundamentals*. New York: The Macmillan Company, 1972.

Scripps, Samuel H. *American Dance Festival Award Program*, Durham, NC: Duke University, Page Auditorium, June 11, 1989.

Seckler, Beatrice. Interview by author, March 19, 1989, New York, NY.

Shakers Labanotation Score. New York: The Dance Notation Bureau.

Shanahan, Carl. Interview by author. June 10, 2004, New York, New York.

Shattuck, Roger. *The Banquet Years*. Toronto: Random House of Canada, revised edition, 1968.

Shawn, Ted. *Dance We Must*. Pittsfield, MA: The Eagle Printing and Binding Company, 1950.

_____. *Every Little Movement*. Pittsfield, MA: The Eagle Printing and Binding Company, 1954.

_____. *One Thousand and One Night Stands*. Garden City, New York: Doubleday & Company, 1960.

Shelton, Suzanne. *Divine Dancer: A Biography of Ruth St. Denis*. Garden City, New York: Doubleday & Co., 1981.

Sherman, Jane. *Soaring*. Middletown, CT: Wesleyan University Press, 1976.

_____. *The Drama of Denishawn Dance*. Middletown, CT: Wesleyan University Press, 1979.

_____. "The Humphrey-Weidman Company: A Personal View." *Dance Chronicle 3* (1980): 331-336.

_____. *Denishawn: The Enduring Influence*. Boston: Twayne Publishers, 1983.

Sherman, Jane and Barton Mumaw. *Barton Mumaw, Dancer*. Brooklyn, NY: Dance Horizons, 1986.

Siegel, Marcia B. *At the Vanishing Point*. New York: Saturday Review Press, 1972.

_____. *Days on Earth*. New Haven, CT & London: Yale University Press, 1987.

Sketches From Chronicle. Program, Martha Graham Dance Company, 2005, New York Season at City Center.

Soares, Janet Mansfield. *Louis Horst. Musician in a Dancer's World*. Durham, NC: Duke University Press, 1992.

Sobel, Bernard. *A Pictorial History of Vaudeville*. New York: The Citadel Press, 1961.

Sorell, Walter, ed. *The Dance Has Many Faces*. Third Edition. Chicago, IL: a cappella books, an imprint of Chicago Review Press, 1992.

Sorell, Walter. *The Dance through the Ages*. New York: Grosset & Dunlap, 1967.

Sorell, Walter. "Weidman Returns to Lexington 'Y'." *Dance News*, May 1972, 1, 2.

_____. *Looking Back in Wonder: Diary of a Dance Critic*. New York: Columbia University Press, 1986.

Stodelle, Ernestine. "Humphrey-Weidman: Their Theory of Movement." *Focus on Dance 11* (1962): 18-21.

_____. *The Dance Technique of Doris Humphrey*. New Jersey: Princeton Book Company, 1978.

_____. *Deep Song: The Dance Story of Martha Graham*. New York: Schirmer Books, 1984.

Stodolsky, Ellen. "Charles Weidman and the Theatre Dance Company, Spenser Memorial Church, Brooklyn; Expression of Two Arts Theatre, NYC, June 14, 1973; June 24, 1973," *Dance Magazine*, September 1973.

St. Denis, Ruth. "The Independent Art of the Dance." *Theatre Arts Monthly 8* (1924): 367-72.

_____. "Music Visualization." *The Denishawn Magazine*. Vol. 1, No. 3 (1925): 1.

_____. *An Unfinished Life*. New York: Harper & Brothers Publishers, 1939; copyright renewed HarperCollins Publishers, 1967.

St. Denis, Ruth and Ted Shawn. *Ruth St. Denis Paper, 1915*; "Denishawn Dancing Technique." Dance Collection, New York Public Library. Folders 361-374.

Staff, Donald and Deli Sacilotta. *History and Process Printmaking*. New York: Holt, Rinehart and Winston, Inc., 1978.

Stephen, Edith. "Modern Dance—A Technique or Philosophy." *The Dance Observer* (January, 1955): 12.

Strauss, Richard. *Ein Heldenleben*. Produced by David Mottley, New York Philharmonic. Compact disc MK37756, CBS Records, 1983.

Sullivan, Michael. *Great Art and Artists of the World: Chinese and Japanese Art*. New York: Franklin Watts, Inc., 1966.

Taterkiewicz, Wladyslaw. "The Great Theory of Beauty and Its Decline." *The Journal of Aesthetics and Arts Criticism 31* (Winter 1972): 165-180.

Terry, Walter. "Moderns in Review." *Dance News*, September 1947, 4.

_____. "The Legacy of Isadora Duncan & Ruth St. Denis." *Dance Perspectives 5* (Winter 1960): 5-60.

_____. *Miss Ruth*. New York: Dodd, Mead & Company, 1969.

_____. *Ted Shawn, Father of American Dance: A Biography*. New York: The Dial Press, 1976.

_____. "An effort to save the masterpieces of modern dance." *Smithsonian*, October 1980, 61-9.

Terry, Walter. *How to Look at Dance*. New York: William Morrow and
    Company, 1982.
    _____. "Chipmunk at Jacob's Pillow." *Time Magazine*, July 28, 1947,
    54.
    _____. *The New York Times*, June 30, 1985.
Terry, Walter and Jack Rennert. *100 Years of Dance Posters*. New York:
    Universe Books, 1975.
Tharp, Twaya. *Push Comes to Shove*. New York: Bantam Books, 1992.
Thomas, Bob. *Astaire: The Man, the Dancer*. New York: St. Martin's Press,
    1984.
Time Magazine. V. 49, January-March 1947, 65, 66.
Todd, Arthur. "Broadway Callboard." *Dance News*, August 1950, 8.
    _____. "Broadway Callboard." *Dance News*, October 1950, 10.
    _____. "Broadway Callboard." *Dance News*, January 1951, 3.
    _____. "The Opera Ballet Enigma: and What Four Choreographers Have
    Done About It." *Dance Magazine*, April 1951, 22, 23, 36-8.
Torbert, Leonard William. *Broadway Bound: A Guide to Shows That Died
    Aborning*. Lanham, MD: The Scarecrow Press, 1983.
Towner, Janet. Interview by author, June 11, 1989, Scripps Award, Durham,
    North Carolina. Tape recording.
    _____. "Charles Weidman's Choreographic Process in the Creation of
    Visualization, or From a Farm in New Jersey." M. S. thesis, University of
    Oregon, 1990.
Tuchman, Barbara W. *Practicing History*. New York: Ballantine Books, 1982.
*Ukiyo-e Prints And The Impressionist Painters: Meeting of the East and the
    West*. Exhibition: Tokyo, Japan, 1980.
Variety. Obituaries, June 23, 1975.
Vitak, Albertina. "Dance Events Reviewed." *The American Dancer*, March
    1937, 18, 19.
    _____. "Dance Events Reviewed." *The American Dancer*, January
    1939, 23, 43, 46.
    _____. "Dance Events Reviewed." *The American Dancer*, May 1939,
    38.
    _____. "Dance Events Reviewed." *The American Dancer*, May
    1940, 16, 17, 36, 37.
    _____. "Dance Events Reviewed." *The American Dancer*, February
    1941, 19.
Waldorf, Wilella. "'Sing Out, Sweet Land!' A Salute to Folk Music," *New York
    Post*, New York Theatre Critic's Reviews, Vol. V, No. 24, December 28,
    1944: 48-50.

Weidman, Charles. Papers, Special Collections, The New York Public Library for the Performing Arts (MGZMD 99), New York, New York.

_____. Interview by Marian Horosko, 1966-67. Oral History, Dance Collections, New York Public Library, New York, New York.

_____. "Popular Sports Steps." *Dance Lovers' Magazine*, June 25, 1925, vol. 4, no. 2.

_____. "Random Remarks." *The Dance Has Many Faces*. Third Edition. Chicago, IL: a cappella books, an imprint of Chicago Review Press, 1992.

Weiner, Hans. "The New Dance and Its Influence on the Modern Stage." *The Drama Magazine 19*, November 1928, 36-39.

Whitman, Walt. *Leaves of Grass*. New York: Random House; The Modern Library, original edition, 1891-1892.

Wright, Frank Lloyd. *The Japanese Print: An Interpretation*. New York: Horizon Press, 1967.

Wynn, David. "Three Years with Charles Weidman." *Dance Perspectives 60* (1980): 5-49.

Webster Family Encyclopedia. Humphrey, Edward, ed. The Webster Publishing Company Ltd., 1984. s.v. "Loti, Pierre," by Charles G. Hill; s.v. "Transcendentalism" by Lewis Leary; s.v. "Japan" by Chitoshi Yanaga; s.v. "Nebraska" by Marvin F. Kivett; s.v. "Cowboys" by Joe B. Frantz; s.v. "Homesteading" by Paul W. Gates; s.v. "Frontier in American History" by Ray A. Billington; s.v. "Rollerskating" by Alvin M. Levy; s.v. "Needlework" by Cornelia Wagenvoord; s.v. "Panama" by Paul D. Simkins; s.v. "Panama Canal Zone" by Walter A. Payne; s.v. "Emerson, Ralph Waldo" by Lewis Leary; s.v. "Whitman, Walt" by James E. Miller Jr.

Webster's New Universal Unabridged Dictionary, Second edition.

Yonemura, Ann. *Yokohama: Prints from Nineteenth-Century Japan*. Washington, D.C.: Smithsonian Institution, 1990.

Index

529

530

532

George Eastman House, 181
George Peabody College, 87
Georgi, Yvonne, 475
Gerrard, Saida, 11, 260
Gerrard, William, 276
Gershwin, Ira, 6, 154, 157, 274, 276
Gershwin Preludes (Weidman), 154 455
Gershwin Theatre, 274
Gesture, ii, 4, 9, 22, 25, 28, 50, 58 60, 92-96, 99-103, 106, 110, 117, 131, 165, 166, 173, 199, 209, 211, 212, 221, 222, 225, 240, 249, 258, 261, 276, 284, 287, 302, 311, 312, 325, 349, 353
Ghigliotti, Robert, 33
Ghilberti, Lorenzo, 188
Gibran, Kahlil, 135
Giglio, Santo, v
Gilbert, Douglas, 66
Gilford, Henry, 171, 200-203, 209
Gilliam, Bryan, 138
Gilpin, John, 2
Giordano, Gus, 163
Giordano, Umberto, 21
Giselle (Coralli-Perrot), 189
Glenn, John, 144, 153-155, 158
Global Dance Dramas, ii, 134
Gnossienne (Shawn), 83, 88, 109, 127, 224, 249, 312
Gnossiennes I & II, (Ito), 83
Goff, Chrristine, vi
Golden Mean, 188
Gordon String Quartet, 171, 200
Gore, Clyde, 294, 297
Gorham, Robert, 16, 33, 91, 92, 111, 122, 124, 130, 168
Gorney, Jay, 268
Gorska, Leja, 158
Graf, Herbert, 170

Graham, Georgia, 16, 77, 111, 113, 114, 120, 125
Graham, Martha, ii, 5, 9, 10, 15, 19, 22, 23, 31, 33-35, 55-57, 70, 75, 78-80, 84, 86, 91, 92, 94, 103-105, 108, 119-126, 128-131, 133, 136, 137-140, 145, 146, 149, 158, 169, 170, 190, 198, 204, 210, 213, 216, 219, 221, 223, 224, 233, 234, 238, 239, 286, 296, 297, 302, 312, 313, 315, 316, 328, 338, 339
Graham, Mary, 120, 125
Grand Street Follies, 135
Grandy, Maria, 308
Gray, Harriette Ann, 1, 11, 212, 236, 300, 331, 357, 474
Gray, Trent, 252, 253, 294-296
Great Depression, 6, 42, 168, 193, 216, 267, 268, 270, 318, 332
Greek Dancer in Silhouette (St. Denis), 57
Greek Scene: Pas de Trois (St. Denis), 57
Greek Veil Plastique (St. Denis) 57, 312
Greenwich Village Follies, 77-79, 130, 131, 138
Grelinger, Els, 464
Grey, Joel, 282
Grieg, Edvard, 144
Grimes, Tammy, 282
Gronau, Ilse, 276
Gross, Sally, 181
Grunn, Homer, 121
Guest, Ann Hutchinson, 28, 29
Guggenheim, Simon, 27
Guild Theatre, 152, 153, 171, 174, 175, 177, 200, 203, 204
Guthman, Louise, 288
Gymnòpédie (Weidman), 457

538

542

544

Rodgers, Richard, 7, 277, 278
Rodin, Auguste, 68
Roerich Society of New York, 238
Rogers, Ginger, 150
Rogers, Helen Priest, 28
Rogosin, Elinor, 182
Rolf, Bari, 315
Roller-skating, 47
Romeo and Juliet, 62
Rommett, Zena, 306
Rooms (Sokolow), 475
Roosevelt, Franklin Delano, 193, 194, 197, 277
Roosevelt, Theodore, 42, 49
Rose, Judy, 314
Rose of Sharon (Weidman), 89, 259
Rousell, Albert, 195
Rubin, Hyla, 275
Rudepoema (Weidman-Humphrey), 170-172, 317, 457
Rudhyar, Dane, 157-161
Ruins and Visions (Humphrey), 251
Rumanian Rhapsody No. 1 (Weidman), 456
Rumba to the Moon, (Weidman), 251, 458
Runes (Taylor), 109
Rousmaniere, Nicole Coolidge, 72
Royal Fandango, The, 134
Roxy Theatre, 473
Ryder, Mark, 12
Ryerson Polytechnic Institute, 314

Sadowska, Theresa, 111
Saint Matthew Passion (Weidman), 2, 7, 20, 33, 89, 90, 96, 109, 163, 199, 221, 224-226, 228, 294, 309, 310, 329, 333, 346, 461
Saint-Saens, Camille, 32, 33, 300, 311

Saints, Sinners and Scriabin (Weidman), 30, 251, 293, 334, 351, 460
sakoku, 72
Salome, 83
Salutation to the Depths, A (Weidman-Humphrey), 157-160, 456
Salut au Monde (Tamiris), 195
San, Kongo, 134
Sandor, Gluck, 195, 198
Sands, Dorothy, 135
Santaro, Mikhail, 7, 30-32, 108, 289-292, 294, 296-301, 338, 351
Sargeant, Winthrop, 152
Sasche, Leopold, 21
Satie, Erik, 83, 158
Saudades (Weidman), 287, 459
Savery, Gail, 172
Savery, Helen, 266, 269, 270
Savonarola, 31, 108, 153, 231, 293, 334, 455
Scanlon, Jennifer, 3, 303
Scarf Dance (Humphrey), 77
Scheffer, Lenore, 111, 130
Scheherazade (Fokine), 83
Scherzo (Weidman), 456
Schlaffer, Betty, 276
Schlenck, John, 156
Schlundt, Christina L., 128
School for Husbands, The, 168, 273, 275, 462
Schulman, Jennie, 298
Schultz, Patricia, vi
Schurman, Nona, iii, v, vi, 1, 2, 3, 6, 11, 12, 18, 19, 44, 103, 105-107, 156, 163, 174, 182, 196, 201, 215, 219, 220, 222, 223, 230, 232, 234, 237, 243, 247, 252, 313, 473, 474
Schwarz, Kaleigh, vi

550

United Fruit Company, 245
United Scenic Art Union, 135
University of Calgary, 306
University of Michigan, 92
University of Nebraska, 45, 46, 55,
  61
University of North Carolina, 340
University of Oregon, 475
University of Toronto, 314
University of Washington, 315
Unsung, The (Limón), 108, 226
Utamaro, Kitagawa, 74, 75, 80, 81
Utamaro (Ichinohe), 80

Valentino, Rudolph, 26, 27, 58, 252,
  357
Valse à la Loïe (St. Denis), 77, 78,
  114
Valse Caprice (Humphrey), 312
Vanoff, Nicholas, 156
Varner, Jack, 58
Varone, Doug, 303
Vaudeville, i, 4, 26, 39, 46, 47, 52-
  54, 56, 57, 61, 65-67, 92, 120,
  121, 124, 126, 128, 149, 176, 277
Vaughan, Clifford, 16, 113, 115,
  117, 144, 150
Veen, Jan. (See Wiener, Hans)
Venable, Lucy, 464
Verdi, Giuseppe, 21
Village Voice, The, 327
Villa-Lobos, Heitor, 171
Virden, Dorothy Murphy, iii, vi, 11,
  294, 297-301, 351, 355
*Visualization, or From a Farm in
  New Jersey* (Weidman) 7, 33,
  311-313, 329, 461
Vitak, Albertina, 239, 248, 249
Voices of Spring (Shawn), 111, 114

Volk, Scott, 313
Volpone (Weidman), 459
Voltaire, 25, 196

Wagner, Richard, 21
Wainer, Lee, 278
Waiting for Godot, 463
Wald, Lillian, 132, 133
Waldorf, Wilella, 280
Walker, June, 275
Wallmann, Margareta, 146, 147
Walnut Theatre (Philadelphia), 266
War Between Men and Women, The
  (Weidman) 28, 284, 287, 288,
  353, 357, 459
Warburg, Anita, 315
Waring, James, 302
War Dance for Wooden Indians
  (Weidman), 251, 458
War Poem, A (Sokolow), 204
Warrior (Ito), 83
Waters, Ethel, 6, 272, 273
Water Study (Humphrey), 95, 111,
  153, 154, 170, 218, 267
Watt, Nina, 3, 303
Wayne State University, 12, 30, 289
Webb, Clifton, 272, 273
Weidman, Charles Edward, Jr.,
  awards, 17, 27, 33, 34, 36, 299, 314
  beliefs, 15, 16, 29, 63, 89, 90, 147,
    148, 182
  birth, 43, 44
  Broadway, ii, 4, 6, 7, 9, 20-22, 25,
    29, 37, 66, 155, 168, 171, 176,
    197, 207, 239, 262, 265, 266-269,
    272-282, 284, 286, 288, 299, 314,
    341
  childhood, 4, 13, 14, 23, 26, 39, 45,
    46, 50-52, 55, 56, 58, 65
  comedy, 17, 22, 24, 35, 94, 166

552

Weidman, Ruth, 50
Wells Fargo Company, 45
Westbrook, Frank, 12
We Weep for Spain (Delza), 204
Wheeler, Pearl, 113, 120, 123,
   129, 150, 151
White, E. B., 288
White, Stanford, 67
Whitman, Walt, 39, 73, 85-87, 185,
   195
Whitney, Cornelius, 36
Wiener, Hans, (Jan Veen), 189
Wigman, Mary, 146, 147, 180, 189,
   238
Wild, Mindy Franzese, vi
Wilkes-Barre Ballet Theatre, 2, 337
Williams, Anne Dunbar, 11, 260
Wilson, Charles, vii, 300, 301, 359
Wilson, Paul, 33, 252, 253, 260, 294,
   296
Winter Garden Theatre, 276
Winton, Sid, 126, 127
With My Red Fires (Humphrey),
   5, 108, 196
Wodinski, Jan, 33
Wolenski, Chester, 3
Wolfe, Ian, 270
Woman's Christian Temperance
   Union, 45
Woodford, Charles Francis, 167-169,
   207, 213, 245, 269
Woodford, Charles Humphrey, vii,
   168
Woodford, Joyce Trisler, 306
Woodward Hotel, 29, 288
Workers Dance League, 196
Works Progress Administration,
   185, 194
Worth, Billie, 279
World War I, 57, 120
World War II, 6, 260

Wray, John, 278
Wright, Frank Lloyd, 76, 79
Wynn, David, 11, 16, 20, 234, 303,
   338, 341, 342

Xochitl (Shawn), 5, 9, 16, 92, 109,
   114, 116, 121-128, 130, 316
Xoregos, Shelia, 306

Yacco, Sada, 69, 70
Yeats, J. B., 78
Yoga, 4, 104
   charkas, 104
YM-YWHA (92nd Street), 170, 171,
   287, 306, 357, 459, 473
Yokohama Harbor, 112-113
York University, 314
Young Tramps (Becque), 195

Zahn, Anita, 239
Zall, Deborah, 285
Zane, Arnie, 36, 181
ZaZa (Belasco), 67, 69
Ziegfeld Follies, 131, 143
Zilbert, Maurice, 209